Justice Denied: Exploring Inequities in the Legal System

This volume focuses on injustice in the criminal justice system in England and Wales and discusses the current barriers to achieving justice. The book draws on contributions from established and emerging scholars as well as insight from professional practice to provide insight into the contemporary challenges in distinct areas of injustice through original analysis and argument. Topics covered include the theory of punishment, criminal justice, access to justice, climate justice, migrant justice, and barriers to justice. The volume will be of interest to researchers, academics and policy-makers working in the areas of criminal law, criminology, sociology of law and human rights law. Focused on the legal system of England and Wales, the issues raised are relevant for an international readership.

Ed Johnston is Associate Professor of Criminal Justice and Procedure and the Faculty Research Lead at the University of Northampton, UK.

Claire-Michelle Smyth is Associate Professor of Law at Kingston University, UK.

Routledge Contemporary Issues in Criminal Justice and Procedure
Series Editor Ed Johnston
Is an Associate Professor of Criminal Justice and Procedure at the University of Northampton, UK.

Neurolaw in the Courtroom
Comparative Perspectives on Vulnerable Defendants
Edited by Hannah Wishart and Colleen M. Berryessa

Contemporary Challenges in the Jury System
A Comparative Perspective
Nicola Monaghan

Implementation of Rights for Crime Victims in Theory and Practice
Lessons from India
Anupama Sharma

Justifying Punishment
Perspectives from Post-Communist Europe
Edited by Jakub Drápal

International Perspectives of Neuroscience in the Youth Justice Courtroom
Edited by Hannah Wishart and Ray Arthur

Poor Defence Lawyering in Criminal Proceedings
A Comparative View
Edited by Ashlee Beazley, Michele Panzavolta and Andrew Sanders

The Digital Courtroom
Participation, Attendance, Engagement and Consumption
Lisa Flower

Justice Denied: Exploring Inequities in the Legal System
Edited by Ed Johnston and Claire-Michelle Smyth

For more information about this series, please visit: https: // www.routledge.com/Routledge-Research-in-Legal-History/book-series/CONTEMPCJP

Justice Denied: Exploring Inequities in the Legal System

Edited by Ed Johnston
and Claire-Michelle Smyth

Routledge
Taylor & Francis Group
LONDON AND NEW YORK

First published 2026
by Routledge
4 Park Square, Milton Park, Abingdon, Oxon OX14 4RN

and by Routledge
605 Third Avenue, New York, NY 10158

Routledge is an imprint of the Taylor & Francis Group, an informa business

British Library Cataloguing-in-Publication Data
A catalogue record for this book is available from the British Library

ISBN: 978-1-032-80379-1 (hbk)
ISBN: 978-1-032-80426-2 (pbk)
ISBN: 978-1-003-49682-3 (ebk)

DOI: 10.4324/9781003496823

Typeset in Galliard
by Apex CoVantage, LLC

Contents

Cases

Andrew Malkinson v The King [2023] EWCA Crim 954
Atkinson (1978) 2 All ER 460.
Attorney General for Jersey v Holley [2005] UKPC 23
Attorney General v X [1992] 1 IR 1
Attorney General's Reference No. 126 of 2006 (H.). [2007] 2 Cr. App. R. (S.) 59
Boyd (1980) 2 Cr App R (S) 234.
Cain [1976] QB 496.
Campbell v Mirror Group Newspapers Ltd [2004] UKHL 22
Carla Foster v R [EWCA] Crin 1196
Casey v Planned Parenthood 505 U.S 833 (1991)
Chahal v UK (1996) 23 EHRR 413
City of Akron v Akron Centre for Reproductive Health 462 U.S 416 (1983)
*Cowcher v Cowcher [*1972] 1 W.L.R. 425, 430
David Caley and others [2012] EWCA Crim 2821.
Davis v Johnson [1979] A.C. 264
Dobbs v Jackson Women's Health Organisation 597 U.S 215 (2022)
Dossetter (1999) 2 Cr App (S) 248.
Eves v Eves [1975] 1 W.L.R. 1338, 1341
Foakes v Beer (1884)
Foster v R [2023] EWCA Crim 1196
Gleeson [2003] EWCA 3357.
Goodyear (2005) EWCA Crim 888.
Great Peace Shipping Ltd v Tsavliris Salvage (International) Ltd [2003] Q.B. 679.
Grobbelaar v News Group Newspapers and Ltd [2002] 1 W.L.R. 3024
Hassini v West London Magistrate's Court [2017] EWHC 1270 (Admin).
HJ (Iran) [2010] UKSC 31
Hollington and Emmens [1986] Crim LR 270.
Hussey v Palmer [1972] 1 W.L.R. 1286, 1290
Jones v Kernott [2012] 1 A.C. 776
K and Fornah [2006] UKHL 46

Lloyds Bank Plc. Appellants v Rosset and Another Respondents [1991] 1 A.C. 107

Lumsdon & Ors, R (On the Application Of) v Legal Services Board [2014] EWHC 28 (Admin)

Magor and St. Mellons Rural District Council v Newport Corporation [1952] A.C. 189 191

Merkur Island Shipping Corporation Respondents v Laughton and Others Appellants [1983] 2 A.C. 570

Miller v College of Policing [2021] EWCA Civ 1926

Mosley v News Group Newspapers [2008] EWHC 1777 (QB)

MWB Business Exchange Centres Ltd v Rock Advertising Ltd [2019] A.C. 119, 131

NFU Mutual Insurance Society Limited Society Ltd v Khedir (2022) EWHC 437 (QB)

NFU Mutual Insurance Society Limited Society Ltd v Khedir (2022) EWHC 437 (QB)

Norris v Ireland (1988) 13 EHRR 186

Norris v Ireland 13 EUR HR Rep 186 (1988)

Paddington Garden Company One Ltd v Rasool (2022) EWHC 2081 (QB)

Paddington Garden Company One Ltd v Rasool (2022) EWHC 2081 (QB)

Pinnel's Case (1602)

Plaku and others [2021] EWCA 568.

R (on the application of Zenovics) v Secretary of State for the Home Department [2002] I.N.L.R. 219

R (Begum) v Special Immigration Appeals Commission [2021] UKSC 7, [64] (Lord Reed).

R (European Roma Rights Centre) v Immigration Officer at Prague Airport (United Nations High Commissioner for Refugees intervening) [2005]

R (European Roma Rights Centre) v Immigration Officer at Prague Airport (United Nations High Commissioner for Refugees intervening) [2005] 2 AC 1, para. 28.

R (ex parté Begum) v Special Immigration Appeals Commission [2021] UKSC 7

R (on the application of AAA and ors) v The Secretary of State for the Home Department (UNHCR Intervening) [2023] UKSC 42

R (on the application of Jesse Quaye) v Secretary of State for Justice [2024] EWHC 211 (Admin)

R (Smith) v Home Secretary [2006] 1 A.C. 159

R (Smith) v Secretary of State for the Home Department [2005] 3 WLR 410.

R v AB & Ors [2023] EWCA Crim 2003

R v ABQ (2024) EWCA Crim 310

R v Ahluwalia (1993) 1 ALL ER 153

R v Atkinson [1978] 2 All ER 460

R v Bains (2023) EWCA Crim 1586

R v Baldry (1852) 21 LJMC 130, 2 Den. CC 430
R v Baldwin (2021) EWCA Crim 417
R v Bass (1953) 37 Cr. App. R. 5
R v Bel (2021) EWCA Crim 1461
R v Best [1909] 1 KB 692
R v BGW (2023) EWCA Crim 1198
R v Bond (2024) EWCA Crim 406
R v Booth and Jones (1910) 5 Cr App R 177
R v Bourne [1938] 3 All ER 615
R v Bourne [1938] 3 All ER 615
R v Brackenbury (1903) 17 Cox CC 628
R v Cain [1976] QB 496
R v Catt [2013] EWCA Crim 1187
R v CH (2020) EWCA Crim 1736
R v Chaaban [2003] EWCA Crim 1012
R v Challen [2021] EWCA Crim 680
R v Clinton (Jon Jaques) [2012] EWCA Crim 2
R v Cook, Williams (2023) EWCA Crim 649
R v Cornick [2015] 1 Cr. App. R. (S.) 69
R v Crowe and Myerscough (1917) 81 JP 288
R v David Caley and others [2012] EWCA Crim 2821
R v Duffy [1949] 1 All ER 932.
R v Finch (2021) EWCA Crim 377
R v Goodyear (2005) EWCA Crim 888
R v Gore (2022) EWCA Crim 219
R v Griffiths (2021) EWCA Crim 1872
R v Gulzar (2023) EWCA Crim 630
R v Gurpinar (Mustafa) [2015] 1 Cr App R 31
R v Hellyer (2021) EWCA Crim 550
R v Herbert [2024] EWHC 211 (Admin)
R v Honeyman (2021) EWCA Crim 1324
R v Hoskin (2022) EWCA Crim 1633
R v Iercosan [2023] EWCA Crim 934
R v Jackson [2023] EWCA Crim 735
R v JD (2023) EWCA Crim 317
R v Jenkins (2021) EWCA Crim 1179
R v JW (2023) EWCA Crim 1257
R v Knight and Thayre (1905) 20 Cox CC 711
R v Law (2021) EWCA Crim 1985
R v *Male and Cooper* (1893) 17 Cox CC 689
R v Markham and Edwards [2017] 2 Cr. App. R. (S.) 30
R v *Martin* [2020] EWCA Crim 1798
R v Miller (1895) 18 Cox CC 54
R v Newman (2024) EWCA Crim 415
R v Noble (2023) EWCA Crim 492

R v Nugent (2021) EWCA Crim 1535
R v Plaku and others [2021] EWCA Crim 588
R v Qayum (2022) EWCA Crim 454
R v Quayle and the Secretary of State for Justice [2024] EWHC 211 (Admin)
R v Richardson (Adam) [2005] EWCA Crim 1408
R v Richfield (2024) EWCA Crim 116
R v Rochford [2010] EWCA Crim 1928
R v Secretary of State for the Home Department, ex parte Furber [1998] 1 All ER 23
R v Secretary of State for the Home Department, Ex Parte Hindley [2005] UKHL 51
R v Secretary of State for the Home Dept, ex p Venables, R v Secretary of State for the Home Dept, ex p Thompson [1997] 3 All ER
R v Simmonds (2023) EWCA Crim 1063
R v Slack (2023) EWCA Crim 522
R v Smith [2002] UKHL 51
R v Taylor [2024] EWCA Crim 615
R v Thompson [1893] 2 QB 12
R v Thornton (No 1) [1992] 1 All E.R. 306
R v Thornton (No 2) [1996] 1 W.L.R. 1174
R v Turner [1970] 2 QB 321
R v Verdins (2007) VSCA 102
R v Verdins (2007) VSCA 102.
R v Voisin (1918) 13 Cr. App. R. 89
R v Wellington (2021) EWCA Crim 294
R v Wilson (2023) EWCA Crim 673
R v ZA [2023] EWCA Crim 596
R. (on the application of Zenovics) v Secretary of State for the Home Department [2002] I.N.L.R. 219
Roe v Wade 410 U.S 113 (1973)
Rogers v Hawken (1898) 67 LJQB 526
S.K. v The United Kingdom (application no. 28774/22)
Sempra Metals Ltd (formerly Metallgesellschaft Ltd) v Inland Revenue Commissioners and another [2008] 1 A.C. 561
Shah and Islam [199] INLR 144
SM (PSG, Protection Regulations, Regulation 6) Moldova CG [2008] UKAIT 00002
Solle v Butcher [1950] 1 K.B. 671
T v United Kingdom (1999) 7 BHRC 659
Thornberg v American College of Obstetricians and Gynaecologists 476 U.S 747 (1986)
United Scientific Holdings Ltd v Burnley Borough Council [1978] A.C. 904
V v United Kingdom [1991] ECHR 24888/94
V. v United Kingdom (2000) 30 EHRR 121

Venables v News Group Newspapers Ltd [2019] EWHC 494 (Fam)
West, Re [2014] EWCA Crim 1480 (CA (Crim Div)).
Westdeutsche Landesbank Girozentrale Respondent v Islington London Borough Council Appellant [1996] A.C. 669
Whole Women's Health v Hellerstedt 579 U.S 582 (2016)

Legislation

Abortion (Amendment) Regulations 2022
Abortion Act 1967
Aliens Act 1905
Aliens Restriction Act 1914
Aliens Restrictions Order 1920
Borough of Tamaqua, PA Code, §260–61 Statements of Law, para F, as inserted by Ordinance No 612 of 2006.
British Nationality Act 1948
British Nationality and Status of Aliens Act 1914
British Nationality and Status of Aliens Act 1918
British Nationality and Status of Aliens Act 1922
British Nationality and Status of Aliens Act 1933.
British Nationality and Status of Aliens Act 1943
Children Act 1908
Children and Young Persons Act 1933
Commonwealth Immigrants Act 1962
Commonwealth Immigrants Act 1968
Conservation of Habitats and Species Regulations 2017, as amended.
Constitution of Ecuador (2008).
Constitution of Ireland 1937
Constitutional Reform Act 2005
Convention Relating to the Status Refugee 1951
Coronavirus Act 2020
Coroners and Justice Act 2009
Crime (Sentences) Act 1997
Crime and Disorder Act 1998
Criminal Justice Act 1991
Criminal Justice Act 2003
Domestic Abuse Act 2021
Equality Act 2010
Georgia's Living Infants Fairness and Equality (LIFE) Act 2019
Homicide Act 1957
Human Rights Act 1998

Illegal Migration Act 2023
Immigration Act 1971
Immigration Act 1999
Immigration Act 2014
Immigration and Asylum Act 1999
Immigration Rules Appendix Family Reunion (Protection)
Immigration Rules Part 11: Asylum
Judicial Review and Courts Act 2022
Kyoto Protocol to the United Nations Framework Convention on Climate Change (adopted 11 December 1997, entered into force 16 February 2005).
Law of the Rights of Mother Earth (Bolivia, 2010) art 3.
Legal Aid, Sentencing and Punishment of Offenders Act 2012
Magistrates' Court Sentencing Powers) (Amendment) Regulations 2023
Murder (Abolition of Death Penalty) Act 1965
Nationality and Borders Act 2022
Offences Against the Person Act 1861
Ordinance No 612 of 2006, Borough of Tamaqua, PA.
Police, Crime, Sentencing and Courts Act 2022
Post Office (Horizon System) Offences Act 2024
Powers of Criminal Courts (Sentencing) Act 2000
Protection from Harassment Act 1997
Public Order Act 1986
Safety of Rwanda (Asylum and Immigration) Act 2024
Sentencing Act 2020
Serious Crime Act 2015
Sexual Offences Act 2003
Stalking Protection Act 2019
Terrorism Prevention and Investigation Measures Act 2011.
Texas Heartbeat Act 2021
United Nations Educational, Scientific and Cultural Organization Convention on Wetlands of International Importance especially as Waterfowl Habitat (adopted 2 February 1971, entered into force 21 December 1975) (Ramsar Convention).
United Nations Framework Convention on Climate Change (adopted 9 May 1992, entered into force 21 March 1994).
Vienna Convention on the Law of Treaties 1969.
Voyeurism (Offences) Act 2019
Wildlife and Countryside Act 1981

Abbreviations

ADHA	Attention Deficit Hyperactivity Disorder
APP	Authorised Professional Practice
ASD	Autism Spectrum Disorder
BAME	Black, Asian, Minority Ethic
BCM	Better Case Management
CJA	Criminal Justice Act
COP	College of Policing
CRIMPR	Criminal Procedure Rules
CPS	Crown Prosecution Service
DBE	Dame Commander of the British Empire
ECHR	European Convention on Human Rights
E&W	England and Wales
KC	Kings Counsel
LASPO	Legal Aid, Sentencing and Punishment of Offenders Act
LIP	Litigants in Person
MOJ	Ministry of Justice
MVAWG	Male Violence Against Women and Girls
NPCC	National Police Chief's Council
PACE	Police and Criminal Evidence Act
PCSC	Police, Sentencing and Courts Act
RCCJ	Royal Commission on Criminal Justice
SA	Sentencing Act 2020
PTPH	Plea and Trial Preparation Hearing
PTSD	Post-Traumatic Stress Disorder
RJ	Restorative Justice
VOM	Victim Offender Mediation

Contributor Biographies

Lisa Mary Armstrong is a socio-legal researcher with a background in law and criminology. Her doctoral research looks at women's experiences of remand in Scotland and incorporates poetry and creative writing as methods. She has a broad range of teaching experience and has worked in the volunteer sector with children and young people in an advocacy capacity for over ten years. Lisa Mary is also a research associate at Glasgow University based in the Scottish Centre for Crime and Justice Research and has conducted qualitative research into women's experiences of community custody. Her research interests focus primarily on women and children's experiences of the criminal legal system, children's rights, and the use of creative arts in criminal justice and community settings.

Clare S. Allely is a professor of forensic psychology at the University of Salford (England) and an affiliate member of the Gillberg Neuropsychiatry Centre at Gothenburg University (Sweden). Clare is an honorary research fellow in the College of Medical, Veterinary and Life Sciences (Institute of Health and Wellbeing, University of Glasgow). She is also an Associate of The Children's and Young People's Centre for Justice at the University of Strathclyde (Scotland). Clare acts as an expert witness in criminal cases involving defendants with autism spectrum disorder and contributes to the evidence base used in courts on psychology and legal issues through her published work. She has authored *The Psychology of Extreme Violence: A Case Study Approach to Serial Homicide, Mass Shooting, School Shooting and Lone-actor Terrorism* (2020; Routledge) and *Autism Spectrum Disorder in the Criminal Justice System: A Guide to Understanding Suspects, Defendants and Offenders with Autism* (2022; Routledge).

Dominic Carrington is a senior lecturer in law at the University of Northampton as well as a practising barrister. Dominic was called to the Bar in 1996 and is a member of Middle Temple. His practice involved criminal law defence and prosecutions as well as immigration law and general common law. Dominic was the programme leader of the undergraduate law programme at GSM London in partnership with Plymouth University. Presently he is the module leader on criminal law, criminal litigation, and legal skills at the University of Northampton. His research is on areas on race and the legal profession as well as the criminal justice. He is an external examiner for London Metropolitan and St Mary's, Twickenham University.

Rupert Dunbar is a senior lecturer at Kingston University Law Department. His research tests and debates notions of justice and legal certainty. He has studied the European Union and approaches adopted by its Court of Justice, arguing for improvements in justice and certainty in its case law. His wider research has included human rights, environmental protection, and artificial intelligence.

Ed Johnston is Associate Professor in Criminal Justice and Procedure and the Faculty Research Lead at the University of Northampton. Ed has published in various criminal justice journals, including the *Criminal Law Review*, the *International Journal of Evidence and Proof*, and *Journal of Criminal Law*. He is the co-author of *Criminal Procedure and Punishment* (Hall and Stott, 2018). He has published a number of books and edited collections, including Ed Johnston and T. Smith, *The Law of Disclosure: A Perennial Problem in Criminal Justice* (Routledge 2020); Ed Johnston and T. Smith, *Criminal Procedure and Punishment* (3rd edition) (2023); Ed Johnston, R. Erbas and D. Jasinski, *A Comparative Analysis of Pre-Trial Procedure in Europe: The Search for an Ideal Model* (2020); Ed Johnston, *The Role of the Defence Lawyer* (2021); Ed Johnston, D. Jasinski, A. Phillips, *Analysing Organised Crime, Financial Crime and Criminal Justice* (Routledge, 2023); Ed Johnston, *Covid 19 and Criminal Justice: Legacy and Impact in England and Wales* (Routledge 2023); and Ed Johnston, *Challenges in Criminal Justice* (Routledge 2022). Ed's research interests include disclosure, the role of the defence lawyer, the demise of adversarialism, and fair trial rights.

Sally Kennedy is a research fellow in criminology at Deakin University, Victoria, Australia. Sally examines issues with individual rights and fairness within domestic and transnational justice environments, including the relationships between transnational online offending, extradition, autism, and the reluctance of national courts to shift the trial forum, which creates complex legal geographies and concerns about sovereign power. Her work includes the examination of high-profile cases and the impact of potential prison conditions on the extraditee's physical and mental health if surrender occurs. Sally also has experience with other transnational and domestic justice issues such as consular assistance, alcohol-related restrictions, and risky driving. She works primarily with qualitative data and has experience in thematic and legal case analysis, often within a comparative context.

Olayinka Lewis is a senior lecturer in law at the University of Essex and a practising solicitor specialising in immigration, nationality, and international refugee law. He has over a decade's experience in UK immigration law and practice. He obtained his PhD in law in 2021 and holds an LLM and an LLB. He is Immigration Lead at Essex Law Clinic and delivers training to volunteers and third-sector organisations, as well as advising clients on a vast range of immigration and asylum issues including nationality, asylum, applications under the Immigration Rules, and representations to the Home Office. He previously worked as Director of the RGU Law Clinic and lecturer at RGU, Aberdeen. He has presented at national and international conferences including GAJE, South Africa, 2022; SLSA, Derry, 2023 and LSA, Puerto Rico, 2023. He has published on UK immigration and asylum issues. He currently researches immigration and nationality issues with a focus on the hostility of UK immigration law and policy.

Luke Marsh is Associate Professor and Deputy Director (JD Programme) at the Faculty of Law, Chinese University of Hong Kong. He has held visiting positions at law schools including Oxford, Cambridge, Waseda (Tokyo), Nottingham, Columbia (New York), Auckland (Australia), UCLA (California), and University College London. Luke has published widely on the English criminal process, examining the erosion of the adversarial process and protections for the accused. He is the editor (with Máximo Langer and Mike McConville) of *The Research Handbook on Plea Bargaining and Criminal Justice* (forthcoming). Luke is a barrister of England & Wales and a door tenant at 25 Bedford Row, London.

Mike McConville was Founding Dean of the Faculty of Law, Chinese University of Hong Kong, where he is now Emeritus and Honorary Professor. Mike was formerly Head of the School of Law, University of Warwick, and Walter E. Meyer Professor, New York University. Mike's books include *Negotiated Justice* (with J. Baldwin, 1977), *The Case for the Prosecution* (with A. Sanders and R. Leng, 1991), *Watching Police Watching Communities* (with D. Shepard, 1992), *Standing Accused: The Organisation and Practice of Defence Solicitors in Britain* (with J. Hodgson, L. Bridges and A. Pavlovic, 1994), *Slippery Customers* (with M. Clarke and D. Smith, 1994), *Jury Trials and Plea Bargaining* (with C. Mirsky, 2005), *Criminal Justice in China: An Empirical Study* (with S. Choongh, D. Wan Choy, W. Hong Chui, I. Dobinson and C. Jones, 2011), *Criminal Justice in China* (with E. Pils, 2013), *Criminal Judges* (with Luke Marsh 2014), and *The Myth of Judicial Independence* (with Luke Marsh 2020).

Sarah Moore's research focusses on justice policy, particularly as it relates to changing courtroom experiences/processes, in both the family and criminal courts. She is currently involved in two projects. The first is a collaboration with Dr Alex Newbury (University of Brighton) that examines the impact of the recent reforms to Legal Aid in England and Wales. Their book, *Legal Aid in Crisis* (Policy, 2016) argues for a more litigant-focused approach to Legal Aid and support. She is also the lead investigator for a GW4-funded study that examines the introduction of cameras to courtrooms in England and Wales (with co-investigators from the University of Bristol, Cardiff

University, and the University of Exeter). Sarah has particular expertise in designing focus groups and in-depth interviews. She also has experience of questionnaire design, creating datasets, and quantitative analysis.

Alex Newbury's research focuses on the court system and access to justice, particularly from the perspective of the court user. She is currently collaborating with Dr Sarah Moore (University of Bath) in a socio-legal investigation of the impact of the reduction of legal funding for both litigants and staff in the family courts. Initial findings were published as a book, *Legal Aid in Crisis: Assessing the Impact of Reform* (Policy Press, 2016). Previously, she worked as a Legal Aid family law solicitor. She has particular expertise in empirical research including undertaking face-to-face qualitative interviews and observing court proceedings and restorative justice group conferences. She has been an invited speaker for youth charities (Only Connect, a London-based charity) and at MOPAC (the London Mayoral Office Police and Crime Committee in relation to youth crime).

Rebecca Penfold, St. John's Buildings, is a specialist defence criminal barrister. She also defends in regulatory criminal cases ranging from animal welfare and environmental offences to fire safety. She fundamentally believes in access to justice and to that end engages in social mobility programmes. She works towards improving the Bar for all, offering support through mentoring more junior members of the Bar and sitting on various Bar committees. Rebecca has a particular interest in improving the experience for women working within the criminal justice system and is Chair of the Women in Criminal Law Manchester sub-committee.

Claire-Michelle Smyth is Associate Professor of Law at Kingston University. She has published widely in the area of human rights law including *Social and Economic Rights in Ireland* (2017); '"Restrictive" Abortion Laws as Torture in International Law' (2016) 34(9) Irish Law Times 127, with S. Donoghue; 'Abortion for Foetal Abnormalities in Ireland: The Limited Scope of the Irish Governments response to the A, B and C Judgment' (2013) 20 European Journal of Health Law 1; 'The Impact of the Economic Crisis on Socio-Economic Rights' in Tanya Ni Mhuirthile and James Gallen (eds) *Law Responsibility and Vulnerability* (Routledge, 2021); 'Repealed the Eighth' in Claire-Michelle Smyth, Jack Thompson and Richard Lang (eds) *Contemporary Challenges in Human Rights Law* (2020); 'Social and Economic Rights; The Struggle for Equivalent Protection in International Law' in Lora Wildenthal and Jean Quataert (eds) *The Routledge History of Human Rights* (2nd Ed, Routledge 2019). Claire-Michelle has also previously edited two collections: *Contemporary Challenges in Human Rights Law* (2020) with Jack Thompson and Richard Lang (eds) and *The Future of Human Rights in the UK* (2017) with Richard Lang (eds).

Simon Sneddon is an associate professor of learning and teaching and Deputy Head of Law at the University of Northampton. Simon's work focuses on the impact of firearms crime on societies and different perspectives of environmental justice. He is currently working on two projects. The first looks at the impact of human food consumption on environmental, ecological, and social injustice, and the second is a longer monograph looking at the exclusionary impact of green technology on marginalised communities.

Clare Wade KC, Garden Court Chambers, is an experienced defence silk with particular expertise in representing women and those facing the most serious of crimes. She also possesses a successful track record in appellate work. Ranked as Tier 1 in the Legal 500 and Barrister of the Year at the Women in Law Awards 2020, Clare has a particular interest in women's justice and was commissioned by the government to undertake the Domestic Homicide Sentencing Review in a further call for action to address a culture of misogyny throughout the criminal justice system.

Ian Warren is a senior lecturer in criminology at Deakin University, Geelong, Australia. He has researched a wide range of socio-legal topics that invoke the critical analysis of legal rulings including the sentencing of drug offenders and the legal impact of cognitive impairments in criminal trials. Ian's research encompasses both domestic and comparative studies.

Hannah Wishart is a lecturer in law and the Programme Leader for the LLB at the University of Sunderland. Her research integrates neuroscience and psychology to advocate for changes in criminal law doctrine and legal practice concerning developmentally immature children. She completed her PhD at the University of Manchester in 2023, focusing on developmentally immature children, neuroscience, and the defence of diminished responsibility. Hannah has published peer-reviewed journal articles and books on the relevance of neuroscience in youth justice, the abolition of the doctrine of doli incapax, and the unfair treatment of developmentally immature children within the English criminal justice system. In 2024, she received a British Academy/Leverhulme grant to support a project examining police charging decisions regarding young offenders. Additionally, she has secured funding from the SLSA and the UKRI policy fund.

1 Introduction

Ed Johnston and Claire-Michelle Smyth

Justice is often perceived as an ideal – the goal of a fair and equitable society. But when we interrogate the real-life mechanisms of justice within legal systems, it quickly becomes apparent that the delivery of justice is fraught with tensions, contradictions, and systemic barriers. In England and Wales, the justice system operates under a legal framework designed to uphold the rule of law, protect rights, and ensure accountability.

However, as this volume demonstrates, the reality of justice often diverges from its theoretical aspirations. While justice is a concept universally upheld in principle, its practical application is influenced by political, economic, and social factors that often lead to inequalities in how it is administered. While some aspects of justice remain functional and accessible, many others are fundamentally flawed or inaccessible to certain groups. For some, justice is a tangible reality; for others, it is an elusive promise. This volume critically examines the structures, policies, and practices that contribute to both justice and injustice in contemporary England and Wales, highlighting areas where the system falls short and where reform is urgently needed. The following chapters analyse the impact of judicial discretion, systemic inequalities, economic constraints, racial disparities, and gender biases in the justice system, illustrating the deep-rooted issues that influence legal outcomes.

This book is a collaboration between established and emerging scholars, practitioners, and experts from fields as diverse as criminal justice, family law, environmental justice, and human rights. It draws upon legal doctrine, empirical research, and professional experience to paint a comprehensive picture of how justice operates – and fails to operate – in different contexts. From the family courts to the criminal justice system, from racial disparities to the treatment of migrants, each chapter reveals distinct challenges that undermine the fairness and efficacy of the justice system. Moreover, the book interrogates the extent to which law reform efforts have succeeded or failed in addressing these systemic issues, assessing both legislative changes and grassroots advocacy as potential avenues for progress.

In this introduction, we provide an overview of the key themes that run through the book and set the stage for the discussions that follow. We explore the evolving concept of justice, the tensions between justice and legal certainty,

DOI: 10.4324/9781003496823-1

and the systemic barriers that prevent justice from being realised for all. These discussions are framed within broader theoretical perspectives, including from legal positivism, critical legal studies, feminist jurisprudence, and restorative justice. By situating legal injustices within these frameworks, we provide a deeper understanding of how justice is shaped by ideology, social structures, and institutional power.

Dunbar's chapter opens with the idea that justice is frequently in tension with legal certainty. Judicial discretion to achieve justice in individual cases can conflict with the need for clear and predictable rules, and legal scholars debate which of these aims should be prioritised. This chapter engages with leading thinkers such as Habermas, Raz, and Twining to explore this tension, examining how figures like Dworkin, Cardozo, Radbruch, and Weber have approached the issue. English law has historically responded to this challenge by balancing common law (certainty) with equity (justice). However, as Dunbar argues, the merger of these traditions has led to an evolving contextual approach. He explores whether justice or certainty should be prioritised in different legal contexts and how contemporary courts navigate these competing demands. The chapter also draws on case law to illustrate instances where courts have struggled with this balance, leading to divergent decisions that raise questions about the consistency and fairness of legal reasoning.

In Chapter 3, McConville critically examines theories explaining the transformation of the criminal justice process in England, Wales, and the United States, particularly the rise of plea bargaining. He discusses key theories related to caseload pressures, professionalisation, political economy, and bureaucratisation and argues that while theories about courtroom workgroups and managerialism offer insights, they lack empirical robustness. McConville questions whether these changes genuinely serve justice or whether they have introduced further inequalities and inefficiencies into the system. He also examines the extent to which plea bargaining disadvantages marginalised defendants, highlighting concerns about coercion, wrongful convictions, and disparities in sentencing outcomes. Using historical data and contemporary case studies, McConville demonstrates how systemic pressures influence plea negotiations, often prioritising efficiency over fairness.

Chapter 4, by Marsh, continues the criminal justice theme and investigates significant shifts in the English and Welsh criminal justice system that have undermined traditional justice principles. Marsh explores how efficiency-driven reforms have transformed the police interview process, pre-trial detention, the adversarial system, and the guilty plea. The chapter demonstrates that procedural protections for defendants have eroded, leaving many vulnerable to wrongful convictions or coercive plea deals and raising profound questions about the future of criminal justice. Furthermore, he examines how the legal profession's evolving role – from defence advocacy to prosecutorial discretion – has contributed to a system more concerned with case throughput than with substantive justice. By incorporating first-hand accounts from legal practitioners and defendants, Marsh provides a detailed and humanised perspective on the consequences of these changes.

In Chapter 5, Newbury and Moore explore the impacts of Legal Aid cuts and the Covid-19 pandemic on access to justice for unrepresented litigants (LiPs) in the family courts. Drawing on qualitative research, they highlight the barriers posed by legal jargon, imbalances of power, and digital inequalities. The authors argue that while these issues have long existed, austerity measures and pandemic-related changes exacerbated the struggles of LiPs, making justice even more elusive for many families. They also provide policy recommendations aimed at improving access, including suggestions for more robust pro bono support, alternative dispute resolution mechanisms, and clearer procedural guidance for self-represented litigants.

In the sixth chapter, Lewis critically examines the UK's shifting immigration policies and their impact on asylum seekers. He illustrates how the Illegal Migration Act 2023, among other legislative measures, significantly restricted access to asylum by creating legal and practical barriers that violate international legal obligations. By exploring these changes, He illustrates how migrants often find themselves trapped in bureaucratic and legal limbo. He also highlights the systemic biases that disproportionately affect asylum seekers from certain regions, questioning the fairness and consistency of immigration policies. Lewis concludes by advocating for a more humane, legally compliant approach to migration justice.

Wade and Penfold, in Chapter 7, ask if the law is failing women who kill. This chapter highlights that women who kill their abusive partners frequently struggle to access just outcomes, due to the rigidity of existing defences such as loss of control and diminished responsibility. The authors examine the gender biases embedded in legal frameworks and how historical stereotypes about female defendants continue to shape judicial reasoning. Wade and Penfold argue for a broader understanding of coercive control as a form of self-defence and call for legal reform to better account for the lived experiences of women trapped in abusive relationships. The authors consider two primary failings in the law: (1) there remains a lack of proper understanding of what amounts to a loss of control in law and the partial defence is too restrictive; (2) loss of control and diminished responsibility are defences which operate against a background of stereotype, misogyny, and negative perceptions of women who kill. They also compare the situation in England and Wales with another jurisdiction in which this is an emerging area: New Zealand, in the case of Karen Rudelle. In considering the failings, the authors suggest that it is time for this area of law to modernise and for the harm caused ('social entrapment') to victims of controlling and coercive behaviour to be recognised as a true legal harm, such that the partial defences to murder are remodelled accordingly.

The eighth chapter continues in the orbit of criminal justice as Carrington examines the issues through a racial lens. He examines the impacts of racial biases in the English and Welsh criminal justice system, focusing on the Magistrates' and Crown Courts. Statistical analysis demonstrates that Black, Asian, and minority ethnic (BAME) defendants are overrepresented and often receive harsher sentences than white counterparts. The composition of the judiciary and its lack of diversity further exacerbate disparities. Carrington explores how systemic biases affect case outcomes, with an emphasis on the influence of judicial discretion, jury composition, and racialised perceptions of defendants. Additionally, he assesses recent legal reforms, such as the Judicial Review and Courts Act 2022, and their potential impact on racial justice.

In the ninth chapter, Smyth and Johnston explore the history, legislation, and criminalisation of abortion in the UK, examining the legal framework established by the Abortion Act 1967 and its continued restrictions under the Offences Against the Person Act 1861. They trace the origins of reform movements from the 1930s, highlighting the public health and social justice concerns that culminated in David Steel's Medical Termination of Pregnancy Bill of 1966. Despite the liberalisation introduced by the 1967 Act, abortion remained criminalised outside the Act's provisions, placing significant authority in the hands of medical professionals and upholding severe legal consequences for those who act outside its scope. Smyth and Johnston also discusse the legal and ethical justifications for punishment, drawing on theories of retribution, prevention, denunciation, and reparation. They examine how the increased use of medical abortions, along with legislative amendments during the COVID-19 pandemic, reshaped access to abortion but has not decriminalised the procedure. Case studies, including *R v Cutt* and the prosecution of Carla Foster, illustrate the harsh realities of legal enforcement particularly for vulnerable women. Further, the authors evaluate the international legal perspective, noting increasing calls for decriminalisation by human rights bodies. Comparisons with recent developments in Ireland and France highlight a shifting global consensus towards reducing legal restrictions on abortion. Ultimately, Smyth and Johnston argue that the criminalisation of abortion in England and Wales serves primarily punitive purposes, often disregarding the well-being of affected individuals, and calls for a re-evaluation of the current legal framework.

In Chapter 10, Armstrong examines misogyny and restorative justice. She argues that tackling misogyny requires multiple tactics rather than a single approach or method. While legislation can play an important part in increasing awareness, it cannot change attitudes; activism, strategic approaches and education-based interventions are all key to prevention. Restorative justice (RJ) can be particularly effective in tackling prejudice against women by promoting dialogue, education, and empowerment. It can encourage empathy, enable the prejudices held by the harmer to be explored and challenged openly in a safe environment, and allow victims to express their feelings. By helping tackle the problem at the root, restorative justice helps dismantle attitudes and gender stereotypes and offers an opportunity for replacing prejudice with understanding and respect. As a practice, RJ is increasingly being sought by those affected by serious crime, for example, hate crime, domestic abuse, and sexual offences. Although particular challenges can arise in the restorative process in serious cases, when facilitated by experienced practitioners, it can allow victims to move forward and recover from the effects of crime. In this chapter, we first outline the difficulties in using the law as a response to misogyny before exploring the potential ways that RJ could be used to tackle these behaviours, focussing on recent developments in England and Wales.

Chapters 11 and 12 focus on issues around crime and the mind. In Chapter 11, Kennedy, Alley, and Warren examine the sentencing of offenders with mental, developmental, or neurological impairments in England and Wales. They evaluate how these guidelines influence judicial decision-making and assess their effectiveness in ensuring fair and appropriate sentencing. By analysing case studies and legal judgments, the authors highlight how mental health conditions impact culpability, rehabilitation prospects, and sentencing outcomes. The authors also explore broader societal implications, questioning whether the current legal framework sufficiently accommodates individuals with cognitive and psychological impairments.

In Chapter 12, Wishart critically examines the sentencing framework for children and young people convicted of murder, focusing on recent reforms introduced by the Police, Crime, Sentencing and Courts Act 2022. She explores the tension between punishment and rehabilitation, questioning whether the current system appropriately considers developmental immaturity and neuroscientific evidence regarding adolescent brain development. Wishart assesses case law and sentencing patterns, arguing that the rigid application of sentencing guidelines can disproportionately impact young offenders. The chapter concludes by advocating for a more nuanced and individualised approach to sentencing that balances accountability with rehabilitative principles. In the final chapter, Sneddon explores issues around justice and nature. The author highlights that while justice in England and Wales is often viewed as a fundamental ideal, its practical delivery is fraught with challenges.

This introduction explores the evolving concept of justice, emphasising its tensions with legal certainty and systemic barriers that prevent its full realisation. The book interrogates various aspects of injustice, from racial and gender disparities to economic and institutional obstacles, environmental justice, and immigration policies. By engaging with legal scholarship, empirical research, and professional practice, it highlights how justice is frequently denied to marginalised groups. The introduction also examines the intersection of law, power, and social inequality, questioning whose interests the justice system truly serves. By framing these discussions within broader philosophical and legal theories, it sets the stage for an interdisciplinary exploration of contemporary justice challenges. Ultimately, this book calls for urgent reforms to ensure that justice is not a privilege for the few but a lived reality for all.

The chapters in this volume reveal a justice system at a crossroads. While certain legal reforms have been heralded as progress, systemic failures persist. The tension between justice and legal certainty, economic and institutional barriers, racial and gender disparities, and shifting policy landscapes all contribute to making justice inaccessible for many. A recurring theme throughout this volume is the need for an approach to justice that is more holistic, responsive, and adaptable to the realities of those it seeks to serve. Justice should not be a theoretical construct but a tangible reality that individuals, regardless of their socio-economic background, race, gender, or mental state, can access and experience fairly. The current legal system, while built upon principles of fairness and equity, often falls short due to the rigid structures that govern it. Procedural barriers, funding constraints, and bureaucratic inefficiencies create gaps between the law's intent and its practical outcomes.

The need for intersectional reform is particularly pressing. As demonstrated by the discussion on Legal Aid cuts, the lack of adequate representation continues to disenfranchise those most vulnerable in society. The erosion of procedural safeguards in criminal trials, particularly in the context of plea bargaining and efficiency-driven justice, threatens the very foundation of due process. Similarly, the challenges faced by women who kill in self-defence highlight the persistent failure of the legal system to incorporate contemporary understandings of domestic violence and coercive control into legal defences. The disproportionate impact of sentencing guidelines on children and young people further exemplifies how rigid laws can fail to account for human development and rehabilitation.

The marginalisation of racial minorities within the criminal justice system remains one of the most pressing issues requiring reform. The overrepresentation of BAME defendants in the justice system, coupled with harsher sentencing outcomes, underscores the need for systemic changes that address both explicit and implicit biases in judicial processes. The increasing reliance on digital court hearings, while expedient, raises concerns about access to justice for those who lack technological resources or literacy, particularly within marginalised communities. Ensuring a legal system that works for all means prioritising accessibility, transparency, and fairness over expedience and administrative efficiency. Moreover, the book highlights the troubling treatment of asylum seekers and the ways in which legislative changes have made it increasingly difficult for those fleeing persecution to secure refuge. The UK's shifting immigration policies raise serious ethical and legal concerns regarding its adherence to international obligations. Justice for migrants is not just about legal recognition but about fundamental human rights and dignity.

While this volume cannot not claim to offer a single solution to these deeply entrenched issues, it does serve as a call to action. Scholars, policymakers, legal practitioners, and activists must work collectively to address these failings and move toward a justice system that is truly equitable. Legal education and public discourse must also play a role in reshaping how justice is understood and delivered. The need for continuous legal evolution cannot be understated.

A just society is one where laws are not only fair in their drafting but also in their application. It is a society where systemic biases are actively dismantled, where legal protections are meaningful and accessible, and where individuals feel confident that they will be treated with dignity and fairness. This book, through its diverse contributions and critical engagements, hopes to contribute to this ongoing conversation, inspiring reforms that align legal practice with the ideals of justice that underpin it. Only by recognising the current system's failings and actively working toward solutions can we hope to bridge the gap between the ideal and the reality of justice in England and Wales.

We hope you find this book stimulating and perhaps it can act as a springboard for a deeper examination of the issues proffered in this collection.

Ed & Claire-Michelle,
February 2025

2 Ripe for Justice?

Rupert Dunbar

Introduction

This contribution considers the relationship between justice and legal certainty. The aims of justice (achieving the right outcome in an individual case) and certainty (providing clear rules to guide future conduct) are seen by many as law's two ultimate goals.[1] There is often a tension between them. This is teased out in the first part, with indication of where prominent scholars sit concerning their preferences. The second part explores how this tension has been resolved historically in England and Wales through equity and the common law. With these two bodies of law now delivered simultaneously, the chapter considers how substantively we may decide whether justice or certainty is preferable in a given case by developing a typology. Finally, the chapter highlights some of the most contentious topics and demonstrates aspects of the justice and certainty conundrum which underpins them. A conclusion identifies that while justice and legal certainty are essential to the functioning of law, certainty is often given lesser billing.

Justice and Certainty

The tension between justice and legal certainty has long been recognised by scholars to be problematic. John Rawls went as far as to call it 'one of the tangled questions of political science'.[2] To some, it is the 'duality of law'[3] and encompasses all that law is seeking to achieve.[4]

1 See especially Jürgen Habermas, *Between Facts and Norms* (William Rehg (trans), Polity Press 1997) 199; John Rawls, *A Theory of Justice* (revised edn, Harvard University Press 1999) 52–53 and Robert Alexy, 'The Dual Nature of Law' (2010) 23(2) *Ratio Juris* 167.

2 John Rawls, *A Theory of Justice* (revised edn, Harvard University Press 1999) 52–53.

3 Robert Alexy, 'The Dual Nature of Law' (2010) 23(2) *Ratio Juris* 167, 173–174.

4 Joseph Raz, 'Legal Principles and the Limits of Law' (1972) 81 *Yale Law Journal* 823, 841; Jürgen Habermas, *Between Facts and Norms* (William Rehg (trans.), Polity Press 1997) 199; Lord Denning, *The Discipline of Law* (Butterworths 1979) 293; Stefano Bertea, 'Certainty, Reasonableness and Argumentation in Law' (2004) 18 Argumentation 465, 475; and William Twining, *Karl Llewellyn and the Realist Movement* (2nd edn, CUP 2012) 157.

DOI: 10.4324/9781003496823-2

One sees that an approach that focuses purely on achieving a 'fair' outcome could mean that participants struggle to organise their affairs. We would have a blurred line concerning the 'definitional stop' between the legal and non-legal. All manner of unexpected factors may be considered in the courtroom to achieve the seemingly cosmological 'right' outcome, based not only on applying rules but something – everything – more.

Conversely, the pursuit of legal certainty alone would render law rigid, inflexible, and impractical. Change or modernising rules would not be possible as certainty alone would be paramount. Courts would be reluctant to fill gaps in the law or respond to novel circumstances satisfactorily. Principles would be few, and it is likely that text would be paramount, with literal interpretations prevailing over purposive ones.[5]

With absolutism in justice or certainty providing the prospect of two different dystopias, a blending of the two aims seems desirable. But in what proportions? Here, scholars disagree profoundly. It is possible to loosely place scholars along a continuum of certainty and justice based on their vision for utopia. Max Weber expressed a strong preference for legal certainty, asserting that the 'modern judge is like a vending machine'[6] who (for a fee) 'disgorges the judgment with its reasons mechanically derived from the Code'.[7] Weber encouraged this approach in the interests primarily of the economy. He highlighted the English common law as his antithesis and expressed surprise at its success, putting this down essentially to the diligence and skill of lawyers in persevering through an antiquated system.[8]

Gustav Radbruch suggested that 'positive law, secured by legislation and power, takes precedence even when its content is unjust and fails to benefit the people, unless the conflict between statute and justice reaches such an intolerable degree that the statute, as "flawed law," must yield to justice'.[9]

5 Although some argue that purposive interpretation is more certain than textual interpretation in certain contexts, such as Miguel Poiares Maduro in 'Interpreting European Law: Judicial Adjudication in a Context of Constitutional Pluralism' (2007) 1(2) *European Journal of Legal Studies* 137, 147.

6 M Weber, *Economy and Society* (Guenther Roth and Claus Wittich (eds), University of California Press 1978) 886.

7 Ibid.

8 For discussion, see Emmanuel Melissaris, 'Is Common Law Irrational? The Weberian "England Problem" Revisited' (2020) 55(4) *Northern Ireland Legal Quarterly* 378.

9 Gustav Radburch, 'Statutory Lawlessness and Supra-Statutory Law' (first published 1946) (Bonnie Litschewski Paulson and Stanley L Paulson (trans)) (2006) 26(1) *Oxford Journal of Legal Studies* 1, 6–7. Radbruch had a second formulation along similar (though not identical) lines: '(2) Where there is not even an attempt at justice, where equality, the core of justice, is deliberately betrayed in the issuance of positive law, then the statute is not merely "flawed law", it lacks completely the very nature of law. For law, including positive law, cannot be otherwise defined than as a system and an institution whose very meaning is to serve justice'.

It is frequently noted that Radbruch developed this formula as a consequence of specific challenges presented by the Nazi regime.[10] Prior to this, he had been seen as adopting a more conservative approach in which laws passed in accordance with the rules set by the relevant legal system ought simply to be applied by judges. HLA Hart suggested Radbruch underwent a 'conversion'[11] in now providing a margin of discretion, although certainty is still promoted above justice: Only intolerable injustice warrants juridical modification.

BN Cardozo cites Munroe Smith in highlighting that it is not only intolerable injustice that may cause us to wish to deviate from legal certainty. Instead, 'if a rule continues to work injustice, it will eventually be reformulated'.[12] The language reflects some reluctance, as it is suggested that 'the attempt to do absolute justice in every case would make the development and maintenance of general rules impossible'.[13]

Ronald Dworkin famously developed a hypothetical super-judge called Hercules. As one might imagine, a super-judge is not created to be overly cautious, and Dworkin suggested that Hercules would 'test his interpretation of any part of the great *political* structure and decisions of his community by asking whether it could form part of a coherent theory justifying the network as a whole'.[14] While it is possible that the network/community may by its nature dictate a more conservative interpretation, Dworkin clearly anticipates a fuller role for the judge than that suggested by Radbruch. Dworkin's assertion that morality forms a part of law and law's interpretation also implies an outlook which is more concerned with justice than certainty,[15] not least because we are not super-human and so may not with certainty anticipate what Hercules will decide![16]

Lord Denning wrote extra-judicially that '[t]he law must be certain. Yes, as certain as may be. But it must be just too'.[17] Of course, Lord Denning had the opportunity to put his vision of the appropriate balance between certainty and justice into practise. It is fair to say that while suggesting in abstract that law must be as certain as may be, in outcome Lord Denning showed a strong

10 See, for example, Raymond Wacks, *Understanding Jurisprudence: An Introduction to Legal Theory* (6th edn, OUP 2020) 35–36.

11 HLA Hart, 'Positivism and the Separation of Law and Morals' (1957–58) 71 *Harvard Law Review* 593, 616. See also Stanley L Paulsen, 'Lon L. Fuller, Gustav Radbruch, and the "Positivist" Theses' (1994) 13(3) *Law and Philosophy* 313, 315–316 and Deniz Coskun, *Law as a Symbolic Form: Ernst Cassirer and the Anthropocentric View of Law* (Springer 2007) 328.

12 BN Cardozo, *The Nature of the Judicial Process* (Yale University Press 1921) 23, citing M Smith, *Jurisprudence* (Columbia University Press 1909) 21.

13 Ibid.

14 R Dworkin, *Law's Empire* (Hart Publishing 1986) 245 (emphasis added).

15 For example, R Dworkin, *Freedom's Law: The Moral Reading of the American Constitution* (Harvard University Press 1996).

16 See similarly, Ofer Raban, *Modern Legal Theory and Judicial Impartiality* (Glasshouse Press 2003) 78–79.

17 Lord Denning, *The Discipline of Law* (Butterworths 1979) 293.

preference for justice that 'didn't hesitate to exercise his discretion even when there was clearly no room for any'.[18]

Famously, Lord Denning returned to the (lower) Court of Appeal because it was possible to be more influential there than in dissent at the House of Lords.[19] Lord Denning's substantive justice excursions from the Court of Appeal included a short-lived attempt to introduce common mistake in equity (allowing a contract to be rescinded) on a more flexible basis than that available under the common law[20] and a new model for trusts to be imposed 'whenever justice and good conscience require it'.[21] This was based on the concept that 'equity is not past the age of childbearing'.[22] As we shall see, equity is a branch of law which is historically more flexible than the common law. However, this did not prevent the conclusion of others that even for equity, 'its progeny must at least be legitimate'.[23]

Lord Denning's approach often led to creative tension, most notably with more conservative judges, one of whom accused Lord Denning of 'naked usurpation of the legislative function'.[24] In this light, it is not surprising that Lord Denning welcomed the importation of the purposive interpretative style, which is characteristic of EU courts.[25] So great was Lord Denning's preference for justice that he proved consistently willing to confront one of the hallmarks of the common law system in its name: precedent.[26] Lord Diplock famously suggested that this amounted to a 'one-man crusade'.[27] One wonders what Weber would have made of this crusading judge far removed from his ideal of the vending machine.

Having laid out a continuum upon which scholars disagree concerning the appropriate balance between justice and certainty, let us now see how the England and Wales answered this challenge.

Justice and Certainty: Equity and the Common Law

The tension between justice and legal certainty is one with which every legal system must wrestle. It is fair to say that the English and Welsh answer to

18 Emmanuel Melissaris, 'Is Common Law Irrational? The Weberian "England Problem" Revisited' (2020) 55(4) *Northern Ireland Legal Quarterly* 378, 379.
19 Lord Denning, *The Discipline of Law* (Butterworths 1979) 287.
20 *Solle v Butcher* [1950] 1 KB 671 *cf Great Peace Shipping Ltd v Tsavliris Salvage (International) Ltd* [2003] QB 679.
21 *Hussey v Palmer* [1972] 1 WLR 1286, 1290 (Lord Denning M.R.).
22 *Eves v Eves* [1975] 1 WLR 1338, 1341 (Lord Denning M.R.).
23 *Cowcher v Cowcher* [1972] 1 WLR 425, 430 (Bagnall J).
24 *Magor and St. Mellons Rural District Council v Newport Corporation* [1952] AC 189, 191 (Lord Simonds).
25 Anthony Arnull, 'The Law Lords and the European Union: Swimming with the Incoming Tide' (2010) 35(1) *European Law Review* 57, 58.
26 Hazel Carty, 'Precedent and the Court of Appeal: Lord Denning's Views Explored' (1981) 1(1) *Legal Studies* 68.
27 *Davis v Johnson* [1979] AC 264, 325 (Lord Diplock).

this has been a remarkable one which has given rise to a significant amount of history. It saw the division of justice and legal certainty into recognisable, institutional functions separated from one another. Over time, these subsequently united, although the extent to which they conflate with one another remains hotly contested by academics over 150 years on.[28] It is still possible today to trace rules back to their equitable or legal origins, and it matters in their application. For example, equity, based in fairness and justice, may ask whether you come to it with 'clean hands', whereas the common law would be more circumscribed in beginning its enquiry with your cause of action, not your motive or past.[29]

In the 1300s, common law's circumscription became problematic: To have a cause of action, one's claim needed to fit within established 'writs'. King Henry VIII's Provisions of Oxford (1258) precluded the creation of new writs, and so the common law was destined to remain both rigid and limited. However, the King, as the fountain of all justice, remained a valuable resource to which citizens could turn in order to plead their 'case' where the common law would be of unsatisfactory or no assistance (the King's prerogative including the power to deal with 'unjust judgment' and 'default of justice').[30] This alternative path to justice was steadily used, and Watt notes, interestingly, that the 'Black Death' (1346–1353) increased usage of equity as common law courts became overwhelmed.[31] The Chancellor oversaw the dispensing of justice on the King's behalf, and in this period the Court of the Chancery (equity) expanded.

By the time of the famous *Earl of Oxford* case (1615), two recognisable 'legal' avenues were available to claimants: Defects in the King's common law could be resolved through access to the King's Court of Chancery (equity), although it was rationalised that common law's judgments remained in place while equity merely acted on the 'conscience' of the parties (in this case preventing enforcement of the common law as a result).[32] It may have long seemed clear which body of law (if necessary) took precedence, and this was confirmed by King James I in this case: Equity prevails. Nonetheless, equity follows the common law wherever possible. Moreover, equity acts on the conscience, whereas common law acts in *rem* (the thing itself). In the intervening years equity also came to be seen as a body of rules rather than a divine or political whim of the King or his Chancellor.[33]

28 For discussion, see Warren Barr and John Picton, *Pearce and Stevens' Trusts & Equitable Obligations* (8th edn, OUP 2022) 8–10.

29 See, for example, *Grobbelaar v News Group Newspapers and Ltd* [2002] 1 WLR 3024.

30 Gary Watt, *Trusts and Equity* (10th edn, OUP 2023) 4 citing *Leges Henrici Primi* 10.1 (LJ Downer (ed and trans), OUP 1972) 108.

31 Ibid.

32 For discussion see ibid 10 and JE Penner, *The Law of Trusts* (12th edn, OUP 2022) 7–8.

33 Richard Clements and Ademola Abass, *Complete Equity and Trusts: Text, Cases, and Materials* (5th edn, OUP 2018) 7–9.

Equity became popular, arguably too popular. This caused significant delays for claimants, and 'by the nineteenth century, because of the backlog of administration in the Court of Chancery, escape was often sought in the other direction.'[34] With the passing of the Judicature Acts 1873–5, the competition ended, and legal and equitable rules could be applied in all courts. The unification of the courts provided the prospect that 'omnicompetent judges would deploy whatever doctrine and use whatever remedy met the needs of the case'.[35]

In both the institutional and substantive senses, we see some answer to the justice or certainty question, but on reflection, it is a little limited. Institutionally, we picked neither the dystopia of pure justice nor that of pure certainty; instead, we had schizophrenic oscillation between the two, based on which building one happened to be standing in at the time. *Earl of Oxford* confirmed that in a clash, equity (justice) prevails, yet caution in exercise of this jurisdiction is evident (equity will follow the common law where possible).[36]

Substantively, after the Judicature Acts 1873–5, both common law and equity could be applied. Setting aside the debate as to whether common law and equity's waters now mingle or simply run side-by-side, it should be noted that each element is subject to change.[37] Common law evolves and in the process sporadically injects new justice conceptions, even though at times, caution is palpable.[38] Equally, equity is not a license to simply do the right thing; we can recall that Lord Denning's flexible approach was often too much for equity to bear. Over time, the need for equity to intervene was also lessened by some greater flexibility in the common law, while simultaneously, the basis on which equity would intervene was more informed by its rules than by unfettered discretion 'by precedent out of principle'.[39] Each body of doctrine came to be a more pragmatic mix of the certain and the just within itself. With a more nuanced and mixed set of rules for judges to apply, the question becomes, in which circumstances is legal certainty or justice to be preferred? Legislators also face a similar question.

34 Gary Watt, *Trusts and Equity* (10th edn, OUP 2023) 8.

35 Patrick Polden, 'Mingling the Waters: Personalities, Politics and the Making of the Supreme Court of Judicature' (2002) 61(3) *The Cambridge Law Journal* 575, 577.

36 See, for example, *Stack v Dowden* [2007] UKHL 17, [33], [54].

37 For discussion of this 'fluvial' occurrence, see *United Scientific Holdings Ltd v Burnley Borough Council* [1978] AC 904, 925 (Lord Diplock).

38 See, for example, the protracted debate over whether compound interest should be awarded under the common law, decided three to two against in *Westdeutsche Landesbank Girozentrale Respondent v Islington London Borough Council Appellant* [1996] AC 669 and three to two for in *Sempra Metals Ltd (formerly Metallgesellschaft Ltd) v Inland Revenue Commissioners and another* [2008] 1 AC 561.

39 *Cowcher v Cowcher* [1972] 1 WLR 425, 430 (Bagnall J).

Justice and Certainty: Developing a Typology

John Rawls was more hesitant than many of the scholars I placed along the continuum in part one. Rawls first suggested that even where laws and institutions are unjust, it is often better that they be consistently applied. In this way, those subject to them at least know what is demanded and can try to protect themselves accordingly[40] before adding, '[o]n the other hand, it might be better in particular cases to alleviate the plight of those unfairly treated by departures from existing norms'.[41] For Rawls context was decisive.

Recognising that courts have the capacity to draw upon both common law and equitable concepts, and that both common law and equity incorporate justice and legal certainty in a more varied way than was previously the case, the question becomes how to apply this varied palette. We can attempt to put flesh on Rawls' intuition by developing a non-exhaustive typology of indicators to inform this decision.

Personal/Impersonal

Law can be personal and can feel personal. Imagining a divorce between people who have spent decades together, we would be surprised if the judge were not able to take into consideration their personal circumstances when making provision for dividing their assets.[42] If in a separate context, we have a violation of an individual's human right, perhaps a trespass against their dignity, then we would expect nothing less than a full and fair resolution. In both these situations, arguably, legal certainty is less relevant than justice and has fewer merits.

In contrast, imagine a company dealing with rules of incorporation or (dare I say) tax. A company is well placed (perhaps too well placed) to navigate rules and mitigate adverse outcomes. Certainty is more acceptable as a primary concern than would have been the case if we advised our poor citizen in advance (with certainty) that they would suffer an indignity and they should take steps to avoid it; there certainty would just serve another indignity, and only justice would do. Companies often indicate that uncertainty is their primary challenge, and certainty is often treated as a paramount concern in commercial contexts.[43]

Significant/Minor Impacts

Law failing to take account of, or to protect, specific differences between us linked strongly to our identities simply will not do. We have discrimination

40 John Rawls, *A Theory of Justice* (revised edn, Harvard University Press 1999) 52.

41 Ibid.

42 Judges are so empowered under the Matrimonial Causes Act 1973.

43 Lord Mance, 'Should the Law Be Certain?' *The Oxford Shrieval Lecture* (11th October 2011) 3 <www.supremecourt.uk/docs/speech_111011.pdf> accessed 11 November 2024).

laws to address these specific problems, and we apply them as an overlay or protective backstop to multiple areas of law.[44] Recognising that justice may not satisfactorily be achieved across multiple areas (even if sought), discrimination rules function as a justice finesse across what may be a series of unsatisfactory rules pursuing different justice agendas and delivering different certainties. The focus of discrimination rules is – appropriately – on what is right.

At the opposite end of the importance spectrum, speed limits often cover long stretches of road on which it may be safe to drive faster but where (logically) the highest speed will be determined by the lowest maximum safe speed on that part of that road. The impact on the driver is minor, and even though a more just approach is possible, it is not desirable.[45] In land law, there are many cases in which neighbours enter into battles over placement of fences or other minor inconveniences visited from next door. Judges often remark pointedly on the excessive time, cost, and effort in resolving disputes which grow out of all proportion to their origins.[46] Of course, this concept is also encapsulated in the maxim *de minimis non curat lex*: The law is not concerned with trifles.

Precedent (Following or Setting)

Clearly, in a common law system, the concept of precedent is of immense importance. Precedent was deemed so important that prior to 1966, even the House of Lords could not depart from its own previous decisions. It later empowered itself to do so, describing precedent as an 'indispensable foundation upon which to decide what is the law and its application to individual cases' as '[i]t provides at least some degree of certainty upon which individuals can rely', but adding 'too rigid adherence to precedent may lead to injustice in a particular case and also unduly restrict the proper development of the law'.[47] Essentially, previously decided cases are 'normally binding', but the House can 'depart . . . when it appears right to do so'. The more entrenched a principle is, the more hesitant will – and should – be the court to dislodge

44 Equality Act 2010, Introductory Text indicates *inter alia* its application to Ministers of the Crown, employment, public procurement, increasing equality of opportunity and rights, and responsibilities in family relationships.

45 It was recently found in Wales, however, that a default 20 mph restriction imposed across multiple roads takes preference for certainty too far. The Transport Secretary acknowledged, 'There is generally universal support for 20mph being targeted in areas where there are schools [etc.] . . . [b]ut in many areas, routes that shouldn't have been included, were'. Jack Grey, Cemlyn Davies, and Tink Llewellyn, '20mph Wales: Some Roads to Revert to 30mph after Backlash' (*BBC News*, 20 April 2024) <www.bbc.co.uk/news/uk-wales-68859568> accessed 10 November 2024.

46 Lord Hoffmann notes 'a particularly painful form of litigation. Feelings can run high and disproportionate amounts of money are spent'. Martin George and Antonia Layard, *Thompson's Modern Land Law* (8th edn, OUP 2022) 212–213 citing *Ian Wibberley Building Ltd v Insley* [1999] 1 WLR 894, 895 (Lord Hoffmann).

47 House of Lords, *Practice Statement (Judicial Precedent)* [1966] 1 WLR 1234.

it.[48] Many may be relying on it and need to reorganise their affairs in light of any change. In contrast, where there is no clear precedent, the judge's discretion and capacity to do justice in a specific context increases.[49] Judges may also consider whether their decision (or comments) may set a new precedent, being more cautious as a result or even declining to comment if they do not deem it necessary.[50]

Capacity to Navigate

The capacity for a subject to navigate certain rules will increase our preference for certainty, in contrast to circumstances where such rules would not helpfully/realistically guide behaviour for most (for example, relatively few may look at divorce law before getting married). The forward-looking element of legal certainty compared with the more backward-looking merits of justice was brought into sharp focus by the Women Against State Pension Inequality (WASPI) regarding women who have had to work longer due to changes in pension ages:

> WASPI agrees with equalisation [between men and women], but does not agree with the unfair way the changes were implemented . . . with little or no notice and much faster than we were promised . . . with not enough time to re-plan for our retirement.[51]

Aside from timing, certain groups of people cannot easily navigate certain but less just rules; vulnerable members of society would clearly suffer if preference were given to certainty with the expectation that citizens will take evasive action where necessary. Concerning adult welfare, courts have inherent jurisdiction to provide justice,[52] but it is also notable that vulnerability emerges in different contexts and that more refined legislation pursues protection, for example of consumers when dealing with companies.[53] These rules derogate from long-entrenched precedents of contract law, and they prioritise justice over certainty due to capacity of participants.

48 See, for example, continued adherence to *Pinnel* (1602), which rigidly rejected part payment of debt despite the misgivings of judges dating to *Foakes v Beer* (1884). For discussion, see Janet O'Sullivan, *O'Sullivan & Hilliard's the Law of Contract* (10th edn, OUP 2022) 108–113.

49 HLA Hart famously termed this the penumbra of uncertainty. HLA Hart, *The Concept of Law* (first published 1961, 3rd edn, OUP 2012) 12.

50 See, for example, Lord Sumption exercising such restraint concerning part payment of debt in *MWB Business Exchange Centres Ltd v Rock Advertising Ltd* [2019] AC 119, 131.

51 WASPI <www.waspi.co.uk/background-information/> accessed 10 November 2024.

52 Inevitably, the debate then becomes whether the 'piecemeal, contentious, and confused approach to the development of the law' which develops is satisfactory or whether more certainty is needed. Laura Pritchard-Jones, '"Palm Tree Justice": The Inherent Jurisdiction in Adult Welfare Cases' (2023) 86(6) *Modern Law Review* 1358, 1389.

53 For instance, The Unfair Terms in Consumer Contracts Regulations 1999.

Ultimately, where time is limited or the subject of legal rules will not be able to adapt, preference should be given to justice.

Large Number/Small Number

The idea here is that certainty gains in importance when we look to those rules which impact large numbers of people in contrast to justice, which is more easily applied to smaller numbers.

For example, in interpreting a contract, the court has underlying principles of contract law but will seek to understand the specific understanding shared by the two parties to that contract even if this means drawing on a wider range of evidence.[54] The legal system, in this context, is providing quite a bespoke service and delivering justice. In contrast, rules covering all of society, such as tax or criminal law, usually have as their starting point rigidity and neutral application to all, providing certainty.[55]

Resources and AI

To put it bluntly, achieving legal certainty often costs less than achieving justice. The time and resources necessary to do justice were among the things that caused claimants to return to the doors of common law courts from those of equity. More narrow admission of evidence and the prevention of a string of witnesses and counter-witnesses clearly lessens the length and cost of cases (for state and claimant). But it means the 'truth' (and justice) is less attainable. Similarly, brief and more simple legislation is easier and quicker to pass. It will also often be easier to interpret. The convoluted nature of some recent statutes has drawn the ire of judges, notably a provision that needed to be read in conjunction with other pieces of legislation to be made sense of![56] Of course, over-simplification can give rise to gaps in the law which can prompt further uncertainty and litigation, but pursuit of absolute justice in each instance will be costly.

An important future note on this regards artificial intelligence (AI). AI will work effectively in imposing clearer rules; for example, AI might struggle with enforcing a rule not to block a junction unreasonably but a rule not to stop in a yellow box will be easily enforced by it. Automated law enforcement through technology could well see us shift towards legal certainty in rule

54 See, for example, the detailed analysis of whether a course of previous dealing between parties implied certain terms in *McCutcheon v David Macbrayne Ltd* [1964] 1 WLR 125.

55 Indeed, in modifying its approach to precedent, the House of Lords singled out criminal law as an area for caution. House of Lords, *Practice Statement (Judicial Precedent)* [1966] 1 WLR 1234.

56 *Merkur Island Shipping Corporation Respondents v Laughton and Other Appellants* [1983] 2 AC 570.

formulation, perhaps admitting justice arguments at the review stage with a human in the loop.[57]

Prevailing Winds?

When debating whether to move the law on or develop it in a particular way, judges will often openly debate whether the matter is best left to Parliament. This reflects a broader concern that 'it is undesirable for judges to become involved in controversial issues of public policy, because their decisions would be less certain and predictable, and because judges would become more vulnerable to criticism in the political arena'.[58] How aware the individual judge should be of the political moment is debatable and may feel like an uncomfortable topic for those who view the law as being separate from politics. The reality of the moment is that there is erosion in public perceptions of the rule of law across Europe and the US. This is occurring at a time when populism is on the rise (which may not be a coincidence). Where justice is pursued rather than certainty, there is more fertile ground for debate (your vision of substantive justice may not be the same as my vision of substantive justice). Politicians may successfully label judges and the legal profession as having certain predilections in the eyes of the public. More rigid adherence to legal certainty lessens the scope for political criticism and the risk of law's exclusion, but it does so at the cost of doing what the individual judge and wider profession may see as the 'right thing' in a given case.

With an indicative typology, let us now turn to some recent legal developments and tease out the justice and certainty factors at play.

Justice and Certainty: Problematic Contemporary Case Studies

i) Criminal Law and Review of Convictions

Criminal law seeks to lay down some of the clearest directions possible so as to enable individuals to live life within its rules and to understand the ramifications of breaching the law. It applies to all of us, so we may think that certainty is paramount, but it is simultaneously very personal for both victims and perpetrators. Accordingly, it is not just the *actus reus* that is needed to complete an offence but also the *mens rea*. It is a mix of certainty and justice

57 AI has successfully been used in the UK to detect mobile phone usage and failure to wear seatbelts with a human in the loop (deciding whether to issue a fine). Mobile Phone and Seatbelt Detection Trial (ends March 2025), *National Highways*, 'privacy notice' <https://nationalhighways.co.uk/about-us/privacy-notice/mobile-phone-and-seatbelt-detection-trial-ends-march-2025-privacy-notice/> accessed 7 November 2024.

58 Anthony Lester, 'English Judges as Law Makers' (1993) *Public Law* 269, 270.

in a very specific formulation. *Mens rea* rests on either intention, recklessness, negligence, or strict liability.[59]

However, this formulation would still not be able account for the difference between somebody stealing a loaf of bread in desperation to feed themselves and another stealing a diamond to order to sell on the black market: Both would be guilty of theft under Section 1 of the Theft Act 1968. However, sentencing guidelines provide judges with guidance and discretion. Our bread theft is likely to be less well planned (less culpability), and the value of the item would be considered (below £200 compared with above £1,000).[60] Stealing the diamond to order also increases the seriousness, another aggravating factor, whereas the bread thief is in a difficult or deprived personal circumstance, which includes poverty, and poverty is a mitigating factor that reduces the seriousness. Our diamond thief may face close to six years in prison, but our bread thief will likely escape with only a fine.[61]

In short, while every court must follow the guidelines, the court can derogate if 'it would be contrary to the interests of justice to do so'.[62] Through the *actus reus*, *mens rea*, and sentencing stages, there is a progression from applying rules that promote legal certainty towards those that promote justice. Overall, in our example, we see a wide difference in treatment based on ostensibly the same initial offence: Certainty is frontloaded, but justice tempers it in a rearguard action.

Interestingly, one of the most problematic areas of criminal law has recently been when to reopen or review cases. High-profile miscarriages of justice in the Malkinson case and the Post Office scandal drew much public attention. Andrew Malkinson was convicted of rape in 2004 and served 17 years in prison, but no DNA evidence linked him to the case. The Criminal Cases Review Commission (CCRC) turned down requests to review his case in 2009 and 2018 but eventually accepted the request in 2023.[63] As a result of advancements in DNA technology, from at least 2008, there was awareness that DNA was present that did not belong to Malkinson, the victim, or the victim's partner,[64] but despite this, it was only after a charity externally

59 Jeremey Horder, *Ashworth's Principles of Criminal Law* (10th edn, OUP 2022) 171–237.

60 Sentencing Council, 'Sentencing Guideline, Theft – General' (1 February 2016) <www.sentencingcouncil.org.uk/offences/magistrates-court/item/theft-general> accessed 8 November 2024.

61 The Sentencing Act 2020, s. 125 requires considering the financial circumstances of the defendant (e.g. insufficient means) in setting the fine after seriousness has been established.

62 Sentencing Act 2020, s. 59(1).

63 *Andrew Malkinson Inquiry*, 'Chronology' <https://andrewmalkinson.independent-inquiry.uk/andrew-malkinson/> accessed 10 October 2024.

64 This was a breach of the disclosure regime whereby the prosecution was required to alert the defence to the existence of this evidence. See Attorney General's Office, *Attorney General's Guidelines on Disclosure: For Investigators, Prosecutors and Defence Practitioners* [2024] for the latest disclosure rules.

commissioned DNA tests that produced confirmatory evidence in 2023 that the CCRC finally referred the case to the Court of Appeal.[65]

Beyond the shocking facts of the Malkinson case – which are now subject to an inquiry – there is the suggestion that the CCRC has generally been too cautious in its mandate. The test of whether to refer a case to Court for review is whether there is a 'real possibility', meaning there 'is more than an outside chance or a bare possibility, but which may be less than a probability or a likelihood or a racing certainty'.[66] On this basis, the success rate (upholding convictions) of around 70% suggests the test is being applied too stringently.[67] Resources are limited, and the CCRC has said it needs more staff.[68] In the Malkinson case, when refusing a second application for review, the CCRC also took into account cost of DNA testing.[69]

Similarly to Mr Malkinson's case, the process of individually reviewing and (where appropriate) overturning convictions in the Post Office scandal concerning financial errors in the Horizon programme for which individual postmasters were blamed proved a slow one. Because of this, the government took the unprecedented step of quashing convictions for hundreds of people *en masse*.[70] This caused concern for some,[71] who viewed it as extensive reach from the government into what would typically be an issue reserved for the judiciary. For our purposes, it is interesting to note that the government was keen to provide certainty (arguably with broad stroke justice) but proves willing to risk quashing correct convictions in the mix where the judicial process (and more nuanced application of justice) would not.

The unique nature of criminal law means that it often encompasses multiple aspects of our typology which push us in opposite directions towards either justice or certainty. The solutions have been innovative, with headline offences clear but personal circumstances lessening punishments. The balance between

65 See *Andrew Malkinson v The King* [2023] EWCA Crim 954 for discussion of relevant grounds.

66 Lucy Welsh, Layla Skinns, and Andrew Sanders, *Sanders & Young's Criminal Justice* (5th edn, OUP 2021) 581 citing *Criminal Cases Review Commission, ex p Pearson* [2000] 1 Cr App R 149.

67 Ibid.

68 'Our finance budget allocation in 2022/23 was significantly below our requirements. Inadequate resource makes it more difficult to fulfil our purpose of finding, investigating, and referring possible miscarriages of justice. There is a risk that the CCRC finds it more challenging to secure support for its objectives, plans and initiatives which will impact delivery of services. Substantial CCRC time is absorbed in dealing with 'satellite' resource issues rather than focussed on reviewing cases'; CCRC, *Annual Report and Accounts 2022/23* (2023) 62. Staffing levels were also indicated to be 20% below requirements.

69 Dominic Casciani, 'Andy Malkinson: DNA Evidence Identified Three Years after Rape Conviction' (*BBC News*, 16 August 2023) <www.bbc.co.uk/news/uk-66513959> accessed 10 November 2024 citing file released to Mr Malkinson.

70 Post Office (Horizon System) Offences Act 2024.

71 See, for example, Hannah Quirk, 'The Post Office Scandal and the Separation of Powers' (2024) 2 *Criminal Law Review* 91.

justice for individuals wrongfully convicted and certainty in finality of prosecutions sees divergent approaches at current. Arguably the knee-jerk reaction to the Post Office scandal is not matched by approaches to reviews of convictions elsewhere. Too little, too much, and inconsistency across the piece.

ii) Cohabitation and the Home

I have previously mentioned the discretion provided to judges in the case of divorce. Where couples choose not (or cannot afford) to get married, there is no equivalent provision in spite of misconceptions concerning 'common law' marriage, meaning cohabitees can be in a vulnerable position.[72] This is especially so concerning any equitable entitlement to the 'shared' property.

Cohabitees who break up often need to rely on the principles of equity manifested primarily in the resulting and constructive trust. Where a party has made a financial contribution the resulting trust suggests they are entitled to an equivalent share. The clarity associated with this has proven attractive, and Lord Neuberger in particular has advocated it as a favourable approach for reasons of legal certainty.[73]

However, the common intention constructive trust is increasingly the mechanism by which disputes are being resolved. Even if a resulting trust is present, where the parties intend and share an understanding of a different arrangement, this will be honoured by the courts. Herein lies the challenge: Parties are often not on good terms, and conversations will often not be easily recalled. This poses particular challenges for the party who has not made a financial contribution, especially in 'sole names' cases in which only one party's name is registered as the legal owner, giving rise to the presumption that they are fully entitled to the whole in equity property too. In joint names cases, both parties are registered as legal owners, meaning there is evidence of an intention to share (presumably) on equal terms.

Notable cases in the House of Lords[74] and now the Supreme Court[75] have addressed this issue but only for joint names cases. However, tantalising statements were made concerning sole names cases that hinged on open criticism of Lord Bridge's famous dictum that where there is not evidence of an intention to share in sole names cases,

> direct contributions to the purchase price by the partner who is not the legal owner, whether initially or by payment of mortgage instalments,

72 The existence of 'common law marriage' has been described as a 'wide-spread myth' *Stack v Dowden* [2007] 2 AC 432, [45] (Baroness Hale).

73 Ibid [123–127] (Lord Neuberger).

74 *Stack v Dowden* [2007] 2 AC 432.

75 *Jones v Kernott* [2012] 1 AC 776.

> will readily justify the inference necessary to the creation of a constructive trust. But, as I read the authorities, it is at least extremely doubtful whether anything less will do.[76]

The consequence of this is that if one party is prudent enough to pay the mortgage instalments, they will have a share, while if the other pays for holidays, food, clothes, childcare, cars, insurance, pets, etc., they will not. These elements can only be used in quantifying the share, not in establishing the share in the first place, even if (in real terms) the expenditure/contribution is greater from that party than the other.

In this conundrum, one can see the familiar battle lines of certainty and justice emerging. Lord Bridge's approach is easy to apply with direct contributions easy to ascertain. The legal owner will not be at risk of losing equity in their home through inadvertent conduct or allowing 'other' non-financial contributions to the home. Any mortgagees or other externally interested parties will be dealing with a simpler asset. In counter, it seems disagreeable that a party who contributed an awful lot is left with nothing if their contribution does not fit within a narrow, albeit certain, formula.

In advancing the certainty argument, Lord Neuberger noted that '[a] change in the law, however sensible and just it seems, always carries a real risk of new and unforeseen uncertainties and unfairnesses.'[77] Lord Neuberger also said that 'the law of resulting and constructive trusts is flexible enough . . . and it would be a disservice to the important causes of certainty and consistency if we were to hold otherwise'.[78]

In defence of justice, Lord Hope stated '[w]hether or not Lord Bridge's observation was justified in 1990, in my opinion the law has moved on, and your Lordships should move it a little more in the same direction . . .'.[79] In recognising the certainty argument as the prevailing winds against which justice must struggle, Lord Hope suggested that the progress has been modest but acknowledged that any alignment of this area with rules applied to divorce proceedings would mean '[t]he law would then become more flexible (and so better able to avoid injustice) but at the price of uncertainty. . . . But already there is a good deal of uncertainty'.[80]

Baroness Hale adopted the conceptual distinction of the personal and commercial, observing that 'the behaviour of people living together in an intimate

76 *Lloyds Bank Plc. Appellants v Rosset and Another Respondents* [1991] 1 AC 107, 133 (Lord Bridge).

77 *Stack v Dowden* [2007] 2 AC 432 [102] (Lord Neuberger).

78 Ibid [106] (Lord Neuberger) *cf* 'the fact that couples (whether married or unmarried) rarely make agreements about their respective shares in their homes, and to the enormous inflation in property prices which has made the division of ownership by reference to initial financial contributions artificial and potentially productive of injustice.' *Jones v Kernott* [2012] 1 AC 776, 796 (Lord Collins).

79 Ibid [26] (Lord Hope).

80 Ibid [27] (Lord Hope).

relationship may be different from the interpretation to be put upon similar behaviour between commercial men' and 'an outcome which might seem just in a purely commercial transaction may appear highly unjust in a transaction between husband and wife or cohabitant and cohabitant.'[81]

It is notable both how judges divide into camps for certainty and justice and how aspects of our typology emerge in their reasoning. The wait continues for the sole name case that comes before the Supreme Court, where we shall see if certainty or justice will be preferred in this area.

iii) Rwanda Flights

The former government's decision to conclude a treaty with Rwanda for processing asylum seekers made many headlines.[82] It revealed tensions between the legal discipline and the government of the day. It also resulted in increased suggestions that the UK may leave the European Convention of Human Rights.[83]

The Supreme Court was called upon to decide whether the Rwanda policy was lawful but was at pains to point out that 'court is not concerned with the political debate surrounding the policy'.[84] Specifically, it had to determine whether there was a risk of refoulement for asylum seekers, meaning the returning of an applicant to a country where they are likely to face persecution. The decision of the court was unanimous: The definition of refoulement applied was international, and further supported by the ECHR (incorporated into UK law by the Human Rights Act 1998),[85] and the decision concerning the (un)safety of Rwanda was based on a wide range of evidence.[86] What more could the court do? Yet pointedly, after the judgment was handed down, the

81 Ibid [42] (Baroness Hale). For discussion of the constructive trust's role in commercial contexts, see Ying Khai Liew, 'Making Sense of Agreement-Based Constructive Trusts in the Commercial Context' (2022) 4 *Journal of Business Law* 330.

82 See, for example, Charles Hymas, 'Ministers Threaten to Quit over Rwanda Flights Law' *The Daily Telegraph* (London, 5 December 2023) and 'The Magical Thinking Behind Britain's Rwanda Bill: Law's Should Be Rooted in Reality' *The Economist* (14 December 2023; online) <www.economist.com/britain/2023/12/14/the-magical-thinking-behind-britains-rwanda-bill> accessed 18 November 2024.

83 See, for example, Paul Seddon, 'Tories Must Back ECHR Exit to Survive, Says Jendrick' (BBC News, 30 September 2024) <www.bbc.co.uk/news/articles/cy0lqzjwqx8o> accessed 18 November 2024. Note that with the change of government from Conservative to Labour in July 2024, the prospect of leaving the ECHR has lessened for the foreseeable future.

84 *R (on the application of AAA and ors) v The Secretary of State for the Home Department (UNHCR Intervening)* [2023] UKSC 42, [2] (Lord Reed and Lord Lloyd-Jones).

85 Ibid [28].

86 *Inter alia* United Nations High Commissioner for Refugees, possible previous instances of refoulement, previous UK case law, statements of the UK at international meetings, Foreign, Commonwealth and Development Office comments/records and events concerning the Rwanda/Israel similar bilateral agreement.

then Prime Minister (Rishi Sunak) indicated he 'disagreed' with it.[87] He also indicated acceptance of it and noted the importance of the rule of law in the UK. However, within seconds, in the same speech, he detailed that emergency legislation was necessary to prevent further domestic legal challenges. Moreover, the risk of challenge to the legislation could not be ruled out due to the European Convention on Human Rights (ECHR), with the Prime Minister indicating a willingness to leave this 'foreign' court if necessary.

This case, at first glance, does not reflect a problem of balancing justice and legal certainty. From the court's perspective, the issue of refoulement was clear and the evidence concerning Rwanda was clear. What is noticeable was that for the government it was not, or – as some suspect – the government was not willing to admit how clear it was. The circularity of Rwanda being safe simply because the government said so was humorous to many.

For the government, the paramount concern was finding a clear deterrent to boat crossings in the channel. For the UK Supreme Court, the primary concern was to apply law (international and domestic). For the government, certainty meant a path to ensuring that flights would take off unencumbered by legal challenges; for the court, certainty meant providing clear rules to prevent refoulement. This case was a tale of different visions of justice and certainty.

The nub of the argument thus was whether the judgment of Rwanda as a safe country was a legal one or a political one? The government presented it as a political one, and the court of public opinion did not seem to have been overly questioning of the government's position. The legislation also 'disapplied' parts of the Human Rights Act 1998 (incorporating the ECHR) to its subject matter.[88] The marginalisation of law in the Rwanda policy demands our attention. We know that political questions are challenging for the judiciary and give rise to contention. Here, the more significant question could arguably be cast as a legal one, let alone the multitude of smaller legal questions that interrelate with the larger one. Yet through the force of legislation, the government was able to place the issue as purely political and place it beyond the reach of key provisions of domestic law.

Murmurings resulted, but there has been no revolution in the name of upholding the rule of law. The assurance that law provided for individuals was lifted in the name of getting a policy 'done'. Lawyers may say "shame on you" but law should look at itself too. How has law ended up being so vulnerable to politics? And how can that tightrope be walked?

Of course, if the Supreme Court had done the government's bidding, there would have been no reason to marginalise domestic courts in this area. This is certainly not the suggested solution here; the court should apply the law. But

87 PM remarks on Supreme Court Judgement (Prime Minister's Office, 10 Downing Street, 15 November 2023) <www.gov.uk/government/speeches/pm-remarks-on-supreme-court-judgement-15-november-2023> accessed 1 November 2024.

88 Safety of Rwanda (Asylum and Immigration) Act 2024, s. 3.

it behoves the court, and lawyers, to recognise that public perception seems to be that it is fire against fire, politics of politicians against politics of lawyers. If the law is, as has been argued throughout this contribution, a blend of justice and certainty, we as lawyers should ensure that we highlight equally the aspect of certainty that sets law apart from politics.

Whether one likes it or not, law is in a precarious state when the government openly mocks 'lefty lawyers'[89] and marginalises courts with little apparent public backlash. The lesson of the Rwanda saga is certainly not that the court should have neglected asylum seekers to appease the government. The lesson is that when the court sought to draw on the reserves of legitimacy present within the law (often attributable to levels of legal certainty), it found little. Had the law been more revered, the idea that a factual judgment could be dislodged simply by passing legislation that said the opposite would have gained less traction. The spectre that other protected rights in the form of the ECHR could be removed to suit a shorter-term vision of justice would also have been unimaginable.

Foreign courts, lefty lawyers, 'Enemies of the People' (Brexit)[90] – in spite of the change in government such slogans to politicise law appear to have been somewhat successful in eroding confidence in the law (beyond legal circles at least!). At a time when competing visions of justice have never seemed more divergent and fractious, it may be prudent for lawyers to place some emphasis on legal certainty.

Conclusion

Ultimately, law is a balance between the aims of certainty and justice; a model based exclusively on either is doomed to fail. England and Wales recognised this and had a quite remarkable, albeit somewhat schizophrenic, structural answer. In recognition that in each case it may be necessary to deliver a blend of certainty ***and*** justice rather than certainty ***or*** justice, unification took place through the Judicature Acts. Now, courts are empowered to deliver a delicately blended solution to the specific case before them, with common law and equity blending justice and certainty within themselves, too. But when should justice or certainty be preferred? This has troubled academia for centuries, and in practice it will depend on multiple factors including the area of law, the claimants, and perhaps even the politics of the day. We have seen that some of the most pressing legal challenges of today can be traced to the classic tension between justice and certainty.

Yet on the cover of this book, justice takes centre stage, and it will do so for many other law books, too. Courses and research centres at universities often adopt

89 Monidipa Fouzder, 'Sunak Criticised for "Startling Ignorance" over "Lefty Lawyer" Attack' (*Law Society Gazette*, 8 March 2023) <www.lawgazette.co.uk/news/sunak-criticised-for-startling-ignorance-over-lefty-lawyer-attack/5115357.article> accessed 8 October 2024.

90 The cover of the *Daily Mail* (4 November 2016) newspaper showing senior UK judges.

justice as an integral part of their titles; people march for justice. Legal certainty receives lesser billing. It is less exciting and less prominent, but it is essential for providing law with the legitimacy it needs. Certainty provides law with an identity which is separate from politics and the (often) unanswerable question of what is 'right'. Certainty lessens the risk that law can successfully be marginalised by politicians.[91]

On this reading, each investment in justice (where not universally agreed upon) draws on the wider resource of legal certainty present within the law. Sometimes justice, dramatic justice is needed, but only through careful nurturing of legal certainty can we ensure that law will be there when we need it most: in the name of justice.

91 Interestingly, we see similar developments in the US, including from the other side of the political divide with President Biden's criticism of the US Supreme Court's decision on Presidential immunity. See Andrea Shalal, 'Biden Warns Supreme Court Presidential Immunity Ruling Is "Dangerous Precedent"' (*Reuters*, 2 July 2024) <www.reuters.com/world/us/biden-make-remarks-Monday-evening-immunity-ruling-by-supreme-court-2024-07-01/> accessed 17 October 2024.

3 Plea Bargaining and the State

Mike McConville

Introduction

In this chapter, I assess some of the literature relating to plea bargaining with emphasis upon the principal theories advanced to explain the transformation of the criminal justice process, primarily in England and Wales.[1] Based on my ongoing research, I review explanations relating to the origins of plea bargaining as well as those which seek to account for its modern formation as a guilty plea system.

The discussion highlights concerns, which are, I argue, fundamental to a proper engagement with the 'socio-legal' enterprise. These have not been stockpiled and are not *ad personam*. Indeed, I have often changed my approach, sometimes exhuming ill-supported ideas previously placed in shallow graves for yet other unsteady public showings.[2] What follows can be seen in part as self-criticism of earlier work, which sometimes evokes a sense of mild embarrassment.

Far from wishing to discourage innovative and cutting-edge theory, I want to encourage adventurous scholarship, proposing new theories and solutions even if they lack the expected rigorous empirical underpinnings or are undercut

1 I am not here concerned with issues such as the ethics of plea bargaining or the risk posed to innocent defendants. On these, see, for example, RL Lippke, *The Ethics of Plea Bargaining* (OUP 2011); J Roberts and J Ryberg, *Pleading Guilty: Ethical Perspectives on Sentencing the Self-Convicted* (Hart Publishing 2023); RK Helm, 'Constrained Waiver of Trial Rights? Incentives to Plead Guilty and the Right to a Fair Trial' (2019) 46(3) *Journal of Law and Society* 423. For an overview of the many issues in plea bargaining, see Máximo Langer, Mike McConville, and Luke Marsh (eds), *Research Handbook on Plea Bargaining and Criminal Justice* (Edward Elgar 2024).

2 The primary examples here have their origins in J Baldwin and M McConville, *Negotiated Justice* (Martin Robertson, 1977) and McConville et al., *Standing Accused* (OUP, 1994). While the soundness of the empirical basis of each book has, I would argue, withstood subsequent scrutiny, far too many of my follow-up articles on plea bargaining were in the exposé genre, and both books place too much emphasis upon the line workers and fail to engage with my current theoretical understandings, which advance a broader state-centred project in the hands of the Senior Judiciary and the Executive, as I flag later in this chapter.

DOI: 10.4324/9781003496823-3

or later refuted. Although then, I raise more than an eyebrow at some strands of scholarship, I acknowledge that my own theories and opinions are tentative and that others are lacking in rigorous empirical or documentary support.[3]

Overall, I emphasise an often-overlooked issue which is part of the title of this volume: namely 'the legal system'. I will suggest that popular conceptions/theoretical constructions in the plea bargaining literature are inadequate, misleading, inward looking, and even dangerous. I will also suggest that authors and teachers have too readily resorted to approaches which offer students an 'oven-ready' dish that is easy to digest but poisonous to intellectual inquiry. The overriding purpose is to depreciate the market value of ideas and approaches that should no longer be traded in the academic stock exchange.

An underlying theme is that the 'law in context' approach is flawed; instead, researchers should follow an approach based upon 'the context of law'. I hope the following discussion will illustrate the difference between these pathways, the former beginning and ending with the law, the latter providing the setting in which the law is best viewed and of which it may only be a small part.[4]

Section One: Models and Bargaining

One tranche of literature (and a popular approach in textbooks) seeks to understand plea bargaining as linked to 'models' of criminal justice, and it is useful to give these outline consideration.[5] I begin with a brief visit to the 'red light' district of academic research and teaching: Herbert Packer's models of the criminal process.[6] As is notorious, Packer proposed that criminal justice systems could be better understood as involving a contrast between, on the

3 In key areas, there must be a reduced demand for 'evidence' precisely because the state has filtered it or removed it or continues to hide it from public scrutiny.

4 Incidentally, it so happens that a focus on plea bargaining rather than its setting additionally runs the risk of overstating its importance in structuring not only guilty pleas but also the wider criminal justice system.

5 These models have attracted a vast critical literature as well as stimulating the proposal of yet more models such as to remind the reader of Alexander Pope: 'The increasing prospect tires our wandering eyes, Hills peep o'er hills, and Alps on Alps arise!': *An Essay on Criticism*, 1709.

6 Herbert Packer, *The Limits of the Criminal Sanction* (Stanford University Press, 1968). Packer himself captured the essence of the two models: 'If the Crime Control Model resembles an assembly line, the Due Process Model looks very much like an obstacle course'. Herbert L Packer, 'Two Models of the Criminal Process' (1964) 113 *University of Pennsylvania Law Review* 1, 14). The following notes do not represent a review of Packer's work, which has rightly enjoyed a favourable critical reception in academic and practitioner circles. For a fuller review, see John Griffiths, 'Ideology in Criminal Procedure or a Third "Model" of the Criminal Process' (1970) 79 *Yale Law Journal* 359; Malcolm M Feeley, 'Two Models of the Criminal Justice System: An Organizational Perspective' (1973) 7 *Law & Society Review* 407 (1973); Abraham S Goldstein, 'Reflections on Two Models: Inquisitorial Themes in American Criminal Procedure' (1974) 26 *Stanford Law Review* 1009, 1009; Peter Arenella, 'Rethinking the Functions of Criminal Procedure: The Warren and Burger Courts Competing Ideologies' (1983) 72 *Georgia Law Journal* 185; Kent Roach, 'Four Models of the Criminal Process' (1999) 89 *Journal of Criminal Law and Criminology* 671. It is a 'red light' area because it is seductive but at base unattractive.

one hand, 'crime control' and, on the other, 'due process'. Packer's depiction of crime control as involving a value system which viewed 'efficiency' in the suppression of crime as more important than the freedom of individuals in their confrontation with the state led many commentators to identify plea bargaining with crime control, thereby allowing uncritical observers and students to end their inquiry into the significance of plea bargaining rather than seeking understanding of it.

Three short observations may be made on this. First, a point that Packer himself sometimes forgot is that these conceptual models were not intended to be descriptive of any system but rather provided ways of formulating questions about a system of which the observer knows nothing.[7] They should accordingly not be used to impute some quality to plea bargaining. Second, using these labels risks ignoring the importance of class, race, gender, and distributive inequality in any critical analysis.[8] Third, at a theoretical level, as McBarnet discussed,[9] due process can be argued to be *for* crime control, the former existing as an ideology to mask a crime control function. This perspective should lead, at least, to a more critical interrogation of the place of plea bargaining within criminal justice beyond the simplified labels.

Section Two: Modern Characterisations of Plea Bargaining

At this point, it is helpful to look at approaches that have become increasingly popular in the literature as modern forms of criminal justice have become entangled in various rules and procedures. While there are differences in approaches, for present purposes, two may be discussed together: 'bureaucratisation' and 'managerialism.'

In this context, bureaucratisation seeks to portray criminal justice as set within a regulated, rule-bound hierarchy the purpose of which is to produce standardised outcomes. Closely allied to this is the idea of managerialism.[10] Here, while still accepting the rule-bound character, the emphasis is placed upon a management philosophy expressed in rules, regulations and key performance indicators which celebrate control through professionalism. In the

7 I am not here concerned with exploring other models that have been proposed for the same reason.

8 For reasons which appear, I am here concerned not with these issues but with a wider focus upon the state itself.

9 Doreen McBarnet, *Conviction* (Macmillan 1983).

10 See further M Feeley and J Simon in Nelken (eds), *The Futures of Criminology* (Sage 1994) 173–201; G Ritzer, *The McDonaldization of Society* (Pine Forge Press 2004). I have discounted the attempt to portray plea bargaining within the context of 'courtroom work groups', which are said to rest upon relationship networks through shared goals for which the principal advocates provided no convincing evidence: J Eisenstein and H Jacob, *Felony Justice* (Little Brown 1977), on which see Arlene Sheskin, 'Trial Courts on Trial: Examining Dominant Assumptions' in James A Cramer (ed), *Courts and Judges* (Sage 1981).

literature, each seeks to achieve the business-related outcomes of 'efficiency' and 'economy'.[11]

In England and Wales, both approaches have led to excellent ethnographic studies which have collated and sought to explain a mass of detailed rules, procedures, and regulations which beset modern criminal justice systems.[12] Additionally, they have convincingly described how those affected have adjusted or been forced to adjust their behaviours to accommodate these bureaucratic structures,[13] sometimes in direct compliance and sometimes adopting 'easing' practices which go unnoticed or are tolerated by the system.

Despite this, the general approach has significant limitations which are easily overlooked.[14] A focus on the production line of 'justice' – the microculture of the shop floor and its workers – commonly overlooks the corporate entity which directs and runs the business, the role of the state, and thus the politics of criminal justice. In turn, this runs the risk of confusing reasons with justifications proffered by judges and policy-makers[15]: Either efficiency or economy is seen as the motor force of the system rather than rationalisations for it, and 'rights' are seen as part of 'system balance' rather than as fundamental to a legitimating ideology.[16] These outcomes are a result not only of the bounded nature of the conceptual tools relied upon but of the fact that at base, the analytical tools utilised are characterisations rather than theories.

Langer advanced a much more sophisticated and theoretically informed account based on the concept of 'administratisation'.[17] He argues that in many

11 In passing, it should be noted that although they are rarely differentiated in the literature, these are distinct concepts: Efficiency refers to the way in which outcomes may be achieved using the least resources; economy, on the other hand, seeks to minimise waste and optimise productivity.

12 See, for an excellent account, Jenny McEwan, 'Truth, Efficiency and Cooperation in Modern Criminal Justice' (2013) 66 *Current Legal Problems* 203.

13 For a theoretical account, see Malcolm Feeley, 'Two Models of the Criminal Justice System: An Organizational Perspective' (1973) 7 *Law & Society Review* (Spring).

14 An excellent example which avoids many of the pitfalls is Daniel Newman, *Legal Aid Lawyers and Their Quest for Justice* (Hart 2013). See also Daniel Newman, 'Still Standing Accused: Addressing the Gap between Work and Talk in Firms of Criminal Defence Lawyers' (2012) 19 *International Journal of the Legal Profession* 1. For an earlier account, see Mike McConville et al., *Standing Accused* (OUP 1994).

15 This is seen most starkly when the policy documents are written by judges seeking executive action. See, for example, Sir Robin Auld, *The Criminal Courts Review* (Royal Courts of Justice 2001); Sir Brian Leveson, *Review of Efficiency in Criminal Proceedings* (Judiciary of England & Wales January 2015).

16 In England and Wales, defendants who are the object of plea bargaining are clothed in these factitious 'rights' including the right to legal advice, the right to plead guilty or not guilty, the right to refuse a sentence discount, the right to go to trial, etc.

17 Máximo Langer, 'From Legal Transplants to Legal Translations: The Globalization of Plea Bargaining and the Americanization Thesis in Criminal Procedure' (2004) 45 *Harvard International Law Journal* 1; Máximo Langer, 'Plea Bargaining, Conviction without Trial, and the Global Administratization of Criminal Convictions' (2021) 4 *Annual Review of Criminology* 377.

jurisdictions, over the past three decades, plea bargaining should be understood together with other mechanisms which have been introduced to impose criminal convictions without trial. Viewed collectively, these mechanisms have brought an administratisation of criminal convictions in two respects: They represent a shift of authority and *de facto* power to decide who gets convicted, for which crime, and to which sentence, from judges and juries to prosecutors, the police, and other administrative agencies; these essentially administrative determinations occur in non-public settings where defendants waive rights traditionally associated with criminal adjudication. This spread of plea bargaining and equivalent mechanisms implies, Langer argues, the spread of an administrative model of criminal adjudication around the world. This impressive account lifts analysis away from a narrow focus on line-workers and invites consideration of how and why this process is occurring and what this means for the political/judicial organisations which allow or encourage it.

Before returning to these accounts, I turn to discuss the history of plea bargaining which does involve theorisation.

Section Three: The Origins of Plea Bargaining

In this section, I discuss two favoured theories[18] accounting for the origins and subsequent rise of plea bargaining as they relate to criminal justice in England and Wales from the late Victorian period onwards.[19] Although plea bargaining came to public and academic prominence in England and Wales only around 1970 in the case of *Turner*,[20] there is an open question as to whether it existed prior to this and if so, in what forms. Should historical research demonstrate that guilty pleas were bargained at a much earlier period, the causes need to be identified, and questions should be raised as to how it remained concealed for so long. Testing theories explaining the rise of plea bargaining is, accordingly, vitally important if understanding is to proceed.

The most popular generalisable (i.e. non-jurisdictional) theory locates the rise of plea bargaining in increased 'professionalisation' associated with the entry of lawyers into an existing lay process and their impacts upon evidence,

18 I do not give credence to the view that plea bargaining is caused by 'caseload pressure', notably promulgated by George Fisher in *Plea Bargaining's Triumph: A History of Plea Bargaining in America* (Stanford University Press 2003). The theory is undermined by Milton Heumann's empirical work on courts at different historical moments: M Heumann, 'A Note on Plea Bargaining and Case Pressure' (1975) 9(3) *Law & Society Review* 527. For reviews of this theory and contrary data, see M Vogel, 'The Social Origins of Plea Bargaining: Conflict and the Law in the Process of State Formation, 1830–1860' (1999) 33 *Law & Society Review*, 1; Mary Vogel, 'Plea Bargaining: A Misreading of the Common Law in Modernity' in Maximo Langer, Mike McConville, and Luke Marsh (eds) *Research Handbook on Plea Bargaining and Criminal Justice* (Edward Elgar 2024); and M McConville and C Mirsky, *Jury Trials and Plea Bargaining* (Hart 2005).

19 In examining reported cases, I have taken 1890 as an arbitrary starting point.

20 [1970] 2 QB 321.

procedure, and substantive law. According to this 'lawyerisation' theory,[21] the introduction of lawyers necessarily complicated evidence and procedure (and ultimately the law itself), slowing the process at every juncture so as to render the adversarial trial, as John Langbein's described it,[22] absolutely 'unworkable as an ordinary dispositive procedure' and thereby providing a catalyst for the creation of plea bargaining as a speedier and cheaper alternative. Despite its superficial attraction, this theory turned out to lack grounding in empirical data in the home of its sponsors, the United States of America, and it has now been replaced by more persuasive jurisdictionally specific explanations.[23]

Regarding Victorian England,[24] I tested the theory against large samples[25] of serious cases heard in the Old Bailey in London between 1890 and 1912,[26] perhaps a fair representation of practices elsewhere,[27] the Old Bailey handling around 20% of all serious criminal cases in England and Wales over this period.[28] Despite citizens being the driving forces of prosecutions,[29] there was

21 See, for example, John Langbein, 'Understanding the Short History of Plea Bargaining' (1979) 13 *Law & Society Review* 261; Lawrence Friedman and Robert Percival, *The Roots of Justice: Crime and Punishment in Alameda County, California, 1870–1910* (UNC Press 1981). The theory was subject to the historiographical limitation that in a number of states such as New York, the office of public prosecutor and the presence of front-rank defence lawyers *predated* the rise of plea bargaining by many decades: Mary Vogel, 'Plea Bargaining under the Common Law' in Darryl K Brown, Jenia I Turner, and Bettina Weisser (eds) *The Oxford Handbook of Criminal Process* (OUP 2019).

22 See John Langbein, 'Understanding the Short History of Plea Bargaining' (1979) 13 *Law & Society Review* 261, 265.

23 See Mary Vogel, *Coercion to Compromise: Plea Bargaining, the Courts and the Making of Political Authority* (Oxford Socio-Legal Studies 2007); Mike McConville and Chester Mirsky, *Jury Trials and Plea Bargaining* (Hart 2005). These authors demonstrate that plea bargaining's rise in Boston and New York City, respectively, was intimately bound to transformations in local political culture. Indeed, for example, long before the sudden emergence and dominance of plea bargaining, the system extant in New York City was marked by an adversarial culture replete with defence lawyers of the highest learning and standing.

24 For convenience, I refer to the period 1890–1912 as 'Victorian' although Queen Victoria's reign ended in 1901. As far as the criminal justice system is concerned, the principal characteristics remained for some years notwithstanding such reforms as the introduction of an criminal appellate system.

25 For 1897, for example, I examined all cases reported (n = 893) in the Old Bailey for that year.

26 The case reports are *The Proceedings of the Old Bailey, London's Central Criminal Court, 1674–1913* <www.oldbaileyonline.org/>. The reports must be treated with caution because they are an incomplete record without, for example, accounts of pre-trial discussions (if any) between the parties or full transcripts of the trial proceedings.

27 The qualification 'perhaps' because, notwithstanding the high proportion of cases dealt with at the Old Bailey and a measure of consistency secured by the fact that trial judges travelled around the country on circuit, local variations may have occurred in regions with strong local cultures and traditions, and this should be the subject of future research.

28 See Mike McConville, 'English Plea Bargaining in Context: A Revisionist History of Plea Bargaining' in Maximo Langer, Mike McConville and Luke Marsh (eds) *Research Handbook on Plea Bargaining* (Edward Elgar 2024).

29 There being no organised system of public prosecution (the office of Director of Public Prosecutions instituted in 1879 was involved in only a few cases bearing upon the interests of the state).

a significant presence of lawyers such that one would, under the lawyerisation theory, expect lawyered trials to be beset with complexity and at least the glimmerings of an emergent plea bargaining. Over this period, prosecutors had the benefit of state-supported solicitors for investigation and counsel for both trial preparation and presentation. Additionally, 25% or more defendants secured legal representation by private means.

Despite this, there was no evidence that the presence of lawyers resulted in procedural or evidential complexity. In the great majority of cases, trials were not in any real sense adversarial. It was routine for trials to be held within a few weeks of the alleged criminal occurrence, with little time for factual or legal investigations. The law reports illustrate that the court processed 20 or more defendants in a single day without encountering procedural or evidentiary obstacles.[30] Trials, whether attended by or without legal representatives, were predominantly concerned with establishing the facts in a setting where evidence and procedure was straightforward[31] or readily settled by the judge without recourse to appellate review.[32] In short, lawyerisation did not result in complications to evidence and procedure and accordingly, any such driver for plea bargaining was absent.

A second theory, popularised in the USA, is that plea bargaining was facilitated by the introduction of lesser pleas: That is, once prosecutors could charge a full offence but then offer a reduction to a lesser offence (e.g. murder to manslaughter; robbery to theft; theft to handling; assault with intent to inflict bodily harm to simple assault), the door would open to a system of bargaining. As part of this, it was argued that once judges were accorded sentencing discretion, they were free to 'reward' those who pleaded guilty to a lesser charge with a lesser sentence, again triggering plea bargaining. In Victorian Britain, there is no evidence to support either strand of this theory.[33]

Over the whole period examined, offences in England were already graded in degrees of seriousness, as they are today, and there was no 'moment' when this changed to induce plea bargaining. Moreover, sentences were determined by the seriousness of the offence and the criminal/personal biography of the defendant and were not influenced by the nature of the plea. This is demonstrated in joint-defendant cases where one defendant pleaded guilty and

---

The Crown Prosecution Service was not established until 1986; see Prosecution of Offences Act, 1985, c. 23.

30 If necessary, the court day could be prolonged to deal with any unexpected interruption or to handle the volume of cases presented.

31 The same jury might hear several cases in succession and return verdicts without retiring.

32 At this time, the rulings of the trial judge were almost always dispositive, the Court of Criminal Cases Reserved rarely intervening and only then at the invitation of the trial judge. See Phil Handler, 'The Court for Crown Cases Reserved, 1848–1908' (2011) 29 Law & Hist Rev 259. In exceptional cases, evidence might be extensive with occasional disputes over such matters as admissibility.

33 For New York City in the nineteenth century, see: Mike McConville and Chester Mirsky, *Jury Trials and Plea Bargaining* (Hart 2005).

the other went to trial. In a plea bargaining system, in such cases, the theory would predict a lesser sentence to follow the guilty plea, but this did not happen. An example is the joint-defendant case of *Joseph Gold* (21, tailor) *and William Marcus* (21, dealer):[34]

> The defendants were jointly charged with feloniously uttering counterfeit coin, the trial taking place on 24th April, the alleged offence in the previous month on 14th March. Charles Brewster, tobacconist, gave evidence that Gold went into his shop, asked for a packet of Woodbine cigarettes price 1d, tendered a florin and was given 1s 11d change. Mr. Brewster testified that after Gold left the shop, he tested the florin and found that it was light. He then went to the shop door and saw Gold walking in the High Street with Marcus and shortly afterwards saw Gold come out of the Post Office and join Marcus on the street. He sent for the police and Gold was arrested. When cross-examined, he stated that he was certain that he saw Gold and Marcus together. His testimony was supported by Agnes Woodman who was present when Gold bought the cigarettes. Alfred William Hall, chemist, then testified that Gold had bought strapping there, tendered a florin and was given 1s 11d change, the florin then being found light. Mr. Hall stated that, having gone to his door, he saw Marcus running away and caused his arrest. Police Sergeant Ely White gave details as to the arrest of each defendant and the result of searches: Gold was found with various amounts of good money, some chocolate and a court plaster; on Marcus, two packets of woodbines were found. Marcus, who was legally represented by Mr. J. E. Y. Radcliffe, stated that he did not know Marcus, that the money and items found on him were acquired through buying and selling at markets and that this was mistaken identity. Under cross-examination, Marcus said that he ran away because he had seen Gold being arrested and was nervous because he had never been in trouble before. Neither defendant was known to have a prior criminal record. Marcus was convicted. Although Gold, who was legally represented by Mr. David White, pleaded guilty, there was no reward or sentence discount both defendants receiving five months' hard labour.

Other such cases were dealt with in a similar way.[35]

Behind these theories (and implicit in much of the literature discussing bureaucratisation and managerialism) is the assumption that the change alleged to have occurred was to a pre-existing system that was adversarial. As far as late Victorian England is concerned, while there were instances in which witnesses

34 23 April 1912.

35 See, for example: *Thomas Meredith and Edward Haycock* 14 May 1912; *Reuben Liberman and Benjamin Fiddler* 9 January 1912.

were questioned, challenged, and, as in *Gold and Marcus* (discussed earlier) cross-examined, it would be misleading to describe this as adversarial. Legal arguments were rare, although when they occurred, lawyers were certainly equipped to engage the issues involved. In the absence of an opportunity for pre-trial investigation, with trials held on the heels of the alleged criminal occurrence, there was an inadequate basis for mounting a searching inquiry of the facts at trial. Testimony generally consisted of witnesses reciting their version of events subject (at most) to limited cross-examination, with defendants themselves incompetent to testify in most cases until after the Criminal Evidence Act 1998.[36]

Section Four: The Structural Changes to Criminal Justice

Although plea bargaining rightfully deserves a place in the history of criminal justice, it is, when placed in context, simply part of how the criminal justice system has been restructured since Victorian times. This restructuring has turned the system on its head such that the roles of the participant units and their relational powers have been transformed, utilising covert alliances and methods at variance with common law understandings repeatedly proclaimed by the judges. The principal architects of this system transformation lie not in case law or legislation but in the actions of the Senior Judiciary in concealed alliance with the Executive.

The Senior Judiciary started to become actively engaged in the management and restructuring of criminal justice soon after the close of the Victorian era. Although the Court for Crown Cases Reserved had been superseded in 1908 by the Court of Criminal Appeal,[37] the new structure failed to achieve consistent decision-making on matters of law, in large measure because the court was reluctant to lay down generalisable rules. Furthermore, trial judges often sat on appeals from their own cases, with the result that divergent practices between trial judges continued or became entrenched. A new oversight mechanism was introduced in 1912 in the form of the Judges' Rules, and these are central to understanding the restructuring of criminal justice, the relationship of trial judges to the Senior Judiciary, the methodology employed, the links between Senior Judges and the Executive, and the underlying involvement of the police.

The police role in the criminal trial had in fact evolved rapidly with the end of the Victorian era because of emerging detention and questioning practices. From their earlier, largely administrative involvement as carriers of information given to them by complainants and witnesses with some also from defendants,

36 Although the Act simply made defendants competent as witnesses, a failure to testify left defendants open to adverse comment by the judge as well as by the prosecution.

37 Established by the Criminal Appeal Act 7 Edw. 7. C following a series of notorious miscarriages of justice.

the police began to subject defendants to custodial questioning and to transmit to the court the fruits of their interrogation.[38] For their part, trial judges offered divergent views on whether the practices of some police forces relating to detention and custodial questioning were lawful and whether any resulting 'confessions' were admissible.[39]

The pivotal resolution came with the Judges' Rules, initially formulated in 1912, revised in 1918, re-issued in 1930, and revised again in 1964. These rules came to set out the powers of the police in relation to arrest, detention, and custodial interrogation and the related rights and entitlements of affected citizens. Although they had little immediate impact, the Rules were pivotal in many ways. First, they were a radical departure in terms of judicial methodology: Whereas the common law was founded in a forensic tradition in which law was made by testing through argument at trial and on appeal, these rules functioned as law emanating from announcements by the Senior Judiciary without any form of juridical scrutiny.

Second, as we shall see, over time this mechanism emboldened the Senior Judiciary to introduce its application in other areas. Third, from early on, and in contradiction of the 'independence' of the judiciary and the separation of powers supposedly at the heart of the constitution, the Rules were the product of a secret alliance with the Executive (hidden from public view for almost one hundred years) which, records show, actually authored a number of the Rules and/or blocked others.[40]

Fourth, the Rules instantiated a practice of detention and custodial interrogation that thereby placed police evidence at the heart of the construction of the prosecution case at major trials,[41] with appellate and trial judges discarding accepted principles[42] and condoning dubious practices and both the

38 The main reason for this change was a change in how the police behaved *in practice* rather than any change in the law. Indeed, this switch is a good example of how practice led to changes in the legal powers of the police rather than the reverse. A contributory factor was that the First World War regulations (DORA) gave the police additional powers of questioning and arrest on failure to answer, and it seems that this helped create an expectation that they could do the same even after the wartime powers had been discontinued.

39 See *R v Baldry* (1852) 21 LJMC 130; 2 Den CC 430; *R v Thompson* [1893] 2 QB 12; R v *Male and Cooper* (1893) 17 Cox CC 689; *R v Miller* (1895) 18 Cox CC 54; *Rogers v Hawken* (1898) 67 LJQB 526; *R v Brackenbury* (1903) 17 Cox CC 628; *R v Knight and Thayre* (1905) 20 Cox CC 711 in which Channell J. accurately said, 'little assistance can be obtained from the cases reported'; *R v Best* [1909] 1 KB 692; *R v Booth and Jones* (1910) 5 Cr App R 177; *R v Crowe and Myerscough* (1917) 81 JP 288.

40 The details are discussed in Mike McConville and Luke Marsh, *Criminal Judges* (Edward Elgar 2014) and, more specifically, Mike McConville and Luke Marsh, *The Myth of Judicial Independence* (OUP 2020).

41 For an account of case construction, see Mike McConville, Andrew Sanders, and Roger Leng, *The Case for the Prosecution* (Routledge 1991).

42 As in *R v Bass* (1953) 37 Cr App R 51 setting aside the principle that witness evidence should not be presented as independent if it was in fact the product of collaboration, in this case covering over police perjury.

judiciary and the Executive disregarding reform recommendations.[43] Fifth, the Rules necessarily placed defendants and defence lawyers at a disadvantage in their relations with the police, when considering whether or when to plead guilty, at trial or on appeal, with defendants accorded no substantive rights, even of access to a lawyer, in the Rules themselves.[44] Sixth, the whole process initiated by the Judges' Rules authorised a judicial practice whereby slippery language was used to disguise the reality of what was happening and of its importance,[45] the difference between 'judicial observations' and 'law' eventually becoming non-existent.[46]

Although the Judges' Rules excited considerable comment when they were issued in 1964,[47] their real significance did not become clear until much later. On the one hand, the Rules formally re-distributed powers and rights as between police and citizens. The police, who had been instrumental in pressuring the Executive in private to give them extended powers and to not allow cautions to be issued to citizen/suspects early in the investigation,[48]

43 Notoriously, ignoring altogether the clear recommendation of the Royal Commission on Police Powers and Procedures (1929) which had been set up following widespread concern over police questioning practices. The RCPPP made the following recommendation: 'We . . . recommend a rigid instruction to the Police that no questioning of a person in custody, about any crime or offence with which he is or may be charged, should be permitted. This does not exclude questions to remove elementary and obvious ambiguities in voluntary statements, under No. (7) of the Judges' Rules . . . but we would extend the prohibition to cover all persons who, though not in custody, have been charged and are out on bail while awaiting trial' (para. 169, *Report*, Cmd. 3297).

44 Belatedly, in the 1964 iteration, accompanying Administrative Directions outlined some qualified 'rights', but these had no force of law since they were annexed to but not part of the Rules. Moreover, it was not until the 1970s that defence solicitors became routinely available to defendants and not until after the Police and Criminal Evidence Act 1984 as a right. For an excellent account of the development of legal aid, see Tom Smith and Ed Cape, 'The Rise and Decline of Criminal Legal Aid in England and Wales' in Asher Flynn and Jacqueline Hodgson (eds) *Access to Justice & Legal Aid* (Bloomsbury 2017).

45 About the Judges' Rules (1964), for example, the leading expert, Professor JC Smith remarked, 'There is one quite fundamental question concerning the Judges' Rules to which there appears to be no clear answer. Do the Rules forbid the Police to question persons in custody or do they merely advise them that if they do question such persons, the answers may be inadmissible in evidence'. JC Smith, 'Questioning by Police: Further Points' (1960) *Criminal Law Review* 347. Professor Smith and other commentators were unaware that the Rules had been cooked up in secret with the Executive.

46 *R v AB & Ors* [2023] EWCA Crim 2003 (see below).

47 There was much debate in academic circles as to the status of the Rules (whether administrative guidance or law) and their internal contradictions, while the Police Federation (representing lower ranks) was upset because its members had not been consulted at all on the drafts. There was little critical comment made on earlier iterations partly because academics and practitioners had a much more deferential attitude towards the judiciary at earlier times and partly because of the way in which the Rules were placed into the public domain. In fact, the first iteration in 1912 went almost completely unnoticed until an afternote reference appeared in the case of *R v Voisin* (1918) 13 Cr App R 89.

48 The principal source of information on the implications of draft Judges' Rules to address concerns over 'law and order' came from the Metropolitan Police, which exerted considerable

were now free to detain anyone they considered might be associated with or implicated in any crime and to subject them to forms of interrogation they considered appropriate without external scrutiny or oversight, and those held in this custodial environment would be held without lawful access to a legal adviser. They also had created a methodology by which the Senior Judiciary, liaising in secret with the Executive, would come to assume near-absolute control over the architecture of the criminal justice system and its principal component parts. It is in this setting that plea bargaining is to be understood.

Plea bargaining did not officially appear (admitted reluctantly by the judiciary and then in disguised form) until 1970 with the Court of Appeal case of *Turner*.[49] Whether this was a recognition of a widespread pre-existing practice among practitioners or only of some judges and barristers[50] is yet to be determined, but of more consequence here is the fact that this announcement by the Court of Appeal was artfully formulated in such a way as to suggest on the one hand a disapproval or banning of plea bargaining while on the other leaving the door open for its widespread adoption in cases involving lesser pleas (i.e. practically all criminal prosecutions).[51]

Plea bargaining took on special significance because it was introduced into an ambiguous legal setting in which there was no framework of support for defendants and where the very existence of 'law' was confused by a canopy of 'advice', 'guidance', and 'rules' which emboldened and encouraged the police and prosecution as it enfeebled the defence.

Plea bargaining also constituted a disciplinary measure that the Senior Judiciary would come to perfect in relation not only to barristers but to trial judges themselves and which would, like the Judges' Rules, substantially re-shape power arrangements within the courtroom. At the outset, the framework was widely described by commentators as the Turner Rules reflecting the understanding that the schema set out in *Turner* should be followed but was not

influence in private on the Executive and the Lord Chief Justice, particularly with the assertion that up to 70% of serious criminal cases would be damaged or lost if proposals to administer an early caution were adopted.

49 *R v Turner* (1970) 54 Cr App R 352. The appeal had been triggered by the public complaints of the defendant's solicitor (extraordinarily for the time made on television and in the newspapers), who had been excluded from clandestine discussions in the judge's chambers where by convention, only barristers were permitted.

50 There are a few indications that bargaining occurred before this date as a local practice, probably more evident in small circuit courts where relations between bench and bar were much closer than in London.

51 For further discussion, see Luke Marsh, 'A Portrait of Guilt from England and Wales: Defending against State-Induced Pleas' in Maximo Langer, Mike McConville, and Luke Marsh (eds) *Research Handbook on Plea Bargaining and Criminal Justice* (Edward Elgar 2024).

'law'. Indeed, the judgment of the Court of Appeal, delivered by Parker LCJ, put the matter as follows:

> Before leaving this case, which has brought out into the open the vexed question of so-called "plea-bargaining," the court would like to make some observations which may be of help to judges and to counsel and, indeed, solicitors.

This opening gambit – nothing more than 'observations' – enabled the Senior Judiciary over time to exercise control over all the parties through what was in substance, and came to be acknowledged, as a punitive framework.

Although the Court in *Turner* said, 'Counsel must be completely free to do what is his [sic] duty, namely to give the accused the best advice he can and if need be advice in strong terms' this became a duty to transmit to defendants the sentence 'discount' that an early guilty plea would attract, a duty that could be enforced by a trial judge who decided that counsel had not done enough to exert pressure on a reluctant defendant.[52] As the observations morphed into rules under the Criminal Procedure Rules (effectively another construct of the Senior Judiciary), the duty of defence counsel was extended to making good deficiencies in the prosecution case. And, after further 'variations,' an authoritative judgment said the following[53]:

> The starting point is *R v Turner* (1970) 54 Cr App R 72, [1970] 2 QB 321 which represented a change in practice and which sought to regulate the way in which judges could give indications as to sentence and to restrict the kinds of indication they could give. *It represented the law for 35 years* until [a decided case] introduced a variation by allowing an additional kind of indication to be given in strictly defined conditions. Those conditions included the indication being given in open court and in the presence of the defendant. Subject to these variations, *Turner still does represent the law* (emphasis supplied).

Here again, the lack of candour and the use of disingenuous language allowed the introduction into English law of a practice (plea bargaining) earlier routinely described by the Court of Appeal itself as 'foreign' and having 'no place in English law'.[54]

The introduction of plea bargaining was also part of another disciplinary process: that exercised by the Senior Judiciary over trial judges. The control

52 See Mike McConville and Luke Marsh, 'Adversarialism Goes West: Case Management in Criminal Cases' (2015) 19 *International Journal of Evidence & Proof* 172.

53 *R v AD & Ors* [2021] EWCA Crim 2003.

54 *R v Atkinson* [1978] 2 All ER 460.

system has matured since *Turner*, from one in which trial judges, as those who had seen and heard the witnesses, had effective discretion over sentence (subject exceptionally in aberrant cases to review by the Court of Appeal) to one in which sentencing is heavily constrained by the Senior Judiciary. This again involves sleight of hand.

The framework of sentencing is effectively set out in *Sentencing Guidelines* laid out in the Sentencing Code, a product of the Sentencing Council. The Sentencing Council is heavily judge laden[55] and purports to provide 'guidelines' to assist judges. Although sentencing guidelines are supposed to help make sure that judges and magistrates in courts across England and Wales take a consistent approach to sentencing,[56] the Sentencing Code requires judges to follow the guidelines unless it is not in the interests of justice to do so. The result of this development is that trial judges are now placed within a Senior Judicial wedge: They must at the outset of trials enforce the plea bargaining 'law' by which defendants are presented with the offer of a sentencing 'discount' for a guilty plea, and, if there is a conviction, they must, with little room for departure, comply with sentencing guidelines laid down by the Sentencing Council, as illustrated in the following example[57]:

> *Iercosan*: The judge found the offending had been planned. He found that the offence fell on the cusp of Categories 1 and 2 and that the starting point, taking into account the aggravating factors, was 10 years' imprisonment.
>
> The judge then reduced that starting point to nine-and-a-half years to reflect personal mitigation and then he applied, *as he had to*, the 25 per cent credit for the guilty plea, reducing the sentence to one of seven years and one month (emphasis supplied).[58]

55 Headed by the Lady Chief Justice, judicial appointments are made by the LCJ with the agreement of the Lord Chancellor; non-judicial appointments are made by the Lord Chancellor with the agreement of the LCJ following open competition.

56 I am not here concerned with appropriateness of individual guidelines, this being the subject of many major works including Andrew Ashworth and Rory Kelly, *Sentencing and Criminal Justice* (7th edn, Hart 2021). For a penetrating review of the difficulties in linking policy changes to real-world decisions, see Rebecca K Helm and Bethany Growns, 'Methodological and Analytical Strategies in Guilty Plea Research: Combatting Myths and Informing Evidence-Based Research' in Máximo Langer, Mike McConville, and Luke Marsh (eds) *Research Handbook on Plea Bargaining and Criminal Justice* (Edward Elgar 2024).

57 It should be noted that nevertheless, formally the appellate court will not interfere with findings of fact except in rare circumstances; see *R v Taylor* [2024] EWCA Crim 615: 'this court will not interfere with findings of fact made by a sentencing judge unless they are: internally inconsistent; inconsistent with an uncontroverted fact; or otherwise irrational'.

58 *R v Iercosan* [2023] EWCA Crim 934, at paras 18 and 19.

Section Five: Some Implications of the Changes

We can begin by noting that the changes I have outlined have resulted in collateral damage to what were celebrated by judges as 'principles' of the common law process:

- The principle that evidence must be independently tested had to give way in the face of prosecution evidence routinely resting upon collaborative police evidence.[59]
- The principle that a confession is not to be admitted if brought about by 'fear of prejudice, or hope of advantage exercised or held out by a person in authority, or by oppression' had to give way since this is the very purpose of plea bargaining.
- The principle that guilt is to be determined by an assessment of the evidence was replaced by guilt through attribution linked to the plea.
- The principle that the sentence must be based upon what was deserved had to give way because of the requirement that the discount must be given not only to the penitent and the remorseful but in equal measure to the calculating, the feckless, the unrepentant, and the vindictive.
- The principle that sentence determinations should be made primarily upon the facts of the case gave way to the idea that controlling 'guidelines' are created which seek to anticipate all possible factual matrices.[60]
- The principle that the judge hearing the case is best placed to calibrate the sentence gave way to what discretionary determinations the Court of Appeal feels able to make.

There are many such 'principles' that appear to have been compromised or sacrificed, but there are much more important consequences to the changes to which I now turn.

Those collateral changes to principles have been, I argue, ones to the ideologies fostered to shore up the image of the common law rather than to the fabric and architecture of the system. To understand this in terms of theory, we need to set aside some of the undergrowth which invariably gathers around such discussions.

While everyone is agreed that there have been major changes in criminal justice, to focus on those of most recent heritage, however radical some appear, risks falling into several pitfalls. Thus, 'bureaucratisation' and 'managerialism' throw the spotlight on present-day actors and alleged upending modifications to their work environment, an approach which, while enriching our understanding of the practical outcomes of policy changes, commonly assumes, as

59 This was a direct result of a decision to allow police evidence that would otherwise rest on perjury: *R v Bass* (1953) 37 Cr App R 51.

60 The result is a Sentencing Compendium which rivals in dimension that of the Encyclopaedia Brittanica.

Malcolm Feeley has pointed out, a golden past which never existed, evident in any examination of court proceedings in Victorian England.[61] This is also true of theorisation based upon metamorphosis.

Under this explanatory framing, changes to the system assume a move, in the words on one of its advocates,[62] 'away from established adversarial values, rules, and practices . . . eroding what were once regarded as core rights and freedoms in the name of efficiency, security and justice for victims'. It is not clear whether metamorphosis is offered as a metaphor for a changed form natural to that occurring in certain biological species such as tadpoles or, like Gregor Samsa, as a phenomenon explicable only in supernatural terms, the sociological equivalent of transubstantiation. In either event, the analysis rests upon a pre-existing condition (adversariness/due process) which did not exist, fails to locate change within the executive–judicial alliance, and is accordingly unclear about the direction of travel.

The Senior Judiciary adopted a similar metaphysical explanatory framework when they sought to present a radical transformation in criminal justice. In more concise form, the Senior Judiciary sought to explain changes, including to the roles of defence and prosecuting lawyers, as already having occurred through a surreptitious change in culture unnoticed by the rest of the legal profession.[63] Part of this theoretical confusion, to use the terminology of Damaška, can be located in how the common law in England and Wales presented itself as lying within a 'reactivist' state, one that favours self-management and a horizontal structure consisting of a series of relatively disconnected agencies ('coordinate officialdom') such as prosecutors and courts, which are largely autonomous. In fact, this has been, like cosmetics painted on an old crone, a presentational coating applied primarily through the ideology of 'judicial independence' and 'separation of powers'. The reality is that the

61 Until at least recent times, defendants in England and Wales, for example, had no right of access to legal advice during custodial interrogation and no right to a state-supported lawyer at trial. The former was introduced only after a string of miscarriages of justice and a collapse in confidence in police integrity during interrogations through the Police and Criminal Evidence Act 1984. The latter came about in serious cases only with a 'devil's bargain' when defence lawyers agreed to assist the administration of justice by agreeing to committals from the lower courts without testing the state's evidence if the defendant was legally represented under the Criminal Justice Act 1967 c.80 (committal proceedings were eventually abolished in 2013).

62 Jacqueline Hodgson, *The Metamorphosis of Criminal Justice* (OUP 2020) at (xi): 'Due process and fair-trial guarantees have become subordinate, altering the core functions of criminal justice professionals in sometimes fundamental ways and distorting the criminal process balance between effective investigation and prosecution, on the one hand, and the protection of the presumption of innocence, on the other. Preoccupations with prevention, securitization, and a managerialist form of bureaucratic efficiency . . . have been elevated to the objectives against which criminal justice success is measured (at xi–xii, citation omitted)." Setting aside the conflation of concepts which informed analysts have kept separate, the image promoted is an upset in 'balance' leading to a lost golden age of due process and fair trial guarantees.

63 See: *R v Chaaban* [2003] EWCA Crim 1012.

state is highly 'activist', but it conducts its business behind the scenes in secret alliance with the Senior Judiciary.

This hidden activist arrangement has both ideological underpinnings and practical demands. The principal ideological prop has been left to the incessant claims of 'judicial independence' punctured only by the release (after many years) of departmental files demonstrating deep collusion between the Executive and the Senior Judiciary and by the more modern practice of guiding judges in advance to recommend what the Executive wants as the outcome of a 'judicial' policy review.[64] The practical demands of an activist state are seen in the quest for predictability, which gives rise to the dislike of party control and aversion to trials (however qualified both have been in practice) and hence the preference for rule-based decision making fostered by centrally determined rules including plea bargaining and sentence guidelines.

As a side effect, the role of the police has also been transformed. Having been little more than carriers of information from the parties to the court in Victorian times, on their own initiative the police took on a central role in evidence acquisition (sanctioned by a willing judiciary), which over time became greatly assisted by its ability to exert influence in private on the Executive during revision of the Judges' Rules and on the Executive in the run up to the Police and Criminal Evidence Act (PACE), 1984. Once, however, the system could no longer rely upon the veracity of police-induced confession evidence, the application of plea bargaining rules to the earliest stage of prosecutions resulted in a substantial reversion in the police role to its Victorian heritage.

Plea bargaining has, as we have noted, contributed to other structural effects. The position of defendants, already enfeebled by lack of defenders and legal aid, was further diminished by barristerial 'advice' that transformed into a duty to convey plea bargaining demands enforced, if thought desirable, by the intervention of trial judges. And more than this, plea bargaining with its close relation, sentencing guidelines, has helped to dilute if not yet remove local discretion from the courts through common rules which straddle the regions, counties, and countries.[65]

Moving away from detailed ethnographic studies and from accordingly a focus on line workers, we see how, over the years, as the state itself has changed, the way in which it structures criminal justice and the levers of control has also shifted. The criminal justice function extant in Victorian society was delivered through 'trustworthy' trial judges drawn from society's elite

64 As seen in the reports of LJ Auld and the Leveson Inquiry discussed in McConville and Marsh, *The Myth of Judicial Independence* (2020). This is much more significant than the 'judicial gymnastics' employed by the House of Lords/Supreme Court to distinguish precedents that they did not wish to follow.

65 Added to this is the rapid dissolution of local magistrates' courts.

with decision-making at trial in the hands of juries drawn from male property owners and other 'reliable' sections of a hierarchical society.

Trial judges, unencumbered by appellate overview, guided trials which functioned in much the same way whether or not attended by defence lawyers, the basic information/evidence relied upon coming from the parties with little police input. This citizen-initiated[66] but structurally elite system had an internal logic and dynamic with, even in the early nineteenth century, few links to an embryonic Executive.[67]

The appellate procedure put in place in 1908 operated in form rather than substance. As a budding Executive began a close association with the Senior Judiciary through formulation of the early Judges' Rules, police detention and questioning practices became legitimated and without effective restraint after 1929, when the Executive ignored recommendations from the Royal Commission to stop the practice. From the 1960s, a more mature and highly developed Executive began its domination of the Senior Judiciary and started a major re-structuring of criminal justice elements of which, such as the subjugation of juries, 'democratised' following the Morris Committee Report,[68] remain work in progress.

Plea bargaining has played a part, but only part, in this re-shaping, its impact less on the decision-making of defendants themselves and more on the organisational role of the police, the professional standing of defence lawyers, the victims of crime, and the relational position of trial judges to the Senior Judiciary. Rather than being a free-standing instrument of change, plea bargaining has been an instrument, along with others, by which change is sought to be secured.

Criminal justice has *not* been inverted from an imaginary adversary process to one that is something less, but the component parts of the pre-existing process have had their role functions changed and for some their role performance. Even if their conflicts have not been stolen, victims for example, who figured prominently in trials in Victorian times, have little (and often no) role in guilty plea cases and a distant and often imperfect relationship with the trial process. As a result of strict enforcement of plea bargaining rules/laws and the related Criminal Procedure Rules, defence lawyers, lionised by judges in

66 In a minority of cases, such as coinage and 'espionage', prosecutions might be initiated through state agencies.

67 Attempts to move governmental administrative units away from a dependency on patronage following the Northcote–Trevelyan report (1855) were resisted for years by the department responsible for criminal justice (the Home Office). See McConville and Marsh, *The Myth of Judicial Independence* (2020); John Greenaway, 'Celebrating Northcote/Trevelyan: Dispelling the Myths' (2004) 19(1) *Public Policy and Administration* 1.

68 *Report of the Departmental Committee on Jury Service* (Cmnd. 2627, 1965). Actually, such was the residual distrust of 'ordinary people' serving on juries that implementation of the Committee's proposals was delayed until the Juries Act 1974 and following the introduction of minority verdicts by the Criminal Justice Act 1967.

the legitimating ideology of the past, are handcuffed in what they can achieve for their clients while under an obligation to make good deficiencies of the prosecution. Trial judges, once monarchs of the trial, now operate in a more enfeebled environment their authority compromised by actions of the Senior Judiciary.

Over the years, in England and Wales, criminal justice has developed as a 'goal-directed and boundary-maintaining' structure.[69] With the combined actions of the Executive and the Senior Judiciary[70] – the secretly conjoined twins of the constitution – criminal justice has moved towards a highly centralised, non-discretionary, disciplinary system, its precepts increasingly enforced by the Senior Judiciary and operating in different guises; its ideological and legitimacy claims expressed through rationalisations based in 'efficiency' and 'cost-effectiveness'; and its pronouncements/judgments shrouded in casuistic language of which Cicero would have been proud.

69 David Knoke, *Political Networks: The Structural Perspective* (Cambridge University Press, 1990).

70 Much of this alliance was deliberately kept hidden from Parliament as the 1964 Judges' Rules were formulated: see Mike McConville and Luke Marsh, *The Myth of Judicial Independence* (2020). Of course, this account is in need of more validation through access to files charting the role of the Home Office and the Lord Chancellor's Department. These files often remain locked away from public scrutiny and require careful reading given that key documents may be missing.

4 Guilty Pleas in Criminal Justice

Putting Just on Ice

Luke Marsh

Introduction

This chapter explores the role that defence lawyers play in the criminal process when advising clients on plea and of the increasing pressure that is placed on them to ensure their timeliness. It draws on contemporary and historical sources in making the case that the credit system for early guilty pleas now dominates the exchange between defendants and their legal representatives, rendering otiose traditionally important features of their legal training. In shedding light on the changing perceptions of the defence lawyer's role in relation to the protection they can afford their clients, I will show how the rapid development of a guilty plea incentive system has taken hold of the criminal process at the accused's expense.

Three perspectives on the topic are broadly identified: the political, the ethical, and the structural. Adopting each of these perspectives in turn, the chapter sets out ways in which the interplay of the dimensions can impact the delivery of justice and adversely so in the realm of the guilty plea process. In this account, the discussion is construed in the light of a particular understanding of the criminal process characterised as a system ruled by efficiency in which there is little tolerance for other conflicting working ideologies. Further, procedural justice has given way to a system embodied by state-induced pleas, an umbrella concept used throughout which takes the discussion beyond narrow references to plea bargaining, a practice which English judicial authorities have sought to officially disavow.

Whereas sentencing in England and Wales has traditionally been grounded in wide judicial discretion and a resistance to a structuring of the decision-making process,[1] I show how this understanding has been abandoned in the domain of guilty plea discounts. The conclusion drawn is that the working credo of the justice system – the earlier a defendant enters a guilty plea, the

1 For a historical account, see D Thomas, 'Judicial Discretion in Sentencing' in L Gelsthorpe and N Padfield (eds) *Exercising Discretion – Decision-Making in the Criminal Justice System and Beyond* (Willan Publishing 2003), Chapter 3.

DOI: 10.4324/9781003496823-4

greater the gain – distorts the adversary ideal, changing a system founded on the presumption of innocence to one instead inimical to a defendant's right to a fair trial, once deemed '[a] key moral basis of the adjudication of criminal disputes'[2] where the accused is presumed to know whether they are guilty or not from the outset regardless of the extent of case disclosure.

Understanding State-Induced Pleas

As has been well documented in the literature, plea bargaining (to which the court is not a party, though the prosecution must abide by its view if it seeks the court's approval) is not allowed in England and Wales, the practice having been sharply rejected (albeit inconsistently) by courts since its 'discovery' in *Turner*[3] in 1970.[4] Following *Goodyear*,[5] an 'advance indication of sentence' (which does not reduce charge(s) but tells the defendant where s/he would stand if they entered a guilty plea) is permissible. While it can be argued that the issues of principle are much the same – and if one is acceptable, why should the other be disapproved? – whatever the terminology settled upon, both serve a common purpose: the potential and official incentive to avoid trials.

Such judicial innovations, amounting to trial avoidance mechanisms, rely on *state-induced guilty pleas* to operate. Adopted in earlier work,[6] the term encompasses all practices commonly referred to as 'plea bargaining', covering, for example, direct or indirect offers from state officials (police, prosecutors, and judges) to reduce a sentence in return for a guilty plea; practices variously referred to as 'charge bargains'[7]; and most germanely here, non-individuated sentence discounts. In this regard, the principal source of state-induced guilty pleas in England and Wales is the sliding scale discount framework, which incentivises guilty pleas through its 'credit' regime (i.e. usually an entitlement of a discount follows a plea of guilty).[8]

Even with distinctions in language, policy, procedure, and practice, all trial avoidance measures implemented by English courts are connected by their capacity for creating coercive pressures upon defendants' decision-making

2 M McConville and L Marsh, *Criminal Judges* (Edward Elgar 2014) 2. See generally, R Goss, *Criminal Fair Trial Rights: Article 6 of the European Convention on Human Rights* (Hart Publishing 2014).

3 54 Cr App R 352.

4 See, for example, *Dossetter* (1999) 2 Cr App (S) 248: 'Plea bargaining, in the sense of seeking to extract from the judge an indication of sentence which he will give if a particular defendant pleads guilty, forms no part of English criminal jurisprudence'.

5 (2005) EWCA Crim 888.

6 See, for example, M McConville and L Marsh, *Criminal Judges* (Edward Elgar 2014) 2.

7 This includes offers to reduce the number of charges or alter charges from more serious to less serious offences or offers to present the 'facts' (the basis of the guilty plea) in a favourable light.

8 A one-third discount requires a guilty plea at the 'first opportunity' (discussed later). A one-quarter discount where a guilty plea is entered at the first appearance at the crown court; one-tenth if entered on the first day of trial.

owing to the methods through which guilty pleas are incentivised. Allied to this standard concern is the heightened political pressure upon the justice agencies, which has led to a barrage of austerity measures. Counter-intuitively, depleted capacity within criminal justice has been augmented by a fire sale of the court estate nationwide,[9] leading to the creation of emergency 'Nightingale' courts, which continue to operate under crisis-management conditions. The consequences of deep fiscal cuts have also proven to be severe on personnel, with heavy attrition of available criminal lawyers, large numbers of whom have left the profession.[10]

Much focus now lies with the criminal case 'backlog', the swollen size of which generates alarmist political messaging, with other formal statements of policy (the product of the legislature, the higher ranks of the civil service, and the Senior Judiciary) claiming with dubious effect to lessen the stranglehold the logjam has had on criminal courts.[11] The next section further explores some of these issues while considering implications for the accused and criminal justice practitioners amidst this systemic turmoil.

Injustice and the Politics of Managed Decline

Highlighting mismanagement of the criminal justice system has long been a feature of political discourse between the dominant parties in England and Wales.[12] In securing the public vote after a 14-year period in opposition, the new Labour government of 2024 commenced its first term with a panicked stocktake of the country's criminal justice infrastructure. Speaking on the lack of capacity in prisons, the incoming Lord Chancellor and Justice Secretary began with a doom-mongering address:

> When no cells are available, suspects cannot be held in custody. This means vanloads of dangerous people circling the country, with nowhere to go. The police would have to use their cells as a prison overflow, keeping officers off the streets. Soon, the courts would grind to a halt, unable to hold trials. With officers unable to act, criminals could do whatever

9 Taking magistrates' courts as an example, as at 1 April 2000, they 'were divided into 328 independent Petty Sessional Areas, and administered locally by Magistrates' Courts Committees', see B Chapman and S Niven, *A Guide to the Criminal Justice System in England and Wales* (2000) Home Office, 19. According to the Sentencing Council's website, there are now approximately 150 lower courts remaining.

10 See, for example, T Kirk, 'More than 2,000 Criminal Trials Abandoned Due to Crumbling Courts and Lawyer Shortages', *The Standard* (23 September 2023).

11 See M McConville and L Marsh, 'Tipping the Scales of Justice – Covid-19 and Detention without Trial' in E Johnston (ed), *Covid-19 and Criminal Justice – Impact and Legacy in England and Wales* (Routledge 2023).

12 The literature on the interplay of politics and criminal justice is extensive but, for example, see S Hynes, *Austerity Justice* (Legal Action Group 2012) and M Tonry, *Punishment and Politics – Evidence and Emulation in the Making of Crime Control Policy* (Willan Publishing 2004).

> they want, without consequence. We could see looters running amok, smashing in windows, robbing shops and setting neighbourhoods alight. In short, if we fail to act now, we face the collapse of the criminal justice system. And a total breakdown of law and order.[13]

Rather than representing political insight, this instigation was in fact a clarion call of the obvious, with warnings from leadership figures within the legal profession foreshadowing those of the Justice Secretary:

> Turning to the state of the justice system where the central issue is a lack of Government investment. I put it bluntly: The criminal and justice systems are at the point of structural failure. From front to end of the criminal justice system the picture is bleak. Police back-office staff, who traditionally processed statements and evidence for trial purposes, have been decimated. . . . The court estate is dilapidated, and prisons are full. (Sam Townsend KC, Chair of the Bar)[14]

No independent observer would likely reach any other conclusion regarding the crisis of incapacity facing British justice today. In response, a decision by government to release prisoners who have served less than half of their sentences was implemented. This policy was announced alongside the Prime Minister's dumbfounding admission that 'the situation' in prisons is 'worse than I thought it was'.[15] Yet across the entirety of the justice system, evidence of systemic rot abounds. Prominent markers in the system's lineage of decline include the plight of the accused facing pre-trial detention. Untried (i.e. presumptively innocent) defendants have been confronted with criminal courts' inability to provide a trial date, which has resulted in lengthy pre-trial detention periods stretching far beyond those envisaged by Parliament when it legislated for the Custody Time Limits regime.[16]

Relatedly, the politically thorny issue of system delay, which became more visible during Covid-19,[17] has resulted in a scale of stasis which has plagued other aspects of the process, including the timing of plea. By way of snapshot,

13 S Mahmood, speech given at HMP Five Wells. See Government Press Release (12 July 2024): 'Lord Chancellor sets out immediate action to defuse ticking prison "time-bomb"' <www.gov.uk/government/news/lord-chancellor-sets-out-immediate-action-to-defuse-ticking-prison-time-bomb> accessed 31 October 2024.

14 S Townsend, *Inaugural address*, Lincoln's Inn, 9 January 2024, 4.

15 This was reported widely in the press but is astonishing bearing in mind that Sir Keir Starmer was not only a criminal barrister but the Director of Public Prosecutions (2008–2013) before he switched to politics. Moreover, the data on prison occupancy has long been a matter of public record.

16 See further, L Marsh, 'The Wrong Vaccine: Custody Time Limits and Loss of Liberty during Covid-19' (2021) 41 *Legal Studies* 693–709.

17 See M McConville and L Marsh, 'Criminal Justice in a Time of Covid-19: Paralysis and Prognosis' (2020) 170 *New Law Journal* 7906.

there remain an estimated 68,000 cases waiting to be dealt with in the Crown Court, there is an average wait of almost 700 days from the offence to a verdict in the Crown Court, and the available data indicates the situation as to delay is getting worse.[18] Indeed, the Government's decision to automatically release prisoners 40% of the way through their sentence (rather than the half-way point) under the standard determinate sentences 40 (SDS40) scheme has been a direct consequence of the realisation that the case backlog is becoming insurmountable.[19]

The objective of this chapter, however, is not to diagnose the ills of the justice system (politically infected though they may be).[20] Rather, it seeks to provide explanatory context to the ethical challenges confronted by criminal lawyers in an advisory environment in which plea decisions are increasingly governed by haste and efficiency. The defence lawyer–client advisory landscape warrants serious attention because there is a prevailing consensus among the Senior Judiciary, the Crown Prosecution Service (CPS), and a number of related government departments and agencies that the administration of justice is best served by very timely pleas. This implication may also seem to have an obvious solution: fewer cases going to trial. This has led, concomitantly, to the claim that a systemic need for early guilty pleas justifies structural arrangements that enlist the defence in propping up the surrounds of this sentencing framework. As will be shown, the issue's fixture within the practice of criminal courts is both pernicious and permanent.

It is against this backdrop that the next section serves to inject a dose of realism as regards the functionally restricted position of the modern criminal lawyer working under the auspices of the Criminal Procedure Rules (CrimPR). An enduring image of the adversarial advocate has allowed the system to shield from view a more obsequious figure, short-changing the accused as to the measure of protection their representative can provide on plea.[21]

18 The National Audit Office has said the aim of the Ministry of Justice (MoJ) of reducing the crown court backlog from its record high to 53,000 by March 2025 was 'no longer achievable'. See C Hymas, 'Reducing Court Case Backlog "Unachievable", says audit office', *The Telegraph*, 24 May 2024.

19 Although see M Dathan, 'Thousands of Prisoners Recalled to Jail after Early Release', *The Times* (1 November 2024).

20 For a detailed, considered response on the causes of the current malaise in criminal justice, which was published during the pandemic, see the government's 'Independent Review of Criminal Legal Aid' by Sir C Bellamy (Bellamy Review, 29 November 2021).

21 For more background, see L Marsh, 'A Portrait of Guilt from England and Wales: Defending against State-Induced Pleas' in M Langer, M McConville and L Marsh (eds) *Research Handbook on Plea Bargaining and Criminal Justice* (Edward Elgar 2024).

The Ethics of False Symbolism

In the preface to his classical study of advocacy, Richard Du Cann wrote of the English adversarial system:

> In our system the Judge presides somewhat like a referee on the football field, blowing his whistle from time to time for an infringement but not actually kicking the ball himself save in very limited or exceptional circumstances. In such a climate advocacy flourishes. In [this system] [one] will find some of the most brilliant flowers which this climate has nurtured. He may find one or two weeds as well. If the system were changed these might be eradicated. But to curb the natural abilities of the advocate would at the same time rob him of his independence and freedom which are the real strengths of the English system, and it would assuredly rob him of his individuality which is one of its fascinations.[22]

A more sombre portrait of the adversarial ideal in fact emerges. Even though Du Cann's now anachronistic image of the judge and barrister in criminal courts had met its near-total demise following the introduction of the CrimPR in 2005,[23] an embellished stereotype of the adversarial advocate is still promoted, typically by those instrumental in their role transformation. For example, Leveson LJ explained,

> It is a critical test of the freedom inherent in our democratic society that those accused (usually by the State) of committing criminal offences can and should be represented by capable criminal advocates, independent in spirit who, subject to the rules of law and procedure which operate in our courts and to the dictates of professional propriety, are prepared to put the interests of their clients at the forefront and irrespective of personal disadvantage.[24]

Whereas once an advocate owed his/her principal duty to the client, this did not set aside their public duty, namely a duty to the administration of criminal justice and the preservation of integrity within the system.[25] Indeed, it can still be said that a barrister's individual reputation for integrity remains paramount

22 Du Caan, *The Art of the Advocate* (Penguin 1964, reprinted 1993) 3.

23 For a full account, see M McConville and L Marsh, *Criminal Judges* (Edward Elgar 2014) ch 6.

24 *Lumsdon & Ors, R (On the Application Of) v Legal Services Board* [2014] EWHC 28 (Admin) (20 January 2014)), [at 1].

25 Lord Denning put it thus: 'It is a mistake to think he is the mouthpiece of his client to say what he wants; or his tool to do what he directs. He is none of these things. He owes an allegiance to a higher cause. . . . He must disregard the most specific instructions of his clients, if they conflict with his duty to the court. The code which requires a barrister to do all this is not a code of law. It is a code of honour.' Cited in Du Caan, *The Art of the Advocate* (Penguin 1964, reprinted 1993) 35–36.

to this day. But a duty to preserve integrity within the system raises a series of ethical concerns when the organising principles of the system alter in ways unrecognisable and often contradictory to traditional understandings propagated of the wider systemic role assumed by criminal lawyers:

> Criminal justice practitioners are often the principal agents for change, being able to encourage, facilitate, or impede the reform efforts of others. Indeed, to a very considerable extent, practitioners comprise the linchpin that determines the success or failure of any reform endeavour.[26]

Not so with the sea change that occurred with respect to the notion of the adversarial advocate under the CrimPR, with sanctions for resistance[27] leading to a far more precarious working relationship with judges.[28] The gap between the symbolism of defence lawyers and their rapid fall from favour in criminal practice is best encapsulated by the following judicial pronouncement, itself a response to resistance shown by counsel to the expectations placed on them under the CrimPR:

> The lawyer's duty is ***not to give the accused advice on what to do***. The lawyer's duty is to explain the statutory obligation that he has and to explain the consequence which follow from ***disobedience*** of it.[29]

As argued elsewhere, this code created an equivalence of obligations on prosecutor and defence alike,[30] resulting in confused understandings of the precise scope of the defence lawyer's duty to the administration of criminal justice and loyalty to the accused. Key among these is the problem of an 'overriding' duty to a court which has an overriding interest in factors aligned with governmental interests, namely fiscal efficiency or, in common parlance, cost savings. This prompts important questions. For example, what is the advocate to do when financial incentives are heavily weighted towards early disposal of the case with limited (if any) interrogation of the state's case against its client?[31]

26 A Rutherford, *Criminal Justice and the Pursuit of Decency* (OUP 1993), 120.

27 It should be noted that Leveson LJ, appointed President of the Queen's Bench Division in October 2013, made the recommendation that sanctions for failures to comply with the CrimPR should be increased: *Review of Efficiency in Criminal Proceedings*, Final Report, January 2015 (The Leveson Review), section 7.4.

28 Where a barrister showed resistance to the case management approach of a judge which he deemed in conflict with his duty to his client, this was ultimately labelled by the Court of Appeal a systemic threat: '[his conduct], if it was to become the norm, will cause our present system to collapse' *West, Re* [2014] EWCA Crim 1480 (CA (Crim Div)) [at 55].

29 *Rochford* [2010] EWCA Crim 1928 at para 25, per Hughes LJ (emphasis added).

30 This rewired defence role is underscored by the duty to remedy flaws in the prosecution case. See Rule 1.3, where the defence are expected, under fear of sanction, to notify the court and all parties 'at once . . . of any significant failure' of compliance.

31 Empirical research confirms that financial incentive structures in place for defence lawyers heighten this risk. See, for example, D Alge, 'The Effectiveness of Incentives to Reduce the Risk of Moral Hazard in the Defence Barrister's Role in Plea Bargaining' (2013) 16(1) *Legal Ethics* 162; D Newman, *Legal Aid Lawyers and the Quest for Justice* (Hart 2013).

Historically, it was the barrister's high professional standards and spirit of independence that most enabled them to safeguard defendants from the risk of succumbing to pressure emanating from the bench.[32] Nowhere is this threat more pronounced than when advising clients on plea. But in this regard, the modern-day advocate is a mimicry of Du Cann's exemplar, now wed to a procedural structure that prohibits much of that spirit.[33] Under the plea discount system, as I describe, lawyers must repress any historical urge to be 'gladiator of the accused'.[34] Indeed, such is the shift seen in the reduced role defence lawyers perform in the majority of cases that sufficient exposure in the tank of contemporary criminal justice would surely drown, as DuCann might put it, 'the hopes of many embryo Marshall Halls'.[35]

These puncture marks (political, procedural, and ideological in origin) have left a deflated workforce, delimited in function, demoralised by acceptance of its diminished role, and, in real terms, defunded by egregious Legal Aid cuts.[36] With these grass-roots realities of criminal practice in England and Wales in mind, the next section discusses further dilemmas that arise when frontline lawyers collide with a system structure predicated on very early disposals.

Bargaining 'Guilt': Exploring Plea Incentives

If a defendant pleads not guilty to a criminal allegation, the prosecution must, if they can, prove the case beyond any reasonable doubt to the satisfaction of the jury, or, as is more common, the magistrates' court. While this had always been a cardinal and fundamental principle of the English Constitution, the volume of criminal business dealt with by courts has made *control* of proceedings, it is said, a precarious matter for the state:

> At present something of the order of 75 per cent of all Crown Court cases result in pleas of guilty; if in all those cases the defendants were *out of defiance* or otherwise to insist on each detail of the case being proved to the hilt the administration of criminal justice would be in danger of collapse.[37]

32 An arc of empirical research from the 1970s through to the CrimPR era supports a continuing perspective of defendants being 'pressured' into pleading. See, for example, J Baldwin and M McConville, *Negotiated Justice* (Martin Robertson 1977); D Newman, *Legal Aid Lawyers and the Quest for Justice* (Hart 2013).

33 Of course, this is not to disparage the ranks of existing senior lawyers who commonly display the highest standards of advocacy. The point here is that the permissible mould for future lawyers under the CrimPR is a discouraging one, with an aptitude for fearless advocacy no longer a metier of incoming 'talent'.

34 R Du Cann, *The Art of the Advocate* (Penguin 1964) 46.

35 Ibid 30.

36 The Bellamy Review explained that many systemic issues of criminal justice have been underpinned by a lack of resourcing of the entire system for a decade and more.

37 *R v David Caley and others* [2012] EWCA Crim 2821 per Hughes LJ [at 6], emphasis added.

The positioning here of defendants as the potential cause of system malfunction is unsubtle.[38] And despite research having attested to the myth of the overburdened trial system,[39] the claim that courts would grind to a sudden halt without guilty plea discounts remains a pervasive force among those steering the direction of travel for procedural and sentencing reform. Accordingly, the focal point on 'efficiency' in criminal justice policy[40] continues to fixate on reducing the overall number of trials. In this regard, the evolution of sentencing guidelines has been instrumental.[41]

The Growth of a Reduction Principle

While the notion of 'credit' for a guilty plea is nothing new, first identified as an under-the-counter principle in English common law in the 1970s,[42] the prominence of its existence has been amplified over successive iterations of sentencing policy.[43] Until 2003, the availability of a 'discount' was simply an accepted practice by a sentencing judge. Subsequently, it was formally introduced by section 144 of the Criminal Justice Act 2003, which states the following (without acknowledging the fact of a discount):

1. In determining what sentence to pass on an offender who has pleaded guilty to an offence in proceedings before that or another court, a court must take into account –

    a. the stage in the proceedings for the offence at which the offender indicated his intention to plead guilty, and
    b. the circumstances in which this indication was given.

Placing the importance of the timing of plea on a statutory footing was then bolstered by the Sentencing Guidelines Council a year later when it produced

38 Research has contested the enduring claim by state officials that a late guilty plea by defendants is a major cause of trials collapsing on or shortly before the trial day. See, for example, M McConville and L Marsh, *Criminal Judges* (Edward Elgar 2014) Ch 4.

39 M Tonry, for example, has said '[t]he empirical evidence in support of this belief is weak': 'Setting Sentencing Policy Through Guidelines' in S Rex and M Tonry (eds) *Reform and Punishment – The Future of Sentencing* (Willan Publishing 2002) 97.

40 See L Marsh, 'Leveson's Narrow Pursuit of Justice: Efficiency and Outcomes in the Criminal Process' (2016) 45(1) *Common Law World Review* 51–67.

41 All the English Council's guidelines are available on the Council's website (see <www.sentencingcouncil.org/uk/>). For further on their development, see for example A Ashworth and JV Roberts, 'The Origins and Nature of the Sentencing Guidelines in England and Wales' in A Ashworth and JV Roberts (eds) *Sentencing Guidelines: Exploring the English Model* (OUP 2013) 1–12.

42 The position that a guilty plea attracts a lighter sentence than a conviction following a not guilty plea was crudely enunciated, for example, in *Cain* [1976] QB 496, although note that this initial endorsement of plea bargaining was later subject to the caveat of the *Turner* rules.

43 See for example *R v Atkinson* (1978) 2 All ER 460; *R v Boyd* (1980) 2 Cr App R (S) 234; *Hollington and Emmens* [1986] *Criminal Law Review* 270.

its inaugural guideline on *Reduction in Sentence for a Guilty Plea* ('*Guideline*'), an amendment to which occurred in 2007. Para 2.2 provides us with the 'reduction principle':

> A reduction in sentence is appropriate because a guilty plea avoids the need for a trial (thus enabling other cases to be disposed of more expeditiously), shortens the gap between charge and sentence, saves considerable cost, and, in the case of an early plea, saves victims and witnesses from the concern about having to give evidence. The reduction principle derives from *the need for the effective administration of justice and not as an aspect of mitigation.*

With a few large sweeps of the brush, evidence of remorse was no longer a relevant consideration, and credit for a guilty plea given to a defendant to reflect their admission of guilt rather than being found guilty after trial was wholly reconfigured to reflect other state objectives. Whereas once plea bargaining (and by necessary implication here, sentence discounts) was claimed by state apparatus to be solely for the benefit of *defendants,*[44] cost/time saving (i.e. advantages to the justice *system*) was no longer an organisation value that required the embroidery of legitimating rhetoric to mask it.

The Sentencing Council for England and Wales (which replaced the Sentencing Guidelines Council and was set up in 2010) then produced a revised version of the *Guideline* on 1 June 2017. Of note, and in the lead-up to its introduction, consultations on proposed features of the new guideline had led the question to circulate as to whether defendants should in fact be provided with a 'large incentive to plead guilty'. The then Chairman of the Sentencing Council, Lord Justice Tracy, responded defensively:

> In fact, the proposed guideline reaffirms the recommended levels of reduction found in the existing guideline issued by the Sentencing Guidelines Council in 2007. Indeed, the proposed guideline *caps the reduction possible* at one third, whereas under the existing guideline the reduction of one third was only a "recommendation". Under the proposals it is a maximum.

His Lordship continued, revealing the grand ambition of those tasked with shaping criminal justice policy behind the scenes:

> Moreover, the aim of the Council's new guideline is not to provide any additional incentive to defendants to plead guilty; *rather it aims to bring forward the point in the court process at which pleas are entered.* Nothing

44 See, for example, *Report of the Royal Commission on Criminal Justice* (RCCJ) (1993; Cm 2263) 113, para 51.

> in the existing or proposed guideline undermines the defendant's right to a fair trial. The proposed guideline is intended to clarify the various levels of reduction available, and to promote a more consistent approach to the awarding of plea-based sentence reductions.[45]

In the event, alongside a 'cap' on the maximum discount, the recognised rationale for providing a defendant's admission of guilt with credit was re-identified within the 2017 *Guideline*[46]: [It] (a) normally reduces the impact of the crime upon victims; (b) saves victims and witnesses from having to testify; and (c) is in the public interest in that it saves public time and money on investigations and trials.[47]

Explaining the Council's Singular Vision on Pleas

While there is some representation on the Sentencing Council from key stakeholders in criminal justice, it should be noted that members of the judiciary constitute a majority of its 14 members. Michael Tonry has described a judicially stacked approach to sentencing councils as 'a bit like putting foxes in charge of the henhouses'.[48] His disquiet stems from the notion that 'judges [whom] by training and ideology are especially committed to the desirability of judicial discretion and reluctant to establish sentencing rules that constrain that discretion'.[49]

Tonry's primary concern with a dominant judicial coalition responsible for the oversight (and development of) sentencing guidelines was *inverted* under the tenure of Sir Brian Leveson, the inaugural Chair of the Council (2009–13), making it clear in his 2015 *Review of Efficiency in Criminal Proceedings* (The Leveson Review),[50] which foreshadowed the 2017 *Guideline*, that he sought to make '*alterations* to the culture which surrounds practices in the criminal courts'.[51] Far from shoring up judicial power, these alterations would result

45 Originally published as a 'Letter to the Editor' in the *Criminal Law Review* (2016), 7, 489–90.

46 Available at <www.sentencingcouncil.org.uk/overarching-guides/crown-court/item/reduction-in-sentence-for-a-guilty-plea-first-hearing-on-or-after-1-june-2017/>

47 With this chapter, I do not seek to critique this rationale, which has been done elsewhere. See M McConville and L Marsh, *Criminal Judges* (Edward Elgar 2014) ch 8.

48 M Tonry, *Punishment and Politics – Evidence and Emulation in the Making of Crime Control Policy* (Willan Publishing 2004) 102. Lord Taylor had earlier made the judicial position explicit: judges required 'the widest range of measures, and the broadest discretion to deploy them either individually or in combination. . . . The best approach to sound sentencing is to leave it to the judiciary to exercise their experience and judgement', quoted in I Dunbar and A Langdon, *Tough Justice – Sentencing and Penal Policies in the 1990s* (Blackstone 1998) at 106.

49 Ibid 102.

50 The Leveson Review, para 193.

51 Ibid para 322. Emphasis added.

in a fundamentally constrained version of discretion in the realm of sentence discounts for guilty pleas. Indeed, Leveson had pedigree on this specific issue:

> Over the last few years, schemes intended to remedy the proliferation of late guilty pleas and ineffective case management have been developed in different court centres in different ways. To ensure consistency of approach (which is particularly important in relation to sentencing), it has therefore been essential to create a national scheme allowing a limited degree of local variation to reflect conditions within particular circuits.[52]

Part of the national solution to inconsistent approaches to securing early guilty pleas was a defining initiative entitled Better Case Management (BCM)[53] which sought to implement many of the changes to procedure advocated by Leveson (and, among others, Sir Robin Auld)[54] to address problems of process including 'transitory not guilty pleas which later result in cracked trials.'[55]

As far as his mission was concerned, Leveson was explicit:

> Part of the solution to improving the efficiency of the whole system is to acknowledge the critical role that the defence can play whether in relation to advising clients as to discount and the benefits of entering an early guilty plea.[56]

Leveson continued,

> The first hearing at the Magistrates' Court has developed into the critical hearing for those cases where a not guilty plea is entered.[57] . . . the Magistrates' Court also has a significant part to play in ensuring that as many suitable cases as possible are brought into the [Early Guilty Plea] scheme. *Identifying Early Guilty Plea cases should be particularly useful for indictable-only offences, where there is no Plea before Venue hearing in the Magistrates' Court.* Given that the Sentencing Guideline on Guilty Pleas now has to be read in light of decisions of

52 Ibid para 166.

53 This was introduced nationally in January 2016 and was designed to improve evidence handling and case management in relation to proceedings in Crown Courts.

54 As I have written elsewhere, many of Leveson's endeavours were generated by the aspirations of Auld's review. See, for example, M McConville and L Marsh, *The Myth of Judicial Independence* (OUP 2020) Chapter 7.

55 See the BCM Handbook (2018) at 5 <www.judiciary.uk/wp-content/uploads/2018/02/bcm-guide-for-practitioners-05032018.pdf>

56 The Leveson Review, para 99.

57 Ibid, para 101–02.

> the Court of Appeal and is presently undergoing revision, *it would be helpful if the Sentencing Council could, when a revised Guideline is issued, clarify the meaning of the 'first reasonable opportunity' to indicate a plea of guilty.*[58]

It took no stretch of the imagination, therefore, to envisage the 2017 *Guideline* in tandem with the BCM policy ushering in a monoculture of procedural obligations surrounding the advisory stage of a defendant's plea.

Courtroom Culture Under the 2017 Guideline

The 2017 *Guideline* and BCM which proceeded it entrenched a new criminal procedural model in England and Wales in which the role of credit for a guilty plea became the overriding element upon which criminal defence lawyers advise clients. Under this culture, a systemic preoccupation with this one matter from judiciary has manifested. Lawyers are given a reminder to advise clients on credit at their first appearance. Further confirmation of that is sought when a case is transferred to the Crown Court (via the BCM form). Once the case arrives in the Crown Court, a Plea and Trial Preparation Hearing (PTPH) form places further emphasis on the need to advise a client on credit for a guilty plea. To compound matters, judges are trained to inculcate the benefits of early guilty pleas, actively investigating whether such advice has been given to the accused.[59] This feature of the pre-trial process has sidelined other fundamental duties, including whether the accused has been advised on the elements of an offence.

Despite the unremitting approach taken to secure early guilty pleas with the assistance of defence counsel, the joined forces of BCM and the 2017 *Guideline* did not provide a complete guard against the problem of counsel seeking to litigate the boundaries of precisely when a client's '*first opportunity*' to enter a plea arises, thereby allowing them to receive maximum credit. Involvement from the Court of Appeal was thus required to tackle aberrant lawyers challenging the correct application of the sentence discount framework. A three-line whip was provided for by Lord Justice Holroyde, Mrs Justice Cheema Grubb DBE, and Mr Justice Bourne who ensured that a highly restrictive approach would be followed by those formerly less anchored to the aims of the system.

58 Ibid, para 120, emphasis added.

59 This is reflected in Rule 3 of the Criminal Procedure Rules which was amended, from 2 October 2017 (Criminal Procedure (Amendment No. 3) Rules 2017, SI 2017/755), by the insertion of a new provision (r 3.13(2)): 'At the plea and trial preparation hearing the court must – (a) satisfy itself that there has been explained to the defendant, in terms the defendant can understand (with help, if necessary), that the defendant will receive credit for a guilty plea' (this provision is now reflected in r 3.16(3) of the latest version of the CrimPR).

Plaku: *Reinforcing Structures of Case Management on Plea*

R v Plaku and others[60] ('*Plaku*') was a conjoined appeal involving three defendants and an attorney general's reference for an unduly lenient sentence. While the facts surrounding *Plaku* are of less interest here, it must be explained that of the three appellants, two had been convicted of 'Indictable only' offences.[61] This mattered, according to the appellants,[62] because of the established position in relation to the mode of trial for offences that they were charged with. In sum, both appellants accused of indictable only offences were not able to enter a plea of guilty to the magistrates as they had no jurisdiction to hear the case. In other words, any delay to their plea, at least until the first appearance in the Crown Court (the PTPH), should not, it was submitted, preclude them from receiving the full discount for a guilty plea. Put differently, the first opportunity to plead could not occur in the magistrates' court.

In one technical sense, the appellant's submissions had force. Regardless of plea, a first appearance hearing must be held in the Crown Court in light of the procedural rules that apply to indictable only offences. As such, there is something perverse about requiring a decision on plea from a defendant when a plea cannot legitimately be entered. Acceptance of the appellant's submissions on this point would have had enormous repercussions as far as scope for providing effective representation is concerned. This is because, ordinarily, there are approximately four weeks from the first appearance in the magistrates' court to the first appearance in the Crown Court (although the system stasis highlighted earlier can prolong the listing of case hearing dates). Of course, with prosecution disclosure post-committal being an unpredictable weak point of the criminal process,[63] different cases will progress to different extents. In his review, Leveson, by implication, conceded this very point:

> [S]trong local judicial oversight is needed to hold both the CPS and defence to account if defendants continue to enter late guilty pleas *when no significant change in the evidence or the charge has occurred since the case was sent from the Magistrates' Court.*[64]

As such, there would be cases where a significant change in the evidence or the charge *had* occurred by the time a plea could be legally entered at the PTPH stage in the Crown Court, placing some defendants at a plain disadvantage in

60 [2021] EWCA 568.

61 Plaku was accused of conspiracy to supply class A drugs (Indictable Only); Bourdon was tried for stalking and other similar offences (Either Way), whereas Smith was convicted of aggravated burglary (Indictable Only).

62 Plaku and Smith.

63 See, for example, E Johnston and T Smith (eds), *The Law of Disclosure – A Perennial Problem in Criminal Justice* (Routledge 2021).

64 The Leveson Review, para 140, emphasis added.

terms of the advice they would receive were they mandated to commit to their position on plea in the lower court. And yet this is precisely the position that the Court of Appeal cemented in *Plaku*. Due to the introduction of the BCM form,[65] which is now completed at all magistrate's courts during the first appearance and which allows for a defendant to indicate their plea, the Court held that the 'first available opportunity' to plead is at that same juncture, *regardless of the legal barrier to its entry until the Crown Court*.

By allowing the credit system to operate on the basis of an *indication*, not the entering of a plea, criminal courts circumvent the procedural barrier that a plea cannot be formally entered until it reaches the Crown Court. In doing so, the Court of Appeal validated the courts' practice of recording 'indications', allowing judges to substantially reduce the time counsel had to offer advice on plea, and, it follows, the level of prosecution disclosure that might inform that advice. Moreover, an uncompromising stance was set forth: Firstly, the one-third discount for an early guilty plea will only be given where an indication that the defendant wants to plead guilty is given at that first stage of proceedings. This stands even if a defendant is charged with a serious offence requiring a trial in the Crown Court, where, as stated, one cannot even enter a plea in the magistrates' court.

Secondly, while the 2017 *Guideline* made clear that a formula is applied to the sliding scale discount regime, specifically a one-third discount is given where the plea is *clearly* indicated at the first opportunity, *Plaku* results in a more unforgiving bargain laid down for defendants: a one-third discount is given only where the plea is '*unequivocally* indicated'. Where any sliver of doubt as to plea is conveyed to the court (e.g. even if a lawyer specifies that their client is 'likely' to plead guilty) that will not suffice, catapulting to new heights the level of certainty required of defendants who find themselves at this most vulnerable entry point to criminal proceedings.

The Problem with Plaku

While the importance of guilty pleas *to the system* is apparent from the preceding discussion, reliance on a sliding scale discount to incentivise guilty pleas is replete with challenges *for the accused*. In many ways, *Plaku* is a paradigm example of criminal justice putting its administrative needs in front of those it seeks to punish; nowhere in the system is the notion that efficiency has supplanted fairness more graphically exemplified.[66]

65 The BCM form must be used in all cases and uploaded to the Digital Case System (DCS) when a case is committed and to the Common Platform.

66 The willingness to prioritise efficiency gains over the risk to innocent defendants entering wrong pleas was on display before the advent of the CrimPR regime with the Runciman Commission: 'It would be naïve to suppose that innocent persons never plead guilty because of the prospect of the sentence discount . . . [But against this risk] must be weighed the benefits to the system' (RCCJ) (1993; Cm 2263) 110–111, paras 42–45.

While it is conceivable that precipitating 'closure' to a case might earlier spare genuine victims the ordeal of giving evidence in some cases,[67] it entirely disregards the existence of the growing trend of backlogs and system delay, which has resulted in 'victim attrition'[68] and further ignores the harsh corollary that defendants must make an accelerated decision with potential for their immediate loss of liberty. Moreover, even if it can be understood that the production of an unequivocal indication of guilt at the very first hearing in criminal cases will furnish the state with cost savings, these are quantified by removing the need for the CPS to be 'trial ready'. It is the lack of trial readiness by the CPS at the commencement of court proceedings that should animate real concern. If '[i]nadequate preparation is the enemy of good advocacy',[69] the demands placed upon an accused's plea by *Plaku* pay no attention to the present advisory landscape. Often, disclosure at the early stage of a first appearance will be limited, delayed or incomplete and that makes 'proper advice' on plea fanciful.

Leveson's own view on what is expected of defence at the early stage a plea is sought is symptomatic of system blind spots that facilitated the judgment in *Plaku*:

> By the time of entering a not guilty plea, I would expect the parties to have already been in discussions and for each to have a *clear understanding of the issues* which require determination at the trial.[70]

As would be familiar to any criminal practitioner, this idealist vision does not coincide with reality on the ground.[71] The notion of taking meaningful instructions when only a prosecution summary is provided is problematic for several reasons. Setting aside that (1) growing numbers of unrepresented defendants bring with them the attendant risk of failing to understand that they should plead guilty only if they are in fact guilty[72]; (2) a body of research has demonstrated how certain ethnic minorities have pleaded guilty less often *and later* than white defendants, often because of a community-based climate of distrust of the justice system[73]; and (3) non-disclosure has led to an untold

67 Of course, there are citizens who *want* to give evidence.

68 J Ames, 'Victims Abandon Rape Trials Due to Acute Backlog of Cases' *The Times* (25 July 2024).

69 Sir B Jeffrey, *Independent Criminal Advocacy in England and Wales* (MoJ, 2014).

70 The Leveson Review, para 102.

71 Ibid para 178. The evidence against Leveson was written by no less than his own pen: 'One of the major issues [is] the present failure of the police and the CPS to meet deadlines for disclosure'.

72 It is understood that 'in the first six months of 2023 over 50% of magistrates' court trials conducted on the Common Platform involved unrepresented defendants.' See S S Townsend, *Inaugural Address*, Lincoln's Inn, 9 January 2024, 4.

73 See, for example, R Hood, *Race and Sentencing* (OUP 1992).

number of miscarriages of justice,[74] courts have fundamentally misunderstood the extent to which an accused person relies on the advice of their representative in helping them to make a potentially life-altering decision.

Various factors operate upon that lawyer–client exchange that might serve to heighten risk factors typically associated with unsafe pleas. Central amongst them is that decision-making takes place in a context where their contact with counsel is likely to have been very limited and their case likely handled through a hearing that will be expected to be brief, contending for court time with countless other first appearances and bail applications before the bench.[75] Aside from the obvious difficulties stemming from advice on an outline of the evidence,[76] the first appearance is not conducive to the development of a defendant's trust with their lawyer.[77] What is more, a significant number of first court hearings are covered by a pupil barrister or junior practitioner. The fact that the least experienced, most poorly paid lawyers are chaperoning clients at this vulnerable stage has become an ethically suspect feature of the advisory landscape.

In any event, the *Plaku* precedent results in a coercive presentation of the available evidence. An inescapable cost (i.e. an enhanced penalty) is imposed on the accused in situations where the production of further evidence is necessary for a better understanding of the prosecution case against them. The whole point of due process is to reach decisions in an informed manner. Yet the compelling of defence lawyers to *speculate* on the possibility of further (unknown) evidence being later disclosed, rather than basing advice on its actual production, places the integrity of plea decisions in jeopardy.[78]

Conclusion

On the interplay between values and criminal justice, Walter Miller once said,

> Ideology and its consequences exert a powerful influence on the policies and procedures of those who conduct the enterprise of criminal justice,

74 See, for example, F Belloni and J Hodgson, *Criminal Injustice* (Macmillian 2000).

75 A report by the NGO Fair Trials has drawn attention to evidence of this risk in the context of young defendants: *Young Minds, Big Decisions* (October 2022).

76 I have explained elsewhere why counsel might have good reason to avoid placing reliance upon 'prosecution summaries': M McConville and L Marsh, 'Adversarialism Goes West: Case Management in Criminal Courts' (2015) 19(3) *The International Journal of Evidence and Proof* 172–189.

77 As the Bellamy Review (para 9.14) documents, 'the evidence to the Review is that at the first hearing in the Magistrates' Court, many cases are taken "on the hoof" with the defence representatives trying to absorb what may be quite complex facts and take instructions from the client, with very little time to do so, while the client, who has not previously seen the evidence either, is under pressure to decide on a plea at that first hearing in order to earn the maximum credit.'

78 An expectation placed on the shoulders of criminal lawyers which runs contrary to the court's mantra: 'The criminal law is not a game to be played in the hope of a lucky outcome.' See for example *R on the application of Hassini v West London Magistrate's Court* [2017] EWHC 1270 (Admin) echoing the oft-cited words of Auld LJ in *R v Gleeson* [2003] EWCA 3357 ([at 36])).

> and . . . the degree and kinds of influences go largely unrecognised. Ideology is the permanent hidden agenda of criminal justice.[79]

In an extension of this, when one triangulates the political, ethical, and structural issues outlined in this chapter, criminal proceedings in England and Wales are seen to be monopolised by a transparent agenda: the production of early guilty pleas. While any system of justice will necessarily have pragmatic considerations impinging upon it, the prevailing ideology of efficiency has been elevated to such an expansive degree that the further 'shrinking' of defence capacities has ensured its incorporation into a state-induced (i.e. coercive) plea system.

Under the CrimPR, the adversarial advocate already struck an elusive figure in criminal courts. Having been lionised for the protections they once offered the accused, independent counsel have buckled under the growing weight of alterations to their function (propped up sometimes by a judiciary acting in gesture only). In this vein, the Criminal Division's judgment in *Plaku* saw the Court of Appeal endorse a far more stringent approach to decision-making about plea discounts, and, in doing so, fully realise the long-held goal of the Sentencing Council (and Guidelines Council before it) to capitalise on the pre-trial role played by defence in securing guilty pleas. Part of the issue here is those indications are now expected at a very advanced stage of proceedings, whereby lowered obligations of disclosure necessitate the turning of defence representatives into *agents of speculation.* A role that once involved the sensitive weighing of evidence against elements of an offence has morphed into an exercise in second-guessing the shape of prosecution evidence that might unfold, a challenge made more difficult by inexperience and the financially precarious position that accompanies the junior lawyers ordinarily tasked with such hearings.

A worrying corollary of this new plea environment is the courts' perception that defendants surely know *whether or not* they are guilty of the crime charged. Only allowing full 'credit' for admitting culpability in this context, especially where criminal allegations are nuanced and sufficient disclosure is wanting, is anathema to traditional understandings of *legal* guilt. Structural arrangements to facilitate this binary view of accused persons can introduce profound unfairness where the innocent are confronted with a sliding scale of 'reward' geared towards them most heavily when, antithetically, they face most risk of entering a wrong plea. Calibrated to 'bargain' hardest with defendants who may not truly understand what they have to lose in 'taking the discount', the end result is not just expedited but *amputated* 'justice'.

79 Walter B Miller, 'Ideology and Criminal Justice Policy: Some Current Issues' (1973) 64 *Journal of Criminal Law and Criminology* 141–162 at 142.

5 Access to Justice in the Family Court

An Exploration of Key Issues and Barriers to Justice

Alex Newbury and Sarah Moore

Introduction

In this chapter, we analyse key barriers to justice that became prevalent after the cuts to Legal Aid following the Legal Aid and Sentencing of Offenders Act 2013 (LASPO), which affected the majority of family law matters and was then exacerbated by the Covid-19 pandemic. We evaluate the impact of these barriers and explore the extent to which they have remained as live issues since the end of the pandemic, arguing that they risk becoming endemic within court processes if more is not done to alleviate them.

Legal Aid in England and Wales underwent radical reform in 2013 following the cuts brought by LASPO. Amongst other things, the act prompted a significant retrenchment in Legal Aid, especially for civil law cases, where casework decreased by roughly two-thirds in the first year following the introduction of the LASPO reforms.[1] There is now consensus that the cuts went too far and have had deleterious effects on access to justice.[2] The marked under-use of extraordinary case funding has raised particular concern, being a ring-fenced budget for those cases where there is a possible breach of the European Convention on Human Rights, including cases involving vulnerable litigants.[3]

As a direct result of these cuts, there was a collapse of Legal Aid services across England and Wales and dispersal of many highly trained and dedicated Legal Aid family lawyers. Facing a lacuna of advice and support, those pursuing civil law cases are now left with few options but to navigate the system by themselves to seek a 'do it yourself' form of justice.[4] Successive government-sponsored reviews and commissions have indicated that the cuts to funding

1 L Trinder, R Hunter, E Hitchings, J Miles, R Moorhead, L Smith, M Sefton, V Hinchly, K Bader, and J Pearce, *Litigants in Person in Private Family Law Cases* (Ministry of Justice 2014).

2 House of Commons Justice Committee, 8th Report, *Impact to Changes of Civil Legal Aid under Part 1 of LASPO 2012* (HMSO 2015).

3 Ibid 15–16.

4 S Moore and A Newbury, *Legal Aid in Crisis: Assessing the Impact of Reform* (Policy Press 2017).

DOI: 10.4324/9781003496823-5

have led to a sharp increase in litigants in person (LiPs), that is, people representing themselves in court.[5]

The impact of this shift was just starting to be documented when the Covid-19 pandemic hit in 2020. This caused court proceedings to slow and become more volatile, and judges and barristers adapted their roles to accommodate the challenges faced by LiPs in the courtroom.[6] This was then further compounded by a shift to online hearings in their entirety due to the pandemic, a shift which remains for many regular family law cases. As so much of the work of the family court was face to face, the vast majority of these services were reduced to almost nil during the first lockdown in spring 2020 (save for emergency public law child protection cases, which are beyond the remit of this chapter). Most court hearings went online, and the family court became manned by a few court staff with no in-person hearings taking place in court buildings. Although there was a gradual return to some hearings, the subsequent lockdowns over the next 18 months meant matters became increasingly dealt with online as a 'new normal', and much routine work has remained this way in many family courts. As we examine in this chapter, what started as emergency measures have become entrenched in the system, with unintended, far-reaching consequences for access to justice.

Concern amongst legal academics[7] about the impact of the cuts to Legal Aid on access to justice for those people who cannot afford private legal representation resulted in the formation of CLOCK.[8] This is a legal outreach–research group composed of universities that train undergraduate law students to act as legal companions for LiPs. They are trained to support litigants in navigating the court process and then to support them in representing themselves at

5 See generally L Trinder, R Hunter, E Hitchings, J Miles, R Moorhead, L Smith, M Sefton, V Hinchly, K Bader, and J Pearce, *Litigants in Person in Private Family Law Cases* (Ministry of Justice [MoJ] 2014); Lord Chief Justice of England and Wales, Senior President of Tribunals, *Transforming our Justice System* (2016); The Fabian Society, *The Crisis in the Justice System in England and Wales: The Bach Commission on Access to Justice – Interim Report* (2016); R Lee, T Birch, and M Humphries, *Survey of Civil Legal Aid Providers in England and Wales: Informing the Review of Civil Legal Aid* (PA Consulting 2024).

6 L Trinder, R Hunter, E Hitchings, J Miles, R Moorhead, L Smith, M Sefton, V Hinchly, K Bader and J Pearce, *Litigants in Person in Private Family Law Cases* (MoJ 2014).

7 A Barlow, R Hunter, J Smithson and J Ewing, *Mapping Paths to Family Justice: Resolving Family Disputes in Neo-Liberal Times* (Palgrave Macmillan 2017); S Moore and A Newbury, *Legal Aid in Crisis: Assessing the Impact of Reform* (Policy Press 2017); S Wong and R Cain, 'The Impact of Cuts in Legal Aid Funding on Private Family Law Cases' (2019) 41 *Journal of Social Work and Family Law* 3; J Mant, *Litigants in Person and the Family Justice System* (Hart Publishing 2022).

8 See https://clock.uk.net/ for more information. For further insight into CLOCK, see J Krishnadas, 'Legal Needs across the Family Justice System: Who Needs What, Where, and When? The Contribution of CLOCK, a Community Outreach System in England and Wales' in M Maclean, R Treloar, and B Dijkterhuis (eds) *What Is a Family Justice System For?* (Bloomsbury 2022) 171.

court hearings, akin to a McKenzie friend.[9] There is a dearth of research focusing on the experiences of both LiPs and their student legal companions. The student companions are uniquely placed to offer insight and reflect on both the tensions and challenges of being *in loco* solicitor, but they lack the legal qualifications and thus the ability to truly offer legal advice and guidance to litigants. Indeed, they are strictly told by their institutions that it is essential that they only assist and befriend and that they be clear when they introduce themselves to litigants that they cannot offer legal advice. As a voluntary service, CLOCK operates out of university law schools in a small number of locations throughout the country.[10] Thus, although the work carried out is undoubtedly valuable, it represents a drop in the ocean of unmet legal need amongst unrepresented litigants throughout the country. This brings into sharp relief the significant gap left by the near abolition of Legal Aid in family cases[11] and thus the lack of access to trained, dedicated Legal Aid lawyers to support and advise litigants.

Methodology

This chapter grew from empirical work carried out following the publication of our initial book about the impacts of the Legal Aid cuts, which drew on one of the author's former roles as a Legal Aid family solicitor.[12] The research, funded by the British Academy, consisted of a series of focus groups with three consecutive cohorts of legal companions involved in supporting LiPs: one prior to the pandemic, one during lockdowns, and one later in the Covid-19 pandemic.

Companions are trained in a variety of areas including family law, financial issues, mediation, the role of CAFCASS,[13] and the impact of domestic abuse. The companions commit to doing one shift, about four hours, per week over an academic year. In the initial stages of the research, these shifts took place face to face at the family court, and the participants in the first focus group were able to reflect upon their in-person experiences in meeting with litigants at court and supporting them with their issues in trying to navigate the court process. The latter two focus groups occurred after the start of the pandemic

9 For more on McKenzie friends, see Judiciary.co.uk (2022) *Guidance from the President's Office: McKenzie Friends* at <www.judiciary.uk/wp-content/uploads/2022/07/pfd-guidance-mckenzie-friends.pdf> accessed 8 July 2024.

10 CLOCK operated out of university law schools in the respective Court Centres in Keele, Stoke-on-Trent; Brighton, Sussex; Canterbury, Kent; Salford, Greater Manchester, and Essex. Forthcoming from Birmingham City, Birmingham, and Liverpool John Moores, Liverpool.

11 Except in cases of significant and clearly evidenced cases of domestic abuse when it can still be accessed but requires levels of documentation that may in itself cause a barrier for many litigants, despite the clear need.

12 S Moore and A Newbury, *Legal Aid in Crisis: Assessing the Impact of Reform* (Policy Press 2017).

13 Children and Family Court Advisory and Support Service.

in 2020. The second focus group was during the first lockdown and explored the second cohort of students' experiences of trying to navigate processes that had moved suddenly to virtual platforms, with solely online support for litigants and solely online hearings. The final focus group took place after there had been some attempt to return to normal practice, but much of the work of the family court, and for legal companions supporting LiPs, was still online, with the inherent difficulties and barriers that posed.

The legal companions who took part in the focus groups for this study were all undergraduate law students in their second or final years of study in the south-east of England. The first focus group, carried out in January 2020, just prior to the impact of the pandemic hitting the UK, took place in person over the course of a full afternoon. It was the longest in duration (at around four hours) and elicited rich responses from the participants. We conducted the discussion jointly using a schedule of questions to guide the group. The second focus group took place online in March 2021, during the second period of national lockdown, and the third and final focus group was held in November 2022. We also jointly delivered these sessions over Microsoft Teams. They lasted two to three hours and used the same schedule as that used in the first group. Next, we discuss and reflect in more depth on this point including how the focus groups gave us a sense of the extent to which barriers to justice have shifted over the last three years, in a context of significant change.

LASPO and Its Impact on Access to Justice

Whether measured by backlogs in casework or by more qualitative indicators such as satisfaction with justice processes and outcomes, the Civil Justice of England and Wales – and in particular the Family Court – is nearing crisis point.[14] Recent research shows that LASPO has not succeeded in reducing the numbers of people using the court process to resolve family cases; it has just succeeded in denying them access to trained legal advice and support. This has resulted in delayed or paused court proceedings rather than any actual reduction in the overarching need for legal assistance.[15] The prevailing government view is that the causes of this are partly exogenous – lying in individual litigants' over-use of court as a mechanism for deciding a dispute (and, latterly, the impact of an unforeseeable public health crisis) – and partly endogenous, lying in a long-term failure to modernise court systems and processes. Successive reforms have sought to tackle these perceived problems and include such

14 M Briggs, *Civil Courts Structure Review: Interim Report* (Judiciary of England and Wales 2015); *The Crisis in the Justice System in England and Wales: The Bach Commission on Access to Justice – Interim Report* (The Fabian Society 2016); *Access Denied: The State of the Justice System in England and Wales in 2022* (The Bar Council 2022).

15 L Cusworth, S Bedston, B Alrouh, K Broadhurst, A Akbari, and LJ Griffiths, *Uncovering Private Family Law: Who's Coming to Court in England? Summary* (Nuffield Family Justice Observatory 2021) 1.

diverse measures (over a 25-year period) as the introduction of court fees, the promotion of alternative dispute resolution,[16] the mass closure of court buildings, the launch of an online portal to access,[17] download and in some instances submit forms, the (failed) attempt to make mediation mandatory for divorcing couples, and – most impactful of all – Legal Aid reform.

Civil justice reform was given new impetus with the emergence of austerity politics under the coalition of the Conservative and Liberal Democrat parties in 2010, which focussed on reducing public spending. This prompted the Ministry of Justice (MoJ) to undertake wide-ranging reform to tackle what they conceived to be the twin challenges of litigant over-use of court processes and the need for modernisation. As part of this drive in 2016, Her Majesty's Courts and Tribunal Service launched a £1 billion court reform package aimed at overhauling courts' digital infrastructure. This initially ambitious reform programme was directed towards significantly decreasing costs in the long run by, among other things, introducing an end-to-end digital case management system, piloting the use of online forms, and moving as many hearings as possible online. This reform programme has been mired with difficulties, and in reviewing its progress and outcomes, the National Audit Office[18] noted that it was significantly behind schedule and needed to successively reduce the scope of its programme.[19]

While this digital reform programme was underway, a parallel strand of justice reform was having a genuinely transformative impact on the court user's experience of civil justice processes. Implemented in 2013, LASPO radically reformed the legal aid system in England and Wales, removing Legal Aid entitlement for most litigants pursuing private family law cases. Its effects were not only felt at an individual level but at a system level, too: The sharp reduction in funding for the civil legal aid sector led to a significant shrinking of this sector.[20] The MoJ is currently reviewing[21] the funding structure and organisation of civil legal aid, which has already pointed to the very significant mismatch in demand for civil legal aid services relative to supply.[22]

16 For an extensive review of family dispute resolution processes in a post-LASPO period, see A Barlow, R Hunter, J Smithson, and J Ewing, *Mapping Paths to Family Justice: Resolving Family Disputes in Neo-Liberal Times* (Palgrave Macmillan 2017).

17 <www.gov.uk/government/publications/hmcts-reform-family-fact-sheets/fact-sheet-family-public-law-online-service>

18 *Early Progress in Transforming Courts and Tribunals* (National Audit Office 2018); *Transforming Courts and Tribunals – A Progress Update* (National Audit Office 2019).

19 MoJ, Lord Chief Justice of England and Wales, Senior President of Tribunals, *Transforming our Justice System* (MoJ 2016).

20 S Wong and R Cain, 'The Impact of Cuts in Legal Aid Funding on Private Family Law Cases' (2019) 41 JSWFL 3.

21 <www.gov.uk/guidance/civil-legal-aid-review>

22 R Lee, T Birch, and M Humphries, *Survey of Civil Legal Aid Providers in England and Wales: Informing the Review of Civil Legal Aid* (PA Consulting 2024) 7.

The key effect of LASPO, rather than streamlining the process and enabling the use of mediation or informal agreement, has been to make the experience of pursuing a private family law case harder. In retrospect, perhaps seeking to reduce the use of family courts was always an unachievable objective given that their day-to-day business includes adjudicating on the breakdown of relationships, with all the emotionally charged needs and power imbalances this entails, over matters (housing, children, pensions, financial support) that are at once utterly vital to everyday life and hedged round in complexity and strict legal provisions. Kirwan highlights the lacuna of legal advice and support in a post-LASPO era as the 'delegalised space' of family law.[23] Hitchings et al. argue that most divorcees now end up relying on a patchwork of formal and informal support, with only 56% of divorcees employing a lawyer or legal services companies and a concerning 12% not having any legal advice or support at all.[24]

This has caused a significant increase in people representing themselves through the legal process as LiPs, with a 19% increase in a complete lack of legal representation for either party between 2013 and 2018.[25] As we here establish, this has resulted in significant challenges for many litigants in pursuing their cases that work together to cause real barriers in ensuring a fair hearing and for LiPs' general understanding of the litigation. As these issues frequently hinge around contact and residence for children, financial support, and housing, this is highly problematic, particularly for less resourceful litigants and those with language barriers.

A key impact following the LASPO cuts was the removal of the court desk in many courts,[26] which had previously been manned throughout office hours by court staff who were previously available to hand out paper forms, give advice on fees and the correct forms to use, and accept and process applications; this was cut away, and the forms are now only available online. However, navigation of the government website and finding the correct forms is far from straight-forward for people who might struggle with what the legal terminology means and what is required in terms of supporting documentation. In short, there is limited face-to-face support available for litigants to navigate this, even as a first step in the legal process, which could be exacerbated by the challenge of low digital literacy amongst the population as a whole.[27] In

23 S Kirwan, 'Law and the "Stbx": Online fora and the 'Delegalised Space' of Family Law' (2017) 7(7) *Oñati Socio-Legal Series* 1421.

24 E Hitchings, C Bryson, G Douglas, S Purdon and J Birchall, *Fair Shares? Sorting Out Money and Property on Divorce. Final Report* (University of Bristol, Nuffield Foundation, and Bryson Purdon Social Research 2023) 103–16.

25 *Guide to Family Court Statistics* (MoJ 2021).

26 G Parker-White, 'Family Courts: Fit for the Modern Era? (2024) *The Law Gazette*; Commons Select Justice Committee, '5 HMCTS reductions in staffing' (HoC, 2024) para 131–52.

27 Dept For Science, Innovation, and Technology, *Policy paper: 2. Digital Skills and Inclusion – Giving Everyone Access to the Digital Skills They Need* (gov.uk 2023).

2020, the Office of National Statistics cited that 6.3% adults had never used the internet,[28] a cohort which was also likely to overlap disproportionately with those with low levels of written literacy who therefore would be impacted twice over by the change.

Much has been written about the significant practical and emotional support court-based staff can offer litigants and the need for a physical family court space for this that is not readily replicated online.[29] Smith and Hitchings highlighted the wide-ranging benefits of the emotional support that the physical presence of a supporter, such as a McKenzie friend, can bring[30] and how important it is for litigants to feel both emotionally and practically ready to engage with the court processes and understand the need for engaging with family dispute resolution mechanisms such as mediation.[31]

A lack of legal support has differing levels of impact for different litigants. Those least able to help themselves in comprehending the forms, organising their case, and representing it to the court and mediation or CAFCASS services may fare worst, but Trinder et al highlighted a significant impact for people from any walk of life, even those educated to degree level and with English as their first language. Their research categorised litigants on a spectrum from those who were most challenged to those who were 'apparently competent' and educated but who still frequently failed to comply with court orders or to complete court forms correctly and who still struggled to distinguish between what was *legally* relevant to their case, rather than matters that were emotionally or personally highly significant for them.[32]

Reflecting on one of the author's own experiences as a family law solicitor, and the impossibility for many clients of separating a (lack of) payment of child support from enabling the other partner to have child contact, or their own needs from the court's requirement to make the child's needs of paramount concern, this challenge is not altogether surprising. Mant draws attention to the further need for LiPs to find time to prepare their case, weaving this around their own paid work and childcare commitments. Many of her interviewees 'explained that the only time they had to complete their court preparations was during the evenings and often well into the night', often, she adds, with 'severe consequences for their health and wellbeing'.[33]

28 Office for National Statistics, *Internet Users: UK, 2020* (ONS 2021).

29 R George and R Marsh, 'Do We Need Physical Family Courts?' (2024) 46(1) *Journal of Social Welfare and Family Law* 59.

30 L Smith and E Hitchings, 'Professionals and Partisans: Lessons for Family Lawyers from a Study of Fee-Charging McKenzie Friends' (2019) *Child and Family Law Quarterly* 362.

31 A Barlow, R Hunter, J Smithson, and J Ewing, *Mapping Paths to Family Justice: Resolving Family Disputes in Neo-Liberal Times* (Palgrave Macmillan 2017).

32 L Trinder, R Hunter, E Hitchings, J Miles, R Moorhead, L Smith, M Sefton, V Hinchly, K Bader and J Pearce, *Litigants in Person in Private Family Law Cases* (MoJ 2014) 24.

33 J Mant, *Litigants in Person and the Family Justice System* (Hart Publishing 2022) 2.

This can either be triggered by, or result in, key indicators of vulnerability. Moorhead and Sefton identified these as depression, alcoholism, drug use, terminal illness, being a young lone parent, living in temporary accommodation, having a history of mental illness, previous imprisonment, involvement with social services, being a victim of violence, and illiteracy.[34] The legal companions we interviewed for this study also noted a tendency for litigants in person to be subject to two or more vulnerabilities (a point similarly made by Moorhead and Sefton). For this group, the experience of social isolation, uncertainty and instability, fear and victimisation, and poor health were interrelated. When combined, these factors rendered the task of preparing a legal case overwhelming and often defeated them. These observations point to the overlapping and interacting forms of inequality at work in family law courts in a post-LASPO era, where those in the most precarious financial positions are disproportionately likely to be pursuing especially high-stakes cases and to be doing so alone.

Now, several years on from the outset of the pandemic, the legal landscape is much changed, with a patchwork of differing court practices reported by different CLOCK teams across the country. The post-pandemic approaches adopted by family courts range from emphasising returning to the pre-pandemic in-person court hearings to continuing a substantial number of online hearings. The issues this raises, both potentially positive and negative, will now be explored in greater depth.

Barriers to Justice

This section focusses on a range of barriers to access to justice that are present within the current family court system. Before introducing these barriers, we want to provide a caveat. The legal companions who participated in this study pointed to some benefits of the online hearings, even as they tended to see these as significantly outweighed by the disadvantages that form the focal point of this chapter. These benefits include protecting litigants who have suffered domestic abuse from any risk of direct contact with their attacker, making the process less stressful; eliminating time and travel costs for both litigants and court personnel, which benefit those who are working from home or who have caring responsibilities; and potentially benefiting the environment on a wider scale by reducing travel.

However, these potential advantages were outnumbered by the significant range of disadvantages flagged by our participants. In this section, we argue that the barriers LiPs encounter to justice including a basic comprehension of court processes pose significant strains on family court and the process as a whole. Some of these issues, which would have been unthinkable prior to

34 R Moorhead and M Sefton, *Litigants in Person: Unrepresented Litigants in First Instance Proceedings* (2005), DCA Research Series 2/05, 70.

LASPO and the pandemic, have almost become normalised in a context where 'making the best of a bad situation' has become a guiding principle (it is worth recalling here that for over two years from early 2020, the UK staggered from lockdown to lockdown, with some brief respites and attempts at normality but with the potential of a further uptick in the pandemic casting a long shadow beyond the end of 2022).

Along with significant funding cuts amidst the cost-of-living crisis, this resulted in a legacy of technological, procedural, and societal changes that were made *in extremis* and at speed and that became the new normal. However, what this new normal entails appears to be relatively *ad hoc*, and to some extent it depends on the geographical location and choices of individual family courts. This, coupled with court personnel who are still trying to make sense of how this can fit within the traditional court system and empty public-facing desks in many court buildings, has resulted in a system where the litigant in person can feel truly lost and at sea. The overall consequence is a lack of even basic help or support on something as simple yet vital as knowing the correct forms to complete, let alone any detailed advice or guidance.

Some of the barriers to justice we outlined can be grouped around particular areas. Some emerged prior to the pandemic and remain today; others were exacerbated by the pandemic. Many of the barriers might be characterised as overarching: the pandemic and its fall-out may have shone a starker light upon them, but they are key issues that affect and impede the ongoing access to justice for many litigants. It is important to acknowledge here that some of the barriers are unintentional and inadvertent on the part of the court and potentially unavoidable given the necessary complexity inherent in legal systems. However, the points we highlight coalesce to create particular barriers and tensions for litigants in seeking justice, and it is our hope that shining a light upon them will cause them to be recognised more widely, allowing work to be done at a policy or court level to alleviate at least some of them.

Language Barriers and Legal Jargon

A key issue that the focus group legal companions highlighted as causing barriers to justice throughout the process was the need for relatively sophisticated language, including understanding legal terminology. LiPs need not only to comprehend legal documents and the court process but to prepare and write their cases for the court, including identifying essential information and evidence. Although the Court Service has done much to attempt to make court forms clearer and more accessible, many of the student companions highlighted the length and complexity of some of the main forms used. As a key example, the main form used for applying for private law matters relating to children, such as contact and overnight stays, form C100 Child Arrangements, is 26 pages long and written in terms which many of the focus group students described as impenetrable for many of the LiPs they were assisting, relying as they do on very specific legal terminology. Its full title is *Application under section 8 of the Children Act 1989 for a child arrangements, prohibited steps, or specific issue order, or to vary or discharge or ask permission to make a section 8 order.* It then requires the applicant to tick the correct box for the type of court order they need from that selection.

The problem of a legal form that – due to the complexity of the matters involved – is not (and perhaps cannot, as the system currently stands) written in plain English is exacerbated by many defendants' low language ability and comprehension of many of those that came to the court, sometimes because English was not their first language. In the past, trained solicitors were publicly funded to give not only support and explanation but also advice and case management, and this has now been entirely removed, leaving litigants to struggle alone or with the help of volunteers such as the student legal companions. In one focus group, one and then a number of student companions reflected on litigants attending in-person court with a supermarket plastic bag full of unsorted documents and statements.[35] In the designated CLOCK offices at the court building, the student companions helped litigants bring order to their documents by ranking them in order of importance for their cases. The lengthy court forms and legal terminology were hard to understand, making it even more challenging for litigants to reformulate complex personal matters to fit the justice system's parameters, this system that requires litigants (or their lawyers or legal companions) to convert personal problems into legal cases and align their key concerns with the court's priorities.

Lost in the Process: The Lack of Emotional and Moral Support

As we discussed in our earlier book,[36] the role of the Legal Aid family solicitor at the turn of the 21st century was as much about moral and emotional support in a situation that is frequently acknowledged to be one of the most stressful life events many people ever experience – family break-up often resulting in loss of home and fractured contact with children – as it was about cutting-edge legal advice. This view was borne out by the experiences related by the student legal companions about the emotional support that they were able to offer to the litigants and the extent to which they recognised that some litigants felt lost in the process. The CLOCK administrator reflected that the legal companions' support was frequently sought by people who 'are most afraid of authority and courts . . . [who] think that they might do something wrong to upset a judge and then everything will go against them'. She stated that this meant the job for the legal companions was 'reassuring them that

35 Focus group 1, 30 January 2020.

36 S Moore and A Newbury, *Legal Aid in Crisis: Assessing the Impact of Reform* (Policy Press 2017).

actually the law always is looking for the best outcome for everybody and for the all-round outcome'.[37]

The students in the focus groups frequently came back to the theme of the importance of being physically present and an appreciation of how the small amount of time and support they gave was such a lifeline for people who were cut out of gaining legal advice and support. One reflected on her reasons for volunteering:

> The opportunity to be able to help litigants in person, when you delve into legal aid a little bit more and you realise just how much the cuts impact those that cannot simply afford it, but your little bit of help and knowledge just goes a long, long way, to be able to help them in court, even if it's just by making them feel at ease. That is something. You're giving them something.[38]

The legal companions frequently picked out emotional support as one of the key things there were able to offer litigants. They reflected that even being able to metaphorically hold a hand and 'just being there' as a moral support was of immense value. Elsewhere, we have detailed how the shift to online and then hybrid support arrangements changed their ability to do this work and the effects this had on the quality of support provided.[39] It is, we think, reasonable to think of the reduction of legal advice and support – whether that's from LASPO, and later, the reduction of in-person services in response to the COVID-19 pandemic – as a barrier to justice, given what legal companions told us about the diffuse and practical benefit of their work, pre-pandemic, in offering emotional support.

A Lacuna of Legal Advice

One area of frustration that was an overarching theme from the student legal companions was that they were unable to offer the level of support they wanted to because they were not allowed to give advice. They are explicitly told this during their initial training, and the policy is strictly enforced because of the potential liability for universities and the insurance cover stipulations required in order to supply the service: They provide support, not advice. It is explained to the students that even giving advice about the correct form to submit to the court and being wrong could cost the litigant's court fee (at the time of writing, £255 for a Child Arrangements application and £593 for

37 Interview, 15 July 2022.

38 Focus group 1, 30 January 2020.

39 S Moore and A Newbury, 'Pursuing Family Justice before, during, and after the COVID-19 Pandemic: The Changing Role of Legal Companions and the New Invisibility of Unmet Legal Need' (2024) 2 *Child and Family Law Quarterly* 155.

an application to start divorce proceedings)[40] or delay the litigant's application beyond the time limit.

In short, there were good reasons to prohibit providing legal advice. However, many of the companions asserted that the line between support and advice was difficult to navigate, especially in relation to completing forms (where they knew that a standard C100 form was appropriate, for example, but were unable to convey this to a confused litigant seeking help and clarification about the process). They also expressed frustration about the fact that this restriction was in a context (following LASPO and cuts to Citizens Advice Bureau services) where *no one* is providing advice. The companions regularly told us that the average litigant in person had nowhere else to turn apart from private legal advice that was beyond their financial reach.

The cuts to legal support were then exacerbated by the pandemic because many courts no longer had a functioning face-to-face court office, which was previously open to the public with clerks to answer queries or give any guidance on the forms. There is no in-person advice available for litigants and they are just directed to the government website. As an example of this complexity, from the landing page on the government website for the Form C 100 Child Arrangement form, it is described thus: "Apply for a 'child arrangements', 'prohibited steps' or 'specific issue' order under the Children Act 1989."[41] Although the non-lawyer may reasonably guess that 'child arrangements' means arranging things for children (although it still does not seem as clear as the old terms of 'child contact' and 'residence'), the terms 'prohibited steps' and 'specific issue' are unlikely to mean anything to non-lawyers, without some legal advice, and even more so if English is not their first language, or they have low levels of literacy. In summary, a key barrier to justice is the design of the forms that allow the litigant to access the court system in the first place, the fact that they are now only available online, and the potentially misleading nature of their categorisation. This combines with the legal jargon, the procedures and deadlines, the documentation and a statement, and the fact that the last lifeline of support of the friendly clerk as a face-to-face presence at the court has also been cut.

40 HM Courts and Tribunals Service, *Guidance: Family Courts Fees (EX50)* (2024) <www.gov.uk/government/publications/fees-in-the-civil-and-family-courts-main-fees-ex50> accessed 9 July 2024.

41 HM Courts and Tribunals Service, *Form: Apply for a Court Order to Make Arrangements for a Child or Resolve a Dispute about Their Upbringing: Form C100* (2024) <www.gov.uk/government/publications/form-c100-application-under-the-children-act-1989-for-a-child-arrangements-prohibited-steps-specific-issue-section-8-order-or-to-vary-or-discharge> accessed 15 July 2024.

Navigating the Court Hearing

The court hearing itself was also identified by student legal companions as a point of tension for LiPs. Although an everyday, familiar experience for lawyers and court personnel, these hearings are frequently the first and only time many litigants are inside a court building. Court is an unknown environment, with its own language and rules that can seem impenetrable and incomprehensible and that is accessed via forms strewn with legal jargon. The hearing itself could feel like an interview, presided over by a judge, and now unmediated by a familiar Legal Aid solicitor who might have met with a litigant on several occasions prior to the proceedings and was felt to be 'on their side'.

The student legal companions somewhat mitigated this by being present and taking notes to give moral support as a friendly face in the actual court hearings, including repeating the judges' comments and judgments to litigants who did not grasp the full proceedings, but they still could not give concrete legal advice. Student companions reflected that they felt reluctant to even explain cases in more detail as, as they had already noted, the line between support and advice could be a difficult one to draw.[42] The students reported frustration that litigants actually wanted advice or representation at the court that they were not allowed to provide. Even the term 'Court Legal Companion' on documentation could give the unintentional impression that they had been legally trained. Indeed, one student stated that even the judges sometimes got confused about their role and had asked the student companion to go outside and explain the hearing and judgement in clearer detail to the litigant, which was beyond the level of support they could offer.[43] This highlights the challenges the legal companions face as well as the ongoing problems caused by the lack of both trained legal support and advice for litigants and due process in ensuring justice is done, leaving litigants dissatisfied that their case has been heard fully and not necessarily understanding the outcomes.

IT Barriers

The legal companions who took part in this study highlighted significant technical difficulties that were most acute during the Covid-19 pandemic but to some extent have now become the new normal. Even for the more technologically savvy, the 'brave new world' of Teams, Zoom, and Skype meetings can be problematic, with connection outages and difficulties navigating the varied systems. For many LiPs, these technical problems are significant barriers to justice.[44] Some lack the equipment and the resources to obtain it,

42 Focus group 1, 30 January 2020.

43 Ibid.

44 S Moore and A Newbury, 'Pursuing Family Justice before, during, and after the COVID-19 Pandemic: The Changing Role of Legal Companions and the New Invisibility of Unmet Legal Need' (2024) 36 *Child and Family Law Quarterly* 2, 155.

and even those with access to suitable computer equipment might lack the technical know-how to set up the calls. And online hearings add another layer of communication barriers for people with low literacy or non-native English speakers.[45]

In person, a judge might perceive a litigant's lack of comprehension (for instance through body language) and attempt to clarify in simpler language, but such nuances are less easy to discern in the online environment, especially if poor internet access and connectivity means that information gets lost and communication impeded. The student companions could give these clarifications directly after a hearing in person as long as they did not give advice, but this vital service was much more difficult to provide once cases moved online.

Conclusion

The barriers to justice that we have outlined in this chapter are rendering litigants and their legal needs increasingly invisible. Taken as a whole, these barriers have a compound effect. Technical difficulties make the task of pursuing justice all the harder for the litigant in person whose first language is not English, and a lack of legal advice post-LASPO makes the move to online forms (and their inadequate categorisation) all the more impactful. The reduction in emotional support for litigants makes the emotionally charged court hearing even more difficult to navigate effectively. The result is vast – and still growing – swathes of unknown and unmet legal need as litigants are left to manage these challenges on their own.

On a global level, the pandemic and other crises such as high costs of living and environmental impacts left a mark on many, including a long-term state of exhaustion and struggling to make progress in a world where in one way or another we are always all potentially together online, but at the same time, we are also all separate and in our own individual spaces. People in general, but LiPs in particular, are left attempting to navigate a worldwide web of knowledge but without necessarily the required intellectual and technological tools and knowledge to do so. For court staff and lawyers, the transition to online services almost overnight was an exhausting and demanding process, which in some senses is still ongoing, and that level of exhaustion may mean that the court's ability to respond continues to be reduced.

For the student legal companion, which also reflects on the experience and potential support being offered to litigants, there has been significant change. Previously, the students could meet with litigants face to face at the court building, with the general hubbub and life of the court around. They would see at first hand a litigant in need of help and support and offer it tangibly; now, following the pandemic and the policy drive to more online hearings following LASPO, many processes remain online or are hybrid. In the

45 Focus group 3, December 2021.

early stages of the pandemic, the student companions were present and could support the litigants, but this became less common as the world adapted a new normal. Discussions with CLOCK academic leads from other areas of the country, however, reveal that the practice currently varies among different family courts.

With the move to a hybrid system, the students returned to their CLOCK offices in the court building to see litigants in person, but most hearings are still held online, and litigants continue to find that no one is physically present in court to help them. They now no longer routinely receive the court's online listings, additionally making it much harder to offer the same support they used to provide. Litigants therefore face significant gaps in access to that support and in turn face a potential fundamental lack of justice.

These barriers cause an overarching disintegration in justice and an ailing system that has lost its bearings, creating a world where it has become challenging to maintain even the most important frontline services for child protection cases, leaving much less space and time for the ongoing private law child law and family cases. The situation points to an online world where we are all seemingly connected at the touch of a button, but none of us are really connected in our ability to offer, seek, or gain support. How many are struggling alone, attempting to navigate a system that makes no sense to them and without more support than a government website with a list of forms, attempting to gain justice from the complexity of the legal system but with little support in navigating it?

6 Migrant (In)Justice

Olayinka Lewis

Introduction

One fundamental principle of law requires adherence to international agreements made between states. It therefore follows that where parties or countries ratify a treaty, there is an obligation, in good faith, to adhere to the provisions of the treaty. Furthermore, the disruption of basic human security results from human rights abuses that sometimes lead affected individuals to seek protection outside their country of origin.

As a party to international agreements, the UK demonstrates its commitment to ensuring that the human rights of migrants seeking justice and asylum in the UK are legally protected. However, the right to seek asylum in the UK by persons fleeing conflicted zones is threatened by recent changes to immigration laws in the UK. For example, the discriminatory approach adopted by the Illegal Migration Act 2023 makes it impossible for certain citizens fleeing conflicted zones to seek asylum in the UK, and other barriers changes to legal aid for asylum seekers, arbitrary migration targets, and hostile and deterrent immigration policies. By imposing these barriers to seeking asylum, the UK breaches its obligations under international law and fuels migrant injustice. In this chapter, I combine theory, doctrine, and practical application to examine migrant injustice.

The chapter is divided into four sections. The first section explores the concept of justice and how it permeates various aspects of human life, illustrating the importance of justice beyond the migration discourse. The next section illustrates migrant injustice in UK immigration law and policy especially through the lens of the deterrence and hostile environment policies, the latter policy examined in more depth through legislation from 1905 to 2023. The third section highlights how immigration law and policies have created legal barriers to asylum seekers fleeing conflicted zones to claim asylum in the UK and therefore contributing to migrant (in)justice. The final section concludes this chapter and recommends a pragmatic and sustainable approach to the treatment of migrants and asylum seekers.

DOI: 10.4324/9781003496823-6

The Concept of Justice and Migration

The Rawlsian theory of justice – developed by American philosopher John Rawls – delves into the principles of societal fairness and equity, aiming to establish a framework for a just society.[1] The notion of justice permeates various aspects of society, evident across a rich body of literature. Amartya proposes a shift from the conventional focus on the age-old question of 'What is a just society?' towards exploring comparative justice inquiries.[2] The shift emphasises the importance of comparing justice advancements and injustices reductions, prioritising a practical approach over transcendental answers. While questioning the feasibility of definitively answering the transcendental query, the significance of a comparative framework for evaluating justice is underscored. Similarly, a comparative justice framework is valued for its robustness and effectiveness in justice evaluation without directly addressing the broad question of defining a just society.

Miller's empirical study on social justice principles delves into public perceptions of justice, providing valuable insights into societal understandings of justice and enhances comprehension of societal norms and values, laying a solid groundwork for examining the practical applications of justice theories in everyday contexts.[3] On ecological justice, Baxter's interdisciplinary approach aligns environmental concerns with impartial justice, expanding the discourse on justice theories within modern-day complexities and dilemmas.[4] Robeyns' exploration of ideal theory and feminist perspectives highlights the challenges in establishing truly just societies, particularly in addressing gender inequalities.[5] The concept of justice is pivotal in understanding justice theories in democratic settings,[6] the evolving justice frameworks in response to feminist perspectives,[7] and the interpretative models employed by justices to navigate the convergence of virtue ethics and legal theory,[8] enriching the understanding of justice across diverse contexts.

1 John Rawls, *A Theory of Justice* (Harvard University Press, 1971).

2 Amartya Sen, 'What Do We Want from a Theory of Justice?' (2006) 103(5) *The Journal of Philosophy* 215–238.

3 David Miller, *Principles of Social Justice* (Harvard University Press 1999).

4 Brian Baxter, 'Ecological Justice and Justice as Impartiality' (2000) 9(3) *Environmental Politics* 43.

5 Ingrid Robeyns, 'Sen's Capability Approach and Feminist Concerns' in Flavio Comim, Mozaffar Qizilbash and Sabina Alkire (eds) *The Capability Approach: Concepts, Measures and Applications* (Cambridge University Press 2008) 82–104.

6 Laura Valentini, 'Justice, Disagreement and Democracy' (2013) 43(1) *British Journal of Political Science* 177.

7 Martha Craven Nussbaum, 'Rawls and Feminism' in Samuel Freeman (ed) *Cambridge Companions to Philosophy* (CUP 2002) 488; Martha Craven Nussbaum, 'The Future of Feminist Liberalism' (2013) American Philosophical Association Centennial Series 679.

8 Lawrence B Solum, 'District of Columbia v. Heller and Originalism' (2009) 103(2) Northwestern University Law Review, Illinois Public Law Research Paper No. 09-14; Robert Garner, 'Towards a Theory of Justice for Animals' (2012) 2(1) *Journal of Animal Ethics* 98; Robert Garner, *A Theory of Justice for Animals: Animal Rights in a Nonideal World* (Oxford University Press 2013).

The relevance of justice in migration discourse is paramount, especially concerning the ethical treatment of migrants. Maboloc provides a compelling ethical perspective on migration rights, calling attention to the moral values that should guide migration policies.[9] By emphasising ethical principles and democratic ideals, Maboloc advocates for policies that centre on migrants' rights and welfare. This underscores the critical importance of ethical considerations in shaping migration frameworks, as exemplified by Lister's examination of the intersection of justice and temporary labour migration,[10] underscoring the need for ethical considerations and legal frameworks to ensure fairness for migrant workers and asylum seekers. By addressing the complexities of temporary migration and asylum management, these authors probe the essential role of justice within the broader migration discourse. Grey emphasises the need to uphold migrants' rights within the immigration (and asylum) law framework and proposes that a state's authority to exclude migrants and asylum seekers is constrained by the indirect principle of freedom of migration.[11] This principle stipulates that if immigration (and asylum) laws infringe upon a migrant's fundamental rights, they cannot be lawfully enforced. While this principle is pivotal, it could potentially limit a state's ability to exclude migrants and indeed asylum seekers.

In addressing the issue of human rights violations within the migration (and asylum) context, Cotello and Mann emphasise the importance of accountability for those responsible for such violations. Their discussion stresses the need for a topographical accountability approach that considers the geographic and political landscapes where violations occur, recognising the complexities of addressing these issues across borders.[12] Focusing on accountability is essential for ensuring justice for migrants and asylum seekers and safeguarding their rights. Cotello and Mann emphasise that accountability mechanisms are crucial in combating human rights violations, particularly violence experienced at borders.[13] They underscore the significance of holding states and other actors accountable in managing migration flows and protecting migrant rights.

Climate-induced migration is also gaining increasing significance, especially concerning its intersection with justice theory.[14] The concept of justice is a crucial aspect of the broader migration discourse, particularly in the context of asylum seekers. Upholding individuals' rights to seek asylum – without

9 Christopher Maboloc, 'The Moral Argument for Migration' (2020) 48 *Philisophia* 1501.

10 Matthew Lister, 'Justice and Temporary Labor Migrations' (2014) 29(1) *Georgetown Immigration Law Journal* 95.

11 Colin Grey, 'The Rights of Migration' (2014) 20 Legal Theory 25–51.

12 C Cotello and I Mann, 'Border Justice: Migration and Accountability for Human Rights Violations' (2020) 21 *German Law Journal* 311–334.

13 Ibid.

14 Joachim Wundisch, 'Towards a Non-Ideal Theory of Climate Migration' (2022) 25(4) *Critical Review of International Social and Political Philosophy* 496–527.

viewing it as a problem or a means of excluding people[15] – is essential for achieving justice within the migrant community. However, immigration legislation and policies in the United Kingdom have historically been focused on restricting migrants' rights, influencing their interactions with the immigration and asylum system.

Illustrating Migrant (In)Justice in UK Immigration Law and Policy

The starting point is the Illegal Migration Act 2023 (IMA), an act designed to curb unlawful migration, especially through unsafe and illegal routes,[16] but one that raises numerous concerns.[17] Critically, it appears to promote an unjust society for asylum seekers, diverging from the principles of justice advocated by the Rawlsian theory.[18] It has been described as a dangerous and senseless piece of legislation which will cause untold hardship and suffering to thousands of people and breach international human rights laws,[19] one that could lead to the collapse of the system of international protection for refugees.[20]

Additionally, the legislation raises apprehensions about impeding vulnerable groups' ability to receive assistance, particularly victims of modern slavery.[21] Its provisions constitute a clear breach of the Refugee Convention and undermine the UK's longstanding humanitarian traditions,[22] expressed

15 Rogier van Reekum and Willem Schinkel, 'Instituting the Global: The Racial Analytics of Migration' (2024) *Migration Studies* 12.

16 Section 1(1).

17 From inception as a bill. See generally, Hannah White, '*Illegal Migration Bill Highlights How Expectations of Legislative Scrutiny Have Plummeted*' Institute for Government (2023). Available at https://www.instituteforgovernment.org.uk/comment/illegal-migration-bill-legislative-scrutiny; ILPA describes the bill as an assault on the rights of migrants and on the rule of law. *ILPA Briefing on Illegal Migration Bill for Second Reading in the House of Commons* (13 March 2023). Available at https://ilpa.org.uk/ilpa-briefing-on-illegal-migration-bill-for-second-reading-in-the-house-of-commons-12-march-2023/. The Public Law Project described it as one of the most damaging bills put forward by a British government: *Public Law Project Briefing on the Illegal Migration Bill – House of Commons Second Reading* (March 2023); available at https://publiclawproject.org.uk/content/uploads/2023/03/Illegal-Migration-Bill-briefing.pdf). See also Tom Daly and Calum Dawkins, 'The Illegal Migration Bill Is Not Only Deeply Cruel: But Also a Shameless Attempt to Embolden Extremism' *The Bristol Cable* (Bristol, 13 March 2023); available at https://thebristolcable.org/2023/03/the-illegal-migration-bill-cruel-extremism-small-boats-refugees/.

18 John Rawls, *A Theory of Justice* (Harvard University Press 1971).

19 The Joint Council for the Welfare of Immigrants, '"Illegal Migration" Bill 2023 Briefing' (April 2023). Available at https://jcwi.org.uk/reportsbriefings/illegal-migration-bill-2023-briefing/.

20 Diane Taylor, 'Illegal Migration Bill Could Topple World Refugee System, Lawmakers Told' *The Guardian* (29 March 2023). Available at https://www.theguardian.com/uk-news/2023/mar/29/migration-bill-could-topple-world-refugee-system-mps-told.

21 IOM UK *Statement on UK's Illegal Migration Bill* (20 March 2023). Available at https://unitedkingdom.iom.int/news/statement-uks-illegal-migration-bill.

22 Ibid. See also Convention Relating to the Status Refugee 1951. Art. 31 prohibits the imposition of penalties on refugees on account of illegal entry.

by the former Home Secretary's oral statement during the passage of the Act. Section 1(5) disapplies s. 3 Human Rights Act 1998 (HRA). This section requires primary legislation and subordinate legislation to be compatible with Convention Rights. HRA Section 19 requires a minister in charge of a bill in either House of Parliament to make a statement of compatibility before the second reading of a bill. The former Secretary of State for the Home Department (SSHD) in her oral statement to Parliament acknowledged that the IMA (then a bill) was incompatible with convention rights and instead stated the UK will 'always seek' to uphold international law.[23] The need to circumvent the law superseded the need to deter illegal entry into the UK. Despite the serious concerns from various organisations and the clear lack of compatibility with international law, the government passed the Bill into law.[24] The act raises very serious questions about its aim, and the answer arguably is two-fold: One is to further the aim of deterrence, set out in the Act, and the second is to further the so-called hostile environment policy.

The 'Deterrence' Policy

There is clear evidence that deterrence as a policy has not worked previously. Walsh and Sumption[25] identify two key types of policies to deter people from claiming asylum in the UK: policies that aim to make it easier to remove people to 'safe third countries' without assessing their asylum claim and policies to give fewer rights to refugees who cannot be removed and remain in the UK.[26] The former acknowledge that removing people to their home countries increases the risk of persecution and therefore opts for a safe third country,[27] while the latter penalises asylum seekers who cannot be removed from the UK.

23 The Rt Hon Suella Braverman, *Oral Statement to Parliament – Home Secretary Statement on the Illegal Migration Bill* (7 March 2023). Available at https://www.gov.uk/government/speeches/home-secretary-statement-on-the-illegal-immigration-bill.

24 CJ McKinney, Melanie Gower, Joanna Dawson, *Research Briefing – Illegal Migration Bill: Progress of the Bill* (24 April 2023). Available at https://researchbriefings.files.parliament.uk/documents/CBP-9776/CBP-9776.pdf.

25 PW Walsh and M Sumption, *UK Policies to Deter People from Claiming Asylum* (2023) The Migration Observatory at the University of Oxford. Available at https://migrationobservatory.ox.ac.uk/resources/commentaries/uk-policies-to-deter-people-from-claiming-asylum/.

26 Ibid.

27 *N.S.K. v The United Kingdom* (application no. 28774/22) was the first case that saw the removal of asylum seekers from the UK to Rwanda stopped by the European Court of Human Rights. The removal was in pursuance to a Memorandum of Understanding between the United Kingdom and Rwanda on refugee relocation. The MOU addressed only limited subject matter, and its opposition highlighted the extent to which the UK was failing to uphold international obligations on protection issues. O Lewis and G Gilbert, *Human Rights of Asylum Seekers in the UK* (Written Evidence to the Human Rights Joint Committee of the UK Parliament ASU0004) (2023) <https://committees.parliament.uk/writtenevidence/114168/html/>.

This penalty takes the form of fewer rights ranging from restrictions on family reunification[28] to longer pathways to settlement.[29]

Policy attempts to deter people from seeking asylum outside their country of residence have generally not been completely effective,[30] and the UK is not an exception. The impact of deterrence measures in asylum policies is often limited, as these policies are not always the primary influence on fluctuations in asylum claims[31]; potential asylum seekers' decisions on migration are influenced by factors beyond policy considerations such as a country's overall reputation as safe and welcoming irrespective of any deterrence policies in place.[32] A Home Office report found that potential asylum seekers are not usually fully aware of the policies they will encounter upon arrival, and where they do have some knowledge of these policies, it is the interpretation and perception of the policies (often inaccurate or incomplete) that is most significant in altering behaviour rather than the policies themselves.[33]

The report also found that deterrent strategies to discourage migrants from crossing the border are unlikely to diminish asylum seekers' motivations in the longer term. For instance, refugees of Hazara, Rohingya, Muslim, and Tamil backgrounds specifically had Australia in mind as a destination country when they sought asylum, and despite the restrictive asylum-seeker policy changes, perceptions of Australia as a more highly functioning civil society than other potential destination countries explain why it remains a country of choice for asylum seekers from west and south Asia.[34]

The Hostile Environment Policy

The 'hostile environment' policy is the UK's approach to immigration.[35] Wilcock[36] notes that in its broadest sense, it refers to the gradual introduction of

28 Immigration Rules Appendix Family Reunion (Protection), para. FR2.1.

29 Settlement gives a person the right to live, work and study in the UK for as long as they like and to access benefits if eligible. See also Immigration Rules part 11: Asylum, para. 352Q (i) and (ii).

30 On refugee deterrence policies, see, generally, Henrik Andersson and Kristoffer Jutvik, 'Do Asylum-Seekers Respond to Policy Changes? Evidence from the Swedish–Syrian Case' (2023) 125(1) *The Scandinavian Journal of Economics* 3; Lamis Abdelaaty, 'Do Rights Violations Deter Refugees?' (2023) 49(1) *Journal of Ethnic and Migration Studies* 110.

31 PW Walsh and M Sumption, *UK Policies to Deter People from Claiming Asylum* (2023) The Migration Observatory at the University of Oxford. Available at https://migrationobservatory.ox.ac.uk/resources/commentaries/uk-policies-to-deter-people-from-claiming-asylum/.

32 Ibid.

33 Home Office, *Sovereign Borders: International Asylum Comparisons Report, Section I: Drivers and Impact on Asylum Migration Journeys* (September 2020). Available at https://drive.google.com/file/d/1bZf02_TVvTBiNSOCMTs3XwZgDnc29_vo/view?pli=1.

34 M McAuliffe and D Jayasuriya, 'Do Asylum Seekers and Refugees Choose Destination Countries? Evidence from Large-Scale Surveys in Australia, Afghanistan, Bangladesh, Pakistan and Sri Lanka' (2016) 54 *International Migration* 4, 44.

35 F Webber, 'On the Creation of the UK's Hostile Environment' (2019) 60(4) *Race & Class* 76.

36 Cathy A Wilcock, 'Hostile Immigration Policy and the Limits of Sanctuary as Resistance: Counter-Conduct as Constructive Critique' (2019) 7(4) *Social Inclusion* 141.

selectively restrictive policies, most significantly under New Labour in the late 1990s,[37] and in its narrow sense, it describes the rhetorical and legislative platform of the Conservative/Liberal coalition and the Conservative government from 2010 to 2024. The policy is described as a package of measures designed to make life so difficult for individuals without permission to remain in the UK that they will not seek to enter the UK to begin with or if already present will leave voluntarily; it is inextricably linked to the net migration target intended to reduce inward migration and increase outward emigration.[38] The aim of the policy is to limit the eligibility of certain groups from entering and living in the UK. Under the modern 'hostile' immigration control the very definition of 'illegal' has shifted from being an objective definition of a person's status under the law to a contingent relationship between the person and whichever private or public entity they face in order to obtain a right or entitlement.[39] Although it is noted that the hostile environment policy can be traced back to the 1970s,[40] there is evidence of the existence of hostile provisions in pre-1970s immigration legislation. Notably, these hostile provisions target specific groups. An examination of immigration legislation dating back 1905 reveals this.

Tracing the History of Hostile Immigration Legislation

The Aliens Act 1905 was arguably the first act of Parliament that restricted and controlled immigration within the United Kingdom. Although it was directed towards immigrants generally, it indirectly targeted specific groups – Jews, Lithuanians, Poles, Germans, and Chinese – due to the attitudes specifically relating to British labour movements.[41] The arrival of unprecedent numbers of Jewish refugees from eastern Europe and Russia fleeing persecution created an immense social and economic problem, and as a result, antipathy towards immigrants increased. This ultimately resulted in the act being enacted. A report of the Select Committee on the Sweating System argued

37 H Lewis, L Waite and S Hodkinson, '"Hostile" UK Immigration Policy and Asylum Seekers' Susceptibility to Forced Labour' in F Vecchio and A Gerard (eds) *Entrapping Asylum Seekers: Social, Legal and Economic Precariousness* (Palgrave Macmillan 2017) 187.

38 C Yeo, 'Everything You Need to Know about the "Hostile Environment Policy" for Immigrants' (*Free Movement*, 29 May 2017) < https://freemovement.org.uk/hostile-environment-affect/>. See also M Griffiths and C Yeo, 'The UK's Hostile Environment: Deputising Immigration Control' (2021) 41(4) *Critical Social Policy* 521.

39 S York, 'The "Hostile Environment": How Home Office Immigration Policies and Practices Create Perpetual Illegality' (2018) 32 *Journal of Immigration, Asylum and Nationality Law* 363.

40 B Bowling and S Westenra, 'A Really Hostile Environment: Adiaphorization, Global Policing and the Crimmigration Control System' (2020) 24(2) *Theoretical Criminology* 163; N Yuval-Davis, G Wemyss and K Cassidy, 'Everyday Bordering, Belonging and the Reorientation of British Immigration Legislation' (2018) 52(2) *Sociology* 228.

41 J Pellew, 'The Home Office and the Aliens Act, 1905' (1989) 32(2) *The Historical Journal* 369.

that 'undue stress' had been 'laid on the injurious effect on wages caused by foreign immigration'.[42]

The arrivals were seen as a potential threat to political stability and not for the well-being of poor immigrants to Britain. Irrespective of the concerns of the government, the crucial fact is that the act targeted specific groups that the government deemed a threat to the labour market. Bashford and McAdam noted that the Aliens Act had been analysed by historians and legal scholars as an aspect of the history of British immigration law on the one hand and of British Jewry and British anti-Semitism on the other.[43] Exclusion based on ethnic and religious grounds dominating both analyses.[44] This was the first of many provisions targeting specific groups, and subsequent legislation followed.

The British Nationality and Status of Aliens Act 1914[45] provided a statutory definition of British nationality that was enshrined, for the most part, in common law. The act restricted transmission of British subject status to one generation in the legitimate male line. By creating a distinction between the wife of a British subject and the wife of an alien, the act targeted another specific group. The implication was that a British woman who married an alien became an alien herself,[46] losing the rights and privileges accorded to British nationality.[47] A key concept introduced by the act was the use of the term 'aliens' to refer to non-British subjects. Restricting British citizenship to children of female citizens who married aliens deliberately targeted a specific group who could have been British subjects, seen as a further manifestation of the hostility towards certain groups who were deemed to be less deserving of the rights and protections afforded to British citizens. This term is considered hostile and perpetuates a negative bias toward immigrants or persons deemed to be foreigners, creating an environment in which it is difficult for them

42 See footnote 9, pp 1890, xvii (169), xliii.

43 A Bashford and J McAdam, 'The Right to Asylum: Britain's 1905 Aliens Act and the Evolution of Refugee Law' (2014) 32(2) *Law and History Review* 309.

44 Ibid.

45 British Nationality and Status of Aliens Act 1914 (https://www.legislation.gov.uk/ukpga/Geo5/4-5/17/enacted). Amended by the 1918 (https://duckduckgo.com/?q=British+Nationality+and+Status+of+Aliens+Act+1918&t=ffab&ia=web) and 1922 (https://www.legislation.gov.uk/ukpga/Geo5/12-13/44/contents/enacted) acts. Main amendments revoked certification of naturalisation and acquisition of British nationality by persons born 'out of His Majesty's Dominions', respectively, amongst other things.

46 British Nationality and Status of Aliens Act 1914, S. 10(1). Section 10 was amended by S. 1 of the 1933 Act. Further provisions of S. 10 of the 1914 Act were amended by the 1943 Act, which made special provision for the naturalisation of persons rendering service in connection with the Second World War and restricted the making of declarations of alienage in time of war. It also extended the power to make regulations under Section 19 of the 1914 Act.

47 MP Baldwin, 'Subject of Empire: Married Women and the British Nationality and Status of Aliens Act' (2001) 40 *Journal of British Studies* 522.

to integrate into British society.[48] The targeting of women, a specific group, aligns with subsequent legislation on immigration. The use of certain terms in legislation impacts how certain groups are perceived and can lead to certain unintended consequences.[49]

The Aliens Restriction Act 1914 made it possible to deport, deny, and relocate immigrants from the UK.[50] The act sailed on the anti-immigrant sentiment in an already xenophobic climate. Asylum seekers were treated as prisoners of war rather than victims or civilians fleeing the dire consequences of the First World War.[51] There is also the Aliens Restrictions Order 1920, which imposed constant government surveillance on aliens in the country with the purpose of making assimilation difficult for them.[52] The act also refused entry to anyone deemed 'a lunatic, idiot, or mentally deficient'[53] or if 'for medical reasons his admission is undesirable,' so long as the determination was 'certified by a medical inspector',[54] clearly targeting people with disability, another specific group defined in the Aliens Act 1905 as 'undesirable immigrant'.[55]

While a modern version of this act would be contrary to the Equality Act 2010 and similar legislation protecting people with disability, hostility towards certain groups was evident in pre-1970s immigration legislation. The Alien Restrictions (Amendment) Act 1919 enabled the government to determine a foreigner's nationality in doubtful circumstances[56] while also empowering it to imprison those believed 'likely to cause sedition or disaffection'.[57] This bred a culture of persecution, ill treatment, and isolation of all categories of foreigners living in the UK, not just the 'enemy aliens' that the act intended to target and eliminate.[58]

Subsequent immigration legislation followed this policy of hostility and continued to target certain groups. Of note are Commonwealth citizens. The Commonwealth was seen as a strong bond that bound nations in allegiance to

48 For general information on British nationality from the 18th century, see *British Nationality: Summary* (https://assets.publishing.service.gov.uk/media/5a74d575e5274a59fa7154c7/britnatsummary.pdf).

49 Chinua Achebe, 'The Politics of Language' in B Ashcroft, G Griffiths, and H Tiffin (eds) *The Postcolonial Studies Reader* (2nd edn, Routledge 2006) 268.

50 Section 1.

51 JC Bird, *Control of Enemy Alien Civilians in Great Britain, 1914–1918* (Routledge Revivals) (Routledge 2015).

52 C Reinecke, 'Governing Aliens in Times of Upheaval: Immigration Control and Modern State Practice in Early Twentieth-Century Britain, Compared with Prussia' (2009) 54 *International Review of Social History* 39.

53 Article 1(2)(c) and (d), Alien Restrictions Order 1920.

54 B Taylor, 'Immigration, Statecraft and Public Health: The 1920 Aliens Order, Medical Examinations and the Limitations of the State in England' (2016) 29 *Social History of Medicine* 512.

55 Section 1(3)(b) Aliens Act 1905.

56 Section 2.

57 Section 3.

58 Steven Hirschler, *Hostile Homes: Violence, Harm and the Marketisation of UK Asylum Housing* (Palmgrave Macmillan 2021) 38.

the monarch; there was a sense of partnership amongst British and Commonwealth soldiers fighting together during both World Wars, and this developed a sense of familiarity with Britain. There was an argument for bringing in West Indians to help rebuild the country, but there was an objection to their entry because of their colour and to their claim as British subjects despite their English language abilities; European workers were favoured as they were thought to integrate easily and had no claim as British subjects given that English was not a native tongue.[59] Obstructive practices were used by the government to restrict entry of Commonwealth citizens. A general agreement was reached on a new scheme to reconcile the citizenships of the individual Commonwealth countries with the overall status of British subject. This formed the basis of the British Nationality Act 1948.

The 1948 Act introduced the status of citizen of the United Kingdom and Colonies while retaining the term 'British subject' to cover every citizen of a Commonwealth country. It conferred British citizenship status on all Commonwealth subjects and recognised their right to work and settle in the UK and to be accompanied by their family members.[60] The act did not affect right of entry and dealt with nationality rather than immigration. It expressed a theoretical idea of the meaning of British subject status and laid the foundation for immigration control. The act led to an increase in the number of West Indian and South Asian immigrants to the UK, and this led to resentments that caused race riots and unrest,[61] and the government's panic fuelled the decision to cut the flow of these migrants.[62] The Notting Hill riots in 1958 and Enoch Powell's 1968 'Rivers of Blood' speech formed the background for legislative controls on Commonwealth immigration in 1962 and 1968 legislation.[63]

The Commonwealth Immigrants Act 1962 restricted the admission of Commonwealth citizens to those who had been issued employment vouchers, leading to entry control. The 1968 Act imposed strict quotas and removed automatic right of entry into Britain for Asian British passport holders with the exception of those with a British parent or grandparent and for those born in Britain. The Immigration Act 1971 established temporary work permits and

59 E Smith, 'From the Aliens Act to the "Hostile Environment" the Making of the British Border Control System' in Kahina le Louvier and Karen Latricia Hough (eds) *UK Borderscapes Sites of Enforcement and Resistance* (1st edn, Routledge 2023).

60 British Nationality Act, S. 1.

61 R Hansen, 'The Politics of Citizenship in 1940s Britain: The British Nationality Act' (1999) 10 *Twentieth Century British History* 1, 67.

62 P Brooke, 'India, Post-Imperialism and the Origins of Enoch Powell's "Rivers of Blood" Speech' (2007) 50(3) *The Historical Journal* 669.

63 S Tomlinson, 'Enoch Powell, Empires, Immigrants and Education' (2017) 21(1) Race Ethnicity and Education 1; L Aqui, M Kenny, and N Pearce, '"The Empire of England": Enoch Powell, Sovereignty, and the Constitution of the Nation' (2021) 32(2) *Twentieth Century British History* 238–60.

moved away from the employment voucher scheme. Crucially, the act introduced provisions exempting people from immigration controls if they had a grandfather born in the UK.

The Immigration and Asylum Act 1999 was introduced at the time of high number of appeals for declined applications.[64] The Court of Appeal noted that it was 'badly drafted' legislation that creates a disparity in the treatment of asylum and human rights appeals.[65] The act included provisions on entering and remaining in the UK[66] as well as controversial provisions on the removal of certain persons unlawfully in the UK.[67] It also excluded certain persons from access to welfare and social benefits,[68] and although support was provided to asylum seekers and their dependants,[69] there was no general duty to provide any support.

Prima facie, the possibility of assistance does not seem hostile towards asylum seekers. They do not receive social or welfare benefits until they have received confirmation of their asylum status unless they are in desperate need, but the state will in some circumstances aid them and provide them with a decent life. However, the provisions are overly ambiguous and provide broad discretion to the Secretary of State,[70] whose primary goal is to decrease the number of asylum seekers. Just the bureaucracy required to obtain financial assistance discourages people from coming to the UK unless they are genuinely escaping persecution. The policy is propelled by an 'official discourse' based on the denial of housing and the avoidance of 'home' attachments, which effectively keeps asylum seekers in a state of ontological homelessness and alienation.[71]

The Immigration Act 2014 was one of the most draconian pieces of immigration legislation at the time of enactment; it represented an aggressive attempt by the then coalition government to meet their key policy objective

64 R Thomas, 'The Impact of Judicial Review on Asylum' (2003) *Public Law* 479; R Thomas, 'Evaluating Tribunal Adjudication: Administrative Justice and Asylum Appeals' (2005) 25 *Legal Studies* 462; G Fleming, 'Review of Migration Decision-Making: Rival Goals and Values' (1999) 10 *Public Law Review* 131.

65 *R. (on the Application of Zenovics) v Secretary of State for the Home Department* [2002] INLR 219.

66 Immigration Act 1999, s. 2.

67 P Page and T Hossain, 'State Violence against Migrants: How Immigration Removal Became Normal and How We Are Challenging It Now' (2018) 32 *Journal of Immigration Asylum and Nationality Law* 4, 385.

68 Immigration Act 1999, S. 115.

69 Immigration Act 1999, S. 95 (1).

70 P Billings, 'Alienating Asylum Seekers: Welfare Support in the Immigration and Asylum Act 1999' (2002) 9 *Journal of Social Security and Law* 3, 115.

71 LF O'Mahony and JA Sweeney, 'The Exclusion of (Failed) Asylum Seekers from Housing and Home: Towards an Oppositional Discourse' (2010) 37 *Journal of Law and Society* 2, 285. See also L Scullion, 'Sanctuary to Sanction: Asylum Seekers, Refugees and Welfare Conditionality in the UK' (2018) 25 *Journal of Social Security and Law* 3, 158.

of drastically reducing net immigration.[72] The act introduced a range of measures aimed at creating a hostile environment for individuals in the UK without valid leave by denying them access to various services and benefits.[73] The hostile environment includes limited access to work, housing, health care, bank accounts, and more. It is characterised by a system of citizen-on-citizen immigration checks enforced under S. 22, under which landlords were instructed that they 'must not authorise an adult to occupy premises under a residential tenancy agreement if the adult is disqualified as a result of their immigration status'.[74] This hostile provision forced landlords to discriminate against 'disqualified people', creating the opportunity for disproportionate interference with individual rights if they are indeed prevented from accessing safe and adequate housing solely based upon their immigration status.[75] In addition, the provision risks treating lawful migrants with heightened suspicion and prejudice.

Furthermore, the hostilities of the Immigration Act 2014 is evident in the limitation of the right of appeal to the First-tier Tribunal,[76] the disqualification from renting premises for those without valid immigration status[77] and the imposition of an annual immigration health surcharge.[78] The annual surcharge alongside additional fees for accessing the accident and emergency department and some primary care services not only restricts access to health care but also poses a significant public health risk, exacerbating healthcare inequalities.[79] Restriction on access to essential services lead to missed opportunities for disease prevention in high-risk groups, which could render communicable diseases such as tuberculosis and HIV more prevalent in the wider community.[80] Other provisions prohibit banks from opening accounts for disqualified

72 D Cameron, *Speech on Immigration and Welfare* (25 March 2013). Available at https://www.gov.uk/government/speeches/david-camerons-immigration-speech; M Gower and O Hawkins, 'Immigration and Asylum: Changes Made by the Coalition Government 2010–2015' (House of Commons Library, 24 March 2015). Available at https://commonslibrary.parliament.uk/research-briefings/sn05829/.

73 Independent Chief Inspector of Borders and Immigration, 'The Implementation of the 2014 "Hostile Environment" Provisions for Tackling Sham Marriage' (August–September 2016).

74 E Schatzberger, 'The Immigration Act 2014: "Not on the List You're Not Coming In: Landlords Forced to Discriminate"' (2015) 79(5) *The Conveyancer and Property Lawyer* 395.

75 A Schaap, 'The after Rights of the Citizen of the UK and Its Colonies: Who Is the Subject of the Rights of the Citizen in Britain's Hostile Environment?' (2024) *The International Journal of Human Rights* 1.

76 Immigration Act 2014, s. 15.

77 Immigration Act 2014, s. 21.

78 Immigration Act 2014, s. 38.

79 GM Bowsher et al, 'Immigration Act 2014 Challenges Health of Migrants in the UK' (2015) 385 *The Lancet* Correspondence 9971, 852.

80 HDE Carter and GM Bowsher, 'Hunt's Priorities on Entitlement to Use the NHS Are Wrong' (2013) *British Medical Journal* (Online) 347.

persons[81] and revoke UK driving licenses held by irregular migrants.[82] These provisions reflect the hostile nature of the act, which furthered the government's ambition of stopping irregular migrants from being able to access the essentials of an ordinary life.[83] The deprivation of a normal mundane life further isolates migrants from settled residents, creating a greater division between the two.

The Nationality and Borders Act 2022 (NABA) introduced far-reaching changes to asylum law in the UK.[84] Key changes criminalised asylum, discriminated against asylum seekers attempting to enter the UK,[85] removed the right of appeal for unfounded claims,[86] arranged for removal to safe third countries,[87] lowered the 'particular serious crime' threshold,[88] subjected children to horrific age assessment procedures,[89] and changed to human trafficking law[90] amongst other things. The NABA provisions align with previous immigration legislation that target specific groups. It does not deviate from this key aim and in essence is another chapter in the hostile environment playbook.

A common element in all legislation examined is the targeting of specific groups – a barrier to migrant justice, and although some UK migration laws and policies within the last century have been relatively welcoming where immigration meets certain needs and priorities – like sympathy shown towards Ukrainian refuges in 2022, which echoed the welcome given to the Kindertransport in the late 1930s[91] and the policy towards West Indian immigration in the 1950s – a prevailing theme of hostility can be identified in the majority of UK immigration legislation.

Injustice and Asylum Seekers

Concerns surrounding the treatment of asylum seekers remain pertinent. An analysis of certain provisions within the 2023 IMA demonstrates the continuation of the 'playbook' of targeting specific groups and the injustices embedded in immigration and asylum legislation. Persons seeking asylum in the United

81 Immigration Act 2014, s. 40.
82 Immigration Act 2014, s. 47.
83 H Lewis, L Waite, and S Hodkinson, '"Hostile" UK Immigration Policy and Asylum Seekers' Susceptibility to Forced Labour' in F Vecchio and A Gerard (eds) *Entrapping Asylum Seekers: Transnational Crime, Crime Control and Security* (Palgrave Macmillan 2017) 187.
84 Nationality and Borders Act 2022.
85 Nationality and Borders Act 2022, S. 12.
86 Nationality and Borders Act 2022, S. 28.
87 Nationality and Borders Act 2022, S. 29.
88 Nationality and Borders Act 2022, S. 38.
89 Nationality and Borders Act 2022, S. 52.
90 Nationality and Borders Act 2022, S. 58.
91 C Hill, 'Debating Britain's Role in the World: From Decolonisation to Brexit' (2023) *International Politics*.

Kingdom benefit from protections enshrined in the HRA,[92] which gives effect to certain inalienable rights and freedoms guaranteed under the European Convention on Human Rights.[93] This furthers the UK's obligations under the Convention Relating to the Status of Refugees 1951 by ensuring that the human rights of individuals living or seeking asylum in the UK, are legally protected. This also aligns with the fundamental principle of law that requires adherence to agreements made between states.[94] Permanently prohibiting any person who has ever met the four conditions contained in Section 2 of the IMA targets specific nationalities who do not enjoy the right to enter or remain in the UK without the need to apply for leave and perpetuates discrimination when it comes to seeking asylum.

Section 2(2) (a) to (e) of the act on the conditions for removal from the UK does not acknowledge the right of certain individuals/nationals to seek protection for fear of persecution. The requirement to enter the UK without leave or a visa is based on certain discriminatory classifications contained in the Immigration Rules[95] based on nationality. The UK Immigration Rules divide countries into visa national and non-visa national, and this classification is crucial for determining who can enter the UK without applying for an entry clearance visa: Citizens of non-visa national countries can enter the UK without applying for leave prior to arriving in the UK as a visitor or for any purpose and can stay for up to six months. This means they can seek asylum since there are no limitations to their entry and are therefore not impacted by the provisions of Section 2 and ultimately Section 29 of the Act.

In contrast, citizens of visa national countries require entry clearance in advance of travel to the UK,[96] including most African, Middle Eastern, and Asian countries (Afghanistan, Albania, Algeria, Cambodia, Egypt, India, Iran, Iraq, Libya, Moldova, Pakistan, Rwanda, Somalia, Sudan, Thailand, Ukraine, Venezuela, Yemen, and Zimbabwe amongst others). According to the UN Refugee Agency (UNHCR), more than 7 in 10 of all refugees in need of international protection come from just five countries,[97] and 65% of refugees originate from just Syria, Venezuela, Ukraine, and Afghanistan.[98]

Citizens of these and other visa national countries do not enjoy the benefit of entering the UK without needing to apply for entry clearance. Lord Bingham described this as an apparent attempt to reduce the number of would-be

92 Art. 2 on right to life; art. 3 on prohibition from torture; and art. 8 on right to respect of private and family life.

93 Preamble to the Human Rights Act 1998.

94 Art 26 of the Vienna Convention on the Law of Treaties 1969.

95 O Lewis, *Written Evidence: Legislative Scrutiny: Illegal Migration Bill (IMB0045)* (April 2023) <https://committees.parliament.uk/writtenevidence/119978/html/> accessed 31 May 2024.

96 Appendix VN 3.1 (a), Immigration Rules Appendix Visitor: Visa national list.

97 UNHCR Refugee Data Finder. Available at https://www.unhcr.org/refugee-statistics.

98 Ibid.

asylum seekers from significant refugee-producing countries.[99] This contravenes the provisions of Art. 1A (2), which defines the conditions for a person to be considered a refugee: well-founded fear of persecution for reasons of race, religion, nationality, membership in a particular social group or political opinion; outside one's country; and unwilling to obtain protection in that country, a definition applied in several case laws in assessing the grant of asylum.[100]

Therefore, the law can be described as fundamentally discriminatory against visa national countries, depriving them of the right to seek asylum in the UK. Section 2 specifically targets nationals from countries most in need of international protection and makes removal based on conditions impossible for them to meet. This penalises asylum seekers from these countries and creates barriers for seeking protection in the UK, forcing some to consider illegal entry due to the lack of recognised routes.

The restrictions imposed on these countries go against Art. 31 Refugee Convention 1951. The absence of safe legal routes[101] leaves no choice for some visa nationals fleeing persecution but to resort to illegal entry. This lack of acknowledgment of the rights of individuals/nationals seeking asylum undermines the UK's adherence to international treaties it has signed. The emphasis on immigration enforcement and deportation by politicians often prioritises state sovereignty over international obligations regarding asylum seekers and refugees.[102]

Moreover, S. 3 of the act particularly impacts a vulnerable group: children. The stipulation that unaccompanied children[103] cannot be removed until they reach the age of 18 is more conditional than absolute. This discretionary provision allows the SSHD to potentially overlook this protection and deport unaccompanied children before they reach the age of 18. Additionally, S. 4 of the act showcases a disregard for the UK's international responsibilities under international law. Prioritising removal over an individual's safeguarding or human rights claim signifies a blatant disregard for international law and contravenes Section 6 of the HRA.

Conclusion

The barriers to migrant justice are multifaceted, stemming from both the legal and social challenges facing migrants and those seeking refuge. Immigration

99 *R (European Roma Rights Centre) v Immigration Officer at Prague Airport (United Nations High Commissioner for Refugees intervening)* [2005] 2 AC 1 [28].

100 *Shah and Islam* [199] INLR 144; *K and Fornah* [2006] UKHL 46; *HJ (Iran)* [2010] UKSC 31; *SM (PSG, Protection Regulations, Regulation 6) Moldova CG* [2008] UKAIT 00002.

101 Examples of current safe routes include the Syrian Vulnerable Persons Resettlement Scheme, the Afghan Citizens Resettlement Scheme, and the Ukraine Family Scheme.

102 A Radziwinowiczowna and O Lewis, 'The New Grounds for Deportation of European Union Citizens in the UK' (2023) 61(5) *International Migration* 201.

103 Illegal Migration Act 2023, S. 3.

policies have often rendered migrants as inherently vulnerable to exploitation, with differential socio-legal statuses creating conditions in which forced labour and severe exploitation can thrive.

The UK's immigration policies have undergone significant changes in the past few decades, with a trend towards increasing restrictions and barriers to asylum seekers. These changes have been driven by a range of factors, including concerns about national security, the perceived economic impacts of immigration, and political pressures and have contributed to a climate of increasing hostility and suspicion towards migrants and asylum seekers. As a result, those seeking refuge in the UK have faced growing challenges in navigating the asylum system and accessing the protections they are entitled to under international law.

The practical implications of these changes are significant, as they have profound impacts on the lives of both asylum seekers and all migrants. Instability, extremism, and conflict in regions like the Middle East and Africa have displaced millions of people in recent years, leading to a migration crisis that has tested the limits of the UK's immigration system. The challenges facing migrants are exacerbated by the complex interplay between domestic and global security concerns, as well as the potential impacts of climate change and resource scarcity on migration patterns. Changes to immigration laws have significantly impacted the ability of those fleeing conflicted zones to claim asylum, something that also affects their socio-legal status, which plays a critical role in shaping their vulnerability to exploitation and forced labour and the embedding of hostile provisions in immigration legislation.[104]

The analysis of migrant justice in the UK unveils a multifaceted and dynamic landscape characterised by shifts in immigration regulations that have deeply impacted individuals fleeing conflict zones. Achieving true migrant justice might necessitate a pivot towards a thorough and efficient assessment of the concept of a 'just society', one that integrates social justice principles and offers valuable perspectives into the society's perception of justice. Achieving justice for migrants and asylum seekers requires a thorough examination of the constraints within immigration contexts and advocating for a rights-focused approach to migration governance that safeguards human rights of migrants and asylum seekers.

Through a combination of theoretical, doctrinal, and practical application, this chapter has sought to shed light on the barriers to migrant justice and the implications of these changes, with the ultimate goal of promoting a more just and equitable system for migrants and asylum seekers.

104 P Dwyer, S Hodkinson, H Lewis, and L Waite, 'Socio-Legal Status and Experiences of Forced Labour among Asylum Seekers and Refugees in the UK' (2016) 32(3) *Journal of International and Comparative Social Policy* 182–98.

7 Social Entrapment

Is the Law Failing Women Who Kill?

Clare Wade KC and Rebecca Penfold

Introduction

Domestic homicides[1] appear to be reducing, with 100 recorded in the year ending March 2023. Within that number, however, 70 of the victims were women, who overwhelmingly had been killed by men with whom they were or had been in an intimate relationship. Only 7% of the number of men killed had been killed by a woman.[2] A woman who kills her male partner usually does so when he has a history of perpetrating domestic abuse against her, but there is a lack of forensic understanding as to the motivation for and the circumstances of such killings.[3] This leads to the argument that the law is failing women who kill their abusers, as they are often convicted of murder.[4] These figures perhaps highlight what feminist lawyers have long argued: that killings of men by their female partners are not adequately understood. We question why that is and invite a remodelling of the law.

Coercive Control

The enactment of S. 76 Serious Crime Act 2015 finally introduced the offence of controlling and coercive behaviour on our statute books. Gone should be the days of domestic abuse being limited to physical acts of violence.[5] Section 76

1 Office of National Statistics, 'Homicide in England and Wales: Year Ending March 2023' <www.ons.gov.uk/peoplepopulationandcommunity/crimeandjustice/articles/homicideinenglandandwales/yearendingmarch2023#:~:text=The%20latest%20annual%20homicide%20rate,similar%20(Appendix%20table%204)> accessed 27 June 2024.

2 In the year ending March 2023, 30 of the domestic homicide victims were men (ibid).

3 Many female defendants who report being subjected to controlling and coercive behaviour by the deceased do not appreciate that they are in fact victims of controlling behaviour. For example, in the high-profile case of Sally Challen, it was only upon her remand into custody and her participation in the 'Freedom Programme' that she came to understand the abuse she had endured throughout her long relationship with the deceased.

4 See further *Women Who Kill: How the State Criminalises Women We Might Otherwise Be Burying* by the Centre for Women's Justice <www.centreforwomensjustice.org.uk/women-who-kill>.

5 It is hoped that practitioners now have a firm understanding of what behaviour controlling and coercive covers. The 2015 case of Fariessia Martin (a 22-year-old woman who was

DOI: 10.4324/9781003496823-7

requires coercive behaviour to be repeatedly or continuously performed[6] and for it to have a serious effect on the victim[7] out of fear of violence[8] or causing serious alarm or distress, which has a substantial adverse effect on the victim's usual day-to-day activities.[9] The law, as it is written, is gender neutral.

However, although creating an offence marked a significant milestone, little has been done to afford women access to a viable legal defence when they respond to abuse with a fatal act. The introduction of the offence did not bring with it a recognition of coercive control as a forensic framework for understanding domestic abuse in the context of a killing. This is despite the fact that coercive control can result in either femicide or the killing of the male abuser by the victim. A significant problem for female defendants' inequity is the reluctance to acknowledge 'social entrapment' as resulting from the wrong of coercive control.

In 2019, there was some recognition of this lacuna, and positive change was seen with the Court of Appeal's decision in *R v Challen*.[10] Here, the court overturned the murder conviction based on fresh evidence which included expert opinion that the deceased had controlled the appellant to support the proposition that she was in an abusive relationship. It was advanced on the appellant's behalf that the pattern of behaviour alleged went beyond 'unhappiness' in the marriage and was abuse and entrapment.[11]

When seen in the context of mitigation of or justification for murder, it is Evan Stark's description of the concept of coercive control which is important:

> Coercive control entails a malevolent course of conduct that subordinates women to an alien will by violating their physical integrity (domestic violence), denying them respect and autonomy (intimidation), depriving them of social connectedness (isolation), and appropriating or denying them access to the resources for personhood and citizenship (control). Nothing men experience in the normal course of their everyday lives resembles this conspicuous form of subjugation.[12]

---

convicted of the murder of her abusive partner) highlighted how the system has failed women who kill. No psychiatric report was obtained pre-trial. Details of coercive and controlling behaviour were provided in written instructions to her (all male) defence team but not recognised as such. Non-fatal strangulation and injuries were evidenced in custody material, but these were not disclosed until later in proceedings. Her conviction was overturned on appeal in *Martin* [2020] EWCA Crim 1798.

6 S.76(1)(a).

7 S.76(1)(c).

8 S.76(4)(a).

9 S.76(4)(b).

10 [2019] EWCA Crim 916.

11 It is perhaps easy to recognise now that this was an abusive relationship which would fall within the statutory definition of coercive control under S. 76 Serious Crime Act 2015 when considering the harms that the appellant suffered: anal rape by the deceased as a form of punishment, intimidation, financial control, and attempts to isolate her.

12 E Stark, *Coercive Control: How Men Entrap Women in Personal Life* (Oxford University Press 2007).

Accordingly, the law has failed to keep pace with developments in societal understanding of domestic abuse. In particular, the psychiatric conditions with which many women defendants are diagnosed tend to be an output of the behaviour (coercive control) to which they have been subjected.[13] We submit that coercive control leads to the harm of social entrapment and that this is not recognised in the current legal framework for homicide.

Why does this matter? Women who kill who have suffered a background of coercive control within a relationship[14] are rarely able deploy the full defence of self-defence[15] or to take proper advantage of the partial defences to murder. There remains a lack of proper understanding of what motivates these killings, the harm of entrapment, and what amounts to a loss of control in law:

> It is imperative that as we shift our thinking and understanding from battered woman syndrome concepts to that of the effects of coercive control that may be present without severe violence, we are also able to extend this to be utilised in advancing a successful partial defence. In either situation there is abuse that the abused feels almost impossible to escape.[16]

We agree that 'long has there been academic debate over how a jurisdiction might compassionately deal with a person who kills their abuser'[17] and propose that the law recognise the harm of social entrapment[18] and accordingly remodel the partial defences to murder.

Defending Women Who Kill

As with all homicides, self-defence is a full defence to murder. Loss of control and diminished responsibility are partial defences[19] that lead to a conviction for manslaughter if successfully raised. Defending women who kill requires a particular expertise and understanding of discrete and complex issues.

An examination of the problems posed by the partial defence of diminished responsibility provided under S. 2 Homicide Act 1957 (as amended by the Coroners and Justice Act 2009)[20] is beyond the scope of this chapter. Suffice

13 For example, *Martin* [2020] EWCA Crim 1798 where the appellant suffered from complex post-traumatic stress disorder.

14 These women should properly be considered victims as well as perpetrators.

15 S. 3 Criminal Law Act 1967, as clarified by S. 76 Criminal Justice and Immigration Act 2008.

16 A Clough, 'Coercive Control: Transforming Partial Defences to Murder in England and Wales' (2023) 87(2) *Journal of Criminal Law* 109–112.

17 Ibid 109.

18 A term that has been used by many lawyers and academics in recent years.

19 As set out in Ss. 52–55 Coroners and Justice Act 2009 and S. 2 Homicide Act 1957.

20 S. 52 Coroners and Justice Act 2009 provides that 'A person ("D") who kills or is a party to the killing of another is not to be convicted of murder if D was suffering from an abnormality of mental functioning which – (a) arose from a recognised medical condition, (b) substantially impaired D's ability to do one or more of the things mentioned in subsection (1A),

it to say, however, that in the opinion of the authors, the partial defence is too restrictive as it relies on psychiatric evidence of a recognised medical condition which affected the defendant's mental functioning at the time of the killing. This does not recognise the harm of entrapment. Psychiatric evidence may have a role given that coercive control can affect the mental health of the victim, but mental illness is not the *sine qua non* without which women who are abused will kill their abusers. As commentators have already said: 'the focus needs to be on the abuse and the wrong such behaviour represents, rather than continuing on a path which requires a woman to be deemed "mad"'.[21] Despite the apparent availability of the defences of self-defence and loss of control, it is suggested that the underlying problem is that all defences operate against a background of stereotype, misogyny, and negative perceptions of women who kill.

Self-Defence Is Inaccessible

With respect to self-defence, the law appears to be failing women who kill: 'The law on self-defence (with its masculinist requirements and interpretation of proportionality and reasonableness) remains largely inaccessible to the abused woman who defends herself from an intimate partner's violence and abuse'.[22] When a woman kills a man with whom she has been in an intimate, coercively controlled relationship, she is rarely able to utilise the full defence of self-defence. This tends to be because she has used a weapon.[23] This deprives women of a full defence, 'the legal construction and framing of the use of a weapon as more intentional and more heinous than other methods of killing in loss of control and self-defence pleadings where women are defendants has worked to their great disadvantage'.[24] Usually preferring a knife or other sharp implement, women who use such weapons are perceived

and (c) provides an explanation for D's acts and omissions in doing or being a party to the killing. (1A) Those things are – (a) to understand the nature of D's conduct; (b) to form a rational judgment; (c) to exercise self-control. (1B) For the purposes of subsection (1)(c), an abnormality of mental functioning provides an explanation for D's conduct if it causes, or is a significant contributory factor in causing, D to carry out that conduct'.

21 A Clough, 'Coercive Control: Transforming Partial Defences to Murder in England and Wales' (2023) 87(2) *Journal of Criminal Law* 113.

22 S Edwards and J Koshan, 'Women Who Kill Abusive Men: The Limitations of Loss of Control, Provocation and Self-Defence in England and Wales and Canada' (2023) 87(2) *Journal of Criminal Law* 75.

23 As cited at part 1.4.6 of the Domestic Homicide Sentencing Review, 2023 *All of the Female Perpetrators Who Had Killed a Male Partner Used a Knife or Other Weapon* <www.gov.uk/guidance/domestic-homicide-sentencing-review#domestic-homicide-sentencing-review> accessed 24 July 2024.

24 S Edwards and J Koshan, 'Women Who Kill Abusive Men: The Limitations of Loss of Control, Provocation and Self-Defence in England and Wales and Canada' (2023) 87(2) *Journal of Criminal Law* 78.

to have used disproportionate force to the threat that she faced: 'The use of a weapon to compensate for their physical disadvantage has presented as the main obstacle to successful manslaughter and self-defence pleas. Method of killing is a significant factor in the success of a defence'.[25] If the woman is not under immediate threat, the law does not see her conduct in killing as reasonable. This appears to reflect an unfair presumption of a level playing field between man and woman, irrespective of physical size and force: The person 'who uses a weapon to address the physical disadvantage when encountering a male aggressor is regarded not as levelling the uneven field but as using disproportionate force'.[26] Further, 'reasonable force remains elided with a notion of male proportionality, such that leaving jurors to determine what is a reasonable response of an abused woman depends on their appreciation and understanding of the situation of a woman who is abused, coerced, and controlled'.[27]

Indeed, with manual strangulation, nearly always perpetrated by men against women (nearly always the victims), the law's perception[28] that a killing is aggravated by the use of a weapon can be seen in a much fuller context.[29] It is arguable that had a weapon not been used, then there would be no death and no offence to punish[30] (whether that be murder or manslaughter). However, such arguments tend to fall on deaf ears when it comes to sentencing, which is frequently imposed by adherence to guidelines.[31]

How Myths and Stereotypes Fail Women on Trial for Murder

Intrinsically linked to this issue are the perpetual myths and stereotypes rife within society, including in the criminal justice system even though the Crown Prosecution Service published revised legal guidance.[32] Perhaps the most pervasive myth is that if the domestic abuse had been that bad then she would have left the relationship: 'The question of why the abused person remained in the relationship is often misunderstood and asked without a true picture of

25 Ibid 76.
26 Ibid 77.
27 Ibid 91.
28 Strangulation is not a statutory aggravating factor to sentence for murder (see paragraph 9 to Schedule 21 Sentencing Act 2020) but is an aggravating feature to the offence of unlawful act manslaughter (see Step 2 of the Sentencing Council Guideline 'Unlawful Act Manslaughter').
29 Or indeed when considering the householder defence under S. 76[5A] Criminal Justice and Immigration Act 2008. This appears to provide invariably male householders more of a defence than that available to an abused woman who kills her non-trespasser partner.
30 *R v. Richardson (Adam)* [2005] EWCA Crim 1408, [2005] 5 WLUK 665.
31 Even though the use of a weapon is not a statutory aggravating factor in murder, it is nearly always seen to aggravate the murder for the purpose of sentence.
32 See further at <www.cps.gov.uk/cps/news/there-no-typical-victim-domestic-abuse-cps-says-it-revises-its-legal-guidance-challenge> accessed 24 July 2024.

the constraints a person in such a relationship may suffer'.[33] Even when not made explicit by the prosecution,[34] it is likely that juries are influenced by it. This stigmatises and detracts from where the true focus should be: the actions of the abuser and the impact of those actions on the conduct of the defendant. Those actions can be overt acts of violence or constant 'micro' aggressions and must be considered within the context of the individual relationship.

As Stark argued, coercive control is a heuristic tool.[35] In other words, its deployment will be different in every case. It will depend upon the particular vulnerabilities of the victim and what makes her susceptible to what is, arguably, a form of hostage taking. There may be an idiosyncratic dialogue between abuser and victim which is unique to them and that particular relationship. As many commentators have observed, this means that to outsiders, the abuse can go unnoticed. The domestic context means that coercive control mirrors structural inequalities between men and women while simultaneously perpetuating them. Intersectional issues also go to the specific and personal nature of the abuse in any particular case. They are rarely given the attention they merit within the criminal justice system.[36]

This has been noted to be of particular relevance in cases of women who kill: 'The role intersectionality plays in the psyche of an abused person and their mindset is fundamental, and the criminal justice system need also to take this into consideration'.[37] The role of medical experts (if any) should be to look at where mental health intersects with domestic abuse. Not only is mental disorder a frequent output of domestic abuse, but it can also ground a woman's susceptibility to abuse in the first place. A personality disorder will, for example, increase the gravity of the trigger in a case of loss of control.[38] The interface between coercive control and the fresh evidence going to a dependent personality disorder and traits of bi-polar affective disorder was the basis for the successful appeal of *Challen*.[39]

33 A Clough, 'Coercive Control: Transforming Partial Defences to Murder in England and Wales' (2023) 87(2) *Journal of Criminal Law* 111.

34 For example via the cross-examination of a female defendant or an expert called by the defence.

35 E Stark, *Coercive Control: How Men Entrap Women in Personal Life* (Oxford University Press 2007).

36 There is a reluctance to use, or admit into evidence, the opinions of cultural experts. See further *Women Who Kill: How the State Criminalises Women We Might Otherwise Be Burying* <www.centreforwomensjustice.org.uk/women-who-kill>.

37 A Clough, 'Coercive Control: Transforming Partial Defences to Murder in England and Wales' (2023) 87(2) *Journal of Criminal Law* 119.

38 Conversely, it will not usually be a sufficiently grave condition to satisfy the requirement of substantially impairing the defendant's ability to either understand the nature of her conduct, form a rational judgment or to exercise control. If a psychiatrist is of the view that it is, then there will always be another to espouse the contrary view.

39 [2019] EWCA Crim 916.

Commentators continue to observe that those advocating in court on these cases still use out-dated descriptions such as 'snapped', 'went berserk', 'lost the plot', and 'the straw that broke the camel's back'.[40] Not only do these concepts hark back to the old-style provocation defence which depended on a sudden loss of control, but they are a stark reminder that we still do not have a proper forensic understanding of domestic abuse. They militate against a sophisticated understanding of the dynamic of coercive control because they are seen outside the context of a mounting anger at the experience of loss of liberty and entrapment.

The 'myths and stereotypes' direction in the Crown Court Compendium[41] which, tellingly, appears under the heading 'domestic abuse in context of "loss of control" does little to dispel the dangers of stereotypical and misogynistic assumptions. It refers somewhat euphemistically to 'friction in the relationship' and reduces the complexity of a relationship which is characterised by controlling and coercive behaviour to a binary one which is said to be about exaggeration and/or invented behaviour. In doing so it obviates the need for judges, lawyers and juries to engage with the real harms of domestic abuse and the social entrapment that it causes.

The Domestic Homicide Sentencing Review[42] made it clear to policy makers that attempting to leave a controlling, coercive relationship usually exacerbates the threat to the woman attempting to leave[43] because she is violating

40 H Douglas and A Reed, 'The Role of Loss of Self-Control in Defences to Homicide: A Critical Analysis of Anglo-Australian Developments' (2021) 72(2) *Northern Ireland Legal Quarterly* 271–323, 274.

41 The direction reads 'One of the issues in this trial is the degree to which D was or was not the subject of domestic abuse on the part of W. The prosecution suggest that in so far as there was friction in the relationship D is choosing to exaggerate and/or invent behaviour on the part of the deceased in order to support a defence of 'loss of self-control'. The defence, however, suggest that the deceased was, at times, an abusive partner who mistreated the defendant both physically and mentally; that D was a victim of what we would term these days coercive and controlling behaviour. The defence also suggest that D adopted a strategy of seeking to conceal from others, even those closest to them, the reality of D's life and how D's partner was behaving towards D'. See page 20–12 of *The Crown Court Compendium, Part I: Jury and Trial Management and Summing Up* (Judicial College, June 2023).

42 As cited at part 1.4.6 of the Domestic Homicide Sentencing Review, 2023 *All of the Female Perpetrators Who Had Killed a Male Partner Used a Knife or Other Weapon* <www.gov.uk/guidance/domestic-homicide-sentencing-review#domestic-homicide-sentencing-review> accessed 24 July 2024.

43 Recommendation 6 of the Review states 'if a murder takes place at the end of a relationship or when the victim has expressed the desire to leave then this should be regarded as an aggravating factor and that paragraph 9 of Schedule 21 should be amended accordingly'. In response, the Government stated, 'The seriousness of this will now be recognised in statute. We will add a statutory aggravating factor to Schedule 21 for cases of murder which take place at the end of the relationship or when the victim has expressed a desire to leave the relationship' (see page 19 of 'Domestic Homicide Sentencing Review Government Response to the Independent Review by Clare Wade KC'). The Criminal Justice Bill 2023 (Bill 155 2023–24) proposes 'Murder: end of relationship aggravating factor. In Schedule 21 to the Sentencing

one of the fundamental rules in any controlling and coercive relationship: The victim should not be disloyal to the abuser. As Stark commented, 'The ultimate expression of property rights is the right of disposal illustrated by the statement that frequently precedes femicide "If I can't have you no one will"'.[44] The review assessed that 38% of the femicides considered noted resentment at the end of a relationship as a potential catalyst for the killing.[45] The harm of controlling and coercive behaviour in the background of a relationship is the harm of entrapment.

Problems with the Partial Defence of Loss of Control

The defence has been referred to as 'the product of sustained campaigning to address provocation's gendered inequity'.[46] The partial reform brought about by the enactment of the Coroners and Justice Act 2009 merits proper post-legislative scrutiny.[47]

There is a question as to whether there are conceptual problems with the legislation or whether the lack of a definitive understanding of coercive control is the problem. The introduction of the partial defence was intended to address the gendered history and continuing problems with the defence of provocation. The statutory partial defence to murder 'loss of control' came into force in October 2010 with the enactment of S. 54 of the Act.[48]

It was heralded as a necessary and welcome step forward in modernising the law: 'the Coroners and Justice Act 2009 was certainly a milestone in criminal

Code (minimum terms in mandatory life sentences), in paragraph 9, after paragraph (ba) insert – "(bb) where the offence was committed on or after the day on which section 31 of the Criminal Justice Act 2024 came into force, the fact that the offence was connected with – (i) the end of the offender's intimate personal relationship with the victim, (ii) the victim intending to bring about the end of that intimate personal relationship, or (iii) a belief by the offender as to a thing mentioned in sub-paragraph (i) or (ii)'. However, this legislation is yet to be in force as the passage of the Bill is at report stage in the House of Commons.

44 E Stark, *Coercive Control: How Men Entrap Women in Personal Life* (Oxford University Press 2007) 208.

45 See paragraph 6.2.1 of the Review (As cited at part 1.4.6 of the Domestic Homicide Sentencing Review, 2023 'All of the Female Perpetrators Who Had Killed a Male Partner Used a Knife or Other Weapon' <www.gov.uk/guidance/domestic-homicide-sentencing-review#domestic-homicide-sentencing-review> accessed 24 July 2024).

46 S Edwards and J Koshan, 'Women Who Kill Abusive Men: The Limitations of Loss of Control, Provocation and Self-Defence in England and Wales and Canada' (2023) 87(2) *Journal of Criminal Law* 82.

47 As recommended at Recommendation 17 of the Domestic Homicide Sentencing Review (As cited at part 1.4.6 of the Domestic Homicide Sentencing Review, 2023 'All of the Female Perpetrators Who Had Killed a Male Partner Used a Knife or Other Weapon' <www.gov.uk/guidance/domestic-homicide-sentencing-review#domestic-homicide-sentencing-review> accessed 24 July 2024).

48 While the defence of provocation was modernised with this Act, self-defence was not. See further at *Attorney General for Jersey v Holley* [2005] UKPC 23.

justice for victims of abuse, and it sent a message to twenty first century thinking around relationships, domestic violence and sexual infidelity'.[49] As a result of the introduction of the partial defence, fewer men who kill their female partners are able to rely on the partial defence than they could under the abolished partial defence of provocation. This is possibly because of the preclusion of sexual infidelity in S. 55(6)(c) as a possible trigger. In the Domestic Homicide Sentencing Review, jealousy was found to be a factor in many of the cases of femicide.[50] The unwritten rule 'do not make me jealous' is operative in most, if not all, controlling and coercive relationships.

However, here we expose some of the obstacles which women face when trying to rely on the partial defence. Section 54 provides that

(1) Where a person ("D") kills or is a party to the killing of another ("V"), D is not to be convicted of murder if –

    (a) D's acts and omissions in doing or being a party to the killing resulted from D's loss of self-control,
    (b) the loss of self-control had a qualifying trigger, and
    (c) a person of D's sex and age, with a normal degree of tolerance and self-restraint and in the circumstances of D, might have reacted in the same or in a similar way to D.

(2) For the purposes of subsection (1)(a), it does not matter whether or not the loss of control was sudden.
(3) In subsection (1)(c) the reference to "the circumstances of D" is a reference to all of D's circumstances other than those whose only relevance to D's conduct is that they bear on D's general capacity for tolerance or self-restraint.
(4) Subsection (1) does not apply if, in doing or being a party to the killing, D acted in a considered desire for revenge.

Section 55 provides the statutory definition for 'qualifying trigger':

(2) A loss of self-control had a qualifying trigger if subsection (3), (4) or (5) applies.
(3) This subsection applies if D's loss of self-control was attributable to D's fear of violence from V against D or another identified person.

49 A Clough, 'Coercive Control: Transforming Partial Defences to Murder in England and Wales' (2023) 87(2) *Journal of Criminal Law* 121.

50 As set out at section 6.4 of the review (as cited at part 1.4.6 of the Domestic Homicide Sentencing Review, 2023 'All of the Female Perpetrators Who Had Killed a Male Partner Used a Knife or Other Weapon' <www.gov.uk/guidance/domestic-homicide-sentencing-review#domestic-homicide-sentencing-review> accessed 24 July 2024).

(4) This subsection applies if D's loss of self-control was attributable to a thing or things done or said (or both) which –

(a) constituted circumstances of an extremely grave character, and
(b) caused D to have a justifiable sense of being seriously wronged.

(5) This subsection applies if D's loss of self-control was attributable to a combination of the matters mentioned in subsections (3) and (4).
(6) In determining whether a loss of self-control had a qualifying trigger –

(a) D's fear of serious violence is to be disregarded to the extent that it was caused by a thing which D incited to be done or said for the purpose of providing an excuse to use violence;
(b) a sense of being seriously wronged by a thing done or said is not justifiable if D incited the thing to be done or said for the purpose of providing an excuse to use violence;
(c) the fact that a thing done or said constituted sexual infidelity is to be disregarded.

'Things done and said' requires an assessment of behaviours that can unfairly discriminate against women who kill. Such assessments 'are bound by gendered stereotypes of what male behaviour is acceptable and what female behaviour is acceptable'.[51] We see, again, how myths and stereotypes pervade the law to the detriment of women. The 'serious violence' threshold is high, and while there remains limited understanding of the true impact of coercive control,[52] it only serves to minimise such abuse and does little to help women relying upon the defence. The fact that the statute sets the standard as serious violence underpins why there is such concern around the law failing women in this scenario: The focus is on physical abuse but does not tell us whether non-violent forms of abuse such as financial or emotional manipulation and/or isolation and deprivation constitute 'triggers' pursuant to S. 55(4).[53] The law's failure to recognise the true harm of social entrapment resulting from a coercive and controlling relationship reflects how the law continues to favour male models of behaviour. Furthermore, 'serious violence' falls foul of the same disproportionality hurdle which operates in self-defence.

The inclusion of a 'justifiable sense of being seriously wronged' technically accommodates the theoretical concept of coercive control. It appears that the problem is not necessarily that the current drafting is too prohibitive but rather that coercive control is not understood forensically: Unless there

51 S Edwards and J Koshan, 'Women Who Kill Abusive Men: The Limitations of Loss of Control, Provocation and Self-Defence in England and Wales and Canada' (2023) 87(2) *Journal of Criminal Law* 81.
52 Ibid 84.
53 A Clough, 'Coercive Control: Transforming Partial Defences to Murder in England and Wales' (2023) 87(2) *Journal of Criminal Law* 109.

is an understanding of the harm that coercive control creates, in particular of social entrapment, women will continue to be seriously wronged without true recourse to the statutory defence. As we understand more about the abuse and trauma of coercive control, we see that 'the far reach this behaviour can have, even beyond the remit of a relationship and long after it finishes'[54] and that this 'is astounding'.[55]

The real issue is how this understanding can be translated into a partial defence that is fit for purpose.

Viewing the Limitations in Practice

The facts of *Challen* exemplified the impact of entrapment. As Stark[56] made clear, both in his work and in the expert report he prepared for the Court of Appeal, one of the key emotions on the part of the victim of coercive control is a mounting rage at the incursions into her liberty caused by the entrapment. Killing occurs when harmful manipulation tools such as perspecticide (when an abuse victim loses their ability to know what they know, overwhelmed by their abusers' perspectives, views and opinions) prevent the victim from being able to see any lawful way out of her situation.[57]

The focus of the law has been on the wrong of coercive control as opposed to the harm it causes, when the reality is both the wrong and the harm need to be appreciated if coercive control has a part to play in defences to murder. The concept of entrapment still invokes a populist sense of incredulity, whereas the general view of professionals in the criminal justice system is that they all understand coercive control and that there is no need for training.[58]

In 2021, when 66-year-old Penelope Jackson was tried for the murder of her husband of 24 years, she was recorded on the 999 call as effectively saying that she had felt trapped and that she had killed him because she had 'had enough'. The media reports[59] included a variety of shocking comments that Mrs Jackson said immediately after the killing, including: 'I have killed my husband, or tried to, because I've had enough' and 'bleeding to death

54 Ibid 112.

55 Ibid.

56 E Stark, *Coercive Control: How Men Entrap Women in Personal Life* (Oxford University Press 2007).

57 Conversely, femicide in the domestic context usually occurs when the perpetrator feels threatened in some way and this changes his thinking (see J Monckton-Smith, 'Intimate Partner Femicide: Using Foucauldian Analysis to Track an Eight Stage Relationship Progression to Homicide' 26(11) *Violence against Women* 1267–86, e-print <http://.eprints.glous.ac.uk/id/eprint6896>.

58 The Conservative Government did not adopt recommendation 2 in the Domestic Homicide Sentencing Review.

59 <www.bbc.co.uk/news/uk-england-somerset-58878229 www.theguardian.com/uk-news/2021/oct/19/woman-stabs-husband-tells-police-admit-all-footage-shows-penelope-jackson>.

with any luck' and 'may he rot in hell'.[60] The media had a field day with the footage, largely on the basis that the applicant appeared not to conform to the public's perception of how a woman who kills in a domestic situation should present.[61]

An analysis of the cases which have contributed to the jurisprudence on this discrete area reveals many of the features which were also apparent in *Jackson*.[62] Until 2009, the leading case on the question of whether the loss of control in provocation was *R v Duffy*.[63] As explained by Edwards and Koshan, 'her apparent delayed retaliation upon his provocation (violence against her) together with her use of a weapon (which was regarded as disproportionate) led to a conviction for murder'.[64] On appeal, Duffy's conviction was upheld, confirming J Devlin's finding (at that time) that the loss of self-control must be sudden, thereby revealing the continued obstacles faced by women who killed their abusive partner.

Professor Susan Edwards documented the facts of *Duffy*,[65] which were striking in their contemporaneity from the history of sexual violence and non-fatal strangulation to the matter-of-fact way in which the appellant said that she had killed her husband. Edwards suggested that the law reporting of the case was so brief in terms of the facts that it reflected the seeming irrelevance of that background of domestic violence to the development of the law at the time.

Duffy was interesting in that the facts of the case led to a public campaign for clemency.[66] Feminist activism has led to much of the feminist jurisprudence in this area of law. The enactment of the partial defence of loss of control was intended to assist women who kill by dispensing with the requirement for the killing to be sudden.[67] Women rarely kill suddenly. Instead, killings are frequently planned, as in *Ahluwalia*.[68] Here, the appellant waited until the deceased was asleep before killing him by setting fire to his bed. On appeal, the court 'went some way to recognise the gendered nature of the obstacles the common law on provocation presented to abused women'[69]

60 As cited in judgment on renewed application for leave to appeal conviction, *R v Jackson* [2023] EWCA Crim 735.
61 Advanced as a ground of appeal in *Jackson*, albeit unsuccessfully.
62 [2023] EWCA Crim 735.
63 [1949] 1 All ER 932.
64 S Edwards and J Koshan, 'Women Who Kill Abusive Men: The Limitations of Loss of Control, Provocation and Self-Defence in England and Wales and Canada' (2023) 87(2) *Journal of Criminal Law* 81.
65 S Edwards, 'Justice Devlin's Legacy: Duffy a Battered Woman Caught in Time' (2009) 12 *Criminal Law Review* 851–869.
66 Ibid.
67 Section 54(2) Coroners and Justice Act 2009.
68 (1993) 1 ALL ER 153.
69 S Edwards and J Koshan, 'Women Who Kill Abusive Men: The Limitations of Loss of Control, Provocation and Self-Defence in England and Wales and Canada' (2023) 87(2) *Journal of Criminal Law* 82.

by confirming that the defence of provocation was not negated simply by a delayed reaction.

The legislature attempted to address gender differences by providing that the loss of control need not be sudden in S. 54 of the 2009 Act. However, the dispensation of suddenness remains inconsistent with general perceptions of 'a loss of control'. As sufficient evidence of loss of control must be established for the prosecution to negate before a jury can even consider the other factors in S. 54(1),[70] it is difficult to see how the partial defence is accessible to women. The Law Commission (which was the original architect of the partial defence) did not recommend a requirement for a loss of control on the part of the defendant, yet the legislature retained this.[71] Furthermore, there is no statutory definition of what a loss of control is.[72]

The facts of other high-profile cases demonstrate the hallmarks of a desire to escape entrapment caused by coercive control redolent of the applicant's comments in *Jackson*. In the unsuccessful appeal of *R v. Thornton (No 1)*[73] (where the appellant had stabbed her husband while he was incapacitated through drink), she was recorded by witnesses as having originally said, 'I am going to kill him', 'I didn't intend to kill him', and finally 'it was an accident'. This is a trajectory which is frequently employed by women at first instance in these trials as they struggle to find an acceptable explanation for their conduct in the absence of a legal appreciation of entrapment. In *Thornton (No 2)*,[74] the appellant was able to rely on 'battered woman syndrome' as a characteristic for the purpose of the objective test in the partial defence of provocation and her appeal was allowed.[75]

Edwards also made it clear that all the factors pertaining to coercive control were apparent in *Ahluwalia*.[76] Taylor LCJ described the abject state of the

70 *R v. Clinton (Jon Jaques)* [2012] EWCA Crim 2.

71 'The requirement of loss of self-control was a judicially invented concept, lacking sharpness or a clear foundation in psychology. It was a valiant but flawed attempt to encapsulate a key limitation to the defence – that it should not be available to those who kill in considered revenge', *Partial Defences to Murder* (Law Commission No. 290, 2004), para 3.30.

72 *R v Gurpinar (Mustafa)* [2015] 1 Cr App R 31 at [20] where the Court of Appeal held that it was 'undesirable' to decide that issue. The court appeared to overlook the proposition that the concept of loss of control is defined by a negative condition set out in S. 54(4), which states that 'subsection (1) does not apply if . . . D acted in a considered desire for revenge'.

73 [1992] 1 All ER 306.

74 [1996] 1 WLR 1174.

75 This now has no relevance since *Attorney General for Jersey v Holley* [2005] UKPC 23 and the abolition of the defence of provocation. Provocation as a common law defence to murder under S. 3 Homicide Act 1957 was abolished on 4 October 2010 by S. 56 of the Coroners and Justice Act 2009. Provocation was replaced with the statutory partial defence to murder of loss control as set out in Ss. 54–55 of the 2009 Act.

76 S Edwards and J Koshan, 'Women Who Kill Abusive Men: The Limitations of Loss of Control, Provocation and Self-Defence in England and Wales and Canada' (2023) 87(2) *Journal of Criminal Law* 82.

appellant when he referred to a letter she had written to the deceased before the killing:

> Deepak, if you come back I promise – I won't touch black coffee again, I won't go town every week, I won't eat green chilli, I ready to leave Chandikah and all my friends, I won't go near Der Goodie Mohan's house again, Even I am not going to attend Bully's wedding, I eat too much or all the time so I can get fat, I won't laugh if you don't like, I won't die my hair even, I don't go to my neighbour's house.[77]

This letter provides a stark and bleak background of the impact of coercive control upon this appellant.

Comparison with Other Jurisdictions: The Seminal Case of R v Ruddelle

The New Zealand[78] case of *R v Ruddelle*[79] offers both promise and direction to other jurisdictions on how to approach the knotty issue of women who kill within the background of an abusive relationship. In the early hours of 14 November 2018, Ms Ruddelle (then 58 years old) stabbed her partner to death. There was a history of physical violence (including non-fatal strangulation), sexual abuse, and verbal abuse within the relationship. On 20 February 2020, she was acquitted of murder but found guilty (on a majority verdict) of manslaughter.[80] In perhaps a true expression of compassion and understanding of the history of abuse, Ms Ruddelle was sentenced to 11 months and 2 weeks of home detention.

Of particular importance, the court allowed the expert opinion of Rachel Smith to be admitted into evidence; she had frontline experience, was trained in social entrapment, and was able to provide evidence on cultural background from an intersectional perspective.[81] Paragraphs 16 and 17 of the judgment set out the precis of the expert evidence:

> [16] During the trial, Ms Rachel Smith gave expert evidence about general patterns of ongoing cumulative social entrapment of women experiencing intimate partner violence; entrapment in an ongoing pattern of harm with inadequate safety options. She gave evidence of how overall patterns of coercive control, not just physical violence, can play out in

77 As recited within the case report.

78 It is worth noting that there are no partial defences to murder equating to loss of control and diminished responsibility in New Zealand.

79 [2021] 3 NZLR 505.

80 That is, the jury could not support her claim of self-defence or defence of her son.

81 As detailed in D Tyson, B Naylor, and H Douglas, *Successful Strategies for Improving Access to Justice for Women Who Kill Their Abusers* (2024) Academy of the Social Sciences in Australia <https://doi.org/10.60651/KFYC-3Z13>.

a variety of ways across the lives of these women. She emphasised that victims of intimate partner violence experience their partner's abuse as cumulative, so you cannot look at their response only in a certain moment because intimate partner violence is a form of abuse that takes effect over time. Ms Smith noted that victims often have "heightened sensitivity" to when situations are becoming seriously dangerous because of their long experience of abuse, comparing this sensitivity to experienced drivers scanning for potential hazards on the road. She noted a general pattern in offending by women who are primary victims of family violence, in a study from 2009 to 2015:

> most of those women were inside the home, they were trapped in the kitchen, they were responding to an ongoing assault and they may pick up a knife and they use one or two stab wounds and they don't harm children, they don't commit suicide afterwards, it's actively defending themselves.

[17] Dr Alison Towns' evidence at trial was that social entrapment can lead women to stay in a violent relationship because they believe if they support and love the man he will change. Her evidence was there can be cultural pressure on Māori women, in particular, to nurture and look after people with whom they are or have been in relationships. Under cross-examination, Ms Ruddelle accepted that it was her choice to stay in the relationship and she was not reliant on Mr Ngapera for money, so she was not trapped. Dr Towns' opinion was that Ms Ruddelle had experienced social entrapment, and that her experiences are consistent with those of victims of family violence. She also gave her opinion that, due to her lifetime of trauma, Ms Ruddelle's reaction to a threat did not come from a "rational part of the brain".

It is clear that the multi-faceted nature of abuse, plus the cultural issues were put before the jury, allowed the jury to consider the effects of abuse on victims over time. Clough clearly set out why the case of *Ruddelle* could offer real opportunity for change in England and Wales:

> In New Zealand, the excessive force self-defence case of Ruddelle might provide a particularly interesting comparator. In this case a fifty eight year old female fatally stabbed her partner twice. The relationship was abusive, resulting in a total of sixteen calls to police in a period of four years. She had previously sought help from a women's refuge and protection orders. The fatal event occurred during an argument at their home, observed by her fourteen year old son. Evidence of social entrapment had been introduced at her trial – an explanation of the barriers faced in leaving such a relationship. Though her claim of self-defence itself, in regard to both herself and her son, had failed, a finding of manslaughter was returned. The judge had additionally noted that "the jury did see

this as a case of excessive self-defence', and a lenient home detention sentence was passed of eleven months and two weeks. This shows similarities to the current stance in English law – if self defence fails, might loss of control fill the gap? However, such a sparing sentence might remain elusive. Perhaps the use of social entrapment evidence as utilised in the case of Ruddelle might prove to be beneficial.[82]

Remodelling Partial Defences to Include Social Entrapment

In considering the failings with the current state of the law, we suggest that it is time for the law to modernise and recognise the social entrapment experienced by victims of controlling and coercive behaviour as a true legal harm and to remodel the partial defences to murder accordingly. We favour Clough's route:

> Legislate for a partial defence of coercive control, to operate much as the other partial defences to murder do. Modelled on the offence itself and the evidence of which courts find admissible, this defence could allow evidence of controlling behaviour and social entrapment to show why a victim felt trapped in their situation and prisoner within their own life, desperately acting from self-preservation of mind as well as body.[83]

By adopting a more forensic understanding of domestic abuse, rather than an over-reliance upon psychiatric evidence to validate such abuse, the law can better meet the needs of the women it is currently failing. The prevailing approach pathologises women for what is arguably a logical and predictable reaction to a harm which is not yet fully appreciated in law: social entrapment. When we consider the concept, 'it is not about entrapment in the relationship but entrapment in the abuse. This is because separation is not the same thing as safety'.[84] Presenting realistic real-world support options to victims of coercive control is essential for painting the most accurate picture possible of the lives lived and obstacles faced as to the nature of the entrapment.[85]

When considering practicalities, we suggest that more allowance is needed for expert evidence including from cultural experts to address stereotypes and assumptions.[86] Many practitioners will be alive to the resistance from the

82 A Clough, 'Coercive Control: Transforming Partial Defences to Murder in England and Wales' (2023) 87(2) *Journal of Criminal Law* 118.

83 Ibid 120.

84 J Tolmie, *Defending Victims Survivors Who Use Violence against Their Abusive Partners Using an IPV Entrapment Framing* (International Feminist Legal Network Conference, 2024) <www.feminist-legal.com/ifln-conference-resources> accessed 27 July 2024.

85 A Clough, 'Coercive Control: Transforming Partial Defences to Murder in England and Wales' (2023) 87(2) *Journal of Criminal Law* 119–120.

86 See further discussion at D Tyson, B Naylor, and H Douglas, 'Successful Strategies for Improving Access to Justice for Women Who Kill Their Abusers' (2024) Academy of the Social Sciences in Australia <https://doi.org/10.60651/KFYC-3Z13>.

criminal courts in England and Wales towards admitting such expert evidence, but one effective strategy around judicial resistance is to utilise the Judicial College's Equal Treatment Bench Book alongside Criminal Procedure Rule 19.[87] Such evidence can provide real value in dispelling myths that women should endure abuse rather than resort to defending themselves. In particular,

> 'over the past decade, there has been a paradigm shift away from an understanding of intimate partner violence as consisting of a one-off or series of isolated physical incidents towards a more comprehensive and accurate paradigm that accounts for patterns of coercive control'.[88]

Conclusion

Change may be on the horizon. The Law Commission is undertaking a comprehensive review entitled *Defences for Victims of Domestic Abuse Who Kill Their Abusers*, with the aim of publishing a consultation paper in summer 2025. The Terms of Reference[89] recognise that despite reforms to the partial defences of murder,[90] concerns remain as to whether justice is being achieved for victims of domestic abuse who ultimately kill. As set out in the terms, the modern understanding of the effects of abuse on women is to be considered in light of the current defences to murder to ascertain whether further reform is required. We suggest that reform certainly is required as women continue to be failed by the justice system due to a lack of proper understanding of the actual impacts of abuse. The Law Commission's capacity to research comparative law makes them best placed to learn lessons from other jurisdictions, particularly New Zealand.

Clough eloquently sets out the reason for desire for change:

> The criminal law needs to continuously develop in understanding of abuse. . . . We need to acknowledge that victims of coercive control are less visible but not uncommon. Providing legal redress for the many facets of coercive control, as well as providing avenues for lessened culpability when this results in an abuse victim using lethal violence is not merely important; it is vital. When the criminal law is developed and advanced, the behaviour society will not tolerate is illustrated. If we measure abuse only by the severity of injury, we will continue to

87 This governs the introduction of expert opinion evidence in criminal proceedings.

88 D Tyson, B Naylor, and H Douglas, 'Successful Strategies for Improving Access to Justice for Women Who Kill Their Abusers' (2024) Academy of the Social Sciences in Australia <https://doi.org/10.60651/KFYC-3Z13>.

89 Accessed at <https://cloud-platforme218f50a48129 67ba1215eaecede923f.s3.amazonaws.com/uploads/sites/30/2023/11/Domestic-Homicide-ToR-Nov-23.pdf>.

90 Previous reforms have included provocation and battered women syndrome now being recognised in statute as the partial defence of loss of control.

> contribute to injustice. . . . Admittedly, a vital cog to this wheel of justice is a sound understanding of the many facets of abuse that can occur in intimate partner relationships.[91]

The prevalence of the hallmarks of coercive control[92] and the impact of entrapment in the case law suggest that perhaps what needs to change is how we see these killings. It is only recently that policymakers have accepted that they are motivated by violent resistance to the entrapment caused by the control which underpins femicide in the domestic context.[93] Yet the factors are there in plain sight. It may be that until we have an accepted and definitive understanding of domestic abuse as a forensic concept, any statutory change will not have the desired impact.

91 A Clough, 'Coercive Control: Transforming Partial Defences to Murder in England and Wales' (2023) 87(2) *Journal of Criminal Law* 120.

92 As considered in 'Viewing the Limitations in Practice' earlier in this chapter.

93 Schedule 21 of the Sentencing Act 2020 was amended by The Sentencing Act 2020 (Amendment of Schedule 21) Regulations 2024 to include controlling and coercive behaviour as an aggravating and mitigating factor to sentence further to recommendation 5 in the Domestic Homicide Sentencing Review (As cited at part 1.4.6 of the Domestic Homicide Sentencing Review, 2023 'All of the Female Perpetrators Who Had Killed a Male Partner Used a Knife or Other Weapon' <www.gov.uk/guidance/domestic-homicide-sentencing-review#domestic-homicide-sentencing-review> accessed 24 July 2024).

8 Marginalised Justice

Race and Racism in the Criminal Court System

Dominic Carrington

Introduction

On 24 April 2024 at the University of Northampton, (UON), the Criminal Justice Research Group hosted the symposium 'What Is Justice?' The talk was delivered by Professor Dean A. Strang of Loyola University Chicago School of Law and Professor Jon D. Hanson of Harvard Law School. During this discussion, I asked the speakers their opinions on race and justice, and the answer was that when it came to race, there is no justice. In this chapter, I examine whether BME defendants can be treated fairly focusing on both the Magistrates and Crown Courts in England and Wales. I first look at summary justice by focusing on the trials and sentences meted out in Magistrates' Courts, examining the composition of the magistrates and whether there is sufficient representation of ethnic minorities amongst them. I then examine whether this representation has any effect on ethnic minorities and their courtroom outcomes. Using the recent Lord Chief Justice statistics from 2024,[1] I note that at 43% of the judges, women are well represented in the judiciary, and there has been a gradual increase of the number of Black and other minority ethnic judges from 7% to 11%. In 2024, over half of all magistrates, 57%, are women and about 13% of magistrates declared themselves as ethnic minority. In 2014, that figure was 8%.[2]

Then I look at whether the quick summary process creates disproportionate conviction rates for BME defendants.[3] David Lammy, author of the distinguished Lammy Review,[4] indicates that individuals from BME communities

1 Official Statistics Diversity of the Judiciary, 'Legal Professions, New Appointments and Current Post-Holders – 2024' (*Ministry of Justice*, 2024) 13 <www.gov.uk/government/statistics/diversity-of-the-judiciary-2024-statistics/diversity-of-the-judiciary-legal-professions-new-appointments-and-current-post-holders-2024-statistics/> accessed 19 October2024.

2 Ibid.

3 BME stands for Black and minority ethnic. This is not a homogenous group, but for want of a better word, I have chosen to use this term, as many of study authors do as well. Other terms are GEM for global ethnic majority and BAME for Black and minority ethnic.

4 David Lammy, *The Lammy Review: An Independent Review into the Treatment of, and Outcomes for, Black, Asian and Minority Ethnic Individuals in the Criminal Justice System* (2017) 3

DOI: 10.4324/9781003496823-8

form a disproportionately high percentage of the defendants in the criminal justice system compared with their proportions in the general population, particularly on arrest[5] and in prison. After that, I focus on sentencing in the Magistrates' Courts, highlighting the new measures under the Judicial Review and Courts Act 2022[6] to increase the sentencing powers of the magistrates for a single either-way offence from 6 months to 12 months to cover more cases to remove the backlog due to Covid-19. In March 2022, the UK Parliament committee found that the pandemic had exacerbated a growing backlog of cases waiting to be tried in the criminal courts, significantly affecting defendants, victims, and witnesses.[7] The Act lasted 12 months with the Sentencing Act 2020 (Magistrates' Court Sentencing Powers) (Amendment) Regulations 2023, which returned to the magistrates their original sentencing powers.[8] In this chapter, I examine whether the increased sentencing powers had any adverse effect on BME defendants and why there was a change back to the six months.

I then consider the Crown Court, which adopts stronger procedural safeguards to ensure that 'justice' is done.[9] Statistics suggest that you are more likely to be acquitted at the Crown Court than in a Magistrates' Court.[10] In 2023, the conviction rate in the Magistrates' Court was 83.6%, compared with 77.9% in the Crown Court.[11] I first highlight the percentage of BME judges from 2024 statistics to look at diversity.[12] Then I compare the conviction rates of BME defendants with those of White defendants using the Lammy Review and establish that there is little difference, findings that led Lammy to suggest that the jury trial is a success story of the criminal justice system.[13]

The studies examined will demonstrate that the bias in favour of conviction is diminished during a trial. A study in 2020 shows that BME defendants are more likely to be arrested than White defendants and suggest that one reason

---

<https://assets.publishing.service.gov.uk/media/5a82009040f0b62305b91f49/lammy-review-final-report.pdf/> accessed 19 October 2024.

5 Statista, 'Arrest Rate Per 1,000 People in England and Wales from 2006/07 to 2023/24, by Ethnicity' <www.statista.com/statistics/1230734/arrest-rate-england-and-wales-by-ethnicity/> accessed 6 December 2024.

6 S. 13 Judicial Review and Courts Act 2022.

7 UK Parliament Committee, 'Update on Reducing the Backlog in Criminal Courts' <https://committees.parliament.uk/work/8371/update-on-reducing-the-backlog-in-criminal-courts/> accessed 19 October 2024.

8 Magistrates' Court Sentencing Powers) (Amendment) Regulations 2023.

9 Pat Carlen, *Magistrates Justice* (M Robertson 1976).

10 'Conviction Rates for Magistrates' Courts and Crown Courts in England and Wales from 2nd Quarter 2013 to 1st Quarter 2023 <www.statista.com/statistics/1100769/conviction-rate-in-england-and-wales/> accessed 19 October 2024.

11 Ibid.

12 D Steffensmeier and CL Britt, 'Judges' Race and Judicial Decision Making: Do Black Judges Sentence Differently?' (2001) 82(4) *Social Science Quarterly* 749.

13 The Lammy Review, 31.

for the disparity in sentences is that BME defendants tend not to plead guilty, which reduces their chance of a discounted sentence. Finally, I suggest that the jury being a success story should be looked at in line with the miscarriages of justice. Specifically, I look at the database created by the University of Exeter, which has 490 cases between 1970 to 2021, and I highlight one case study.[14] While these are known cases, there are likely many more. Finally, I consider the problem with the Court of Appeal in overturning decisions in the Crown Court.

Race Issues in the Magistrates' Court

Creation of the Magistrates' Courts

The Magistrates' Courts were established in 1285 during the reign of Edward I when 'good and lawful men' were commissioned to keep the King's peace.[15] Since that day, magistrates have covered 95% of criminal cases.[16] All criminal cases begin in the Magistrates' Courts, which consist of two or three lay magistrates or a district judge who can sit alone. The magistrates deal with summary-only offences consisting of most motoring offences and less serious criminal offences. They can also deal with triable either-way offences such as theft or drug offences. They have the power to send indictable-only offences to the Crown Court under S. 51 Crime and Disorder Act 1998.[17]

Composition of the Magistrates

In 2024, there were over 150 Magistrates' Courts across England and Wales[18]; over 12,000 people in England and Wales have volunteered their time to be a magistrate. They can be appointed from the age of 18 and retire at 75, although they are not usually appointed from the age of 70 years.[19] The role is unpaid, and they volunteer for at least 13 days every year. They require no formal legal qualifications but need to demonstrate the following: making fair, impartial and transparent decisions; understanding and appreciating different perspectives; communicating with sensitivity and respect; showing self-awareness and being open to learning; and working and engaging with

14 Dr RK Helm, *Miscarriages of Justice Registry* (Psychology, Data Science, and Law at the University of Exeter Law School) <https://evidencebasedjustice.exeter.ac.uk/miscarriages-of-justice-registry/the-cases/case-search/> accessed 6 December 2024.

15 'Overview of the Judiciary' <www.judiciary.uk/about-the-judiciary/history-of-the-judiciary-in-england-and-wales/history-of-the-judiciary/> accessed 2 February 2024.

16 Courts and Tribunals Judiciary, 'Magistrates, Criminal Proceedings in Magistrates' <www.judiciary.uk/about-the-judiciary/who-are-the-judiciary/magistrates/> accessed 19 October 2024.

17 S. 51 Crime and Disorder Act 1998.

18 Sentencing Council, *Magistrates' Court* <www.sentencingcouncil.org.uk/going-to-court/> accessed 4 April 2024.

19 Courts and Tribunals Judiciary, 'Magistrates Who They Are' <www.judiciary.uk/about-the-judiciary/who-are-the-judiciary/magistrates/> accessed 4 April 2024.

people professionally.[20] Magistrates need to be of good character and undergo mandatory training, and they are assisted by legal advisers who provide advice on law, procedure, and sentencing powers.[21]

The Magistrates' Courts also have district judges who preside over cases. District judges are legally qualified solicitors or barristers who are appointed by the King on the recommendation of the Lord Chancellor following applications to the Judicial Appointments Commission. District judges must have five years practising as solicitors or barristers and must also have sat as a deputy district judge for a minimum of two years or 30 days sitting.[22] Deputy district judges sit on a fee paid basis for a minimum of 15 days a year.

Diversity Figures from 2019 to 2024

In this section, for comparison, I compare the judicial diversity figures in the magistrates from April 2019 to April 2024:

- On 1 April 2019, 12% of magistrates declared themselves BME. There were very few magistrates aged under 40 (5%) compared with 52% of magistrates who were aged 60 or over.[23]
- On 1 April 2020, 13% of magistrates declared themselves as BME, and 82% were aged above 50.[24]
- On 1 April 2021, 13% of magistrates declared themselves as BME, 82% were aged above 50, Asian or Asian British individuals constituted 7% of magistrates, and Black or Black British individuals constituted 4%. Mixed-ethnicity individuals and individuals from other ethnicities each constituted 1% of magistrates.[25]
- On 1 April 2022, 14% of all magistrates identified as BME. Asian or Asian British individuals constituted 7% of magistrates, 4% were Black or Black British, and 1% each were mixed ethnicity or from other ethnicities.[26]

20 Ibid.

21 Ibid.

22 Ibid.

23 Judicial Diversity Statistics 2019 <www.judiciary.uk/judicial-diversity-statistics-2019-2/> accessed 5 April 2024.

24 'Diversity of the Judiciary: Legal Positions, New Appointments and Current Post Holders 2020 Statistics' (Ministry of Justice, 2020) 39 <https://assets.publishing.service.gov.uk/media/5f62b4d98fa8f5106d15640f/diversity-of-the-judiciary-2020-statistics-web.pdf/> accessed 5 April 2024.

25 'Diversity of the Judiciary: Legal Positions, New Appointments and Current Post Holders 2021 Statistics' (Ministry of Justice, 2021) 14 <www.gov.uk/government/statistics/diversity-of-the-judiciary-2021-statistics/diversity-of-the-judiciary-2021-statistics-report#non-legal-and-magistrates/> accessed 5 April 2024.

26 'Diversity of the Judiciary: Legal Positions, New Appointments and Current Post Holders 2022 Statistics' (Ministry of Justice, 2022) 15 <www.gov.uk/government/statistics/diversity-of-the-judiciary-2022-statistics/diversity-of-the-judiciary-legal-professions-new-appointments-and-current-post-holders-2022-statistics#magistrates-1/> accessed 5 April 2024.

Table 8.1 Proportion of Magistrates from Each Ethnic Minority Group by Region, 1 April 2024

Region	*Asian (%)*	*Black (%)*	*Mixed (%)*	*Other (%)*
England and Wales	7	4	2	1
London	12	14	3	2
Midlands	10	4	2	0
North East	5	2	1	1
North West	6	2	1	1
South East	6	4	1	1
South West	3	2	1	0
Wales	3	1	1	1

Source: Diversity of the Judiciary: Legal professions, new appointments and current post-holders – 2024 Statistics (December 2024) Available at https://www.gov.uk/government/statistics/diversity-of-the-judiciary-2024-statistics/diversity-of-the-judiciary-legal-professions-new-appointments-and-current-post-holders-2024-statistics.

- On 1 April 2023, BME individuals constituted 13% of all magistrates, specifically 7% Asian or Asian British, 4% Black or Black British, and 1% each mixed ethnicity or other ethnicities.
- As of 1 April 2024, BME individuals constituted 13% of all magistrates (a 5% increase from 2014 when 8% declared themselves as from an ethnic minority). The breakdown was again 7% Asian or Asian British and 4% Black or Black British, but this time, mixed-ethnicity individuals constituted 2% of magistrates. Individuals from other ethnicities constituted 1% of magistrates.

The figures from 2019 to 2024 show a stable number of around 13% with no significant increase. Although I identified a 5% increase from 2014, this seems to be a slow progression. The diversity figures show some regional variations, with London showing at least double the proportion of Asian magistrates of all but one of the regions and at least treble the Black magistrates of those in all other regions (see Table 8.1).[27]

Effect of Diversity on Treatment of BME Defendants

The importance of representation was stated in the Lammy Review,[28] which quoted the 2015 Crime Survey for England and Wales that found that 51%

27 'Official Statistics Diversity of the Judiciary: Legal Professions, New Appointments and Current Post-Holders – 2023 Statistics' (Ministry of Justice, 2003) 13 <www.gov.uk/government/statistics/diversity-of-the-judiciary-2023-statistics/diversity-of-the-judiciary-legal-professions-new-appointments-and-current-post-holders-2023-statistics#main-points/> accessed 2 February 2024.

28 The Lammy Review, 37.

of people from BME backgrounds born in England and Wales who were surveyed believe that 'the criminal justice system discriminates against particular groups and individuals'.[29] The feeling was more pronounced amongst BME defendants, who were less likely to face magistrates who represented them. The review mentioned the need to remove the 'them and us' culture and, more importantly, to improve the diversity of the magistrates along with other positions.[30]

On 31 January 2016, David Cameron, the prime minister at the time, commissioned a review on racial bias and BME representation in the criminal justice system. He asked David Lammy MP to investigate the possibility of racial bias against Black defendants and other ethnic minorities. The Prime Minister stated, 'We need to ask difficult questions about whether the system treats people differently based on race'.[31] The review was completed in spring 2017 and reflected a growing sense of urgency across party lines to find solutions to the inequity between Whites and the BME community.[32]

David Cameron stated, 'If you are Black, you are more likely to be in a prison cell than studying at a top university. And if you are Black, it seems you are more likely to be sentenced to custody for a crime than if you are white. We should investigate why this is and how we can end this possible discrimination'.[33] David Lammy noted at the time that 25% of the prison population came from BME background while only making up 14% of the overall population in England and Wales and noted the urgency for the review.[34] In 2023–24, people in England and Wales who identified as Black or Black British were arrested at a rate of 17 per 1,000 population compared with 10 per 1,000 for people who identified as White, and 8 per 1,000 of people who identified as Asian or Asian British (see Table 8.2).[35]

David Lammy found that while there were success stories in the Crown Court, which I will examine later in this chapter, there were stark contrasts in the Magistrates' Courts. He found disparities in particular for BME women, who

29 Centre for Justice Innovation, *Building Trust: How Our Courts Can Improve the Criminal Court Experience for Black, Asian, and Minority Ethnic Defendants* (2017) 7 <http://justiceinnovation.org/wp-content/uploads/2017/03/Building-Trust.pdf/> accessed 5 April 2024.

30 The Lammy Review, 6.

31 Prime Minister's Office, 'Review of Racial Bias and BAME Representation in Criminal Justice System Announced (Press Release, 2016) <www.gov.uk/government/news/review-of-racial-bias-and-bame-representation-in-criminal-justice-system-announced/> accessed 5 April 2024.

32 The Lammy Review, 1.

33 Prime Minister's Office, 'Review of Racial Bias and BAME Representation in Criminal Justice System Announced (*Press Release*, 2016) <www.gov.uk/government/news/review-of-racial-bias-and-bame-representation-in-criminal-justice-system-announced/> accessed 5 April 2024.

34 Ibid.

35 Statista, 'Arrest Rate Per 1,000 People in England and Wales from 2006/07 to 2023/24, by Ethnicity' <www.statista.com/statistics/1230734/arrest-rate-england-and-wales-by-ethnicity/> accessed 19 October 2024.

Table 8.2 Arrest Rates per 1,000 People in England and Wales from 2006–07 to 2023–24 by Ethnicity

	White	*Black (or Black British)*	*Asian (or Asian British)*	*Mixed*	*Other*
2006/07	24	57	19	34	21
2007/08	25	59	20	34	22
2008/09	25	60	21	33	22
2009/10	24	60	21	33	21
2010/11	23	61	21	34	21
2011/12	21	55	19	31	18
2012/13	18	48	18	27	16
2013/14	17	46	17	26	16
2014/15	16	45	16	24	15
2015/16	14	44	16	24	15
2016/17	12	38	14	21	13
2017/18	10	35	12	19	11
2018/19	10	32	12	18	12
2019/20	9	32	11	18	18
2020/21	9	29	11	17	18
2021/22	9	27	10	16	17
2022/23	9	20	8	13	8
2023/24	10	17	8	12	9

Source: Arrest rate per 1,000 people in England and Wales from 2006/07 to 2023/24, by ethnicity available at https://www.statista.com/statistics/1230734/arrest-rate-england-and-wales-by-ethnicity/

were more likely to be convicted than White women. Among those tried at Magistrates' Court, 100 White women were found guilty compared with 122 Black women and 142 Asian women.[36] This figure was obtained from a report on Black, Asian, and minority ethnic disproportionality in the criminal justice system in England and Wales, 2016.[37,38] The figures were across England and Wales and looked at all offence types for each group. The Lammy Review focused on the importance of diversity to remove the 'them and us' culture and in turn to build trust and respect for the rule of law. Lammy discusses the steps required to change the diversity of the magistracy,[39] some of which I consider later in this chapter. Lammy did note the difficulty in maintaining

36 The Lammy Review, 32.

37 N Uhrig, 'Black, Asian and Minority Ethnic Disproportionality in the Criminal Justice System in England and Wales' (Ministry of Justice, 2016) 17 <https://assets.publishing.service.gov.uk/media/5a75928440f0b6360e475224/bame-disproportionality-in-the-cjs.pdf/> accessed 19 October 2024.

38 *Prosecutions, Convictions and Remands Data Tool* (Ministry of Justice, 2014) 16 <https://assets.publishing.service.gov.uk/media/5a80a9b2e5274a2e8ab51739/criminal-justice-statistics-december-2014.pdf/> accessed 19 October 2024.

39 The Lammy Review, 31.

proper figures for the Magistrates' Courts.[40] It would also have been interesting to compare whether there were any disparities between the decisions of district judges, who sit alone, and those of the magistrates, who can sit in panels of up to three.

In another section of his review, Lammy observed that no matter how good they are, we need magistrates to be truly representative of the communities they serve, if trust in the criminal justice system is to be maintained.[41] He also observed that we do not have enough BME magistrates. In particular, of those who declared their ethnicity, 20% of defendants who appeared in court in 2015 were from BME backgrounds, compared with 11% of around 16,000 magistrates who declared themselves to be BME; additionally, the proportion of BME magistrates sitting were overwhelmingly middle class and middle aged.[42,43]

Increased Powers of Sentencing in the Magistrates' Court

The sentencing powers of the Magistrates' Court were increased by Section 13(1) Judicial Review and Courts Act 2022, which states in section 224 of the Sentencing Code (general limit on Magistrates' Court's power to impose custodial sentence) –

(b) after subsection (1) insert –
'(1A) The applicable limit is –
(a) 6 months in the case of a summary offence, or
(b) 12 months in the case of an offence triable either way'.[44]

The effect of this section was to increase the sentencing powers of Magistrates' Court for triable either-way offences from 6 months to 12 months. The aim was to reduce the backlog of criminal cases due to Covid-19.[45] Dominic Raab, at the time the Deputy Prime Minister, Lord Chancellor, and Secretary of State for Justice, said, 'This important measure will provide vital additional capacity to drive down the backlog of cases in the Crown Courts over the coming years'.[46] The Howard League argued that 'there is a danger that an increase

40 Ibid.
41 The Lammy Review, 37.
42 Ibid.
43 Ibid.
44 Judicial Review and Courts Act 2022, S. 13(1)(b).
45 UK Parliament Committee, 'Update on Reducing the Backlog in Criminal Courts' <https://committees.parliament.uk/work/8371/update-on-reducing-the-backlog-in-criminal-courts/> accessed 19 October 2024.
46 MoJ Press Release, 'Magistrates' Courts Given More Power to Tackle Backlog' (2022) <www.gov.uk/government/news/magistrates-courts-given-more-power-to-tackle-backlog/> accessed 19 October 2024.

in short prison sentences will also disproportionately impact on minorities within the system'.[47] This lasted less than 12 months when the Sentencing Act 2020 (Magistrates' Court Sentencing Powers) (Amendment) Regulations 2023 reduced the maximum sentence for an either-way offence from 12 to 6 months.[48] The change came into force on 30 March 2023. The Ministry of Justice (MoJ) Quarterly Report from January to March 2023 stated that the outstanding Crown Court caseload fell slightly, down by 0.4% in March 2023.[49] This suggests that increasing the magistrates' sentencing powers did not have the desired effect; however, it is to be noted that the criminal Bar Association did take industrial action to strike from April 2022 until it was resolved in October 2022, which did have an adverse effect on the Crown Court caseload.[50]

In this section, I looked at the creation of the Magistrates' Courts and the purpose of providing swift summary justice. I then covered the composition of the magistrates with a focus of the diversity figures from 2019 to 2024. The figures remain stationary with no significant increase. The importance of diversity was highlighted in the review by David Lammy MP in 2016. In this review, Lammy noted stark contrasts in outcomes and noted the need to improve the diversity of the bench to remove the 'them and us' culture. The increased powers of sentencing by the magistrates from 6 months to 12 months was warned to have an adverse effect on minorities. It seemed not to have the desired effect of reducing the Crown Court backlog, but its short lifespan may be a comfort to BME defendants. Next I consider some of the issues of race in the Crown Court.

Race Issues in the Crown Court

Crown Courts are situated in circuits across England and Wales. A Crown Court trial usually consists of a circuit judge and 12 members of a jury, the principle being that a person is tried by their own peers. This principle goes back to 1215 with the Magna Carta. They differ from Magistrates' Courts in that the trials are by judge and jury, not a lay magistrate or district judge. In the Crown Court, the judge decides points of law, while the jury decides points of fact. The magistrates decide points of law with the assistance of their legal advisers and also decide points of fact.

47 A Coomber, 'Why Extending the Sentencing Powers of Magistrates Is a Bad Idea' (Howard League, 2022) <https://howardleague.org/blog/why-extending-the-sentencing-powers-of-magistrates-is-a-bad-idea/> accessed 19 October 2024

48 Sentencing Act 2020 (Magistrates' Court Sentencing .Powers) (Amendment) Regulations 2023.

49 'Criminal Court Statistics Quarterly: January to March 2023' (MoJ, 2023) 3 <www.gov.uk/government/statistics/criminal-court-statistics-quarterly-january-to-march-2023/criminal-court-statistics-quarterly-january-to-march-2023/> accessed 19 October 2024.

50 Ibid.

Table 8.3 White and Male: Diversity and the Judiciary

Year	*% Black & minority ethnic*	*Judges in post*
1998	1.6	3174
1999	1.7	3312
2000	2.1	3441
2001	1.9	3535
2002	2	3545
2003	2.2	3656
2004	2.5	3675
2005	2.9	3794
2006	3.8	3774
2007	3.5	3545
2008	4.1	3820
2009	4.5	3602
2010	4.8	3598
2011	5.1	3694

Source: www.theguardian.com/news/datablog/2012/mar/28/judges-ethnic-sex-diversity-judiciary#data.

Ethnic Diversity

Table 8.3 presents evolving diversity in the judiciary from 1998 to 2011 with the focus on BME judges. Tellingly, the system changed in 2006 from appointment by a government minister to the new independent Judicial Appointments Commission (JAC). The low of 1.6% in 1998 increased more than three times to 5.1% in 2011, a clear improvement over the old system.

In the 2011 census, the total UK population was 63.3 million people, with 53.1 million in England and 3 million in Wales. BME groups represented 14% of the population: 7.5% Asian (4.2 million), 3.3% Black Caribbean and African (2.4 million), 2.2% mixed or multiple ethnic groups (1.2 million), and 1% other ethnic group (564,000).[51] Ten years later, in the recent 2021 census, the UK had a population of 67.6 million with 57.1 million in England and 3.1 million in Wales. The more recent breakdown was 9.3% Asian (5.5 million), 4% Black Caribbean and African (2.4 million), 2.9% mixed or multiple ethnic groups (1.7 million), and 2.1% other (1.3 million),[52] for a total of 18%,[53] a 4% increase over the ten years. The different groups represented show the difficulty of collating these figures and trying to represent one whole homogeneous group. Asia is vast continent with many different nationalities, but the entire population is just 'Asia'. Africa is of course another vast continent, and there are numerous islands and nations across the Caribbean, yet these

51 ONS, 'Census 2021' 2 <www.ons.gov.uk/peoplepopulationandcommunity/culturalidentity/ethnicity/bulletins/ethnicgroupenglandandwales/census2021/> accessed 19 October 2024.

52 Ibid.

53 Ibid.

Table 8.4 Ethnic Minority Representation among the UK Judicial System, 1 April 2024

Judicial Role	*Percentage (%)*	*Count*
Heads of Division	0	0
Court of Appeal Judges	3	1
High Court Judges	8	8
Deputy High Court Judges	13	17
Judge Advocates, Deputy Judge Advocates	0	0
Masters/Insolvency & Companies/Costs Judges	8	2
Deputy Masters/Insolvency & Companies/Costs Judges	9	3
Circuit Judges	9	59
Recorders	11	93
District Judges (County Courts)	12	50
Deputy District Judges (County Courts)	11	78
District Judges (Magistrates' Courts)	14	17
Deputy District Judges (Magistrates' Courts)	10	8
All court judges	10	336
Presidents, Chamber/Deputy/Vice Presidents	0	0
Upper Tribunal Judge	14	7
Deputy Upper Tribunal Judge	20	10
Tribunal Judge (Salaried)	15	37
Tribunal Judge (Fee-paid)	14	98
Regional, Deputy Regional Tribunal Judge	4	1
Employment Judge (Salaried)	10	16
Employment Judge (Fee-paid)	10	21
Regional Employment Judge	38	3
All tribunal judges	13	193

Source: Diversity of the judiciary: Legal professions, new appointments and current post-holders – 2024 Statistics (December 2024) Available at www.gov.uk/government/statistics/diversity-of-the-judiciary-2024-statistics/diversity-of-the-judiciary-legal-professions-new-appointments-and-current-post-holders-2024-statistics#:~:text=Over%20half%20(57%25)%20of,a%20magistrate%20in%202023%2D24.

populations are lumped together as one. For this chapter, I do recognise these difficulties and note the limitations of term BME for all of these people, but I use it for the want of a better term.

As of 1 April 2024, around 89% of court judges in England and Wales were White, with 11% from BME backgrounds.[54] This is low compared with the 2021 census figures of persons classed as BME. However, across the legal profession as whole, 17% of all barristers, 19% of all solicitors, and 11% of all Chartered Legal Executives declared themselves BME.[55] Individual figures by position are less impressive, for instance only 9% (59) of circuit judges and 11% (93) of recorders being from an ethnic minority.[56] See Table 8.4.

54 'Official Statistics Diversity of the Judiciary: Legal Professions, New Appointments and Current Post-Holders – 2024 Statistics (MoJ, 2024) 6.4 <www.gov.uk/government/statistics/diversity-of-the-judiciary-2024-statistics/diversity-of-the-judiciary-legal-professions-new-appointments-and-current-post-holders-2024-statistics#fnref:17:1> accessed 19 October 2024.

55 Ibid.

56 Ibid.

Effect of Diversity

Lammy[57] focussed on the importance of diversity to remove the 'them and us' culture, in turn building trust and respect for the rule of law. This stems from the argument that people will be more likely to comply with the law when they feel treated in a just and decent way by the actors who enforce the law.[58] He discusses both the need and the steps required to change the diversity of the magistracy and the judiciary more broadly.[59] Until this is achieved, there will continue to be a pervasive sense of 'them and us' among BME defendants.[60] Lammy notes that there is a fundamental source of mistrust in the Criminal Justice System[61] when only 11% of around 3,000 court judges are from BME backgrounds. On average, younger cohorts of court judges are more diverse – 10% are under 40 compared with 4% 60 and over, but even the younger group remains significantly less diverse than the country it serves.[62]

Lammy identified that the application process was not the problem: In 2016–17, 12% (20) of applicants for circuit judge declared themselves as BME, but only 10% (2) received recommendations. In contrast, 88% (149) of applications came from White applicants, and 26% (38) of them were recommended.[63] Lammy identified that in every round from 2006–7 to 2016–17, BME candidates were recommended at lower rates than they applied. Whilst the JAC mentioned earlier has improved from earlier years, there remains a disparity even five years after its formation: From 2019 to 2022, BME individuals were over-represented in applications for judicial appointments but had lower recommendation rates than white candidates.[64]

Across all legal exercises in this three-year period, ethnic minority candidates together constituted 24% of applications (4,025) and 12% of recommendations for appointment (239), a 31% lower rate than that for White candidates during this period.[65] The fact that this did not change from 2006 until 2022 suggests that candidates are being put forward due to meeting the criteria, which is the number of years practising as a solicitor or barrister, but that the application form contains information about ethnicity, which is not

57 The Lammy Review, 31.
58 KA Beijersbergen, AJE Dirkzwager, and P Nieuwbeerta, 'Reoffending after Release: Does Procedural Justice during Imprisonment Matter?' (2016) 43(1) *Criminal Justice and Behaviour* 63, 78.
59 Ibid.
60 The Lammy Review, 31.
61 Ibid 36.
62 Ibid 37.
63 The Lammy Review, 38.
64 *Diversity of the Judiciary: Legal Professions, New Appointments and Current Post-Holders – 2022 Statistics* (Ministry of Justice, 2023) 6 <www.gov.uk/government/statistics/diversity-of-the-judiciary-2022-statistics/diversity-of-the-judiciary-legal-professions-new-appointments-and-current-post-holders-2022-statistics#ethnicity-1/> accessed 19 October 2024.
65 Ibid.

part of the sifting process, and this suggests that qualified candidates are being rejected for their race. This requires further investigation.

I have mentioned that one of the purposes of the creation of the JAC was to make judicial appointments clearer and more accountable.[66] The aim was to replace the 'tap on the shoulder' approach with a meritocratic option. However, the figures I have cited show that problems still exist; Lammy highlighted the issue that the ones doing the hiring tend to hire candidates who look like them and have similar backgrounds.[67] Next I will look at the legal treatment of BME defendants.

Legal Treatment of BME Defendants

While statistics show that you are less likely to be convicted in the Crown Court than in the Magistrates' Court,[68] Lammy showed that BME residents of the UK make up a disproportionate amount of Crown Court defendants (24%), and those who are found guilty are more likely to receive custodial sentences than White offenders (61% compared to 56%).[69] However, Cheryl Thomas found no disparities for BME defendants in the Crown Court and regarded that finding as a success of the English criminal justice system. Rigorous analysis showed that, on average, juries including all White juries do not deliver different results for BME and White defendants.[70] The lesson is that juries are representative of local populations and must deliberate as a group, leaving no hiding place for bias or discrimination.[71] In her 2010 study, which was updated in 2017, Thomas analysed over 390,000 jury decisions between 2006 and 2014 and found remarkably similar jury conviction rates across different ethnic groups. White, Black, Asian, and mixed ethnic defendants are all convicted at rates of between 66% and 68%. BME and White conviction rates were similar across a range of offences, with only minor differences and no overall pattern.[72] It would also appear that the bias in favour of conviction is diminished when there is a jury trial.

In a later study from 2020, people from BME backgrounds made up 23% of people arrested, 21% of people convicted of a crime, and 27% of people in prison, which suggested the unwillingness of BME defendants to

66 Judicial Appointments Commission <https://judicialappointments.gov.uk/> accessed 19 October 2024.

67 The Lammy Review, 39.

68 See Table 8.5.

69 Prime Minister's Office, 'Review of Racial Bias and BAME Representation in Criminal Justice System Announced (Press Release, 2016) <www.gov.uk/government/news/review-of-racial-bias-and-bame-representation-in-criminal-justice-system-announced/> accessed 5 April 2024.

70 C Thomas, 'Ethnicity and Fairness of Jury Trials in England and Wales 2006–2014' (2017) 11 *Criminal Law Review* 860.

71 The Lammy Review, 31.

72 Ibid.

Table 8.5 Conviction Rate for Courts in England and Wales Q2 2013–Q1 2023

	Magistrates court	*Crown court*
Q2 2013	84.7	81.4 in %
Q3 2013	84.3	81.3 in %
Q4 2013	84.3	81.3 in %
Q1 2014	84.4	79.8 in %
Q2 2014	84.3	80.1 in %
Q3 2014	83.8	79.4 in %
Q4 2014	83.8	78.9 in %
Q1 2015	84	79.2 in %
Q2 2015	83.8	80 in %
Q3 2015	83.5	78 in %
Q4 2015	83.6	79.2 in %
Q1 2016	84.3	79.7 in %
Q2 2016	84.7	79.2 in %
Q3 2016	84.2	78.3 in %
Q4 2016	84.6	78.8 in %
Q1 2017	85.5	79 in %
Q2 2017	85.3	79.9 in %
Q3 2017	84.3	80.1 in %
Q4 2017	84.8	80 in %
Q1 2018	84.9	79.8 in %
Q2 2018	84.8	78.7 in %
Q3 2018	84	79.7 in %
Q4 2018	84.8	78.7 in %
Q1 2019	84	79.7 in %
Q2 2019	84.1	80.8 in %
Q3 2020	87.8	84.3 in %
Q4 2020	83.6	82.1 in %
Q1 2021	82.7	81 in %
Q2 2021	83	80.8 in %
Q3 2021	82.3	79.1 in %
Q4 2021	82.3	79.5 in %
Q1 2022	84.2	78.3 in %
Q2 2022	83.8	78.8 in %
Q3 2022	82.7	76.5 in %
Q4 2022	83	78.8 in %
Q1 2023	83.6	77.9 in %

Source: Conviction rates for magistrates courts and crown courts in England and Wales from 2nd quarter 2013 to 1st quarter 2023 available at https://www.statista.com/statistics/1100769/conviction-rate-in-england-and-wales/.

plead guilty.[73] Indeed, 37% of defendants from BME populations pleaded not guilty compared with 27% of White defendants,[74] which then leads to

73 B Yasin and G Sturge, 'Ethnicity and the Criminal Justice System: What Does Recent Data Say on over-Representation?' <https://commonslibrary.parliament.uk/ethnicity-and-the-criminal-justice-system-what-does-recent-data-say/> accessed 6 December 2024.

74 Ibid.

higher custodial sentences for BME defendants who do not receive the sentence reduction due to an early guilty plea, usually 1/3 at the first available opportunity.[75] In 2019, the average custodial sentence was 27.1 months for offenders from BME backgrounds compared with 9.5 months for White offenders.[76]

Lammy, in suggesting that jury trials are a success story, failed to consider the likelihood of miscarriages of justice. The University of Exeter compiled a database for such miscarriages from 1970 to 2021 and identified and included 490 established cases ranging from unreliable witness testimony to false or unreliable confession, false or misleading forensic science, and inadequate disclosure.[77] One defendant, Tonderai Chakwana, a Black man was convicted of rape and served three years in prison before his conviction was overturned because fresh evidence challenged the reliability of the main prosecution witness.[78] The cases in the database are clearly miscarriages of justice, and there are highly likely to be many more. Lammy also highlighted that the Court of Appeal has difficulty overturning decisions.[79]

Sentencing

Researchers on a 2016 study examined Crown Court sentencing for three groups of offences: acquisitive violence, sexual offences, and drug offences and found an association between ethnicity and being sentenced to prison.[80] BME defendants were sentenced to prison much more often than White offenders[81]: Black defendants are 53% more likely to go to prison than White defendants, Asian defendants overall face a 55% higher chance of a prison sentence, and Chinese defendants specifically were 81% more likely to go to prison than White defendants. There was no effect for those of mixed background. Of approximately 21,370 cases studied, there was no statistical link between ethnicity and the likelihood of receiving a prison sentence for

75 Sentencing Academy, 'Sentence Reductions for a Guilty Plea' <www.sentencingacademy.org.uk/sentence-reductions-for-a-guilty-plea/> accessed 6 December 2024.

76 Ibid.

77 Dr RK Helm, *Miscarriages of Justice Registry* (Psychology, Data Science, and Law at the University of Exeter Law School) < https://evidencebasedjustice.exeter.ac.uk/miscarriages-of-justice-registry/> accessed 6 December 2024.

78 Dr RK Helm, *Tonderai Chakwana* (Psychology, Data Science, and Law at the University of Exeter Law School) <https://evidencebasedjustice.exeter.ac.uk/case/tonderai-chakwana/> accessed 6 December 2024.

79 The Lammy Review, 33.

80 K Hopkins, N Uhrig, and M Colahan 'Associations between Ethnic Background and Being Sentenced to Prison in the Crown Court in England and Wales in 2015' (MoJ, 2016) 10 <https://assets.publishing.service.gov.uk/media/5a814a3d40f0b62305b8e241/associations-between-ethnic-background-being-sentenced-to-prison-in-the-crown-court-in-england-and-wales-2015.pdf/> accessed 6 December 2024.

81 Ibid.

acquisitive violence and sexual offences, but there was a strong correlation with drug offences. In these cases, the odds of receiving a prison sentence were around 240% higher for BME offenders than for White offenders.[82] This distinction is stark. If this offence is most common, then it would explain the increased number of BME defendants who are incarcerated.

In a March 2023 ONS report on drug misuse in England and Wales, an estimated 9.5% of people aged 16 to 59 (approximately 3.1 million people) reported having used a drug in the last 12 months; 7.6% reported using cannabis (around 2.5 million people), and 3.3% reported using a Class A drug (around 1.1 million people).[83] Compared with March 2013, these levels are higher. In March 2013, the figures were any drug, 8.1%; cannabis, 6.3%; and Class A drugs, 2.5%.[84] These figures reflect how common drug use is; the criminal offences relate to being in possession of drugs or supplying drugs.[85] Interestingly, Lammy highlights how appeal courts do not change decisions on appeal because they all fall within the broad range of judges' permissible discretion, and they fail to recognise collective differences in how that discretion is applied to BME defendants.[86]

For instance, Lammy discusses how the use of pre-sentence reports (PSRs) has decreased over the last decade.[87] He looked at the use of fast-delivery PSRs prepared on the same day that are not as detailed as the earlier reports. Judges are dissuaded from using PSRs for certain offences such as possession with intent to supply class A drugs, which is the type of offence where the evidence suggests there are sentencing disparities.[88] Lammy suggested that the MoJ should review the use and effectiveness of PSRs in close consultation with his Majesty's Courts and Tribunals Service (HMCTS), the Probation Service, and the judiciary[89] with respect to the sentencing guidelines for drug offences. A hot topic has been decriminalising drugs. There was some attempt to do this when cannabis was reduced to Class C in January 2004, following a recommendation by the Advisory Council on the Misuse of Drugs (ACMD) in March 2002. This lasted until 2009 when it was reclassified as a Class B drug.[90]

In summary, here I have looked at the issue of race, concentrating on the ethnic diversity in the UK judiciary from 1998 until 2011, which encompassed

82 The Lammy Review, 33.
83 *Drug Misuse in England and Wales: Year Ending* (March 2023) 1 <www.ons.gov.uk/peoplepopulationandcommunity/crimeandjustice/articles/drugmisuseinenglandandwales/yearendingmarch2023/> accessed 6 December 2024.
84 Ibid.
85 Ibid.
86 The Lammy Review, 33.
87 Ibid 35.
88 Ibid.
89 Ibid.
90 J Connolly, 'Cannabis Again Reclassified in the UK' (2009) <www.drugsandalcohol.ie/12158/> accessed 6 December 2024.

the creation of the JAC in 2006, after which some improvement was shown. However, figures remain low in comparison with the recent 2021 census of BME individuals in the population, although percentages are higher in specific areas of London and other areas which are highly populated by BME individuals. Amongst other areas, Lammy did seemingly identify and argue that BME defendants' lack of trust in the court system derives from the lack of diversity amongst Crown Court judges.

Next I examined the disparities in the treatment of BME defendants. One issue Lammy found was identifying the jury system as a success whilst acknowledging clear sentencing disparities as well. There was some suggestion that defendants are more comfortable being sentenced by judges who look like them, but this raises the question of whether it is being proposed that harsher sentences are acceptable for BME defendants as long as the judge is non-White as well. Findings from a 2020 study indicated that BME defendants are more likely to receive longer custodial sentences and suggest that this is because they are less likely to plead guilty. And while Lammy argued that jury trials are a success story, he did not consider the 490 confirmed miscarriages of justice between 1970 and 2021 that the University of Exeter compiled in a database[91]; clearly juries are fallible. Finally, the Lammy Review demonstrated the Court of Appeal's difficulty overturning decisions. Race issues are apparent in both the Magistrates and Crown Courts. Next, I highlight different areas of reform for tackling these issues.

Reforms and Conclusion

Magistrates' Courts

In this section, I look at areas of reform to improve the racial issues in both the Magistrates' and Crown Courts. Firstly, Lammy made the following recommendations for the Magistrates' Courts[92]:

Recommendation 1

In a cross-Criminal Justice System approach, agree to record data on ethnicity. This should enable more scrutiny in the future while reducing inefficiencies that can come from collecting the same data twice. While it was a general recommendation, it does set out the importance of collecting data. In particular, the different ethnic groups should be separated to remove the BME category.

91 Dr RK Helm, Miscarriages of Justice Registry (Psychology, Data Science, and Law at the University of Exeter Law School) <https://evidencebasedjustice.exeter.ac.uk/miscarriages-of-justice-registry/the-cases/case-search/> accessed 6 December 2024.

92 The Lammy Review, 7.

Recommendation 11

The MoJ should address key data gaps in the Magistrates' Court including pleas and remand decisions. This should be part of a more detailed examination of magistrates' verdicts with a particular focus on those affecting BME women.

Recommendation 12

The Open Justice initiative should be extended and updated so that it is possible to view sentences for individual offences at individual courts – both Magistrates' and Crown Courts – broken down by demographic characteristics including gender and ethnicity.

Recommendation 15

Set up a body for modern recruitment involving talent spotting, pre-application support, and coaching for 'near miss' candidates for the magistracy.

Recommendation 16

The government should set a clear, national target to achieve a representative magistracy by 2025. It should then report to Parliament with progress against this target biennially.

Recommendation 1 shows the importance of data collection to keep abreast of the situation. This data could be recorded annually and produced online. It is important to remove the BME category and record individual ethnic groups. Recommendation 11 covers the sentencing disparities between White and BME offenders, particularly women, and could include looking at whether there is a like-for-like offence and whether the sentence follows a plea of guilty or a conviction.

Meanwhile, whilst recommendation 12 would go some way towards addressing sentencing disparities, the potential reasons for the stark differences still need to be considered. No two offences are the same, so sentences will differ as well, and I also discussed how the decision to go to trial costs the Defendant the discount of a reduced sentence for an early guilty plea. Recommendation 15 would need some development on the remit of this body and set clear criteria on what they are to do; support and talent spotting could improve the application process but would it improve the success rate? Recommendation 16 should extend beyond 2025 but is a good starting point.

The Crown Courts

In this section, I highlight the 2016 Lammy Review's areas of reform for addressing the Crown Court's race issues and David Lammy's recommendations specific for the Crown Court,[93] although he did make general recommendations that applied to both the Magistrates' and Crown Courts.

Recommendation 15

An organisation such as the Judicial Training College or the Judicial Appointments Commission should perform more modern recruitment, involving talent spotting, pre-application support, and coaching for near miss candidates.

Lammy also suggested that talented BME candidates need to be actively sought out at an early stage in their careers and advised as to how to accumulate the right experience and develop the competencies they will ultimately need to demonstrate in any selection process. The aim is to draw on the widest pool of talent possible and should include finding ways to fast track the diverse pool of lawyers working across the public sector, including the CPS, to become judges.[94]

The judiciary runs work-shadowing programmes, mentoring programmes, and a job application workshop. It also has a positive action mentoring scheme and provides pre-application workshops for first-time applicants and judges seeking to progress.[95]

Recommendation 16

The government should set a clear, national target to achieve a representative judiciary by 2025. It should then report to Parliament with progress against this target biennially.

The first recommendation aligns with successful targeted recruitment strategies used at other organisations such as KPMG and Freshfields which I mention later in this chapter. Work shadowing and mentorship are important for BME candidates who are not necessarily interested in the work and can also encourage applications, as long as care is taken with which barristers' chambers are being targeted.

In April 2023, a programme by the legal profession and the Judicial Appointments Commission, was designed to improve the diversity in the following ways. Formally expanding its support of selection exercises to include all legal roles, this will assist candidates with a clearer path into the judiciary, expand support to CILEX members, and reiterate the importance of varied pathways and fee-paid experience. Increasing the role of judicial guides to support the expansion of candidate selection exercises and candidates.[96] The

93 The Lammy Review, 40.

94 Ibid.

95 Ibid.

96 *Judicial Diversity and Inclusion Strategy Update 2022* (Judiciary of England and Wales, 2022) 11–19 <www.judiciary.uk/wpcontent/uploads/2023/01/14.173_JO_Diversity_and_Inclusion_Updates_DRAFT_FINAL.pdfv/> accessed 9 December 2024.

candidates would benefit from tailored advice, guidance, and access to wider support.[97]

The programme planners expected many applications so they developed a prioritisation approach[98] that included all ethnic minority lawyers. The scheme aimed to help with the process, but planners did not guarantee success. They also aimed to expand the pool to include other legal professionals such as legal executives. However, so far it is not clear if there has been any real progress in successful appointments including how widely it was advertised and uptake among ethnic minority lawyers.

Finally, Lammy discussed how KPMG improved recruitment in 2016–17 by putting inclusion at the heart of its recruitment strategy by actively developing the next generation of leaders from underrepresented groups, offering mentoring and other professional development to BME staff; 37% of their graduate intake was from BME backgrounds. I will also like to mention the Stephen Lawrence Freshfields scholarship programme, which is designed to address the under-representation of Black men in commercial law firms and other careers in the City of London.[99]

Here I covered selected recommendations to improve the diversity of magistrates and the judiciary and ways of building trust. While some of these recommendations are far reaching, time has shown that the figures remain stagnant and do not move in a fast trajectory. Ultimately, a yard stick needs to be established; the 2021 census would be a good start. This can then be reviewed in 5 to 10 years' time. However, the KPMG approach and the Stephen Lawrence Freshfields scholarship programme could potentially move the numbers. Next I provide concluding thoughts on this chapter.

Conclusion

This chapter examined whether BME defendants are treated fairly in the criminal courts with focus on both the Magistrates' and Crown Courts. It established clear disparities within the ethnic composition of the courts in comparison with census numbers. The chapter acknowledged the limitations of the term BME, but used the term for want of a better word and because most researchers use it as well.

Eminent professors from the United States and former Prime Minister David Cameron identified that there are still issues with race and the criminal justice system. It is concerning for the Prime Minister to state publicly that if you are Black, you are three times more likely to go to prison than to a top university. It is more concerning that prison population statistics bear that out: 27% of

97 Ibid.
98 Ibid.
99 'Freshfields Stephen Lawrence Scholarship Scheme' <www.freshfields.com/en-gb/about-us/responsible-business/freshfields_stephen_lawrence_scholarship/> accessed 9 December 2024.

the prison population is BME despite only comprising 13% of the population. The fact that a problem has been identified is a welcomed start to work from. It is far better to realise that there is a problem compared to some thinking that no issue exists.

Firstly, in the Magistrates' Courts, examining ethnic diversity from 2019 to 2024 showed a stagnant figure of 14% BME representation in 2024 against their 18% representation in the 2021 census, an alarming sign that things are not changing fast enough despite schemes being established in about 2020 to improve recruitment. There are regional differences, however: BME representation in the legal field in London is the highest, which is to be expected given the high diversity in that region. The Judicial Diversity Forum's combined statistical report in 2020 discussed the importance of a diverse magistracy,[100] and David Lammy highlighted the need to remove the 'them and us' culture that currently exists. The increase in sentencing powers of the magistrates by section 13(1) Judicial Review and Courts Act 2022 did cause concern regarding the treatment of minorities,[101] but this only lasted 12 months with the power reversed to the original 6 months by Sentencing Act 2020 (Magistrates' Court Sentencing powers) (Amendment) Regulation 2023.[102] Talent spotting and targeted recruitment would help to improve the numbers, but there is concern on the different treatment of BME defendants and the causes for this disparity.

Secondly, the Crown Court differs from the Magistrates' Court in that there are judges and juries. The chapter examined ethnic diversity in the courts from 1998 to 2011, which overlaps with the creation of the independent Judicial Appointments Commission in 2006. It identified some improvement, but the figure of only 11% BME judges as of 2024 is disappointingly low against the 18% BME representation in the general population from the 2021 census. Lammy highlighted the importance of diversity in building trust in the rule of law, and the JAC was established in 2006 to improve the diversity. While there has been some improvement from the old 'tap on the shoulder' which led to only 1.6% BME Crown Court judges in 1998, Lammy argues that the problem is not the application process but the selection process.

He also found disparities in the sentencing of BME defendants, especially for drug offences, and noted that the Court of Appeal was not quick to overturn any discrepancies, although he did find that the jury system was able to judge BME defendants without prejudice, even with all White juries. However, Lammy fails to consider the possibility of miscarriages of justice, whereas the University of Exeter compiled a database of 490 confirmed miscarriages

100 The Combined Statistical Report (2020) 8 <https://judicialappointments.gov.uk/wp-content/uploads/2020/11/20200916_jdf_common_narrative.pdf/> accessed 9 December 2024.

101 S 13 (1) Judicial Review and Courts Act 2022.

102 Sentencing Act 2020 (Magistrates' Court Sentencing powers) (Amendment) Regulation 2023.

from 1970 to 2021. This suggests that we cannot be so certain that the jury trial is a success in the criminal justice system.

The importance of change in both the Magistrates' and Crown Court has been successfully argued in this chapter. It could only focus on selected recommendations, but a Judicial Training College to provide support and assistance would be a welcome starting point. The 2023 programme is new, and it will take some time to examine how many BME candidates have applied. Variations on the KPMG or Stephen Lawrence Freshfields programmes could aid in making candidates and the judiciary more ethnically representative of the UK. The hope is that there will be some positive changes starting with the review planned in 2025.

9 Why Do We Punish? Interrogating the Role of Criminal Law in Abortion Legislation

Claire-Michelle Smyth and Ed Johnston

Introduction

Abortion has long been a subject of legal, political, and ethical debate, with laws fluctuating between liberalisation and restriction depending on prevailing societal and governmental attitudes.[1] Whilst liberalisation led to strides, the more recent trend has been more restrictive legislation. While the US was at the forefront of liberalisation with cases such as *Roe v Wade*[2] and *Casey v Planned Parenthood*,[3] so too is it at the heart of conservatism. The anti-abortion lobby in the US saw several states passing legislation which restricted abortion rights in breach of the principle set down by *Roe v Wade*, resulting in lengthy court battles to overturn the legislation.[4] And in one of these cases, *Dobbs v Jackson Women's Health Organisation*,[5] the Supreme Court overturned *Roe* and *Casey*. This case centred on a challenge to Mississippi's Gestational Age Act, which prevented abortion after the 15th week of pregnancy. Rather than striking down the legislation as it had previously done, the court found that 'the constitution does not confer a right to abortion', which saw a cascade of restrictive legislation being passed in many US states.[6]

Despite the perception that abortion is widely accessible in England and Wales under the Abortion Act 1967, it remains a criminal offence under the Offences Against the Person Act 1861, with the 1967 Act merely providing exemptions under specific conditions. The 1967 Act, whilst it did not legalise

1 M McKeegan, 'The Politics of Abortion: A Historical Perspective' (1993) 3(3) Womens Health Issues 127; A Stensvold, *A History of Pregnancy in Christianity: From Original Sin to Contemporary Abortion Debates* (Taylor Francis 2015); John T Noonan, *The Morality of Abortion: Legal and Historical Perspectives* (Harvard University Press 1970).

2 410 U.S 113 (1973).

3 505 U.S 833 (1991).

4 For example, see *City of Akron v Akron Centre for Reproductive Health* 462 US 416 (1983); *Thornberg v American College of Obstetricians and Gynaecologists* 476 US 747 (1986) *Whole Women's Health v Hellerstedt* 579 US 582 (2016).

5 597 US 215 (2022).

6 For example, see the Texas Heartbeat Act 2021 or Georgia's Living Infants Fairness and Equality (LIFE) Act 2019.

DOI: 10.4324/9781003496823-9

per se, carved out legal exceptions for permissible abortion. In the last decade or so, there has been an unprecedented number of women being investigated and prosecuted for breaches of the Abortion Act 1967. With women's rights advocates[7] and even international forums[8] calling for the decriminalisation of abortion, we seek here examine the role of criminal law in the enforcement of abortion laws in England and Wales.

History of Abortion in the UK

Calls for reform began in the 1930s with the formation of the Abortion Law Reform Association (ALRA), although as a result of the interruption caused by WWII, it was not until the 1950s that debate began in earnest. Whereas later calls for reform were rooted in feminist ideology, initially the rationale was related to public health and social justice.[9] David Steel MP introduced a private members bill in 1965 with the aim of tackling the 'scourge of criminal abortion'.[10]

At the time, the thalidomide scandal was fresh in the minds of the public and members of Parliament, and long before any disability rights movement, the birth of a disabled child was seen as a tragedy for all involved. Legal abortion therefore appeared to be a 'respectable' solution to this public health issue.[11] In addition, population control was seen as a means of addressing poverty, allowing people to restrict the size of their families 'in proportion to their personal resources'.[12]

At the time of these debates in England and Wales, abortion was illegal, and the 1861 Act provided a penalty of up to life imprisonment for an abortion,[13] making no distinction between a third party abortionist or a woman ending her own pregnancy or between different stages of a pregnancy. Nor was there any legislative exception for circumstances where the termination was being

7 For example, see the Royal College of Nursing Position Statement on Decriminalisation of Abortion <www.rcn.org.uk/news-and-events/news/uk-abortion-decriminalisation-031224#:~:text=The%20RCN%20has%20updated%20its,rather%20than%20a%20criminal%20issue> accessed 7 February 2025; Doctors for Choice, 'The Campaign to Decriminalise Abortion' <https://doctorsforchoiceuk.com/the-campaign-for-decriminalisation> accessed 7 February 2025.

8 Human Rights Committee, General Comment 36 (2018) on Article 6 of the International Covenant on Civil and Political Rights, on the right to life, para. 8; Working Group on the issue of discrimination against women in law and in practice, A/HRC/38/46 (2018), para. 35; The Committee on Economic Social and Cultural Rights General Comment 22 (2016), para. 34.

9 K Hindell and M Simms, *Abortion Law Reformed* (Peter Owen Publishers 1971) 136.

10 Hansard, House of Commons, Administration (vol 885, 7 February 1975) <https://hansard.parliament.uk/Commons/1975-02-03/debates/b024c65f-6ab5-418f-a7d8-af883dcbebbe/HouseOfCommons(Administration)> accessed October 2024.

11 Lesley J Reagan, *Dangerous Pregnancies: Mothers, Disabilities and Abortion in Modern America* (University of California Press 2010) 104.

12 Alice Jenkins, *Law for the Rich* (V Gollancz 1960) 82.

13 Ss 58 and 59.

carried out as a result of a risk to the life or health of the mother. This final omission resulted in the common law being tasked with carving out certain exceptions, such as in the case of *R v Bourne*.[14]

In this case, a gynaecologist was charged under the provisions of the 1861 Act when he performed an abortion on a 14-year-old girl who became pregnant as a result of gang rape by five soldiers. This landmark case provided an exception to the Act, with the court stating that

> if the doctor is of the opinion, on reasonable grounds and with adequate knowledge, that the probably consequence of the continuance of the pregnancy will be to make the woman a physical or mental wreck, the jury are entitled to take the view that the doctor is operating for the purpose of preserving the life of the mother.

This exception was welcomed for allowing doctors to perform a legal termination to save the mother's life, but it had the effect of creating a two-tier system. Women who could afford the fees were able to have abortions under this exception, while those who could not were left at the mercy of back street abortionists, and it was generally these women and the medically unqualified abortionists who faced prosecution.[15] It is impossible to know how many illegal abortions were carried out[16] or how many women died or were permanently injured as a result of abortions gone wrong.[17]

Steel's Medical Termination of Pregnancy Bill 1966 was drafted by Professor Glanville Williams, one of the country's most eminent scholars of the criminal law. While Williams himself believed that abortion should be available on request without restriction, the consensus within the ALRA was that this would be seen as too much of a departure from the existing law, particularly given the influence of religion on the debate.[18] As such, Williams drafted a bill that made abortion available under strict medical control and for specific reasons. When introducing the bill to Parliament, Steel emphasised that he was not advocating for 'abortion on request' but instead aimed to eliminate back street abortions and move abortion care into the hands of the medical profession.

14 [1938] 3 All ER 615.

15 BM Dickens, *Abortion and the Law* (MacGibbon and Kee 1966); Paul Ferris, *The Nameless: Abortion in Britain Today* (Hutchinson, 1966) Chapter 3.

16 Estimates vary from 10,000 to 250,000 per annum. See A Cartwright and S Lucas, *Report of the Committee on the Working of the Abortion Act* (Lane Report) (vol 1, 1974) 506.

17 Official figures state approximately 40 per year, but for a variety of reasons, many have suggested that that number is much higher. See G Williams, *The Sanctity of Life and the Criminal Law* (Cambridge University Press 1957) 194.

18 S Sheldon, G Davis, J O'Neill, and C Parker, *The Abortion Act 1967: A Biography of a UK Law* (Cambridge University Press 2023). Whilst the Catholic Church was absolutely opposed to abortion in all its forms, the Church of England had given indications that it would support abortion in limited circumstances, and this support from one of the dominant religions would be essential to the political support for the bill.

The primary objections to the bill from Parliamentary debates can be summarised into four categories. Firstly, members argued that the bill threatened the independence of both doctors and nurses as it provided no avenue for them to refuse to perform, or be involved in the care of a woman undergoing, an abortion on the grounds of conscientious objection. Secondly, the fact that the bill allowed for an abortion where the foetus was suffering from an abnormality could have resulted in the destruction of healthy foetuses given that screening at that stage was not necessarily accurate. Third, the argument that has remained a core of the debate since was that it undermined the sanctity of life. Finally, the most debated and controversial aspect of the bill was that it sought to permit abortions on grounds other than medical reasons. One MP, Jill Knight, argued that the social grounds in the bill were 'so wide and so loose that any woman who felt that her coming baby would be an inconvenience would be able to get rid of it'.[19] While these arguments did not defeat the bill, they did result in several amendments being incorporated prior to passing.[20]

The 1967 Act

The Abortion Act 1967, despite being hailed as 'one of the finest, most humane and far sighted pieces of legislation in the twentieth century',[21] did not repeal the existing 1861 prohibition but rather carved out exceptions as to when and where an abortion would be lawful. As such, the act places 'remarkable authority' in the medical profession.[22]

The consensus that this legislation was overly liberal was supported by the fact that many women from outside of England and Wales travelled to obtain abortions, with the most coming from Ireland, where the Eighth Amendment to the Irish Constitution conferred the unborn with a constitutional right to life on par with that of the mother.[23] The first case in which the Supreme Court of Ireland considered the parameters of this protection came in *AG v X*, more commonly known as the 'X Case'.[24] The case involved a 14-year-old girl pregnant as a result of statutory rape. Her parents wanted to take her to England to undergo a termination, and the Director of Public Prosecutions

19 Hansard, *House of Commons, Medical Termination of Pregnancy Bill, Second Reading* (vol 372, 22 July 1966) <https://api.parliament.uk/historic-hansard/commons/1966/jul/22/medical-termination-of-pregnancy-bill> accessed October 2024.

20 For a full analysis of the debates and amendments which followed, see S Sheldon, G Davis, J O'Neill, and C Parker, *The Abortion Act 1967: A Biography of a UK Law* (Cambridge University Press 2023) 10–13.

21 Editorial 'Let the Act Act' (13 February 1970) Medical News Tribune 14.

22 Jackson, *Regulating Reproduction, Law, Technology and Reproduction* (Hart Publishing 2001) 71.

23 Article 40.3.3

24 [1992] 1 IR 1.

sought to prevent this on the grounds that the unborn had a constitutional right to life which the state was obliged to protect. Evidence was adduced in court that the girl was severely traumatised by her experience and that if she were forced to continue with the pregnancy, there was a real risk that she would end her own life. In coming to its conclusion, the Supreme Court found that the constitutional provision required the court to balance two competing rights to life and that where there was a real and substantial risk to the life of the mother, her right to life outweighed the right to life of the unborn.[25]

In the wake of this case, rather than addressing the issue directly, a further referendum was held which inserted the 13th Amendment into the Constitution in 1992. This amendment made it clear that the 8th Amendment would not restrict the freedom to travel, essentially exporting the Irish Abortion issue to England. It was estimated that during the 1990s approximately 6000 women per year travelled to England to obtain an abortion.[26] This is a trend that continued until the 8th Amendment was repealed in 2018 and the resulting legislative provisions are considered below.

Despite the fact that this situation gave the outward appearance of being a very liberal abortion regime, the 1967 Abortion Act is actually rather stringent in its requirements. Section 1 of the Act requires that two medical professionals declare in good faith that one of the following conditions has been met:

a. That the pregnancy has not exceeded its twenty fourth week[27] and that the continuance of the pregnancy would involve risk, greater than if the pregnancy were terminated, of injury to the physical or mental health of the pregnant woman or any existing children of her family; or
b. That the termination is necessary to prevent grave permanent injury to the physical or mental health of the pregnant woman; or
c. That the continuance of the pregnancy would involve risk to the life of the pregnant woman, greater than if the pregnancy were terminated; or
d. There is a substantial risk that if the child were born it would suffer from such physical or mental abnormalities as to be seriously handicapped.

It is only the first clause here that prescribes a specific gestational period. Where there is a substantial risk that the pregnant woman will suffer a grave and permanent injury, where there is a risk to her life, or where there is a serious foetal abnormality, no gestational limit applies.

25 For further analysis of this case, see A Smyth, 'The X Case: Women and Abortion in the Republic of Ireland, 1992' (1993) 1 *Feminist Legal Studies* 163; C Quinlan, 'Policing Women's Bodies in an Illiberal Society: The Case of Ireland' (2017) 27(1) *Women and Criminal Justice* 51.

26 Doug Payne, 'Record Numbers of Irish Women visit Britain for Abortion' (1999) 319 *British Medical Journal* 592.

27 Initially, the legislation stated that the time limit for Clause A was 28 weeks, but this was reduced to 24 weeks by the Human Fertilisation and Embryology Act 1990.

The vast majority of abortions in the UK are carried out under Clause A. In 2022, 98% of all abortions (247,440) were performed on the grounds that continuation of the pregnancy would pose a risk to the physical or mental health of the pregnant woman. Less than 0.7% of pregnancies were terminated after the 24-week period.[28] The figures give the illusion that abortions under the gestational limit are available on demand, but the procedure is entirely medicalised and not based on a woman's right to choose, although there have been considerable calls for this to change; the British Medical Association in particular stated that abortions under 13 weeks should be carried out at the woman's request and without the requirement for two doctor's signatures.[29] Not only can this cause delays in accessing treatment, it is an outdated requirement. At the time the legislation was enacted, surgical abortion was the only type of abortion available, making it a legitimate inclusion. However, since then, the vast majority are abortions[30] that can be carried out safely at home.[31]

While the grounds set down in the legislation may seem wide, and further that the application of them is generously interpreted by the medical professionals based on the number of abortions performed annually, one significant and critical fact remains: that the procedure when carried out beyond the scope of the legislation is still a criminal offence; ss 58 and 59 leave a potential sentence of life imprisonment for women who terminate outside of the scope of the legislation. Not only does this impact women in terms of gestation and proving a grounds for termination, but also the 1967 Act states that the abortion must be carried out at a hospital.[32] There have been changes to this in recent years which are considered in the next section.

Covid-19 Amendments

Since the increase in medical abortions in very early stages of pregnancy, there have been calls to deregulate and amend the Abortion Act to make specific provision for this. Both the National Institute for Health Research[33] and the

28 Abortion Statistics for England and Wales 2022 <www.gov.uk/government/statistics/abortion-statistics-for-england-and-wales-2022/abortion-statistics-england-and-wales-2022> accessed 19 November 24.

29 British Medical Association, *The Law and Ethics of Abortion: BMA Views* <www.bma.org.uk/media/3307/bma-view-on-the-law-and-ethics-of-abortion-sept-2020.pdf> accessed 19 November 24.

30 In 2022, 86% of all abortions were medical abortion. See Abortion Statistics for England and Wales 2022 <www.gov.uk/government/statistics/abortion-statistics-for-england-and-wales-2022/abortion-statistics-england-and-wales-2022> accessed 19 November 24.

31 BPAS Guide to Early Abortion <www.bpas.org/abortion-care/abortion-treatments/the-abortion-pill/remote-treatment/> accessed February 2025.

32 Section 1(3).

33 P Baraister et al., 'Improving Experience of Medical Abortion at Home in a Changing Therapeutic, Technological and Regulatory Landscape: A Realistic Review' (2022) 12(11) *British Medical Journal* 1.

Medical Research Council have called for deregulation of early medical abortion, pointing out its safety and efficacy.[34]

A medical abortion involves taking two tablets at separate times. Mifepristone ends the pregnancy, and misoprostol, taken one to two days later, expels the foetus. This once necessitated two separate trips to a recognised provider which often caused hardship for women requiring childcare, time off work, etc. In addition, for those needing to travel some distance, there were reports of excessive bleeding on public transport following the administration of the second medication, causing embarrassment and upset.[35] In 2018, the law was somewhat relaxed: The government recognised a woman's address (provided that it was in England or Wales) as a 'class of place' to take the second medication.[36] This meant that for medical abortions, only one journey was required and the second tablet could be taken at home.

During the Covid-19 pandemic and subsequent lockdowns, the Government of England and Wales was required to revisit the provisions for early medical abortions. While it was permissible for people to leave their homes for medical reasons, it was preferrable that as many as possible stayed at home. The Abortion Act was temporarily amended to allow women under 10 weeks pregnant to receive both doses of medication at home rather than attending a clinic.[37] This measure was intended to be temporary but was made permanent in August 2022.[38]

However, it must be borne in mind that these amendments are merely that and that it is still a criminal offence to end a pregnancy outside of the terms of the legislation. Concerns were raised during the debates over these amendments as to how women could fall foul of the legislation. For example, at a clinic, a scan is performed to date the gestation, but under the new regulations, women were taken at their word, and it was argued that they could lie or that even in good faith, a woman could believe she was earlier in her pregnancy based on her last period, even though that method of dating gestation can be notoriously unreliable.[39]

Why Do We Punish?

Before we examine the criminal law specifically in relation to abortion, it is worth setting out some generalities. In England and Wales, persons convicted

34 See J Lord, 'Triumphs and Trials with UK Abortion Law: The Power of Collaboration in Abortion Reform' (2024) (164) 1 *International Journal of Gynaecology and Obstetrics* 5.

35 K Levine and ST Cameron, 'Women's Preference for Method of Abortion and Management of Miscarriage' (2009) 35(4) *Journal of Family Planning and Reproductive Healthcare* 233.

36 J Parsons, '2017–19 Governmental Decisions to Allow Home Use of Misoprostol for Early Medical Abortions in the UK' (2020) 124(7) *Health Policy* 679.

37 Coronavirus Act 2020.

38 Abortion (Amendment) Regulations 2022.

39 D Schonberg, L-F Wang, AH Bennett, M Gold, and E Jackson, 'The Accuracy of Using Last Menstrual Period to Determine Gestational Age for First Trimester Medication Abortion: A Systematic Review' (2014) 90(5) *Contraception* 480.

of criminal offences are sentenced under the Sentencing Act 2020. Section 57(2) highlights that the court, when sentencing offenders, must have regard to the following purposes of sentencing:

(a) the punishment of offenders,
(b) the reduction of crime (including its reduction by deterrence)
(c) the reform and rehabilitation of offenders
(d) the protection of the public, and
(e) the making of reparation by offenders to persons affected by their offences.

There is an exception to these purposes. If the court need to pass a mandatory minimum sentence, there is no need to have any regard to the purpose outlined in S. 57(2).[40]

It is essential to provide a well-founded justification for imposing a punishment on an offender; imprisoning an offender carries significant implications that extend beyond the immediate act of confinement. Firstly, the conditions within prisons are often suboptimal, characterised by overcrowding, discomfort, and potential dangers that can contribute to or exacerbate mental health issues among inmates. Moreover, the adverse effects of imprisonment are not limited to the incarcerated individual alone but can extend to their family members. For instance, the loss of a primary income provider can create financial hardship, children of incarcerated individuals may experience social stigma or bullying at school, and these cumulative effects could ultimately erode public trust in the criminal justice system. Moreover, a sentence that is not well-founded allow the wider public to question the legitimacy and performance of the courts; for instance, currently, 64% of the public believes sentences are too lenient, and only 22% believe sentences are 'about right'.[41]

As such, it is crucial that the courts hand down the appropriate punishment for the offence that has been committed. It is imperative that punishments appear proportionate, allowing the courts to achieve at least one of the five Section 57(2) purposes of sentencing.[42] To achieve proportionality, each sentence should fit into at least one of a few accepted justifications.

40 S.57(3) Sentencing Act 2020.

41 Sentencing Council, Public *Knowledge of and Confidence in the Criminal Justice System and Sentencing: 2022 Research* (2022) 22 <www.sentencingcouncil.org.uk/wp-content/uploads/2022-12-12-P019988-Sentencing-Council_Perceptions_Report_v14_FINAL.pdf> accessed January 2025.

42 For more on the importance of proportionality and sentencing, see S Easton and C Piper, *Sentencing and Punishment: The Quest for Justice* (4th edn, OUP 2016). In Chapter 3, examine how seriousness and proportionality are central to the 'just desserts' approach to sentencing that was endorsed by the Criminal Justice Act 1991. Easton and Piper analyse how the sentence should correspond to the seriousness of the offense, ensuring that the punishment is commensurate with the crime committed.

Retribution

The core principle of judicial punishment is to intentionally inflict suffering on an offender because of his or her illegal behavior. This theory is retrospective in nature, focusing on penalising misconduct that has already taken place. Some argue that this perspective is archaic and driven by an instinct for vengeance. To counteract this impulse for retribution, it is crucial to ensure that any penalty imposed is fair and proportionate to the severity of the offense committed.[43]

Prevention

The primary objective of punishment under this theory is to prevent the recurrence of criminal behaviour, either by reforming the offender or by physically removing them from society. However, an even greater priority is the broader – and forward-thinking – deterrent effect: curbing crime by deterring individuals from offending, restricting their ability to reoffend through imprisonment, or focusing on their rehabilitation to reduce future criminal tendencies.[44]

Denunciation

Punishment under the denunciation framework is justified less by its deterrent effect and more by its role in publicly condemning criminal behaviour. The fundamental purpose is to communicate to society that certain actions are unacceptable. The public's response, often reflected in media discourse and societal reactions, illustrates collective disapproval of the offense. This theory incorporates aspects of retribution by expressing societal condemnation and elements of prevention by warning others that such conduct will not be tolerated. At its core, denunciation seeks to shame the offender and reinforce societal norms by reinforcing the moral boundaries of acceptable behaviour.[45]

Reparation

The reparation view focusses on rectifying the harm caused by criminal acts and fostering the reintegration of offenders into the community. Rather than

43 For a more in-depth analysis of these theories, see A von Hirsch, *Doing Justice: The Choice of Punishments* (North Eastern University Press 1976); MS Moore, *Placing Blame: A Theory of the Criminal Law* (Oxford University Press 1997).

44 For more, see C Beccaria, *On Crimes and Punishments* (Hackett Publishing Company 1986) and J Bentham, *An Introduction to the Principles of Morals and Legislation* (Hafner Press Reprinted 1948).

45 For more, see A du Bois-Pedain, *Transitional Amnesty in South Africa* (Cambridge University Press 2007); RA Duff, *Punishment, Communication, and Community* (Oxford University Press 2001).

emphasising punitive measures, it prioritises making amends and repairing the damage done. The goal is to encourage offenders to take responsibility for their actions and contribute to restoring the balance they have disrupted. In this sense, reparation can be seen as less of a traditional punishment and more of a constructive resolution aimed at both offender rehabilitation and societal healing.[46] In 1954, Andrew Flew put forward five essential criteria that any form of punishment must adhere to: create human suffering; arise as a direct consequence of the offence; be directed at the person who committed the offence; (d) be an intentional creation; and be inflicted by an authorised body[47]

From Flew's perspective, the punishment must make the offender suffer and this suffering must result from the consequence of their criminal offending, fitting with a retribution perspective. The punishment must be aimed at offenders, and the suffering must be intentional; it suffering cannot be an indirect consequence of the crime, and the offender cannot in turn escape criminal sanction because he or she 'has been punished enough'. Finally, the punishment must be meted out by the courts or the police through out-of-court disposal, rejecting vigilante justice.

The Criminalisation of Abortion

One of the most compelling arguments against the urgency of reforming the Abortion Act 1967 was that despite the severity of the potential criminal sanctions, these were never truly policed or enforced, which appears to be borne out in the fact that only three women were convicted of obtaining an illegal abortion between 1861 and 2022.[48]

These are reminiscent of arguments made in the case of *Norris v Ireland* in the European Court of Human Rights involving the criminalisation of homosexual acts.[49] Despite the fact that Mr Norris had never been prosecuted, the *fear* of potential prosecution was sufficient in the eyes of the court to ground a breach of his Article 8 rights. It is this fear that currently hangs over women in England and Wales under the current abortion regime, and it would appear rightly so.[50] Since 2012, investigations and prosecutions have significantly

46 For more, see J Braithwaite, *Crime, Shame and Reintegration* (Cambridge University Press 1989); H Zehr, *Changing Lenses: A New Focus for Crime and Justice* (Herald Press 1990).

47 A Flew, 'The Justification of Punishment' in HB Acton (ed) *The Philosophy of Punishment* (MacMillan 1954).

48 Statistics from the British Pregnancy Advisory Service (BPAS) reported by Maya Oppenheim in 'UK Faces Sharp Rise in Abortion Convictions' (*Independent*, 28 February 2024).

49 13 EUR HR Rep 186 (1988).

50 Statistics show significant increases in cases, with 18 recorded to date in 2023–24 compared with 3 in 2011–12. See <www.statista.com/statistics/303540/procuring-illegal-abortion-in-england-and-wales-uk/> accessed 4 December 2024.

ramped up, with a reported 67 women facing prosecution.[51] Arguably, the investigations ramped up following the case of *R v Catt*.[52] The case involved a woman who ordered abortion medication online and self administered this at home when she was 38 weeks pregnant. She gave birth to a stillborn male child and buried him in an undisclosed location. Mrs Catt was sentenced to eight years in prison which was reduced on appeal to three and a half years. Many of the subsequent prosecutions are not public, with only written judgments, but are reported by journalists.

For example, in 2022, the story of Laura* was reported in the *Sunday Times*.[53] Her abusive boyfriend had purchased abortion pills and coerced her into taking them. Following the pregnancy loss, the police appeared by her bedside and she was taken for questioning. She was sentenced to two years in prison and stated that 'the prosecution said that if I didn't plead guilty, I would likely go to prison for life. I felt like I had no other choice'. In 2022, a 25-year-old woman went into early labour at 31 weeks, and during a C-section, doctors discovered two tablets they believed to be abortifacients. An investigation was launched, and the unnamed woman was charged. Several months after the charge, her barrister petitioned the court to have her bail varied so that she could visit her family in Portugal. The judge at the time said he was 'flabbergasted' that the woman was being prosecuted, adding 'This case in my judgment beggars belief. There can be no conceivable public interest in pursuing it'.[54] Five months later, the CPS dropped the case. The baby survived and continues to live with his mother.

In 2020, Bethany Cox was charged with two offences: On 06/07/2020 at Stockton, with intent to destroy the life of a child capable of being born alive, by a wilful act, namely administering drugs to procure abortion, contrary to Section 58 of the 1861 Act, and thereby causing the child to die before it had an existence independent of its mother. The second charge read: "Between 02/07/2020 and 07/07/2020 at Stockton, being a woman with child, unlawfully administered to yourself a poison or other noxious thing, with intent to procure your own miscarriage." It was not until January 2024 that the case was disposed of when the prosecution failed to offer any evidence and Ms Cox was formally acquitted of all charges.[55]

51 Hansard, Abortion: Offences Against the Person Act (vol 734, debated 15 June 2023) <https://hansard.parliament.uk/commons/2023-06-15/debates/E4D63B08-4128-46D3-AFCD-EF8D377275EC/AbortionOffencesAgainstThePersonAct> accessed February 2025.

52 [2013] EWCA Crim 1187.

53 Cited in O Petter, 'Why Are Women being Arrested for Having Abortions in the UK' *The Independent* (10 August 2022).

54 T Seaward, 'CPS Drops Prosecution of Oxford Mum Accused of Procuring Miscarriage' *Oxford Mail* (9 December 2022).

55 M Brown, 'Teeside Woman Cleared Over Lockdown Abortion Charges after CPS Offers No Evidence' *The Guardian* (9 January 2024).

The most infamous case in recent years is that of Carla Foster. In this case, Ms Foster acted outside the scope of the permitted legislation and ultimately obtained medication via an online service by giving false information. Internet searches and other evidence showed that Ms Foster was aware at the time that her pregnancy was more advanced, and a post mortem on the body showed that the pregnancy was at 32–34 weeks gestation. With no sentencing guidelines for this specific offence, J Pepperall compared it with the previously mentioned case of *R v Catt* and found that the appropriate sentence in this case was three years, reduced to 28 months for an early guilty plea.[56] On appeal, this sentence was reduced to 14 months suspended with the court stating that it was a case which 'called for compassion, not punishment'.[57]

Even where a prosecution is not mounted, the fact that an investigation begins is a traumatic event which can have significant consequences for those involved. For example, in 2021, an investigation was launched into a 15-year-old girl following a stillbirth which was only dropped once the coroner concluded that the pregnancy ended due to natural causes.[58] In February 2024 it was reported by the BBC Katie (a pseudonym) believed she was seven weeks pregnant when she took abortion pills at home. Once she delivered the foetus, it was clear that the pregnancy had advanced beyond 24 weeks. Katie was admitted to hospital, where the medical staff called the police. She was arrested and remains on bail while the investigation is ongoing.[59] Police forces in Southampton, Bournemouth, and Portsmouth have contacted BPAS to request lists of all women who have been denied access to abortion for being over the 24-week time limit.[60]

These stories may well represent the tip of the iceberg, and while in cases such as *Catt* and *Foster*, where an abortion was deliberately undertaken in full knowledge that it was outside of the legislation, they are very much in the minority. Women who have suffered the trauma of a miscarriage or stillbirth are being placed under police investigation and facing possible prison sentences when they are struggling physically and psychologically to come to terms with the loss of a pregnancy. Further, even when we have the very few clear cases of an abortion being carried out beyond the scope of the time limit, the question must be asked as to what is the appropriate sanction, and why it

56 *R v Foster*, 12 June 2023, Sentencing Remarks of the Hon Mr Justice Pepperall <www.judiciary.uk/wp-content/uploads/2023/06/R-v.-Foster-sentencing-remarks-12.6.23.pdf> accessed 4 December 2024.

57 [2023] EWCA Crim 1196 [49].

58 S Das, 'Women Accused of Illegal Abortions in England and Wales after Miscarriages and Stillbirths' *The Guardian* (2 July 2022).

59 E Layhe, A Meisel and D Talwar, *More Women Investigated for Illegal Terminations, Says Abortion Provider* (9 February 2024) <www.bbc.co.uk/news/uk-68305991> accessed 4 December 2024.

60 Z Williams, 'The Women Being Prosecuted in Great Britain for Abortions' *The Guardian* (10 November 2023).

appears that England and Wales are on a mission to make examples of these women.

As we have discussed, there are a number of reasons why punishment is necessary and important in a criminal justice system. The question that remains is how punishment should apply when people breach abortion law. In the appeal judgement of *Foster v R*, Dame Sharpe concluded that 'rehabilitation had already been achieved. Ms Foster presented no risk to her family or the wider public, and there was no prospect of a repetition of this offence'.[61] The court further noted that 'no useful purpose was served by detaining Ms Foster in custody'.[62]

We can conclude then that retribution is the only legitimate reason for imposing a custodial sentence on women in these circumstances is one of retribution, fulfilling Flew's criteria.

A Return to Liberalism

International law has grown consistent in its calls to reduce regulation around abortion and has found in many areas that restrictive abortion laws can amount to inhumane and degrading treatment in contravention of many of the international human rights treaties.[63] More recently, an arguable consensus has been reached that criminal sanctions jeopardise the life and health of abortion seekers,[64] are discriminatory,[65] and violate human rights protections.[66] Consequently, more and more international institutions are calling for the decriminalisation of abortion in all circumstances.[67] The ire of international committees with regards to the law in the UK had primarily been focused on the situation in Northern Ireland, where the provisions of the 1967 Act did not extend. However, this was superceded by the Northern Ireland (Executive Formation etc) Act 2019, which repealed ss 58 and 59 of the 1861 Act and placed a moratorium on all abortion-related criminal proceedings.

61 [2023] EWCA Crim 1196 [50].

62 [2023] EWCA Crim 1196 [49].

63 For further, see C-M Smyth, 'Restrictive Abortion Laws as Torture in International Law' (2016) 34(9) *Irish Law Times* 127.

64 For example, CEDAW Committee, 'General Recommendation No 24, Article 12 of the Convention' (UN Doc. A/54/38/Rev.1) Chapter 1 (1999).

65 Human Rights Council, *UN Special Rapporteur on Torture and Other Cruel, Inhuman or Degrading Treatment or Punishment, Report of the Special Rapporteur on Torture and Other Cruel, Inhuman or Degrading Treatment or Punishment* (UN Doc. A/HRC/22/53) (2013).

66 Human Rights Committee, *General Comment No. 36 on Article 6 of the International Covenant on Civil and Political Rights, on the Right to Life* (UN Doc. CCPR/C/GC/36) (2018).

67 CEDAW Committee, *Report of the Inquiry Concerning the United Kingdom of Great Britain and Northern Ireland under Article 8 of the Optional Protocol to the Convention on the Elimination of All Forms of Discrimination against Women* (UN Doc. CEDAW/C/OP.8/GBR/1) (2018).

Earlier in this chapter, we examined how Ireland previously had extreme abortion restrictions and effectively exported the issue to England, with Irish women travelling to obtain terminations. In 2018, a referendum was held which removed the Eighth Amendment from the Constitution, and The Health (Regulation of Termination of Pregnancy) Act 2018 was enacted and came into force on 1 January 2019. Under this legislation, a woman may terminate her pregnancy on request without providing an explanation up to 12 weeks gestation; however, there is a mandatory three-day waiting period from the initial consultation to the administration of the abortion medication.[68] Outside of this, the legislation contains provisions that allow terminating a pregnancy prior to viability where there is a risk to the health or the life of the mother[69] or, in emergencies, at any stage of the pregnancy.[70] Pregnancies can also be terminated when the foetus is suffering from a fatal abnormality.[71]

The criminal law does still have a role to play in this new legislation. While the law removes any criminality from the pregnant woman, a provider can face up to 14 years in prison for performing an abortion outside of the scope of the legislation.[72] Thus, abortion providers are very careful in how they are operating. The Master of the Rotunda Hospital in Dublin, Dr Malone, spoke of the need to make sure that they erred on the side of caution in terms of the gestation date stating that 'given that there is a 14 year jail sentence for getting this wrong, I can't put my staff in danger where there is ambiguity'.[73] Whilst the legislation is not without its pitfalls, the removal of criminal liability for pregnant women who act outside its scope is most certainly a welcomed step.[74] And beyond Northern Ireland and the Republic of Ireland, there is a movement in Europe to enshrine a constitutional right to abortion. Most recently, France voted to include this freedom in its constitution, and Article 55 of the Slovenian Constitution gives the freedom to decide whether or not to bear children.

Conclusion

It is evident that criminal sanctions for women who terminate their pregnancies beyond the scope of the Abortion Act 1967 are imposed purely on the grounds of retribution for an act that to some is abhorrent. The continued

68 Section 12.
69 Section 9.
70 Section 10.
71 Section 11.
72 Section 23.
73 J Bray, 'Abortion in Ireland: Four Weeks in, How's It Working?' *The Irish Times* (26 January 2019).
74 A Carnegie and R Roth, 'From Grassroots to the Oireachtas: Abortion Law Reform in the Republic of Ireland' (2019) 21(2) *Health and Human Rights Journal* 109; F de Londras and M Enright, *Repealing the Eighth: Reforming Irish Abortion Law* (Policy Press 2018).

criminalisation of abortion in England and Wales is an outdated and punitive approach that disproportionately targets vulnerable women, often at their most desperate and precarious moments. The evidence overwhelmingly suggests that criminal prosecutions serve no legitimate public safety purpose; they do not act as a deterrent, nor do they protect women or society. Instead, they reinforce stigma, undermine reproductive autonomy, and deter women from seeking medical assistance when they need it most. The increased scrutiny of women's reproductive choices, coupled with the chilling effect of potential prosecution, demonstrates a regressive shift in policy that contradicts international human rights standards and the broader movement towards liberalisation seen in other jurisdictions.

The trend towards conservatism and punitive measures promulgates the stigma associated with abortion and has removed bodily autonomy from women, who must jump through endless medical hoops to make decisions about their own bodies. If the objective of abortion law is to safeguard health and well-being, then a punitive framework is fundamentally misplaced. The experiences of Northern Ireland, the Republic of Ireland, and several European nations demonstrate that decriminalisation coupled with accessible healthcare provisions creates a more just and effective system. Rather than punishing women, the legal system should focus on addressing the structural and societal factors that lead them to seek out and self-administer medical abortions in the first place. True progress lies not in criminalisation but in the recognition that reproductive healthcare is a fundamental right, one that must be protected and not penalised. It is time to abandon punitive measures and embrace a legal framework that prioritises compassion, autonomy, and public health over retribution, deterrence, and denunciation.

10 Misogyny, Misconceptions, and Restorative Justice

Lisa Mary Armstrong

Introduction

In 2021, a series of high-profile murders of women in public spaces prompted then Home Secretary Priti Patel to commission an independent inquiry. The inquiry, led by Dame Elish Angiolini, was tasked with investigating the facts and circumstances which enabled serving police officer Wayne Couzens to kidnap, rape, and murder Sarah Everard.[1] Not only did the investigation uncover serious failures in the police vetting process, it also found that institutionalised sexism and misogyny was widespread in the Metropolitan police force. Part 1 of the report made a total of 16 general recommendations including introducing a specific policy for investigating sexual offences including indecent exposure[2] and providing additional guidance and training on the issue for police officers.[3]

The scope of the Angiolini inquiry was later extended to investigate another serving Met police officer, David Carrick, who had been convicted in February 2023 of 49 offences including rape. Angiolini stressed that sexual crimes are borne out of sexism and misogyny as it allows a culture to exist in which the abuse of women and girls is accepted and even normalised.[4]

The brutal murder of schoolteacher Sabina Nessa revealed how male violence against women and girls (MVAWG) is often minimised, trivialised, or worse, ignored when it concerns women of colour.[5] The jailing of two Metropolitan police officers for sharing photographs of murdered sisters Bibaa Henry and Nicole Smallman on WhatsApp evidenced that institutional misogyny was alive and well and running rampant in the Metropolitan police

1 E Angiolini, *The Angiolini Inquiry: Part 1 Report, HC 530* (The Stationery Office 2024).
2 Ibid.
3 Ibid 129.
4 Ibid vii.
5 H Ali, 'Why Has Sabina Nessa's Murder Not Dominated the News? Take a Wild Guess' *The Independent* (London, 22 September 2021) <www.independent.co.uk/voices/sabina-nessa-murder-media-reporting-b1924887.html> accessed 10 October 2024.

DOI: 10.4324/9781003496823-10

force.[6] These cases illustrate how gender can intersect with other characteristics such as race and class. Patricia Collins-Hill, Bell Hooks, Kimberley Crenshaw, and many others have been instrumental in bringing intersectional feminism to the fore.[7] Intersectionality takes account of the different ways women might experience discrimination and considers how multiple identities overlap and lead to discrimination on many grounds (race, gender, sexual orientation, disability, etc.).[8]

Victims often voice that they play little part in an adversarial system which prioritises winning over promoting justice and where the legal process retraumatises those that dare to come forward.[9] The courts have been repeatedly criticised for giving suspended and unduly lenient sentences to men who have committed violent crimes against women.[10] Such decisions have led to the erosion of trust in the judiciary, police, and politicians and have forced women and women's rights organisations to mobilise and demand a zero-tolerance approach to the epidemic of MVAWG. The Femicide Census reported that in the UK, approximately 78 (53%) women were killed by men.[11] Rather than address the root cause of the problem, women are instead told to modify their behaviour or limits are put on their free movement (Liz Kelly refers to this as 'safety work').[12] Duggan and Mason-Bish write that 'crime control, personal safety and violence has always been conceptualised as a woman's responsibility'.[13]

6 V Dodd, 'Two Met Officers Jailed Over Photos of Murdered Sisters' *The Guardian* (London, 6 December 2022) <www.theguardian.com/uk-news/2021/dec/06/two-met-police-officers-jailed-photos-murdered-sisters-deniz-jaffer-jamie-lewis-nicole-smallman-bibaa-henry> accessed 15 May 2024.

7 R Cseby, *Understanding Intersectional Feminism: Origins, Modern Activism and Critiques* (Global Human Rights Defence, 2022) <www.ghrd.org/wp-content/uploads/2024/03/Understanding-Intersectional-Feminism-August-2023.pdf> accessed 11 October 2024.

8 K Crenshaw, 'Mapping the Margins: Intersectionality, Identity Politics and Violence Against Women of Colour' (1991) 43(6) *Stanford Law Review* 1241.

9 JL Herman, 'The Mental Health of Crime Victims: Impact of Legal Intervention' (2003) 16 *Journal of Traumatic Stress* 159.

10 D Raleigh, 'Serving Soldier Who Beat Woman Unconscious and Boasted about It on Social Media Gets Suspended Sentence' *The Irish Times* (Dublin, 20 June 2024) <www.irishtimes.com/crime-law/courts/2024/06/20/serving-soldier-who-beat-woman-unconscious-and-boasted-about-it-on-social-media-gets-suspended-sentence/#:~:text=He%20said%20he%20had%20to,he%20suspended%20in%20its%20entirety> accessed 25 June 2024.

11 C O'Callaghan and KI Smith, *Femicide Census Report* (Femicide Census, 2021) <www.femicidecensus.org/wp-content/uploads/2024/07/2021-Femicide-Census-Report.pdf> accessed 12 July 2024.

12 FV Gray and L Kelly, 'Contested Gendered Space: Public Sexual Harassment and Women's Safety Work' (2020) 44(4) *International Journal of Comparative and Applied Criminal Justice* 265.

13 M Duggan and H Mason-Bish, 'A Feminist Theoretical Exploration of Misogyny and Hate Crime' in I Zempi and J Smith (eds) *Misogyny as Hate Crime* (2022 Routledge) 33.

This chapter considers how misogyny is currently defined in law and policy before outlining recent developments in misogyny and hate crime laws in England and Wales (E&W). Given the failure of the criminal legal system (CLS) to address the issue of gendered crime, there has been a move towards looking at alternative ways of 'doing justice' including restorative, transitional, and procedural justice and therapeutic jurisprudence. The concluding section explores the application of restorative justice (RJ) to gendered crimes before considering whether it could be used as a justice mechanism in which victims can challenge misogynistic behaviours within criminal justice and other institutional or organisational settings more generally.

Conceptualising Misogyny

Like sexism, misogyny is deeply rooted in our patriarchal society and can be attributed to masculine gender norms.[14] While women and girls generally know 'misogyny' when they see or experience it, feminist criminologists and legal theorists have found it increasingly challenging to come up with a universal definition.[15] Its precise meaning is notoriously difficult to encapsulate because it can manifest as a wide spectrum of behaviours, some of which we outline here and can be prosecuted under existing laws. At present, there is no legal definition of misogyny, and working definitions are wide ranging, but it can include, although is not limited to, behaviours such as objectifying, belittling or seeking to control women, sexual assault, street harassment (wolf whistling and cat calling), threatening, aggressive, intimidating or violent behaviour, bullying, stalking, rape, and taking pictures without consent.[16]

In 2022 the Crown Prosecution Service (CPS) updated its online guidance on prosecuting public order offences including public sexual abuse.[17] Sexual harassment, for example, can be prosecuted under the Public Order Act 1986, the Sexual Offences Act 2003 (SOA 2003), and the Protection from Harassment Act 1997. SOA 2003 provides that non-consensual sexual touching or attempted sexual touching can be prosecuted as a sexual assault. Indecent exposure is also included under Section 66 of SOA 1993, which states that it

14 PJ Fleming, TL Patterson, CV Chavarin, SJ Semple, C Magis-Rodriguez, and EV Pitpitan, 'Are Men's Misogynistic Attitudes Associated with Poor Mental Health and Substance Use Behaviours? An Exploratory Study of Men in Tijuana, Mexico' (2019) 19(2) *Psychology of Men and Masculinities* 314.

15 SM Wrisley, 'Feminist Theory and the Problem of Misogyny' (2021) 24(2) *Feminist Theory* 188.

16 Mayor of London, 'What is misogyny?' (*Gov.UK*, 2024) <www.london.gov.uk/what-misogyny> accessed 3 May 2024.

17 Crown Prosecution Service, 'CPS Sets Out the Law on Street based Sexual Harassment' (Government of the UK, 2022) <www.cps.gov.uk/cps/news/cps-sets-out-law-street-based-sexual-harassment> accessed 12 October 2024.

is an offence 'if a person intentionally exposes their genitals and intends the person seeing them would be caused alarm or distress'.[18]

When it involves words and behaviour rather than physical or attempted physical contact and there is intention to cause 'harassment, alarm or distress to a victim', Section 4A of the Public Order Act 1986 is more appropriate, or Section 5 if the incident involves sexually threatening or abusive words or behaviour that are considered less serious. The Voyeurism (Offences) Act 2019 criminalised 'upskirting', and the Stalking Protection Act 2019 protect against stalking behaviours, all of which come under the scope of misogynistic behaviours. Due to an increase in the use of the so-called 'rough sex defence', part 6 of the Domestic Abuse Act 2021 incorporated the principle that a person cannot consent to serious harm for sexual gratification. It also criminalises threats to share non-consensual sexual images and videos and non-fatal strangulation.

Traditionally, misogyny, derived from the Greek word *misos* ('hatred') and *gunē* ('woman'), has been described as the 'hatred or dislike or prejudice of women'.[19] Whilst there is no question that hatred against women exists, not all misogynistic behaviours can be said to be motivated by hate. Kate Manne, for example, rejects that misogyny is about a specific hatred or hostility of women or is a psychological condition of individual men; instead, she perceives it as an enduring social phenomenon and the enforcement branch of a patriarchal society.[20] While Wrisley agrees that misogyny is a sociocultural event, she frames this around three specific issues: 'that misogyny scholarship tends to conflate misogyny with sexism, it erases the affective or emotional component of misogyny and it is [replaced] by gendered violence'.[21]

Wrisley is highly critical of divorcing misogyny from its affective roots and explains that it is crucial to draw a distinction between sexism and misogyny:

> [whilst] misogyny should be understood as a negative affective or emotional orientation towards women as a group, sexism should be understood as the institutionalised expression of individual misogyny and that they both work together to maintain and reproduce a system of domination in which women are subjugated.[22]

However, McCarthy and Taylor reject Wrisley's framing of Manne's work. Instead, they argue that 'understanding misogyny as an enforcement

18 Crown Prosecution Service, 'Public Order Offences Incorporating the Charging Standard' (*Gov.UK*, 2022) <www.cps.gov.uk/legal-guidance/public-order-offences-incorporating-charging-standard> accessed 11 October 2024.

19 Oxford English Dictionary, *Misogyny* [online] <www.oed.com/> accessed 17 June 2024.

20 K Manne, *Down Girl: The Logic of Misogyny* (Penguin Books Ltd, 2017).

21 SM Wrisley, 'Feminist Theory and the Problem of Misogyny' (2021) 24(2) *Feminist Theory* 189.

22 Ibid 192.

mechanism' does not mean that 'emotions, feelings and affect' are disregarded as 'misogyny is always demonstrably affective'.[23] Manne is asking us instead to conceptualise misogyny from the perspective of its victims rather than the accused because we cannot possibly know the inner or psychological workings behind every man's misogynistic behaviour.[24]

As technology evolves, how misogyny is experienced by women has also changed significantly. The surge in online misogyny during the pandemic and the rise and reach of misogynists like Andrew Tate spawned a different kind of celebrity influencer and culture. The emergence of incel communities, defined as 'a subculture of men who consider themselves to be involuntary celibate and hold attitudes of misogyny and hatred towards women,'[25] prompted a large government survey across the UK and the USA that explored the 'demographics, beliefs, networks and propensity to violence of Incels',[26] citing poor mental health and social skills as some of the likely reasons behind the rise in men engaging in online and offline misogyny.[27]

Misogyny, Hate Crime, and the Law in England and Wales

In 2016, Nottinghamshire police were the first force to identify, record, and investigate misogyny as a hate crime.[28] This policy change was borne out of a hate crime inquiry conducted by Nottingham Citizens in 2014. Initially, only the five protected characteristics (race, religion, sexual orientation, disability, and transgender identity) were considered in the investigation, but women consistently reported that they were being victimised because they were women[29]: For comparison, victimised men did not perceive gender to be a contributory factor, whereas 38% of women did.[30] The investigation also found that women were not inclined to report misogyny, and 28% of women surveyed admitted that if they were a victim of crime, they would not report it to the police.[31]

23 L McCarthy and S Taylor, 'Misogyny and Organization Studies' (2023) 45(3) *Organization Studies* 457.
24 K Manne, *Down Girl: The Logic of Misogyny* (Penguin Books Ltd, 2017).
25 Commission for Countering Extremism, '*Predicting Harm among Incels (Involuntary Celibates)*' (Government of the UK, 2024) 4 <www.gov.uk/government/publications/predicting-harm-among-incels-involuntary-celibates> accessed 14 June 2024.
26 Ibid.
27 Ibid.
28 S Fish, 'Policing Misogyny As a Hate Crime – The Nottinghamshire Police Experience' in I Zempi and J Smith (eds) *Misogyny as Hate Crime* (Routledge 2022).
29 S Legg and Nottingham Citizens, 'No Place for Hate' (2021) 22(8) *Social and Cultural Geography* 1164.
30 S Fish, 'Policing Misogyny As a Hate Crime – The Nottinghamshire Police Experience' in I Zempi and J Smith (eds) *Misogyny as Hate Crime* (Routledge 2022).
31 Ibid 250.

There were some initial objections to the policy on the grounds that it could be interpreted as police overstepping their powers and creating new legislation.[32] A second concern was that engaging in campaigning was not viewed as a police role, yet it was observed that no similar concerns were raised when police engaged in other hate crime campaigns. Sue Fish, the then Chief Constable of Nottinghamshire Police and the driving force behind the policy, acknowledged that institutional sexism and misogyny were likely behind the different responses to hate crime.[33] There was a worry that adopting the policy would divert police time and resources away from other offences perceived to be more serious, such as modern slavery and child sexual exploitation.[34]

However, Fish attributed this to a lack of understanding among police colleagues of the pervasive nature and scale of misogyny, as well as the barriers to women reporting. In fact, the problem was not that this would open the floodgates and overwhelm police resources but rather how to encourage women and girls to come forward and report. We know that women and girls shy away from reporting gendered crimes out of fear that they will not be believed or taken seriously or nothing will be done.[35] A question that has been posed is whether the police are even the right people to be tackling MVAWG outside of their institutional walls given the pervasive culture of misogyny and sexism that exists within?

However, *Miller v College of Policing*[36] turned this policy on its head when the legality of the police recording policy was challenged. Here, it was deemed that perception-based recording was unfair to the accused because it relied on a victim's version of events without any legal scrutiny. It was ruled that the Hate Crime Operational Guidance issued in 2014 by the College of Policing (COP) conflicted with the appellant's right to freedom of expression. Shortly after the judgement, then Home Secretary, Suella Braverman, issued a new statutory code of practice discouraging police forces from recording Non-Crime Hate Incidents (NCHI).[37]

The decision is likely to impact the way future hate crime is recorded by Nottinghamshire Police Constabulary and other police forces that adopted the misogyny hate crime recording policy. The COP authorised professional practice has now been amended to align with the new Code, which stipulates that personal data can only be recorded where there is a genuine risk of

32 Ibid.
33 Ibid 255.
34 Ibid.
35 Ibid.
36 [2021] EWCA Civ 1926.
37 'New Code and Guidance for Non-Hate Crime Incidents' (College of Policing, 2023) <www.college.police.uk/article/new-code-and-guidance-non-crime-hate-incidents> accessed 15 June 2024.

significant harm or of a future criminal offence being committed against individuals or groups with a particular characteristic or characteristics.[38]

In 2018, the government asked the Law Commission to undertake a systematic review of hate crime and hate speech laws and their development, which were criticised as being 'overly complex'.[39] Hate crimes are prosecuted under the Crime and Disorder Act 1998 (CDA 1998), the Criminal Justice Act 2003 (CJA 2003) and in s.66 Sentencing Act 2020 (SA 2020). There is no standalone offence of hate crime, which is a common misconception. The concept of 'hate crime' was introduced in CDA 1998 and only included racial groups. However, this changed when the extended rules were combined in the SA 2020,[40] and now the category include all protected characteristics. An offence is designated a hate crime when it is committed against someone who was targeted because of their protected characteristics, and that designation aggravates the existing offence.[41]

What constitutes a 'hate' crime is generally misunderstood, which stems in part from its overuse by politicians and the public, as are 'the criteria that must be met to enable a successful prosecution'.[42] For example, hate is not mentioned in any of the legislative provisions. Instead, the recipient must demonstrate that the accused was motivated by hostility or demonstrate hostility towards specific protected characteristics.[43]

McGuire argues that for misogyny to constitute a hate crime, it would require significant changes to the hate crime framework.[44] She explains that it would mean criminalising the perpetrator's attitude towards a specific group, as misogyny is a prejudice against women and not an identity. Instead, she recommends making gender a protected characteristic, although she admits that it may be difficult to prove a particular gender bias.[45] She explains that 'the ability to convict based upon *demonstration of hostility* to a protected

38 Ibid.

39 Law Commission, *Hate Crime: Consultation Paper Summary* (2020) <https://lawcom.gov.uk/document/hate-crime-consultation-paper/> accessed 13 June 2024.

40 C Lewis, *Misogyny as a Hate Crime: Is It All That It Seems? South Wales Business Research School* <https://business.research.southwales.ac.uk/law-research/law-research-blog/misogyny-hate-crime-it-all-it-seems/?utm_source=Twitter&utm_medium=social&utm_campaign=Orlo> accessed 15 July 2024.

41 Law Commission, *Hate Crime: Consultation Paper Summary* (2020) <https://lawcom.gov.uk/document/hate-crime-consultation-paper/> accessed 13 June 2024.

42 K McGuire, 'Extending the Concept, or Extending the Characteristics? Misogyny or Gender?' in I Zempi and J Smith (eds) *Misogyny as Hate Crime* (Routledge, 2022) 41.

43 Ibid.

44 Ibid.

45 Dr Kath Murray argues that sex and gender identity aid our understanding of justice inequalities in the criminal legal system. She advises that recording practices based on gender identity could lead to skewed statistics on offending (and victimisation). Instead, she recommends gathering data on both gender and sex independently to deepen our understanding of the ways they work together and individually. See K Murray, 'Data Matters: Recording Sex and Gender Identity in the Criminal Justice System' (Understanding Inequalities, 2024) <www.understanding-inequalities.ac.uk/

characteristic is crucial'[46] and was inserted to avoid the issues experienced in the United States where legislation centred on motivation, which made it difficult to prove. McGuire notes further that this is why adding misogyny to the protected characteristics would be challenging to prosecute as 'a demonstration of hostility ***towards a protected characteristic*** is an aggravating feature of an actual crime and not a crime in itself.'[47]

In addition, there is no legal definition of hostility. One of the main criticisms of its use is that it relies on an objective proof of hostility.[48] However, the CPS provides the following definition for recording and monitoring crime:

> Any criminal offence which is perceived by the victim or any other person, to be motivated by hostility or prejudice, based on a person's disability or perceived disability; race or perceived race; or religion or perceived religion; or sexual orientation or perceived sexual orientation or transgender identity or perceived transgender identity.[49]

To simplify the law in this area, the Commission was tasked with identifying gaps in protection and reviewing the existing protected characteristics. Once the Commission had concluded its review, they decided against including 'sex or gender' as a protected characteristic. The Commission claimed that it might create victim hierarchies and that given the challenges with low attrition and securing prosecutions in cases involving rape, sexual offences, and domestic abuse, it could exacerbate these problems.[50]

The Commission did, however, recommend extending the offence of stirring up hatred to include the grounds sex or gender to crack down on the surge in extremist incel ideology and associated offending.[51] They also recommended a government review which would look at introducing a specific offence to address public sexual harassment, reasoning that it would be more impactful than adding sex or gender to hate crime laws.[52]

Would criminalising misogyny achieve its intended aim, or are there other ways of addressing the misogyny problem? McGuire points out that the law can only take us so far and highlights the need for 'wider publicity' and

---

news-and-blog/data-matters-recording-sex-and-gender-identity-in-the-criminal-justice-system> accessed 12 October 2024.

46 K McGuire, 'Extending the Concept, or Extending the Characteristics? Misogyny or Gender?' in I Zempi and J Smith (eds) *Misogyny as Hate Crime* (Routledge, 2022) 41.

47 Ibid 43.

48 Crown Prosecution Service, 'Hate Crime' (*Gov.UK*, 2022) <www.cps.gov.uk/crime-info/hate-crime> accessed 12 June 2024.

49 Ibid.

50 Law Commission, *Hate Crime Laws: Final Report* (Law Com No 402, 2021) <https://lawcom.gov.uk/document/hate-crime-report/> accessed 20 June 2024.

51 Law Commission, *Hate Crime: Final Report Summary* (2021) 14–15 <https://lawcom.gov.uk/document/hate-crime-report/> accessed 25 June 2024.

52 Ibid 15.

greater education around these issues.[53] In addition to the significant impact misogyny can have on a woman's sense of self and emotional and psychological well-being, research has shown that it can also deeply damaging to men's mental health outcomes.[54] Victim and survivor perceptions of justice are shaped by their trust in the CLS and their experiences of interacting with legal and criminal justice actors in that system. Carol Smart, a feminist legal theorist, has long warned against relying on the law as a panacea for the sexism and misogyny problem.[55] The law has its limits and should be reserved for serious offences.

The second part of this chapter briefly examines the origins of restorative justice (RJ) and the controversy surrounding its use for gendered harms. While RJ is not a universal cure for the misogyny problem, it is suggested that there is a place for it. However, access to quality training, the referral process and funding are key challenges to expanding RJ in this area.[56]

Restorative Justice and Gender-Based Harms

The inability of the CLS to address the needs of victims and survivors of gendered crimes are well documented, as is its harmful impact on the lives of those who offend and their families.

Despite two or three decades of legal reform driven by feminist activists, victims continue to underreport sexual violence and domestic abuse, and prosecution and conviction rates are still shockingly low. Consequently, victims are left disillusioned with a system that purports to protect and uphold their best interests when the reality is that criminal evidentiary rules and procedures are not designed to take account of victims' rights and needs.

In recent years, there has been a conscious shift away from Western conceptions of justice towards alternative ways of 'doing justice'. One favoured approach has been RJ. The expansion of RJ processes and practices throughout the UK and internationally has led to many working definitions. Described as a theory, philosophy of, or approach to justice, RJ's principal focus is on finding ways to collectively resolve the harm or address the risk of harm that has resulted from crime or conflict. While there is no unified definition of RJ, its principles are clearly defined and understood

53 K McGuire, 'Extending the Concept, or Extending the Characteristics? Misogyny or Gender?' in I Zempi and J Smith (eds) *Misogyny as Hate Crime* (Routledge, 2022) 57.

54 PJ Fleming, TL Patterson, CV Chavarin, SJ Semple, C Magis-Rodriguez, and EV Pitpitan, 'Are Men's Misogynistic Attitudes Associated with Poor Mental Health and Substance Use Behaviours? An Exploratory Study of Men in Tijuana, Mexico' (2019) 19(2) *Psychology of Men and Masculinities* 314.

55 C Smart, *Feminism and the Power of Law* (Routledge 1989).

56 LM Armstrong, 'Is Restorative Justice an Effective Approach for Children and Young People Who Sexually Harm' (2021) 10(4) *laws* 86.

worldwide.[57] Marshall's definition has been used widely by academics and practitioners:

> Restorative justice is a process whereby all the parties with a stake in a particular offence come together to resolve collectively how to deal with the aftermath of the offence and its implications for the future.[58]

Another useful definition of RJ is offered by the European Forum for Restorative Justice (EFRJ):

> An inclusive approach of addressing harm or the risk of harm through engaging all those affected in coming to a common understanding and agreement on how the harm or wrongdoing can be repaired, relationships maintained and justice achieved.[59]

RJ surfaced in the 1970s, mainly in response to the failure of the Western legal system to meet the needs of victims.[60] While there has been disagreement as to RJ's origins,[61] with some tracing its roots to ancient and indigenous practices, its values and principles provide a disparate approach to thinking about criminological theories such as 'deterrence, rehabilitation, incapacitation and the prevention of crime'.[62] Grounded in relational theory, RJ is concerned with 'just relations'.[63] As a collaborative and problem-solving process, it focuses on finding ways to repair the harm as opposed to state-sanctioned punishment and retribution, which are notable features of the CLS.

The theory is that RJ brings together those harmed by crime (or conflict) and those responsible for the harm; it can best be described as a deliberative process as it brings people together to discuss the effects of crime and how

57 K Daly, 'Restorative Justice: The Real Story' (2002) 4(1) *Punishment and Society* 55 and Kathleen Daly, 'What is Restorative Justice? Fresh Answers to a Vexed Question' (2015) 11(1) *Victim and Offenders* 9.

58 T Marshall, 'The Evolution of Restorative Justice in Britain' (1996) 4 *European Journal on Criminal Policy and Research* 21, 37.

59 T Chapman, *Connecting People to Restore Relationships, Practice Guide on Values and Standards for Restorative Justice Practices* (European Forum for Restorative Justice, 2018) <https://efus.eu/wp-content/uploads/2022/02/Concept-paper-Tim-Chapman-Restorative-Justice-an-approach-that-contributes-to-the-prevention-and-mitigation-of-polarisation-at-the-local-and-regional-level.pdf> accessed 13 May 2024.

60 H Zehr, *Restorative Justice? What's That?* [online] <https://zehr-institute.org/what-is-rj/> accessed 20 May 2024.

61 K Daly, 'What is Restorative Justice? Fresh Answers to a Vexed Question' (2015) 11(1) *Victim and Offenders* 9.

62 J Braithwaite, 'Restorative Justice' in M Tonry (eds) *The Handbook of Crime and Punishment* (Oxford University Press 1998) 323.

63 P McCold and T Watchel *In Pursuit of Paradigm: A Theory of Restorative Justice* (2003) International Institute for Restorative Practices 1.

best to respond to and prevent it from happening again.[64] Unlike in criminal procedure, the victim plays a central role within RJ. For example, victims are given the opportunity, if they wish, to explain how the criminal offence has impacted their lives or to seek answers to questions that they would not have been able to ask in a traditional criminal legal setting.

Conversations around the efficacy of RJ usually begin by drawing comparisons with the CLS. Howard Zehr, often regarded as the founder of the RJ movement, proposed that while retributive justice centred on 'violation of the law, restorative justice focuses on the violation of people and relationships'.[65] However, Kathleen Daly, who has been conducting research in the RJ space for over a decade, describes RJ as a 'justice mechanism'[66] and is highly critical of discussing RJ and retributive justice in dichotomic terms.[67] During her observations of group conferences, Daly found that participants would often 'incorporate multiple justice aims',[68] including retributive principles such as 'censure' and elements of rehabilitative and restorative justice.[69] Daly also warns that we must remain realistic about RJ's reparative benefits as there is a gap between RJ's 'ideals' and what it can attain from a practical perspective.[70]

Empirical research has shown that RJ has the potential to aid people in their psychological and emotional recovery from crime[71] and can amplify 'the voices of others and their words, languages and framings of harms and injustices to displace dominant discourses and structures'.[72] Godden writes of rape victims and survivors that providing a space for women to tell their stories of harm is significant, even more than the research on RJ and rape would suggest.[73] For victims, particularly those of gendered crime, being treated with dignity and respect is paramount. Research indicates that victim–survivors tend to rate 'safety, perpetrator accountability and reparation'[74] above 'punishment and

64 J Braithwaite, 'Restorative Justice' in M Tonry (eds) *The Handbook of Crime and Punishment* (Oxford University Press 1998) 323.

65 H Zehr, *The Little Book of Restorative Justice* (Good Books 2002) 58.

66 K Daly, 'What Is Restorative Justice? Fresh Answers to a Vexed Question' (2015) 11(1) *Victim and Offenders* 11.

67 Ibid.

68 Ibid.

69 K Daly, 'Restorative Versus Retributive Justice' (2005) 60 *Criminal Justice Matters* 28.

70 K Daly, *Technical Report 2, Research Instruments in Research 2 (1999) and Background Notes* (South Australia Juvenile Justice Research on Conferencing, Griffith University, 2001) < https://www.griffith.edu.au/__data/assets/pdf_file/0024/223764/2001-Daly-SAJJ-Tech-report-2-Background-notes.pdf > accessed 12 July 2024.

71 H Strang and LW Sherman, 'Repairing the Harm: Victims and Restorative Justice' (2003) *Utah Law Review* 15.

72 N Godden-Rasul 'Repairing the Harms of Rape of Women through Restorative Justice' in Estelle Zinsstag and Marie Keenan (eds) *Restorative Responses to Sexual Violence: Legal, Social and Therapeutic Dimensions* (Routledge 2017) 20.

73 Ibid.

74 JL Herman, 'Justice from the Victim's Perspective' (2005) 11(5) *Violence Against Women* 571.

imprisonment'.[75] However, victims consistently find themselves constrained by the legal process, which renders them non-participants. In a dialogue, all parties can participate in the process in meaningful ways. While RJ has the potential to respect and honour the needs and rights of both victim and offender, it is rarely, if at all, possible to do this within a punitive framework or system.[76] Restorative processes can offer a safe space for all parties to be heard.[77]

Typically, RJ was utilised in youth justice settings and for less serious offences.[78] As RJ initiatives grew, so did the interest in expanding practices to capture gendered crime such as sexual and domestic violence. As early as the late 1980s, this was viewed as highly controversial given that much of feminist activism centred on pursuing criminal legal responses to gender-based harms.[79] This specific branch of feminism which relies on state intervention for MVAWG has come to be known as 'carceral feminism'.[80] Carceral feminism views 'policing, prosecution and imprisonment'[81] as the principal answer to MVAWG.[82]

Zehr recognised the problematic nature of applying RJ principles in practice to serious cases, in particular domestic abuse, and advised those interested in its application to proceed with caution.[83] Empirical evidence on the use of RJ for serious and gendered crime has grown,[84] and many established programmes offer RJ for cases of sexual, intimate partner, and family violence (most notably RESTORE[85]). However, there are still significant barriers to realising it in practice in the UK (e.g. lack of quality training, specialised practitioners, and funding; the referral process). It is useful to revisit some of the key arguments that were set out by those who opposed its use in gendered crime.

Much of the resistance stemmed from concerns around 'safety and accountability'[86] and the perceived danger that MVAWG would be consigned back

75 Ibid.

76 B Hudson, 'Restorative Justice and Gendered Violence: Diversion or Effective Justice?' (2002) 42(3) *The British Journal of Criminology* 616, 618.

77 Ibid.

78 A Crawford and T Newburn, *Youth Offending and Restorative Justice* (Willan 2003).

79 K Daly and J Stubbs, 'Feminist Engagement with Restorative Justice' (2006) 10(1) *Theoretical Criminology* 9.

80 L Goodmark, 'Restorative Justice as Feminist Practice' (2018) 1(3) *The International Journal of Restorative Justice* 372.

81 V Law, 'Against Carceral Feminism' *Jacobin* <https://jacobin.com/2014/10/against-carceral-feminism/> accessed 17 June 2024.

82 Ibid.

83 H Zehr, *The Little Book of Restorative Justice* (Good Books 2002) 58.

84 E Zinsstag and M Keenan (eds), *Restorative Responses to Sexual Violence: Legal, Social and Therapeutic Dimensions* (Routledge 2017); M Koss, 'The RESTORE Program of Restorative Justice for Sex Crimes: Vision, Process and Outcomes' (2014) 29(9) *Journal of Interpersonal Violence* 1623.

85 Ibid.

86 L Goodmark, 'Restorative Justice as Feminist Practice' (2018) 1(3) *The International Journal of Restorative Justice* 372.

to the private sphere.[87] Goodmark explains that carceral feminists view 'the state's willingness to intervene as important progress in the effort to eradicate gender-based harms and are loath to relinquish those gains'.[88] They believe that gender-based harm warrants a state response that should include adjudication. During that time, there was also little understanding of, or empirical evidence for, how RJ would work in practice in these types of cases. Understandably, it was objected to on the grounds that using informal justice processes like RJ to divert men who engaged in violence against women would be perceived as a soft option by the perpetrator and society.[89] There were further concerns that it could compromise a woman's safety due to the power hierarchies/dynamics that are a constant feature in gendered crimes such as domestic abuse. It was envisaged that it might also create opportunities for victim blaming (by family members and supporters) and 'unfair and coerced agreements'[90] or apologies.[91]

Some of the misconceptions were around the processual stage RJ would be utilised in cases involving sexual violence and domestic abuse. Due to the diverse range of models and initiatives, RJ can take place at any stage of the criminal process. For example, it can be offered as a: 'diversion from court; pre-sentence; a component or condition of sentence and at post sentence, as a component of pre-prison release or community sentence.'[92] However, in cases of serious crime, it is usually utilised in the aftermath of the crime. As RJ was a relatively new concept in gendered crime, many of its opponents assumed that it would be offered as a diversion from formal prosecution or at the pre-sentencing stage.[93]

In E&W, progress in this area has been hampered by a lack of training, funding, and information sharing; gatekeeping issues; and inconsistencies amongst police and crime commissioners (PCCs).[94] The All-Parliamentary Group on

87 Ibid.

88 Ibid 374.

89 Nadia Maria Wager, 'A Scoping Review Considering the Applicability of Restorative Justice to Cases of Sexual Assault' *Conference Paper* <www.researchgate.net/profile/Nadia-Wager/publication/263653926_A_SCOPING_REVIEW_CONSIDERING_THE_APPLICABILITY_OF_RESTORATIVE_JUSTICE_TO_CASES_OF_SEXUAL_ASSAUL/links/0deec53b6e2be85740000000/A-SCOPING-REVIEW-CONSIDERING-THE-APPLICABILITY-OF-RESTORATIVE-JUSTICE-TO-CASES-OF-SEXUAL-ASSAUL.pdf> accessed 12 October 2024.

90 Donna Coker, 'Enhancing Autonomy for Battered Women: Lessons from Navajo Peace-Making' (1999) *UCLA Law Review* 47.

91 Paul Gavin, C Kite, C Porter, K McCartan, and P Cawley, 'Restorative Justice in Cases of Sexual Violence: Current and Future Directions in the UK' (2024) 26(4) *Contemporary Justice Review* 393.

92 Restorative Justice Council, *Restorative Justice and the Judiciary Information Pack* (2015) <https://restorativejustice.org.uk/sites/default/files/resources/files/Restorative%20justice%20and%20the%20judiciary%20-%20information%20pack.pdf> accessed 15 July 2024.

93 B Hudson, 'Restorative Justice and Gendered Violence: Diversion or Effective Justice?' (2002) 42(3) *The British Journal of Criminology* 616, 618.

94 Restorative Justice APPG, *Inquiry into Restorative Practices in 2021/2022* <https://rjappg.co.uk/wp-content/uploads/2021/09/RJ-APPG-Inquiry-Report.pdf> accessed 14 May 2024.

Restorative Justice (APPG) initiated an inquiry into the quality and availability of restorative practices in E&W between 2021 and 2022 that highlighted the inconsistencies among PCC regions. The CPS said that while the Victim's Code permits victims of domestic abuse to take part in RJ, the National Police Chief's Council opposed the practice and that RJ should only be offered after consulting and seeking permission from the 'supervisors or experts'.[95]

What we do know is that prevention and education play an important part in tackling misogyny and sexism. Due to its flexible nature, RJ is not restricted to the CLS but can be and has been used in schools, universities, workplaces, and prisons to challenge harmful behaviours where misogyny is the root cause. In this final section, we consider how RJ could be used as a justice mechanism for victims of misogyny.

Misogyny and Restorative Justice

While carceral feminists support the use of the CLS to tackle MVAWG, those who align with anti-carceral feminism and abolitionist movements have consistently argued that the CLS and its institutions are sites of 'violence and injustice'.[96] Consequently, it can be challenging to justify the reliance on the CLS when evidence provides that it rarely delivers for victims or those who offend. However, it should be acknowledged that there are victims for whom it plays an important role in their pursuit of justice and recovery from crime. Clare McGlynn has advised against binary thinking and suggests that there is room for both approaches.[97]

Some feminists believe RJ to be incompatible with feminist visions of justice[98] and that it needs to engage with feminist theoretical perspectives of power, oppression, and gender inequality. In examining young girls as offenders and their experiences of RJ conferencing, Hodgson found that the girls and practitioners held conflicting views about the process. Practitioners, for example, believed RJ to be a positive experience for the girls. This was due to stereotypical assumptions that girls would know how to engage meaningfully with the process because females are perceived as naturally empathetic, caring and nurturing.[99] In reality, however, the girls felt 'disempowered, neglected and targeted'[100] at different points in the legal process.[101]

95 Ibid.

96 C McGlynn, 'Challenging Anti-Carceral Feminism: Criminalisation, Justice and Continuum Thinking' (2022) *Women's Studies International Forum* 93 <www.sciencedirect.com/science/article/pii/S0277539522000553> accessed 12 June 2024.

97 Ibid.

98 L Goodmark, 'Restorative Justice as Feminist Practice' (2018) 1(3) *The International Journal of Restorative Justice* 372.

99 J Hodgson, *Gender, Power and Restorative Justice: A Feminist Critique* (Palgrave Macmillan, 2022).

100 Ibid 35.

101 Ibid.

When Masson and Österman researched the female offender experience of RJ conferencing in E&W, they found that much of the literature on RJ was 'gender blind',[102] tending to focus on 'male normative standards'.[103] As a significant number of women in conflict with the law were once victims,[104] the victim/offender dichotomy is rarely if ever helpful. The literature provides that women's life experiences are usually gendered and characterised by trauma, abuse, addiction, and poor mental health.[105] The authors found that there was little recognition by RJ practitioners of the context in which the women's offending took place (e.g. trauma, mental health, victimisation).[106]

In contrast, Goodman argues that RJ is in fact a feminist practice and entirely compatible with feminism and its principles and practices.[107] She writes that like feminism, RJ elevates women's voices and centres their stories and narratives.[108] Women are often portrayed as passive and devoid of agency in the CLS, where they are relegated to the background. RJ processes differ because their direction is ultimately shaped by the victim.[109]

RJ can be used as a preventative measure to avoid harm or as a means of repairing harm already caused by conflict or crime. Although it is treated as an alternative to, or a supplementary process of the CLS, it can be applied across many different settings within and without criminal legal contexts, for example in rebuilding workplace relationships[110] or tackling misogyny and sexist cultures in a university.[111] RJ can be particularly effective for challenging prejudice and hate against women and girls. Goodmark explains that ending MVAWG requires looking beyond the CLS for solutions and suggests that RJ can encourage men to build empathy and emotional intelligence and see things from the perspective of the victim and those harmed, which is necessary to effect behavioural change.[112]

102 I Masson and L Österman, 'Working with Female Offenders in Restorative Justice Frameworks: Effective and Ethical Practice' (2017) 64(4) *Probation Journal*, 354.

103 Ibid.

104 J Rumgay, 'Twice Punished: When Women Victims Become Offenders' (2005) 60(1) *Criminal Justice Matters* 16.

105 Ibid.

106 I Masson and L Österman, 'Working with Female Offenders in Restorative Justice Frameworks: Effective and Ethical Practice' (2017) 64(4) *Probation Journal* 354, 354.

107 L Goodmark, 'Restorative Justice as Feminist Practice' (2018) 1(3) *The International Journal of Restorative Justice* 374.

108 Ibid 375.

109 Ibid.

110 DL Kidder, 'Restorative Justice: Not "Rights" But the Right Way to Heal Relationships at Work' (2007) 18(1) *International Journal of Conflict Management* 4.

111 J Llewellyn, J MacIssac, and M MacKay, *Report from the Restorative Justice Process at the Dalhousie University Faculty of Dentistry* (1 May 2015) <https://papers.ssrn.com/sol3/papers.cfm?abstract_id=2879539#paper-references-widget> accessed 13 July 2024.

112 Ibid 380.

One of RJ's key strengths is that it can be applied to any stage in the criminal legal process. The Victim's Code states that 'Restorative Justice can take place while criminal proceedings are ongoing, as part of a sentence, after criminal proceedings have finished, or as part of an out of court disposal'.[113] Many countries have adopted RJ-specific models, for example, the conferencing model in New Zealand and South Australia; additionally, sentencing circles and reparation panels are common in Canada and the USA.[114] In Ireland, there are a wide array of models, such as family and restorative conferences, offender reparation panels and victim–offender mediation. The latter is also available in the UK, along with restorative cautioning.[115] Typically, the RJ process involves preparatory meetings with participants separately before all parties involved meet face to face.[116]

One area of criminal law where the use of RJ practices has grown is hate crime.[117] The EFRJ noted that between 2017–18 police recorded 94,098 hate crime incidents in E&W, 17% more than in the year before.[118] A study on RJ and hate crime explored some of the benefits of employing a restorative approach, such as giving the victim a voice and the opportunity to explain to the responsible person how it impacted their life.[119]

While the UK government has declined to extend the protected characteristics to include misogyny, sex, or gender, engaging in RJ dialogue would be one means of challenging and combating hate and prejudice directed against women and girls.[120] Hypothetically speaking, if misogyny were to be treated as a hate or bias crime, RJ could be offered as an alternative disposal in the form of victim–offender mediation or group or community conferencing, which uses direct and indirect meetings or circles to bring together victims, offenders and members of the community. As was highlighted by McGuire previously, as misogyny is perceived as a *prejudice* rather than as an *identity*, making

113 Ministry of Justice, *Code of Practice for Victims of Crime* (2015) <https://assets.publishing.service.gov.uk/government/uploads/system/uploads/attachment_data/file/974376/victims-code-2020.pdf> accessed 12 July 2024.

114 Ibid.

115 K Daly, 'Restorative Justice and Sexual Assault: An Archival Study of Court and Conference Cases' (2006) 46 *British Journal of Criminology* 334.

116 Ibid 9.

117 T Gavrielides, *Restoring Relationships: Addressing Hate Crime through Restorative Justice* (City Pariochial Foundation, 2007) <www.rota.org.uk/sites/default/files/webfm/rota_report_on_hate_crime__rj_july_2007_-_final.pdf> accessed 12 October 2024.

118 T Kazi, 'Restorative Justice, Hate Crime and Migrant Integration' [online] European Forum for Restorative Justice <www.euforumrj.org/en/restorative-justice-hate-crime-and-migrant-integration> accessed 22 July 2024.

119 MA Walters, *Hate Crime and Restorative Justice: Exploring Causes, Repairing Harms* (Oxford University Press 2014) 32.

120 RB Coates, MS Umbreit, and B Vos, 'Responding to Hate Crime Through Restorative Justice Dialogue' 9(1) *Contemporary Justice Review* 7.

misogyny a protected characteristic would require significant changes to the existing hate crime framework.

RJ and the Family Court System

While RJ practices have been used as a supplementary process in cases of domestic abuse in the CLS, victim–survivors of abuse will usually have had some contact with the family court system because of ongoing child contact or divorce proceedings. There is a growing body of evidence that perpetrators routinely use the family courts to further control and abuse their victims.[121] This is often termed legal abuse.[122] Civil legal remedies have been found to be inadequate for addressing these issues as they fail to keep women and children safe and hold perpetrators to account[123]; victims, practitioners, and researchers have consistently reported that survivors are blamed and gaslit during proceedings because there exists a culture of disbelief.[124]

An amendment to Section 1 of the Children Act 1989 also presumes that children should have contact with both parents as a matter of statute. Subsequently when a perpetrators behaviour is challenged, women can find themselves accused of parental alienation.[125] Although this theory has been discredited and rejected by mental health experts and the UN[126] as having no evidential basis, lawyers and courts still use and recognise the concept of parental alienation. Research also shows that mediation and other out-of-court orders can be used inappropriately, which can further traumatise women and children.[127] In addition, poor communication between the criminal courts, child safeguarding agencies, and the family law system can endanger the lives of child victims if crucial information is not shared between all those involved.

121 Post-separation legal abuse is when perpetrators use the law or legal threats to control their victim.

122 Domestic abusers often use the legal system to exert control over their victim. This can be in the form of false allegations against the other parent or economic abuse.

123 R Hunter, M Burton, and L Trinder, *Assessing Risk of Harm to Children and Parents in Private Law Children Cases Final Report* (Ministry of Justice, 2020) <https://assets.publishing.service.gov.uk/government/uploads/system/uploads/attachment_data/file/895173/assessing-risk-harm-children-parents-pl-childrens-cases-report_.pdf> accessed 14 October 2024.

124 Ibid.

125 Parental alienation is a concept coined by psychologist Richard Gardener. According to this theory, children who refuse to have a relationship with an abusive parent have been influenced or indoctrinated by the other parent.

126 R Asalem, *Report of the Special Rapporteur on Violence against Women and Girls, Its Causes and Consequences* UNGAOR 53rd Session (UN Doc. A/HRC/53/56) (2023) <www.dropbox.com/scl/fi/0tuwx2l3ffzm4q28bozev/9.-United-Nations-Report.pdf?rlkey=m22h220et30d51d9p8abocp3c&e=1&dl=0> accessed 12 October 2024.

127 R Hunter, M Burton, and L Trinder, *Assessing Risk of Harm to Children and Parents in Private Law Children Cases Final Report* (Ministry of Justice, 2020) <https://assets.publishing.service.gov.uk/government/uploads/system/uploads/attachment_data/file/895173/assessing-risk-harm-children-parents-pl-childrens-cases-report_.pdf> accessed 14 October 2024.

Daicoff explains that RJ has been used with some success in family law proceedings using the circle model.[128] As restorative circles (or conferences) are a systemic approach to conflict, they can help to 'build empathy, respectful communication and a consideration of the impact of their behaviour on others'.[129] She relays some of the benefits of using RJ in family law where there is family conflict such as community engagement, inviting members of the community who were known to the family to give their 'input and perspective on the issues and to help the family keep to the agreements developed in the circle'.[130] She suggests that it can also assist with 'promoting better post dispute family relationships'[131] and encourages those involved to take responsibility and hold those accountable for any agreements made during the circle process.[132]

Juliet Behrens, however, stresses the importance of designing an RJ model that is sensitive to the context in which domestic abuse operates and prioritises the safety and needs of victim–survivors[133] while also acknowledging that RJ can be empowering as it is primarily justice focussed and seeks to restore the harm. She continues that it allows stories of gendered violence to be told, providing an environment where people can come up with 'creative solutions to victims needs'[134] and increasing the chance of rehabilitating the person who has harmed than in traditional criminal justice processes.[135] However, the prominence given to the presumption of contact (with fathers) and narrow focus on private dispute resolution instead of 'justice' contributes to the systemic issues experienced by women who come into contact with the family courts.[136] There is also a noticeable reluctance by the family courts to investigate past behaviours of domestic violence or to hold perpetrators accountable.[137]

There are situations where the circle process would be unsuitable for families in conflict particularly where there is a considerable power imbalance between participants and community members.[138] For example, 'forcing community norms through a mediation or circle process if oppressive'[139] or misogynistic

128 SS Daicoff, 'Families in Circle Process: Restorative Justice in Family Law' (2015) 53(3) 427 <https://onlinelibrary.wiley.com/doi/abs/10.1111/fcre.12164> accessed 14 October 2024.

129 *Practice Guidance: Using Restorative Circles* (Devon County Council, 2020) <https://proceduresonline.com/trixcms1/media/9641/restorative-circles-practice-guidance.pdf> accessed 20 October 2024.

130 Ibid 430.

131 Ibid.

132 Ibid.

133 J Behrens, 'Meeting the Needs of Victims of Domestic Violence with Family Law Issues: The Dangers and Possibilities of Restorative Justice' (2005) 1(3) *International Journal of Law in Context* 215.

134 Ibid 225.

135 Ibid.

136 Ibid.

137 Ibid.

138 Ibid.

139 Ibid.

could harm female participants and reinforce harmful beliefs that perpetuate MVAWG.[140] In some cultures or religions, divorce is frowned upon or even prohibited, and divorced women are often shamed and ostracised from their families and communities. A common criticism by women's organisations and those opposed to the use of RJ in serious and complex cases is that using RJ in cases involving gendered violence risks minimising the seriousness of the harm women experience,[141] although it should be noted that victim–survivors of gendered violence who engage with the RJ process are usually referred *after* the perpetrator has been convicted. Sensitive and complex cases are also carefully evaluated by experienced facilitators, and it can take months or in some cases years before a meeting is arranged.

Misogyny in Educational and Workplace Settings

For women and girls, educational establishments can be sites of violence and sexual harassment.[142] In a government report which looked at attitudes towards women and girls in educational settings, almost a third of 16- to 18-year-old girls had been exposed to uninvited sexual touching at school, and in 2014, 59% of girls and young women between 13 and 21 had experienced sexual harassment at school that year.[143] Restorative practices are fast becoming a popular tool of conflict resolution within schools. Peace-making circles, dialogue, and mediation are just some of the chosen models adopted in classrooms around the UK.

RJ has been used as a justice tool by university students in the context of sexual harassment.[144] The Dalhousie University case in Nova Scotia concerned a group of female students who lodged complaints under the university's sexual harassment policy about their male colleagues and the misogynistic and offensive things they had posted about them on a private Facebook page.[145] The policy offered formal and informal routes to resolve the issue which included RJ. The men spent around 150 hours participating in 'group sessions,

140 Ibid.

141 Justice Committee, *Restorative Justice: Fourth Report of Session* (HC 2016–17 164) paras 29–30.

142 C Jones, N Farrelly and C Barter, 'UK Prevalence of University Student and Staff Experiences of Sexual Violence and Domestic Abuse: A Systematic Review from 2002 to 2022' (2024) *European Journal of Higher Education* 1.

143 House of Commons, *Attitudes towards Women and Girls in Educational Settings* Women and Equalities Committee (5th Report of Session, 2023) <https://publications.parliament.uk/pa/cm5803/cmselect/cmwomeq/331/report.html> accessed 12 July 2024.

144 C Backhouse, D McRae, and N Lyer, *Report of the Task Force on Misogyny, Sexism and Homophobia in Dalhousie University Faculty of Dentistry* (Dalhousie University, 2015) 1 <https://cdn.dal.ca/content/dam/dalhousie/pdf/cultureofrespect/DalhousieDentistry-TaskForceReport-June2015.pdf> accessed 22 July 2024.

145 Ibid.

workshops, educational sessions and conferences[146] with individuals who had been harmed and other stakeholders. It is interesting to note that the men involved were not required to admit guilt as is usually a requirement of RJ processes embedded in the CLS. Instead, they were asked to give a truthful depiction of events and urged to accept responsibility for their 'individual and collective actions'.[147]

System responses to misogyny and sexism in an employment context are often bureaucratic and closely mirror the adversarial system. Remedies are usually disciplinary in nature such as conduct hearings, sanctions, or civil claims involving gender/sex discrimination and harassment.[148] Furthermore those who do report discrimination and harassment or in some cases criminal behaviour are viewed as troublemakers rather than it 'being dealt with as examples of systemic misogyny.'[149] Neeley suggests that restorative processes can be utilised as an 'organisational learning approach to discrimination'.[150] She argues that organisations tend to respond to grievances with a 'single loop learning model' as their goal is to resolve issues as quickly and efficiently as possible. In terms of their approach, organisations will either pursue the legal route and refute that a discriminatory incident took place or settle out of court.[151] Neeley also reports that implementing restorative processes in the workplace can lead to improvements in what she dubs 'conflict culture'.[152] She highlights one example where prison staff who were tasked with delivering restorative programmes to offenders engaged in a restorative initiative themselves because they recognised that until their relationships with each other improved, they would not be able to work with offenders in a restorative way.[153]

Conclusion

This chapter discussed recent developments in legal policy and the debates surrounding making misogyny a hate crime in E&W. The research evidences that state responses to gender-based harms do little to support the rights and needs

146 Ibid.
147 Ibid.
148 JE Neeley, 'Addressing Sexual Assault in Criminal Justice, Higher Education and Employment: What Restorative Justice Means for Survivors and Accountability' (2021) 31(1) *The Kansas Journal of Law and Public Policy* 1.
149 Baroness Casey Review, *Final Report: An Independent Review into the Standards of Behaviour and Internal Culture of the Metropolitan Police Service* (2023) <www.met.police.uk/police-forces/metropolitan-police/areas/about-us/about-the-met/bcr/baroness-casey-review/> accessed 15 June 2024.
150 JE Neeley, 'Addressing Sexual Assault in Criminal Justice, Higher Education and Employment: What Restorative Justice Means for Survivors and Accountability' (2021) 31(1) *The Kansas Journal of Law and Public Policy* 29.
151 Ibid.
152 Ibid.
153 Ibid.

of victim–survivors and equally fail to rehabilitate or engender change in the beliefs and behaviour of perpetrators of MVAWG. Alternatives like RJ can offer victims and survivors, offenders, and other parties the opportunity to resolve matters through restorative dialogue and meaningful participation. It is, however, important to stress that victims of gender-based harms and prejudice and hate should still be given the choice to pursue state responses. Rather than engage in binary thinking,[154] the misogyny problem requires a multi-faceted approach which may include criminal and civil legal responses and RJ and other forms of therapeutic justice initiatives; however, prevention, education, and feminist and social justice activism also play an important part in helping to eradicate MVAWG.

154 C McGlynn, 'Challenging Anti-Carceral Feminism: Criminalisation, Justice and Continuum Thinking' (2022) *Women's Studies International Forum* 93 <www.sciencedirect.com/science/article/pii/S0277539522000553> accessed 12 June 2024.

11 Sentencing Offenders with Mental Disorders, Developmental Disorders, or Neurological Impairments in England and Wales

A Case Study Analysis

Sally Kennedy, Clare S. Allely, and Ian Warren

Introduction

Following a period of consultation,[1] the Sentencing Council issued a guideline called *Sentencing Offenders with Mental Disorders, Developmental Disorders, or Neurological Impairments* (hereafter 'the Guideline') that came into effect in England and Wales on 1 October 2020.[2] The Guideline should be considered when sentencing an offender over the age of 18 who has such disorders or impairments[3] at the time of the offence or sentencing. It closely resembles the *Verdins* common law principles in Australia and New Zealand,[4] which require sentencing courts to consider various mitigating factors associated with mental impairment, including potential reductions in moral culpability, the suitability of the sentence, the adjustment of general and specific deterrence requirements, and the likelihood imprisonment will have an adverse effect on an offender's mental health.[5]

1 Sentencing Council, *Overarching Principles: Sentencing Offenders with Mental Disorders, Developmental Disorders, or Neurological Impairments – Response to Consultation* (Sentencing Council, July 2020) <www.sentencingcouncil.org.uk/wp-content/uploads/Mental-Health-guideline-response-to-consultation.pdf> accessed 10 June 2024.

2 Sentencing Council, 'Sentencing Offenders with Mental Disorders, Developmental Disorders, or Neurological Impairments' <www.sentencingcouncil.org.uk/overarching-guides/magistrates-court/item/sentencing-offenders-with-mental-disorders-developmental-disorders-or-neurological-impairments> accessed 10 June 2024.

3 We use 'disorder' and 'impairment' throughout this chapter, which reflects the terminology in the Guideline, unless quoting directly from the legal judgments which may use other terminology. Terms differ to phrases preferred by the neurodiverse community, particularly around the use of person-first language. See SM Bury, R Jellett, JR Spoor and D Hedley, '"It Defines Who I Am" or "It's Something I Have": What Language do [Autistic] Australian Adults [on the Autism Spectrum] Prefer?' (2020) 53(2) *Journal of Autism and Developmental Disorders* 677–87.

4 *R v Verdins* (2007) VSCA 102.

5 J Walvisch and A Carroll, 'Sentencing Offenders with Personality Disorders: A Critical Analysis of *DPP (Vic) v O'Neill*' (2017) 41(1) *Melbourne University Law* Review 417–44.

DOI: 10.4324/9781003496823-11

Annex A of the Guideline lists conditions including psychotic illnesses such as schizophrenia; non-psychotic illnesses such as depression, and anxiety disorders such as post-traumatic stress disorder (PTSD); substance use disorders; developmental disorders, which can include intellectual/learning disabilities, autism spectrum disorders (ASD), attention deficit hyperactivity disorder (ADHD), conduct disorders, and personality disorders; dementia; and acquired brain injury. Individuals can demonstrate dual diagnoses or comorbidities. For example, developmental disorders often co-occur with anxiety and depression.[6] During sentencing, the Guideline specifies that 'no adverse inference should necessarily be drawn' if an offender did not have a diagnosis prior to the offending and/or sentence, their condition is subject to differing expert opinions, or a specific disorder cannot be identified.[7] A formal diagnosis is not 'always required'.[8]

A key component of the Guideline is assessing culpability,[9] which 'will only be reduced if there is sufficient connection between the offender's impairment or disorder and the offending behaviour'.[10] The Guideline provides a non-exhaustive list of issues for the court to consider, including an offender's tendency for disinhibited behaviour, the failure to take prescribed medication, the relative importance of complying with treatment to their overall well-being, evidence of 'self-medication' with alcohol and non-prescribed or illicit drugs, and the degree of insight the offender has about their impairment or disorder. The sentencing court must carefully review the circumstances of the case and all relevant materials to determine if the impairment or disorder compromised an offender's judgement, rational choices, and capacity to understand the nature and consequences of their actions.[11]

Impairments and disorders can also play a role in the type of sentence given to the offender.[12] If an offender is:

> on the cusp of custody or detention, the court may consider that the impairment or disorder may make a custodial sentence disproportionate to achieving the aims of sentencing and that the public are better protected and crime reduced by a rehabilitative approach.[13]

6 M Casseus, 'Prevalence of Co-Occurring Autism Spectrum Disorder and Attention Deficit/Hyperactivity Disorder Among Children in the United States' (2022) 26(6) *Autism* 1591–97.
7 The Guideline, Section 1(4).
8 Ibid Section 1(4).
9 Ibid Section 2.
10 Ibid Section 2(11).
11 Ibid Section 2(15).
12 Ibid Section 3; sentencing options include fine/discharge; community orders; requirements for mental health treatment, rehabilitation, alcohol treatment, and/or drug rehabilitation; and custodial sentences.
13 Ibid Section 3(22).

When a custodial sentence is justifiable, the court can consider whether it might weigh more heavily on the offender or could 'exacerbate the effects of impairments or disorders'.[14] Although this should only to be 'taken into account in a limited way', the deleterious impact of incarceration can reduce the length of imprisonment or result in a suspended sentence.[15]

Notably, the court retains considerable discretionary power when implementing the Guideline. Per Section 1(2), an offender's impairment or disorder should always be considered by a sentencing court but will not necessarily have a practical impact on the final determination. The judiciary retain discretionary authority over certain elements of the sentencing process and are 'not bound to follow expert opinion if there are compelling reasons to set it aside'.[16]

In this chapter, we examine a sample of rulings scrutinising the application of the Guideline to investigate how it addresses the inequities offenders with a mental disorder or impairment experience when exposed to the criminal justice system. Following a brief review of the literature that provides compelling justification for the Guideline, we outline the methodology we used to collect and analyse 30 judgments examining its implementation. The results summarise key case characteristics, including offence types, offender diagnoses, and case outcomes. We then identify broad trends in cases where the Guideline was appropriately considered during the original sentence and where the sentence was either reduced or increased on appeal. The potential for the Guideline to generate inconsistencies regarding the relevance of an offender's diagnosis, how a condition is reconciled with public safety, and discretionary approaches involving the role of expert evidence are also examined. The chapter concludes by describing how the Guideline requires continued examination to determine its ongoing impacts in reducing inequities in the determination of criminal sentences.

The Rationale Behind the Guideline

The Lord Chief Justice of England and Wales and President of the Sentencing Council praised the Guideline as 'an important and welcome step forward' for 'an informed and consistent approach to sentencing in this difficult and complex area'.[17] The terms 'informed' and 'consistent' are significant, as prior to the introduction of the Guideline, and despite extensive research indicating that people with mental impairments and disorders are over-represented throughout all stages of the criminal justice system, there had been no formally

14 Ibid.

15 Ibid.

16 Ibid Section 2(13).

17 Sentencing Council, 'New Guideline for Sentencing Offenders with Mental Disorders Published' (22 July 2020) <www.sentencingcouncil.org.uk/news/item/new-guideline-for-sentencing-offenders-with-mental-disorders-published/> accessed 10 June 2024.

sanctioned approach to sentencing these offenders in England and Wales.[18] Observational research identifies high rates of mental disorder and substance misuse among police detainees,[19] with many reporting previous contacts with psychiatric services or experiencing active psychiatric symptoms.[20] Many courtroom defendants experience untreated psychiatric disorders, which validates the use of criminal diversion and mental health treatment orders.[21] Prisoners also display disproportionately high rates of mental disorders compared with the general population.[22]

It is difficult to establish a causal link between a mental disorder or impairment and different types of criminal offending. However, one Swedish study found an increased risk of violent crime amongst individuals with bipolar disorder and comorbid substance misuse.[23] People with ADHD are more likely than those without this condition to have contact with police and are at a higher risk of conviction.[24] Research exploring ASD demonstrates how a

18 OP O'Sullivan and N Eastman, '"Out of the Penal System and into the Hospital Regime?" Judicial Challenges in Sentencing Mentally Disordered Offenders and the Likely Impact of the 2020 Sentencing Council Guideline' (2023) 87(5–6) *Journal of Criminal Law* 417–27.

19 I McKinnon and D Grubin, 'Health Screening in Police Custody' (2010) 17(4) *Journal of Forensic and Legal Medicine* 209–12; A Forrester, C Samele, K Slade, T Craig, and L Valmaggia, 'Demographic and Clinical Characteristics of 1092 Consecutive Police Custody Mental Health Referrals' (2017) 28(3) *Journal of Forensic Psychiatry & Psychology* 295–312.

20 A Forrester and G Hopkin, 'Mental Health in the Criminal Justice System: A Pathways Approach to Service and Research Design' (2019) 29(4) *Criminal Behaviour and Mental Health* 207–17.

21 J Shaw, F Creed, J Price, P Huxley and B Tomenson, 'Prevalence and Detection of Serious Psychiatric Disorder in Defendants Attending Court' (1999) 353(9158) *Lancet* 1053–56; P Brown, I Bakolis, E Appiah-Kusi, N Hallett, M Hotopf, and N Blackwood, 'Prevalence of Mental Disorders in Defendants at Criminal Court' (2022) 8(3) *BJPsych Open* 1–8.

22 S Fazel and J Danesh, 'Serious Mental Disorder in 23000 Prisoners: A Systematic Review of 62 Surveys' (2002) 359(9306) *Lancet* 545–50; S Fazel and K Seewald, 'Severe Mental Illness in 33,588 Prisoners Worldwide: Systematic Review and Meta-Regression Analysis' (2012) 200(5) *British Journal of Psychiatry* 364–73; S Fazel, AJ Hayes, K Bartellas, M Clerici, and R Trestman, 'Mental Health of Prisoners: Prevalence, Adverse Outcomes, and Interventions' (2016) 3(9) *Lancet Psychiatry* 871–81; National Audit Office (Comptroller and Auditor), *Mental Health in Prisons* (National Audit Office, 26 June 2017) <www.nao.org.uk/wp-content/uploads/2017/06/Mental-health-in-prisons.pdf> accessed 10 June 2024; A Forrester, A Till, A Simpson, and J Shaw, 'Mental Illness and the Provision of Mental Health Services in Prisons' (2018) 127(1) *British Medical Bulletin* 101–09; S Stürup-Toft, EJ O'Moore, and EH Plugge, 'Looking Behind the Bars: Emerging Health Issues for People In Prison' (2018) 125(1) *British Medical Bulletin* 15–23; N Rebbapragada, V Furtado, and GW Hawker-Bond, 'Prevalence of Mental Disorders in Prisons in the UK: A Systematic Review and Meta-Analysis' (2021) 7(1) *BJPsych Open* 283–84.

23 S Fazel, P Lichtenstein, M Grann, GM Goodwin, and N Långström, 'Bipolar Disorder and Violent Crime: New Evidence From Population-based Longitudinal Studies and Systematic Review' (2010) 67(9) *Archives of General Psychiatry* 931–38.

24 S Young and K Cocallis, 'ADHD and Offending' (2021) 128(7) *Journal of Neural Transmission* 1009–19.

diagnosis can assist courts to make informed decisions regarding factual and moral culpability.[25]

Individuals with certain mental impairments or disorders, including depression and personality disorders, can experience an increased risk of physical victimisation in prison, while those with psychoses can have negative risk associations.[26] The risk of sexual victimisation is also higher for those with a mental disorder.[27] Imprisonment can be particularly onerous for many people with ASD due to their impaired communication abilities and capacity to develop social relationships or understand the behaviours of others.[28] These traits increase vulnerability to bullying, social isolation, sexual victimisation, and exploitation.[29]

The social processes behind the exercise of sentencing discretion are mediated by an array of policy and procedural objectives across the criminal justice system and its diverse personnel.[30] Within these applied contexts, sentencing law requires that any mitigating impacts of an offender's mental impairment

25 CM Berryessa, 'Judiciary Views on Criminal Behaviour and Intention of Offenders with High-Functioning Autism' (2014) 5(2) *Journal of Intellectual Disabilities and Offending Behaviour* 97–106; CM Berryessa, 'Brief Report: Judicial Attitudes Regarding the Sentencing of Offenders with High Functioning Autism' (2016) 46(8) *Journal of Autism and Developmental Disorders* 2770–73; JB Barry-Walsh and PE Mullen, 'Forensic Aspects of Asperger's Syndrome' (2004) 15(1) *Journal of Forensic Psychiatry and Psychology* 96–107; S Foster, 'Autism is Not a Tragedy – Ignorance Is: Suppressing Evidence of Asperger's Syndrome and High-Functioning Autism in Capital Trials Prejudices Defendants for a Death Sentence' (2015) 2(1) *Lincoln Memorial University Law Review* 9–28; OP O'Sullivan, 'Autism Spectrum Disorder and Criminal Responsibility: Historical Perspectives, Clinical Challenges and Broader Considerations within the Criminal Justice System' (2018) 35(4) *Irish Journal of Psychological Medicine* 333–39.

26 CL Blitz, N Wolff, and J Shi, 'Physical Victimization in Prison: The Role of Mental Illness' (2008) 31(5) *International Journal of Law and Psychiatry* 385–93; JC Daquin and LE Daigle, 'Mental Disorder and Victimisation in Prison: Examining the Role of Mental Health Treatment' (2018) 28(2) *Criminal Behaviour and Mental Health* 141–51.

27 N Wolff, CL Blitz, and J Shi, 'Rate of Sexual Victimisation in Prison for Inmates With and Without Mental Disorders' (2007) 58(8) *Psychiatric Services* 1087–94.

28 CS Allely, 'Experiences of Prison Inmates with Autism Spectrum Disorders and the Knowledge and Understanding of the Spectrum Amongst Prison Staff: A Review' (2015) 6(2) *Journal of Intellectual Disabilities and Offending Behavior* 55–67; CE Robertson and JA McGillivray, 'Autism Behind Bars: A Review of the Research Literature and Discussion of Key Issues' (2015) 26(6) *Journal of Forensic Psychiatry and Psychology* 719–36; P Cooper and CS Allely, 'You Can't Judge a Book by Its Cover: Evolving Professional Responsibilities, Liabilities and "Judgecraft" When a Party Has Asperger's Syndrome' (2017) 68(1) *Northern Ireland Legal Quarterly* 35–58.

29 A Lewis, R Pritchett, C Hughes, and K Turner, 'Development and Implementation of Autism Standards for Prisons' (2015) 6(2) *Journal of Intellectual Disabilities and Offending Behaviour* 68–80; I Michna and R Trestman, 'Correctional Management and Treatment of Autism Spectrum Disorder' (2016) 44(2) *Journal of the American Academy of Psychiatry and the Law* 253–58.

30 C Tata, 'Sentencing as Craftwork and the Binary Epistemologies of the Discretionary Decision Process' (2007) 16(3) *Social and Legal Studies* 425–47; C Tata, *Sentencing as a Social Process: Re-Thinking Research and Policy* (Palgrave Macmillan 2020).

or disorder be considered alongside the purposes of punishment in promoting specific and general deterrence and enhancing public safety.[31] This binary contradiction between lenience and punitiveness[32] provides the major rationale for the implementation of the Guideline, which aims to create:

> a substantial and clear methodological shift in judicial practice, thereby enhancing consistency; with a clear shift from a precedent-based approach to one characterised, instead, by adherence to – or sometimes deviation from – explicit [Sentencing Council] guidance.[33]

To encourage transparency, sentencing judges must explain why their decision was appropriate according to the facts of the case, the nature of the offence and the offender's specific needs.[34] However, there is the potential for the Guideline to 'veer over time towards functioning as a "checklist" of sorts' rather than providing clear principles that support formal sentencing decisions.[35] Courts can also 'privilege consideration of culpability over public safety' to enhance consistency when applying the Guideline.[36]

Methodology

We obtained a sample of 30 criminal cases using the phrase 'Sentencing Offenders with Mental Disorders, Developmental Disorders, or Neurological Impairments Guideline' from the Westlaw UK database on 3 May 2024.[37] The initial search returned 37 hits, which we then manually screened to identify whether each case record discussed the Guideline when determining or reviewing an initial sentence.[38] The final sample comprised 30 cases decided

31 OP O'Sullivan and N Eastman, '"Out of the Penal System and into the Hospital Regime?" Judicial Challenges in Sentencing Mentally Disordered Offenders and the Likely Impact of the 2020 Sentencing Council Guideline' (2023) 87(5–6) *Journal of Criminal Law* 417–27.

32 C Tata, 'Sentencing as Craftwork and the Binary Epistemologies of the Discretionary Decision Process' (2007) 16(3) *Social and Legal Studies* 425–47; C Tata, *Sentencing as a Social Process: Re-thinking Research and Policy* (Palgrave Macmillan 2020).

33 OP O'Sullivan and N Eastman, '"Out of the Penal System and into the Hospital Regime?" Judicial Challenges in Sentencing Mentally Disordered Offenders and the Likely Impact of the 2020 Sentencing Council Guideline' (2023) 87(5–6) *Journal of Criminal Law* 417–27 [426].

34 Ibid.

35 Ibid 425.

36 Ibid 426.

37 The search might not have captured all relevant cases as some rulings may refer to the Guideline in a different way. We aimed with this chapter to provide a preliminary illustrative snapshot of the Guideline's application rather than findings from a complete sample of cases scrutinising its implementation.

38 We excluded one case because the Guideline was only mentioned in reference to another cited case, three cases were excluded because the Guideline was mentioned as not in force at the time of the sentence, and three cases were excluded because the judgments were not available under the authors' university subscription agreements (attempts to access these records via other means were unsuccessful).

between 2020 and the end of April 2024 (2020 n = 1; 2021 n = 10; 2022 n = 5; 2023 n = 10; 2024 n = 4).[39] Each case was closely examined to assess specific facts and identify common trends in the operation of the Guideline. We adapted this case study approach from studies examining the relevance of various mental impairments at different points in the criminal justice system, including sentencing.[40] Using a small sample enabled a detailed examination of the Guideline's application, including specific case facts and legal arguments that 'focus on depth, rather than breadth' of analysis.[41]

Results

We grouped criminal conduct into ten offence classifications[42] and categorised the mental disorder or impairment according to Annex A of the Guideline.[43] Nineteen cases involved appeals against the sentence by the offender, nine

39 *R v CH* (2020) EWCA Crim 1736; *R v Wellington* (2021) EWCA Crim 294; *R v Finch* (2021) EWCA Crim 377; *R v Hellyer* (2021) EWCA Crim 550; *R v Baldwin* (2021) EWCA Crim 417; *R v Jenkins* (2021) EWCA Crim 1179; *R v Honeyman* (2021) EWCA Crim 1324; *R v Bel* (2021) EWCA Crim 1461; *R v Nugent* (2021) EWCA Crim 1535; *R v Griffiths* (2021) EWCA Crim 1872; *R v Law* (2021) EWCA Crim 1985; *NFU Mutual Insurance Society Limited Society Ltd v Khedir* (2022) EWHC 437 (QB); *R v Gore* (2022) EWCA Crim 219; *R v Qayum* (2022) EWCA Crim 454; *Paddington Garden Company One Ltd v Rasool* (2022) EWHC 2081 (QB); *R v Hoskin* (2022) EWCA Crim 1633; *R v JD* (2023) EWCA Crim 317; *R v Slack* (2023) EWCA Crim 522; *R v Gulzar* (2023) EWCA Crim 630; *R v Noble* (2023) EWCA Crim 492; *R v Cook, Williams* (2023) EWCA Crim 649; *R v Wilson* (2023) EWCA Crim 673; *R v Simmonds* (2023) EWCA Crim 1063; *R v BGW* (2023) EWCA Crim 1198; *R v JW* (2023) EWCA Crim 1257; *R v Bains* (2023) EWCA Crim 1586; *R v Richfield* (2024) EWCA Crim 116; *R v ABQ* (2024) EWCA Crim 310; *R v Bond* (2024) EWCA Crim 406; *R v Newman* (2024) EWCA Crim 415.

40 J Walvisch and A Carroll, 'Sentencing Offenders with Personality Disorders: A Critical Analysis of *DPP (Vic) v O'Neill*' (2017) 41(1) *Melbourne University Law Review* 417–44; CS Allely, S Kennedy, and I Warren, 'A Legal Analysis of Australian Criminal Cases Involving Defendants with Autism Spectrum Disorder Charged with Online Sexual Offending' (2019) 66(101456) *International Journal of Law and Psychiatry* 1–11; G Wolf, 'Growing Enlightenment: Sentencing Offenders with Autism Spectrum Disorder in Australia' (2021) 44(4) *UNSW Law Journal* 1701–38; CS Allely, S Kennedy, and I Warren, 'Psychiatric and Legal Issues Surrounding the Extradition of WikiLeaks Founder Julian Assange: The Importance of Considering the Diagnosis of Autism Spectrum Disorder' (2022) 28(4) *Psychology, Public Policy, and Law* 630–43; I Cohen, T Gal, and G Enosh, 'Two Roads Converge: The Interchange Between the Mental Health and Legal Discourses in Sexual Assault Trials' (2022) 32(2) *Social & Legal Studies* 441–63.

41 R Tewksbury, 'Qualitative Versus Quantitative Methods: Understanding Why Qualitative Methods Are Superior for Criminology and Criminal Justice' (2009) 1(1) *Journal of Theoretical & Philosophical Criminology* 38–58 [54]; D Garland, 'Penality and the Penal State' (2013) 51(3) *Criminology* 475–517; V Braun and V Clarke, *Thematic Analysis: A Practical Guide* (Sage Publications 2021).

42 Some cases involved multiple charges considered in the same ruling and some individuals engaged in conduct across multiple offence categories.

43 Dementia and acquired brain injuries were not present in the sample. Five individuals, two of whom were involved in the same case, were classified by the authors as having an 'unspecified' diagnosis that was not explicitly mentioned in the judgment, or the judgment highlighted that giving a specific diagnosis was not possible despite the offender's psychiatric evaluation.

were appeals by either the Attorney General or the Solicitor General questioning the leniency of the original sentence, and two were original sentencing rulings. Additional thematic patterns associated with the operation of the Guideline are presented in the Discussion.

The next four tables summarise descriptive elements for each of the 30 rulings according to four outcomes: no change to sentence after reviewing the initial application of the Guideline (Table 11.1), reconsideration of the application of the Guideline to reduce (Table 11.2) or increase (Table 11.3) the original sentence, or upholding the application of the Guideline but altering the sentence on another basis (Table 11.4).

Discussion

Broader patterns became evident across the sample including diverse factual circumstances and case outcomes, rationales for sentence adjustments, possible inconsistencies with the implementation of the Guideline, the process of balancing the offender's diagnosis against public safety concerns, and key issues associated with expert evidence.

Diverse Case Circumstances

There were no clear trends regarding offence types, diagnoses, or final outcomes across the sample. However, sex offences committed against children and both physical and verbal assaults were common, along with more isolated cases involving drug convictions, theft and robbery, blackmail, and manslaughter. This diversity makes it difficult to draw any firm conclusions regarding the types of criminal conduct involving people with mental disorders or impairment in this sample.

Developmental disorders were most common, including intellectual/learning disability, ASD, and ADHD. However, several other diagnoses were also evident, including bipolar disorder and PTSD. Again, this diversity makes drawing any conclusions from this sample unwise. Notably, 13 offenders had a diagnosis of two or more impairments. This highlights the importance of considering the potential impacts of all diagnoses when determining criminal culpability and an appropriate sentence.

Guideline Already Appropriately Considered

In 14 cases, the original court properly considered mitigating factors associated with the offender's diagnosis under the Guideline. It was common for these appeals to highlight the original court had 'regard to the mitigation available to the appellant, and in particular his mental health issues',[44] and

44 *R v Newman* (2024) EWCA Crim 415 [29].

Table 11.1 Sentencing Outcome 1 – Guideline previously considered appropriately: Sentence unchanged

	Case	*Offence Category and Specific Offence*	*Diagnostic Category and Specific Diagnosis*	*Sentence*
1.	*R v Hellyer* (2021) EWCA Crim 550	*Assault (physical and verbal):* Wounding with intent	*Non-psychotic illnesses:* PTSD *Substance use disorders:* Alcohol	14 years 6 months; 5 years extended license
2.	*R v Jenkins* (2021) EWCA Crim 1179	*Sex offences committed against children:* Downloading indecent photographs of a child; distributing indecent photographs of a child	Unspecified	1 year 8 months
3.	*R v Honeyman* (2021) EWCA Crim 1324	*Drugs:* Possessing Class A drugs with intent to supply *Weapons:* Possession of offensive weapon	*Developmental disorders:* Intellectual/learning disability	3 years
4.	*R v Bel* (2021) EWCA Crim 1461	*Terrorism:* Collecting information useful to a person committing or preparing an act of terrorism	*Developmental disorders:* ASD	2 years; 1-year extended license
5.	*R v Griffiths* (2021) EWCA Crim 1872	*Stealing:* Robbery	*Psychotic illnesses:* Bipolar disorder *Developmental disorders:* Personality disorder	7 years 6 months
6.	*R v Law* (2021) EWCA Crim 1985	*Stealing:* Robbery; attempted robbery	*Non-psychotic illnesses:* PTSD	2 years 8 months in young offender institution; 2 years extended license

(*Continued*)

Table 11.1 (Continued)

	Case	Offence Category and Specific Offence	Diagnostic Category and Specific Diagnosis	Sentence
7.	*NFU Mutual Insurance Society Limited Society Ltd v Khedir* (2022) EWHC 437 (QB)	*Other:* Contempt of court	*Non-psychotic illnesses:* Depression	10 months
8.	*R v Gore* (2022) EWCA Crim 219	*Sex offences committed against children:* Possession of prohibited images of children	*Developmental disorders:* Intellectual/learning disability; ASD	4 weeks suspended for 2 years; 50-day rehabilitation; sexual harm prevention order
9.	*Paddington Garden Company One Ltd v Rasool* (2022) EWHC 2081 (QB)	*Other:* Contempt of court	Unspecified	2 years
10.	*R v Hoskin* (2022) EWCA Crim 1633	*Assault (physical and verbal):* Assault of an emergency worker *Other:* Manslaughter	*Non-psychotic illnesses:* PTSD *Developmental disorders:* Personality disorder	10 years
11.	*R v Slack* (2023) EWCA Crim 522	*Assault (physical and verbal):* Wounding with intent	Unspecified	5 years; 2 years extended license
12.	*R v Bains* (2023) EWCA Crim 1586	*Drugs:* Possessing Class A drugs with intent to supply	*Developmental disorders:* ASD	9 years
13.	*R v Bond* (2024) EWCA Crim 406	*Assault (physical and verbal):* Assault causing actual bodily harm	*Developmental disorders:* ADHD	6 months
14.	*R v Newman* (2024) EWCA Crim 415	*Sex offences committed against children:* Sexual activity with a child; causing or inciting a child to engage in a sexual activity; making/taking indecent photographs of a child	*Developmental disorders:* Intellectual/learning disability	3 years 5 months

Table 11.2 Sentencing Outcome 2 – Reconsideration of Guideline: Sentence reduced

	Case	*Offence Category and Specific Offence*	*Diagnostic Category & Specific Diagnosis*	*Sentence*
1.	*R v Baldwin* (2021) EWCA Crim 417	*Assault (physical and verbal):* Making threats to kill	*Developmental disorders:* Intellectual/learning disability; ASD; ADHD	1 year 4 months in young offender institute ↓ 1 year community order; 15-day rehabilitation
2.	*R v Gulzar* (2023) EWCA Crim 630	*Assault (physical and verbal):* Assault causing actual bodily harm *Weapons:* Threatening another with a bladed article; having a bladed article	*Developmental disorders:* ASD; ADHD	3 years 4 months ↓ 2 years 10 months
3.	*R v Simmonds* (2023) EWCA Crim 1063	*Stealing:* Theft; robbery	*Substance use disorders:* Alcohol *Developmental disorders:* ASD; ADHD	6 years 9 months ↓ 4 years 8 months
4.	*R v BGW* (2023) EWCA Crim 1198	*Kidnapping:* Conspiracy to kidnap; conspiracy to commit false imprisonment *Blackmail:* Conspiracy to blackmail	*Non-psychotic illnesses:* PTSD *Developmental disorders:* ADHD	10 years 6 months; 5 years extended license ↓ 8 years; 5 years extended license
5.	*R v JW* (2023) EWCA Crim 1257	*Sex offences committed against children:* Sexual activity with a child; causing or inciting a child to engage in a sexual activity	*Developmental disorders:* ASD	2 years 3 months ↓ 1 year 6 months
6.	*R v ABQ* (2024) EWCA Crim 310	*Sex offences committed against children:* Rape of a child under 13; causing or inciting a child to engage in a sexual activity; sexual assault; making/taking indecent photographs of a child	*Non-psychotic illnesses:* Depression *Developmental disorders:* Intellectual/learning disability; ASD	22 years; 8 years extended license ↓ 17 years; 8 years extended license

Table 11.3 Sentencing Outcome 3 – Reconsideration of Guideline: Sentence increased

	Case	*Offence Category and Specific Offence*	*Diagnostic Category & Specific Diagnosis*	*Sentence*
1.	*R v CH* (2020) EWCA Crim 1736	*Sex offences committed against children:* Rape of a child under 13	*Developmental disorders:* Intellectual/learning disability; ASD; ADHD	3 years community order; 35-day rehabilitation; £200 fine; £2500 victim compensation + victim surcharge ↓ Curfew added
2.	*R v Wellington* (2021) EWCA Crim 294	*Assault (physical and verbal):* Inflicting grievous bodily harm; malicious communication *Drugs:* Conspiracy to supply controlled drug of Class A; possessing a controlled drug of Class B *Damage:* Damaging property *Blackmail:* Blackmail	Unspecified	5 years ↓ 9 years
3.	*R v Finch* (2021) EWCA Crim 377	*Other:* Recording information for a purpose prejudicial to the safety or interests of the state; making a damaging disclosure relating to deference; failing to comply with a disclosure notice	*Developmental disorders:* ASD	4 years 6 months ↓ 8 years

(*Continued*)

Table 11.3 (Continued)

	Case	*Offence Category and Specific Offence*	*Diagnostic Category & Specific Diagnosis*	*Sentence*
4.	*R v JD* (2023) EWCA Crim 317	*Other:* Attempted rape	*Developmental disorders:* Intellectual/learning disability	2 years suspended for 2 years; 40-day rehabilitation ↓ 4 years
5.	*R v Cook, Williams* (2023) EWCA Crim 649	*Stealing:* Aggravated burglary *Weapons:* Having a bladed article	Unspecified	Cook: 6 years 1 month ↓ 8 years 6 months Williams: 5 years 6 months ↓ 8 years
6.	*R v Wilson* (2023) EWCA Crim 673	*Damage:* Causing criminal damage *Other:* Acts tending and intended to pervert the course of justice; dangerous driving	*Non-psychotic illnesses:* Depression; anxiety	2 years suspended for 2 years; 200 hours unpaid work ↓ Sentence was too lenient; discretion used not to interfere in sentence
7.	*R v Richfield* (2024) EWCA Crim 116	*Assault (physical and verbal):* Assault of an emergency worker; putting a person in fear of violence by harassment *Drugs:* Drug possession *Other:* Arson being reckless as to whether life was endangered	*Substance use disorders:* Drugs *Developmental disorders:* ADHD	3 years community order; 40-day rehabilitation; 1 year mental health treatment ↓ 3 years 4 months imprisonment

Table 11.4 Sentencing Outcome 4 – Other: Guideline previously considered appropriately; sentence altered but not due to Guideline

	Case	*Offence Category and Specific Offence*	*Diagnostic Category & Specific Diagnosis*	*Sentence*
1.	*R v Nugent* (2021) EWCA Crim 1535	*Terrorism:* Dissemination of terrorist publications; Possession of information likely to be useful to the preparation of an act of terrorism	*Non-psychotic illnesses:* Depression; anxiety	3 years 6 months; 1 year extended license ↓ 5 years; 1 year extended license
2.	*R v Qayum* (2022) EWCA Crim 454	*Kidnapping:* Kidnapping	*Developmental disorders:* Intellectual/learning disability	10 years 9 months ↓ 9 years
3.	*R v Noble* (2023) EWCA Crim 492	*Stealing:* Conspiracy to rob	*Developmental disorders:* ADHD	3 years 6 months ↓ 5 years 6 months

most indicated that the original sentence had 'appropriately balanced the aggravating and mitigating factors' per the Guideline.[45] In eight cases, the original sentence had already been reduced due to mitigation attributed to the diagnosis. This indicates that most sentencing courts actively engage with and implement the Guideline.

In other cases where the sentence remained unchanged, appeal courts concluded that the original sentence had not been impacted by the offender's diagnosis. For example, in *Bel*, where a sentence of two years imprisonment and one-year extended license was ordered regarding three offences involving conspiracies to harm another person, the original sentencer expressly questioned whether an ASD diagnosis had any bearing on these offences, even though it clearly had some impact during the trial because:

> the applicant used the diagnosis when it suited him. From what the judge had seen of him at the trial and during the pre-trial hearings and bearing in mind the other evidence in the case, he concluded that the applicant was a highly manipulative person. Although the judge bore in mind his mental disorder, as required by the definitive guideline, he did not find that it had any material effect on sentencing. The way in

45 *R v Law* (2021) EWCA Crim 1985 [22].

> which the applicant exploited his diagnosis of Asperger's Syndrome had been demonstrated at the beginning of the trial when the applicant had refused to wear a [medical] mask, as required. He told the security staff that it was his human right not to wear a mask. He then changed his reason and claimed through his counsel that wearing a mask adversely affected his health in terms of his Asperger's condition.[46]

In *Honeyman*, there was no 'evidence of a sufficient connection between his mental state and his offending behaviour significantly to lower his culpability' or reduce a sentence of three years imprisonment for possessing illicit drugs and weapons.[47] Similarly, in *Hellyer*, no evidence linked the offender's PTSD or the effects of alcoholism to the commission of an intentional assault, nor was it determined that the nine-and-a-half-year prison term would be unduly burdensome.[48]

While the mental disorders and impairments were raised during sentencing in our sample of 30, the discretionary application of Section 1(2) of the Guideline is evident. Under this requirement, the court must consider the offender's impairment or disorder but retains discretion to determine the sentence as deemed appropriate.

Sentence Reduced

Six offenders received sentence reductions after reconsideration of the Guideline on appeal. Five of these offenders had been diagnosed with ASD, and four had co-occurring conditions. Four cases involved offences against the person, including two child sex offences. The reasons for these sentence reductions are particularly noteworthy.

Three appeals examined offender culpability under Section 2 of the Guideline. In *Baldwin*, the court found that a reduction was necessary because psychiatric evidence suggested responsibility for the offence of making threats to kill 'was substantially reduced by mental disorder and learning disability'.[49] Further:

> as the guideline states, where there are competing characteristics, the guideline requires a balancing exercise to reach a fair overall assessment of culpability. That balancing exercise did not occur [. . .] Here the judge made no more than passing reference to the evidence of [the psychiatrist]. He made no assessment of whether the appellant's mental issues reduced culpability. Had he made such an assessment, he inevitably

46 *R v Bel* (2021) EWCA Crim 1461 [26].
47 *R v Honeyman* (2021) EWCA Crim 1324 [29].
48 *R v Hellyer* (2021) EWCA Crim 550 [34, 35].
49 *R v Baldwin* (2021) EWCA Crim 417 [15].

> would have concluded that culpability was reduced. There were no reasons, compelling or otherwise, for the judge not to have followed the opinion of [the psychiatrist].[50]

Baldwin's sentence was reduced from 16 months in youth custody to a 12-month community order with a 15-day Rehabilitation Activity Requirement. Similarly, in *JW*, which involved a conviction for child sex offences by a 19- to 20-year-old offender against his 13- to 14-year-old niece, the court stated that a reduction in culpability was warranted after considering 'the impact of the appellant's disorder on his offending', which reduced the initial sentence from 27 to 18 months imprisonment.[51] ABQ was convicted of serious child sexual abuse offences against her children committed in concert with her partner. Here, the original sentencing remarks did not indicate that any reduction in sentence had been considered regarding the offender's diagnosis of intellectual and learning disability, depression, and ASD and resulting culpability.[52] The original sentence of 22 years imprisonment and eight years on extended licence was reduced by five years.

In two cases, the original sentence was reduced after reconsideration of the offender's potential vulnerability or burden of imprisonment under Section 3(22) of the Guideline. In *Simmonds*, a sentence of six years and nine months in prison for theft and robbery was reduced to four years and eight months because the appeal court found that:

> imprisonment is likely to have a particularly severe impact on the appellant due to her "extreme vulnerability". There are a number of elements to her vulnerability. She suffers from autism (which was of sufficient severity for her to have been placed in a special school) and ADHD. There are evident mental health concerns. She has an alcohol misuse disorder and she is a transwoman.[53]

Similarly, in *BGW*, the initial sentence of imprisonment for kidnapping and blackmail was reduced by two years and six months because:

> the severe impact of custody on the appellant is a factor to be taken into account as an aspect of personal mitigation in his favour. The judge noted that the appellant was "doing well in custody", but that does not, in our view, take account of the substantial obstacles that the appellant has had to and continues to overcome in order to do well. These obstacles are also likely to have an effect on the efficacy of efforts to rehabilitate.[54]

50 Ibid [15–16].
51 *R v JW* (2023) EWCA Crim 1257 [17].
52 *R v ABQ* (2024) EWCA Crim 310 [29].
53 *R v Simmonds* (2023) EWCA Crim 1063 [25].
54 *R v BGW* (2023) EWCA Crim 1198 [40].

These cases highlight the importance of appeal courts in recalibrating sentences after an initial application of the Guideline. This is a common feature of appeal procedures that need to reconcile individualised sentencing with consistency.[55]

Adjusting Lenient Sentences

In seven cases, an original sentence was increased after an appeal by the Solicitor General or Attorney General questioned its leniency. In *Richfield*, the appeal court found a custodial sentence should replace a three-year community order and 40-day rehabilitation activity for the offences of harassment, assault, drug possession, and arson because 'the judge was wrong to have given what must have been the very substantial reductions that she did to take account of Mr Richfield's own drug-induced psychotic state'.[56] That is, interestingly, the judge had factored in the offender's self-inflicted psychosis despite contradictory advice in the Guideline.

In *Cook* and *Williams*, the appeal court took a stronger stance, finding a 'tenuous chain of connection' between the mental disorder or impairment and offences of aggravated burglary and knife possession.[57] On appeal, Cook's custodial sentence was increased by two years and five months and Williams' by two years and six months because the initial sentencer had provided:

> no information about [an impairment] as applicable to these offenders. There were no medical reports and there was no other report. He simply had no proper basis for a conclusion that for these offenders [an impairment] played any part in the offending.[58]

In *JD*, the offender was convicted of the attempted rape of his girlfriend while she was unconscious. Whilst the Attorney General conceded 'strong mitigation in the form of the offender's learning disabilities', the appeal challenged the leniency of a two-year suspended custodial term with corresponding rehabilitation requirements.[59] JD was resentenced to a four-year custodial term on appeal because:

> the circumstances of the offending, even taking into account the offender's learning disabilities and difficulties, were not such as to justify a complete departure from the relevant [sentencing] range and starting point. This was very serious offending, involving almost complete commission of the offence of rape.[60]

55 S Krasnostein, '*Boulton v The Queen*: The Resurrection of Guideline Judgments in Australia?' (2015) 27(1) *Current Issues in Criminal Justice* 41–58.
56 *R v Richfield* (2024) EWCA Crim 116 [25].
57 *R v Cook, Williams* (2023) EWCA Crim 649 [37].
58 Ibid [36].
59 *R v JD* (2023) EWCA Crim 317 [45].
60 Ibid [48].

Similarly, in *Wellington*, 'the material available to the judge did not support the suggestion that mental illness played any part in the offender's participation in the conspiracy' to supply illicit drugs or engage in other violent and threatening offences against the person, as well as several property offences.[61] Wellington was originally sentenced to five years in prison but was released at the time of the Crown appeal. An ensuing increase to nine years imprisonment required his return to custody, with the appeal court emphasising the potential beneficial supervisory effects of this outcome by adding:

> the mental health difficulties affecting the offender were substantially under control at the time of this offending and, in any event, do not go to reduce his culpability for this calculated and serious offence [. . .] The medical evidence suggests that his problems result, at least in part, from substance abuse. That will be avoided in prison and he will have appropriate medication.[62]

Potential Concerns Regarding Section 1(4)

It is clear that first-instance courts may still be coming to terms with the Guideline requirements. Section 1(4) notes nine elements sentencers should consider, but repeated use of the hedging terms 'may' and 'can' could be resulting in or contributing to misunderstandings and inconsistencies that are an inevitable by-product of the sentencing process.

Section 1(4) states a formal diagnosis of a disorder or impairment is not always required. In *Slack*, the judgment mentioned the lack of a 'firm diagnosis' beyond possible depression and poor emotional regulation.[63] Similarly, in *Honeyman*, the appeal court found 'no evidence of a severe and enduring mental illness' despite some documentation cataloguing the offender's borderline learning disability.[64] In *Nugent*, the sentencer remarked on a 'rather elusive diagnosis' based on symptoms of anxiety and depression.[65] Whilst the lack of a medical diagnosis might not have directly affected these decisions, the comments appear to stem from the failure of the Guideline to elaborate on the circumstances where a formal diagnosis is not needed.

Section 1(4) also urges sentencers to be aware of differing expert opinions and diagnoses but offers no additional detail on the desired approach in these circumstances. In *Hoskin*, experts were conflicted about the degree to which the offender's diagnosis contributed to the offence.[66] Therefore, the qualifications of experts and their knowledge about the offender remain discretionary considerations in absence of clear statements within the Guideline.

61 *R v Wellington* (2021) EWCA Crim 294 [38].
62 Ibid [43].
63 *R v Slack* (2023) EWCA Crim 522 [23].
64 *R v Honeyman* (2021) EWCA Crim 1324 [13].
65 *R v Nugent* (2021) EWCA Crim 1535 [20].
66 *R v Hoskin* (2022) EWCA Crim 1633 [33].

Finally, Section 1(4) requires the court to avoid assumptions that some mental disorders are always stable; in fact, an offender's condition at the time of the offence could be different from his or her state during legal proceedings. In *Bel*, the offender's behaviour and comments during psychiatric assessments and court proceedings suggested that he was manipulative and using an ASD diagnosis selectively. Although he claimed he could not wear a mask in court, he was photographed wearing a Nazi-like mask elsewhere, and then he wore a mask after being told that his bail could be revoked. The court concluded that Bel was an 'arrogant young man' who believed he was 'superior to others'.[67] These facts raise concerns about possible non-adherence to Section 1(4).

Balancing Public Safety

An offender's diagnosis must be balanced against the broader aim of ensuring public safety.[68] This might require a rehabilitative rather than custodial disposition that is recognised under Section 3(22) of the Guideline. Alternatively, the risk of recidivism, whether linked to the offender's diagnosis or not, can be so high that public safety must be prioritised over the mitigating elements of the offender's diagnosis. For example, in *Nugent*, the court stated the offender was:

> on the 'borderline' of being a dangerous offender and [the court] decided that the special custodial sentence was adequate for public protection. The danger he presents does not arise from a psychiatric condition which could be treated. There was little or no evidence to suggest that this was the case.[69]

Similarly, in *Bel*, expert reports stated that the offender's:

> lack of internal controls when it came to expressing his views was a likely result of his ASD. This condition would render him vulnerable to the influence of others. If he persisted in his association with such individuals, the risk of harm could increase exponentially [. . .] He was assessed as posing a high risk of harm to the public until such time as he developed internal controls to understand and manage his risk to others. There continued to be identifiable indicators of risk of serious harm, the potential event could happen at any time and the impact would be serious. He was assessed as posing a medium risk of harm to children through radicalisation into right-wing extremism. He was also assessed as a medium risk of harm to himself.[70]

67 *R v Bel* (2021) EWCA Crim 1461 [27].

68 Sentencing Council, *Sentencing Basics* <www.sentencingcouncil.org.uk/sentencing-basics/> accessed 10 June 2024.

69 *R v Nugent* (2021) EWCA Crim 1535 [20].

70 *R v Bel* (2021) EWCA Crim 1461 [16]. This comment seems in stark contrast to other parts of the judgment which tended to disregard the relevance of the offender's diagnosis in the context of past and current behaviour by labelling the offender as manipulative and claiming they used the ASD diagnosis to their advantage.

Appeal courts frequently concluded that the risk to the public necessitated a custodial sentence, with the potential for future risk influencing the length of imprisonment and associated licence periods under relevant dangerousness requirements.[71] Thus, despite concerns that the Guideline could mitigate culpability to outweigh consideration of public safety,[72] courts do not appear to have difficulty weighing these issues.

The Importance of Expert Evidence

This sample clearly highlights the importance of expert evidence. Reports from psychologists, psychiatrists, and other mental health professionals commonly detailed specific aspects of the offender's diagnosis that demonstrated how the impairment was relevant to determining culpability. Expert evidence also emphasised the potential negative impacts of imprisonment, including some cases where the offender was 'on the edge of fitness to receive a custodial sentence'.[73]

For example, in *Newman*, psychological reports detailed the offender's 'extremely low intellectual and adaptive functioning' that would generate 'significant challenges in understanding the consequences of their actions'.[74] The report demonstrated the offender would 'face significantly more difficulties adapting to prison life [and] may struggle to communicate effectively with prison staff and inmates, and he may be at risk of being exploited by others'.[75] Similarly, in *BGW*, the expert report stated that the offender would be 'highly vulnerable in a custodial setting' and at risk of 'self-isolation and significant deterioration in mental health'.[76] In *CH*, the expert report suggested the offender would be 'very vulnerable in a custodial setting' and would find it 'difficult to cope with the change in his environment and interact with other inmates', which could lead to 'bullying and other physical abuse'.[77]

These comments support previous literature emphasising the importance of expert witnesses in criminal trials and sentencing,[78] and reinforce their central-

71 See for example, *R v Finch* (2021) EWCA Crim 377 [47]; *R v Hellyer* (2021) EWCA Crim 550 [37]; *R v Law* (2021) EWCA Crim 1985 [17]; *R v Slack* (2023) EWCA Crim 522 [11]; *R v BGW* (2023) EWCA Crim 1198 [27]; *R v Richfield* (2024) EWCA Crim 116 [14].

72 OP O'Sullivan and N Eastman, '"Out of the Penal System and into the Hospital Regime?" Judicial Challenges in Sentencing Mentally Disordered Offenders and the Likely Impact of the 2020 Sentencing Council Guideline' (2023) 87(5–6) *Journal of Criminal Law* 417–27 [425].

73 *R v Gore* (2022) EWCA Crim 219 [6].

74 *R v Newman* (2024) EWCA Crim 415 [18, 19].

75 Ibid [19].

76 *R v BGW* (2023) EWCA Crim 1198 [31].

77 *R v CH* (2020) EWCA Crim 1736 [11].

78 I Freckelton and D List, 'Asperger's Disorder, Criminal Responsibility and Criminal Culpability' (2009) 16(1) *Psychiatry, Psychology and Law* 16–40; I Freckelton, 'Autism Spectrum Disorders and the Criminal Law' in MR Mohammadi (ed) *A Comprehensive Book on Autism*

ity in the Guideline in helping a court reconcile relevant mitigating and aggravating circumstances. However, psychiatrists and other experts must carefully read the Guideline to ensure testimony considers the Sentencing Council's advice, without providing a general opinion on the punishment itself.[79]

Conclusion

This analysis demonstrates the relevance and applicability of the Guideline to a diverse range of case circumstances. It is crucial for enabling the consideration of mental disorders and impairments during initial sentencing and on appeal. While 13 sentences were adjusted (just over 40% of this sample) and concerns were expressed regarding the application of Section 1(4), the Guideline appears to 'consolidate information, improve judicial knowledge, reduce confusion, and assist the courts in promoting consistency in sentencing'.[80] However, it is equally clear that the courts retain considerable discretion in attempting to reconcile the offender's diagnosis with other relevant aggravating and mitigating factors, including the maintenance of public safety. This research suggests that the Guideline is an important step in addressing the inequities faced by those with mental disorders and impairments confronting the criminal justice system. However, the Guideline does not necessarily ameliorate but rather shifts the emphasis of the inherently discretionary character of sentencing.

Spectrum Disorders (Intech Press 2011) 249–72; I Freckelton, 'Expert Evidence by Mental Health Professionals: The Communication Challenge Posed by Evidence about Autism Spectrum Disorder, Brain Injuries, and Huntington's Disease' (2012) 35(5–6) *International Journal of Law and Psychiatry* 372–79; CM Berryessa, 'Educator of the Court: The Role of the Expert Witness in Cases Involving Autism Spectrum Disorder' (2017) 23(6) *Psychology, Crime and Law* 575–600.

79 PJ Taylor, N Eastman, R Lathan, and J Holloway, 'Sentencing Offenders with Mental Disorders, Developmental Disorders or Neurological Impairments: What Does the New Sentencing Council Guideline Mean for Psychiatrists?' (2021) 218(6) *British Journal of Psychiatry* 299–301.

80 OP O'Sullivan and N Eastman, '"Out of the Penal System and into the Hospital Regime?" Judicial Challenges in Sentencing Mentally Disordered Offenders and the Likely Impact of the 2020 Sentencing Council Guideline' (2023) 87(5–6) *Journal of Criminal Law* 417–27 [427].

12 Searching for Justice

Reforming Sentencing for Children and Young People Convicted of Murder

Hannah Wishart

Distinctive Approaches to Sentencing Children for Murder: 1908–1999

Since the 19th century, the principle that children and young people should be treated differently from adults based on their age has been reflected in our approach to criminal justice; it was not until the late 19th century that 'there were no differences according to age in the method of bringing offenders to trial, in the form of the trial itself, in the punishments that could be imposed or, generally, in the way in which they were enforced.'[1] The Children Act 1908 brought crucial legislative reform, establishing distinct principles and procedures for sentencing children and young people differently from those governing adult offenders. Notably, it created a separate legal process to fairly handle cases of children and young people who committed crimes.[2]

The perspective of children as vulnerable persons in need of welfare protection was the paradigm for the government's approach to those who offend following the enactment of the Children and Young Persons Act 1933 (CYPA). The government insisted that the CYPA guaranteed that the criminal justice system would effectively consider the child's best interests and welfare concerns (Section 44(1)) and maintains that position today. Such a welfarist perspective places significant weight on the criminal justice system for making decisions that align with the child's best interests, from the court removing them from undesirable surroundings to making accommodations to enable them to participate effectively at trial.[3]

1 L Radzinowicz and R Hood, *The Emergence of Penal Policy* (Stevens & Son, 1986) 133.

2 Section 102 of the Children Act (1908). See also The Michael Sieff Foundation, *1908–2008: The Children Act 100 Years on Young Defendants Today* (Report on the Conference hosted on Tuesday the 28th of April, 2009 at Church House, Westminster, London July 2009) 4; S Case, *Youth Justice A Critical Introduction* (Routledge 2018) 30–31.

3 Section 44 requires that 'every court in dealing with a child or young person who is brought before it, a either . . . an offender or otherwise, shall have regard to the welfare of the child or young person and shall in a proper case take steps for removing him from undesirable surroundings, and for securing that proper provisions made for his education and training'; E Eekelaar, 'Beyond the Welfare Principle' (2002) 14 *Child and Family Law Quarterly* 237.

DOI: 10.4324/9781003496823-12

The child's best interests and welfare considerations remain at the forefront of the youth justice system; when sentencing youth under 18, a court must consider the young person's welfare and the principal aim of the youth justice system, which is to prevent them from reoffending (Section 37(1) of the Crime and Disorder Act (1998)). This statute also prohibited young people under 16 who were convicted of murder from being sentenced to death 'reflect[ing] the reduced responsibility and special needs of those committing murder as children or young persons'.[4] Under S. 103 of the Children Act (1908), children and young people are sentenced not to death but to detention in 'such place and under such conditions as the Secretary of State may direct and while so detained shall be deemed to be in legal custody',[5] and this remains unchanged.

Legal commentators have praised these statutes for recognising that welfare-based interventions rather than punitive measures were the best and most just approach to addressing the needs of those under 16 who committed murder.[6] These are precedents for adopting a different approach to children and young people in the English criminal justice system by accommodating and distinguishing their youth and immaturity.[7] However, these provisions failed to give clear guidance on the minimun sentence that a child or young person convicted of murder should serve in detention before being released on parole. This responsibility was left to the Secretary of State (the Home Secretary) to address. In practice, the Secretary of State received recommendations from both the trial judge and the Lord Chief Justice (LCJ) to establish the minimum sentence a person should serve, thus satisfying the deterrence and retributive aims of sentencing.[8]

The rationale for this process was set out in S. 2 of The Murder (Abolition of Death Penalty) Act (1965), which provided that 'no person convicted of murder shall be released on license unless the Secretary of State has prior to such release consulted the Lord Chief Justice together with the trial judge if

4 *R v Secretary of State for the Home Department, Ex Parte Hindley* [2005] UKHL 51, 10. Section 53(1) of the CYPA (1933) extended the abolition of the death penalty provision to those aged 18 years and below, as amended by The Murder (Abolition of Death Penalty) Act (1965). Section 53(2) of the CYPA (1933) provided that where a person under 17 was convicted of an offence, the maximum term of detention would not exceed 14 years.

5 Section 103 of the Children Act (1908).

6 B Lyons, 'Dying to be Responsible: Adolescence, Autonomy and Responsibility' (2010) 30(2) *Legal Studies* 271; R Arthur, 'Rethinking the Criminal Responsibility of Young People in England and Wales' (2012) 20(1) *European Journal of Crime, Criminal Law and Criminal Justice* 4; N Stone, 'Children Who Murder: Indeterminate Sentencing in Law and Practice' (2018) 18 *Youth Justice* 83.

7 Home Office, *Report of the Departmental Committee on the Treatment of Young Offenders* (HMSO, The Moloney Report, 1927) 6; R Arthur, 'Protecting the Best Interests of the Child: A Comparative Analysis of the Youth Justice Systems in Ireland, England and Scotland' (2010) 18 *International Journal of Children's Rights* 218–19.

8 N Stone, 'Children Who Murder: Indeterminate Sentencing in Law and Practice' (2018) 18 *Youth Justice* 83.

available'. In 1991, Parliament authorised the Home Secretary to contravene S. 35(2) of the Criminal Justice Act (1991) and release a child or young person on license if, and only if, the Parole Board recommended their release 'after consultation with the Lord Chief Justice of England together with the trial judge if available'.[9]

Parliament intended to provide more explicit guidance to the Home Secretary on establishing minimum sentences for young people before they are eligible for parole. However, the inclusion in S. 35(2) of the phrase 'after consultation with' inadvertently granted the Home Secretary absolute discretion in parole release decisions.[10] This meant that the Home Secretary had the statutory power to ignore any endorsements by the trial judge, LCJ and Parole Board for a lower minimum term and the early release of any child or young person convicted of murder.

This was evident in the case of two ten-year-old boys who abducted and murdered two-year-old James Bulger in *R v Secretary of State for the Home Dept, ex p Venables, R v Secretary of State for the Home Dept, ex p Thompson*.[11] The crime 'profoundly shocked the nation'[12] because it occurred at a time 'amidst a more fundamental shift towards a neoliberal form of governance which encouraged greater individual responsibility and was less tolerant of indiscipline'.[13]

The media vilified Venables and Thompson before and after the trial because of their heinous killing of Bulger. *The Daily Mail* wrote that 'the boys who murdered James Bulger are evil freaks of human nature who were fixated on killing and causing disaster'.[14] *The Sun* issued the following coupon to the public that was completed and sent to the Home Secretary: 'Dear Home Secretary, I agree with Ralph and Denise Bulger that the boys who killed their son James should stay in jail for LIFE'.[15] In agreement with the public and media's punitive stance, the Conservative then Prime Minister, John Major, gave an interview to the *Daily Star* three days after James Bulger's body was

9 Section 35(2) of the Criminal Justice Act (1991).

10 Note that Section 28 of the Crime (Sentences) Act (1997) transferred the power of the Home Secretary to decide the release of children and young persons to the Parole Board.

11 *R v Secretary of State for the Home Dept, ex p Venables, R v Secretary of State for the Home Dept, ex p Thompson* [1997] 3 All ER.

12 *Venables v News Group Newspapers Ltd* [2019] EWHC 494 (Fam); [2019] EMLR 17, 1.

13 B Byrne and K Brooks, *POST YOT Youth Justice Working Paper 19/2015* (Howard League for Penal Reform 2015) 4.

14 *The Daily Mail*, 17th of February 1993, 6; Quoted by C McDiarmid, *Childhood and Crime* (Dundee University Press 2007) 17.

15 Referenced in D Haydon and P Scraton, 'Condemn a Little More, Understand a Little Less': The Political Context and Rights Implications of the Domestic and European Rulings in the Venables-Thompson Case' (2007) 27 *Journal of Law and Society* 433.

discovered stating that 'society needs to condemn a little more and understand a little less'.[16]

This case attracted significant publicity because the trial judge recommended that both boys be sentenced to eight years in detention to satisfy the requirements of deterrence and retribution for murder, reasoning that

> if the defendants had been adults I would have said that the actual length of deterrence necessary to meet the requirements of retribution and general deterrence should have been eighteen years. However, these two boys came from homes and families with great social and emotional deprivation. They grew up in an atmosphere of matrimonial breakdown where they were exposed to, saw, heard, or suffered abuse, drunkenness and violence. . . . In my judgment the appropriate length of detention necessary to meet the requirement of retribution and general deterrence for the murder, taking into account all its appalling circumstances and the age of the defendants when it was committed is eight years. . . . Eight years is 'very very many years' for a ten- or eleven-year-old. They are now children. In eight years' time they will be young men.[17]

Considering the aggravating factors of the case, the LCJ disagreed with the trial judge's recommendation; he believed that Venables and Thompson should have received a longer sentence and recommended that the defendants should serve a minimum term of 10 years.[18]

The Home Secretary reviewed these recommendations and actually ultimately decided on minimum sentences for both of 15 years. Before this decision, there was significant public concern that the defendants would not be sentenced punitively for their heinous actions. Over 20,000 members of the public signed petitions demanding lengthy and punitive sentences for killing a two-year-old boy that were sent to the then Home Secretary. In a written statement, following questions from the Lord Chancellor's Department about his discretionary powers, he remarked that he had to consider 'the public acceptability of early release' in the case and would 'exercise my discretion to release only if I am satisfied that to do so will not threaten the maintenance

16 'Major on Criminals: "We should Condemn A Little More, Understand A Little Less" Exclusive" The Prime Minister Sets Out His Values For the Nineties' reported in the Mail on Sunday (21st of February 1993) 8.

17 House of Lords, *Judgment – Reg. v Secretary of State for the Home Department, Ex parte V. and Reg. v. Secretary of State for the Home Department, Ex parte T* (House of Parliament, Session 1997–98, 12th of June 1997).

18 J Fionda, 'Case Commentary, R v Secretary of State for the Home Department ex parte Venables and Thompson, the Age of Innocence? – The Concept of Childhood in the Punishment of Young Offenders' (1998) 10 *Child & Family Law Quarterly* 78.

of public confidence in the system of criminal justice'.[19] The Home Secretary's decision to go against the recommendations of the trial judge and the LCJ in favour of a 15-year minimum term is thought to have been made to appease public sentiment.[20]

The defendants challenged the Home Secretary and appealed to the Court of Appeal, and the Divisional Court upheld their appeal. The Home Secretary subsequently appealed to the Court of Appeal in 1998 on the lawfulness of this decision, which resulted in him further appealing to the House of Lords.[21]

Here, the House of Lords ruled that the best interests of the child under S. 44 CYPA (1933) demanded a different sentencing approach for children and young persons convicted of murder than that for adults.[22] Lord Justice Davis and Mrs Justice May, in R *(on the application of Jesse Quaye) v Secretary of State for Justice*,[23] explaining that sentencing and detention HMP (Her Majesty's Pleasure)[24] permitted the Secretary of State to 'consider from time to time whether continued detention was justified. He was entitled to set a provisional and reviewable tariff to reflect punishment and deterrence',[25] but was unlawful for the Secretary of State to follow an irreducible policy disregarding the offender's progress.

The House of Lords found the sentence 'disproportionately long' for two 10-year-old defendants and 'without due regard to the needs of rehabilitation' as laid out in CYPA S. 44 (1933).[26] Lord Woolf specifically remarked that the 15-year minimum term was wholly inappropriate because it amounted to '150% of the applicants' lives so far'.[27] Their Lordships stated that the Home Secretary had given in to public outcry and media attention when he should have remained detached, and they quashed the Home Secretary's appeal, finding that the 15 years was incompatible with his duty to review sentences.[28]

The rationale for this different approach is enshrined in Article 3 of the United Nations Convention on the Rights of the Child (UNCRC), which states that 'the best interests of the child shall be a primary consideration in

19 Hansard (HC Debates), 27th of July (1993) Column 864: written answer. https://hansard.parliament.uk/commons/1993-07-27/debates/a3942995-fa01-44d4-8885-0d79bb7e7fac/WrittenAnswers (Accessed June, 2024).

20 N Stone, 'Children Who Murder: Indeterminate Sentencing in Law and Practice' (2018) 18 *Youth Justice* 84.

21 *R v Secretary of State for the Home Department, ex parte Venables and Thompson* [1998] AC 407.

22 J Fionda, 'Case Commentary, R v Secretary of State for the Home Department ex parte Venables and Thompson, the Age of Innocence? – The Concept of Childhood in the Punishment of Young Offenders' (1998) *10 Child & Family Law Quarterly* 77.

23 [2024] EWHC 211 (Admin).

24 The word 'her' has been used to reflect the reign of Queen Elizabeth 2 in 1996.

25 [2024] EWHC 211 (Admin) at 8.

26 *T v United Kingdom* (1999) 7 BHRC 659 at 24.

27 [1997] 2 WLR 67 at p 92.

28 (1999) 7 BHRC 659 at 24.

all actions concerning children'. Section 37 of the UNCRC also requires that custodial sentences only be used as a last resort and for the shortest appropriate period, particularly in cases of severe offences when there are no other suitable sanctions. It is essential to acknowledge the international significance of ensuring equitable sentencing for children and young individuals, considering both the gravity of the offence and the age of the offender. The UNCRC is an international human rights treaty adopted by the UN General Assembly in 1989 and ratified by the UK in 1991. The Convention places a legal responsibility on England and Wales to recognise that individuals under 18 years of age require special protective status and treatment for their young age and development (e.g. shorter sentences).[29] The aim of the Convention is to prevent prolonged incarceration of children and young people and act in their best interests, and the House of Lords found that the Home Secretary's sentence of 15 years was unlawful and unnecessary.

In response to the House of Lords 1998 ruling, the Home Secretary established a new sentencing policy for children and young persons convicted of murder to address the unlawfulness of his actions. The Department of the Home Secretary would continuously review all tariffs set by his office after half of the initial term and consider any request for a review. In doing so, the Home Secretary would consider factors such as the child/young person's rehabilitative progress during detention and their degree of maturation. He further requested that the representatives of Venables and Thompson provide additional statements to the Department so that he could determine new minimum terms for their parole release.

Venables and Thompson appealed to the European Court (ECtHR) in *V. v United Kingdom*[30] and *T v United Kingdom*.[31] One issue considered was whether the Home Secretary's duty to set the minimum tariff term a person must serve in detention before being released on parole was compatible with the Convention. The European Court held that the Secretary of State had breached several rights encapsulated in the Convention, specifically, the defendants' Article 6(1) right to a fair trial and their Article 5(4) right that 'guaranteed to everyone deprived of liberty the right to have the legality of that detention judicially determined'.[32,33]

Lord Reed stated, 'however dreadful a crime may be, the person accused of committing it has certain rights, including the right to a fair trial' and the ability to effectively participate at trial. These rights are protected internationally

29 Children's Rights Alliance for England, UN Convention on the Rights of the Child, https://crae.org.uk/our-guide-childrens-rights-and-law/laws-protecting-childrens-rights/un-convention-rights-child (Accessed September 2024).

30 *V v United Kingdom* (2000) 30 EHRR 121.

31 *T v United Kingdom* (1999) 7 BHRC 659; *V v United Kingdom* [1991] ECHR 24888/94.

32 Ibid [6].

33 (1999) *BHRC*, 7, 659 [2–4]; K Hollingsworth, 'Judicial Approaches to Children's Rights in Youth Crime' (2007) 19 Child and Family Law Quarterly 48–50.

under the UNHCR and in English law with the Human Rights Act (1998). The public and formal nature of the trial in the Crown Court (e.g. 12 jury members, raised docks, Venables' and Thompson's separation from their parents and the public benches filled with the media and public) would have been intimidating for an 11-year-old irrespective of having social workers present and shorter trial days[34]: 'It seems to me that a child of eleven, who was the primary focus of this attention (and hostility), would be likely to find it even more difficult to cope with, and that it would be likely to affect to a material degree his ability to follow the evidence and to give evidence himself'.[35]

The ECtHR held that Article 6(1) 'requires any criminal charge must be determined by an independent and impartial tribunal',[36] and Article 5(4) entitles the applicant to a periodic review of the lawfulness of his/her detention at a tribunal. Sentencing Venables and Thompson was the role of the courts, not the Home Secretary, and Article 5(4) should have been incorporated into any sentencing decision. Given that the Home Secretary is not an 'independent of the executive', the ECtHR deteremined that he had also breached Articles 5 and 6.

The Shift in Sentencing Children for Murder: 2000–2022

Following the ECtHR's ruling in 2000, Parliament introduced legislation[37] to change how minimum sentences for young people were determined and who set the sentences. This came into effect in November 2000 and pertained applications to the High Court for sentence reductions at the halfway point. The basis of this review is derived from the judgment of the House of Lords,[38] underscoring the need to give distinct consideration to the punishment of children and young people.[39] Lady Hale, while examining the USA Supreme Court case *Roper v Simmons*,[40] reasoned that 'a juvenile's irresponsible conduct was not as morally reprehensible as that of an adult' and also 'juveniles had a greater claim to be forgiven for failing to escape the negative influences around them and that even the most heinous crime was not necessarily evidence of an irretrievable depraved character'.[41] She further remarked that,

> these considerations are relevant to the retributive and deterrent aspects of sentencing, in that they indicate that the great majority

34 (1999) 7 BHRC 659 [78–79].
35 Ibid 78.
36 Ibid 659.
37 See also Section 82A of the Powers of Criminal Courts (Sentencing) Act (2000), repealed by Section 416(1) of the Sentencing Act (2020).
38 *R (Smith) v Home Secretary* [2006] 1 AC 159.
39 See, generally, D Emanuel, C Mawer, and L Janes, 'The Sentencing of Young Adults: A Distinctive Group Requiring a Distinctive Approach' (2021) 3 *Criminal Law Review* 203–217.
40 *Roper v Simmons* 543 US 551 (2005).
41 *R (Smith) v Secretary of State for the Home Department* [2005] 3 WLR 410, 24.

> of juveniles are less blameworthy and more worthy of forgiveness than adult offenders. . . . An important aim, some would think the most important aim, of any sentence imposed should be to promote the process of maturation, the development of a sense of responsibility, and the growth of a healthy adult personality and identity. That is no doubt why the Children and Young Persons Act 1933, in section 44(1), required, and still requires, every court dealing with any juvenile offender to have regard to his or her welfare. It is important to the welfare of any young person that his need to develop into fully functioning, law abiding and responsible member of society is properly met. But that is also important for the community as a whole, for the community will pay the price, either of indefinite detention or of further offending, if it is not done.[42]

In line with the legal precedent established in *Smith*, the Secretary of State implemented a policy allowing prisoners to apply for reviews of their minimum sentences at the halfway points and every two years thereafter. Judges would review the evidence and make a recommendation to the Secretary of State, who was obliged to follow the judge's recommendation. The Secretary of State specified the requirements for reducing a minimum sentence for a child or young person, including evidence of positive changes in the offender's conduct while in detention and any significant developments of the offender's maturity.[43]

Section 269 Criminal Justice Act (2003) (now replaced by Section 416(1) of SA 2020 also provides that for cases after November 200, the trial judge must specify the minimum term a child or young person must serve, not the Home Secretary, and that the trial judge must no longer submit sentencing recommendations to the Home Secretary.[44] The trial judge has sole regard for the statutory aggravating and mitigating factors of the case (now under Schedule 21 S. 9–10 SA (2020) and is barred from being swayed by sociopolitical issues.[45] The trial judge must consider the mitigating factors of the case, such as 'an intention to cause serious bodily harm rather than to kill', the defendant's mental disorder[46] or mental disability that reduced his degree of culpabil-

42 Ibid [25].

43 See further *R v Quayle and the Secretary of State for Justice* [2024] EWHC 211 (Admin) at 15–16.

44 Ibid 10–11.

45 *R v Secretary of State for the Home Department, ex parte Furber* [1998] 1 All ER 23 at 26–27.

46 'Sentencing offenders with mental disorders, developmental disorders, or neurological impairments' came into effect on the 1st of October 2022 and defines a developmental disorder as 'conditions which may be apparent at birth, but always have early enough onset that the individual never quite fitted within the average behavioural range. Behaviour has three main components – thinking (cognitions), feeling (emotions, affect) and actions. Autism, generalised or specific intellectual (learning) disabilities, and personality disorders are examples'. Sentencing Council, Annex A <www.sentencingcouncil.org.uk/overarching-guides/

ity and the defendant's age at the time of the killing.[47] This also includes the consideration of aggravating factors, such as the defendant's degree of planning or premeditation, the victim's vulnerability (i.e., age or disability) and the suffering inflicted on the victim by the defendant before the victim's death.[48] However, it is essential to remember that these factors are not an exhaustive list, and a child/young person's minimum term will differ depending on the case's mitigation and aggravating factors (listed above).

While the CJA 2003 resolved some of the minimum term review issues raised with Venables and Thompson by changing how children and young persons were sentenced for murder, focussing on the 12-year mandatory minimum sentence for youth between 10 and 17 years convicted of murder. As Judge LJ observed in *Attorney General's Reference No. 126 of 2006 (H.)*,[49] there was a problem with applying Schedule 21 and determining the minimum starting point because

> No mathematical table can be produced which calculates the culpability of a young offender with any specific age, and no list, however carefully drawn up, can provide an accurate reflection of the way in which a young offender may or may not have learned from or been damaged by the experiences to which his young life has been exposed.[50]

While this may be an astute observation, the trial judge has the discretion to fix a significantly higher minimum sentence for youth than the 12-year minimum based on perceived aggravating features of the case. In this case, H was 14 years old at the time of conviction and was sentenced by the Court of Appeal to a minimum of 15 years in detention for killing an 11-year-old fellow student, three years higher than the starting point. The Court of Appeal considered H's bullying and sexual abuse of the victim, his calm demeanour, and his use of weapons. In addition, the court remarked that the victim's mental incapacity warranted a higher sentence as Schedule 21 provided explicitly that the court must consider 'the fact that the victim was particularly vulnerable because of age or disability'[51] as an aggravating factor of the case. Even though the appellant had no previous convictions or violent past, he was of low intelligence and emotionally immature for his age.

A further example can be found in *R v Cornick*.[52] This defendant also received 15 years rather than 12. C was convicted of murder for fantasising

magistrates-court/item/sentencing-offenders-with-mental-disorders-developmental-disorders-or-neurological-impairments/#Annex%20A%20-%20main%20classes%20of%20mental%20disorders%20and%20presenting%20features> accessed September 2024.

47 Schedule 21, section 10 (a)–(g).

48 Ibid section 9(a)–(g).

49 *Attorney General's Reference No. 126 of 2006 (H.).* [2007] 2 Cr App R (S) 59.

50 Ibid 2.

51 Schedule 21, Section 10(b).

52 *R v Cornick* [2015] 1 Cr App R (S) 69.

and killing a female schoolteacher at his school with a knife, and the trial judge observed that the aggravating features of the case 'would [have] attract[ed] a starting point of 25 years' if he had been an adult. Considering C's guilty plea and adjustment disorder, the Court of Appeal sentenced him to a fixed term of 20 years.[53]

Current Law: The Police, Crime, Sentencing and Courts Act (2022) Reviewed Minimum Sentences

In light of these criticisms, the Government proposed two legislative changes to sentencing children and young people convicted of murder, laid out in Ss. 127–28 of the Police, Crime, Sentencing and Courts Act (2022) (PCSC). The Government indicated that the Act would change how discretionary life sentence minimums are calculated to ensure that the minimum sentence served in custody reflects the seriousness of the offence and would change the minimum sentence starting points for murder committed as a child to ensure that the seriousness of the offence is taken into account and there is less of a gap between older children and young adults.[54]

Section 128 of the PCSC incorporated Section 27A into the Crime (Sentences) Act (1997), which came into effect on 28 June 2022. This allows offenders under age 18 to request a review for reducing their minimum sentences. Before Section 27A came into force, reviews of minimum sentence for any offender detained by His Majesty's Pleasure occurred on a non-statutory *ad hoc* basis, and minor offenders had the right to apply for a review at the halfway point of their sentence, as laid out in *Smith*. However, those whose sentence was handed down on or after their 18th birthday were not granted the same rights and were ineligible to apply for review. This legal right was removed and confirmed when Section 27A came into force for those aged 18 years and above at the time of their application for review.[55]

Section 128(27A) (4) made it possible for an offender to apply for a further review '2 years after an unsuccessful review at the halfway point',[56] and the Government argued that this change was essential to ensure that all sentences reflected how the offender was maturing throughout their detention. The purpose was to lessen the number of parole reviews offenders who had been convicted of murder at age 18 and convicted of murder but not sentenced until they are over 18 years of age. The Government reasoned that such persons 'are not entitled to reviews, reflecting the fact that adults do not go through the same accelerated development and maturation that children

53 See N Stone, 'Children Who Murder: Indeterminate Sentencing in Law and Practice' (2018) 18 *Youth Justice* 86. See also *R v Markham and Edwards* [2017] 2 Cr App R (S) 30.
54 Ministry of Justice, *A Smarter Approach to Sentencing Consultation Paper 292* (HMSO September 2020) 86.
55 [2024] EWHC 211 (Admin) at 2–3.
56 MoJ (2020) 94.

do'.[57] The Government anticipated that these changes would provide a fairer criminal justice system

> that recognises that offenders who were sentenced to DHMP as children but have since turned 18 in custody are now adults and have passed the age where significant development occurs, while still accounting for the fact that they were children and still maturing when the crime was committed and they were sentenced. Under the new system all offenders sentenced when under 18 would receive the opportunity to apply for one tariff review at the halfway point of their sentence.[58]

However, these reforms were substantially criticised, particularly by the Howard League for Penal Reform (Howard League), which presented written evidence to the Joint Committee on Human Rights' Call for Evidence on the Police, Crime, Sentencing and Courts Bill.[59] The Howard League strongly opposed the PCSC Act, claiming that 'the overall tenor and message of the Bill is extremely punitive and sets a worrying precedent in terms of illiberal leadership'.[60] The group believed that these changes would directly contradict the core tenets of the review rights of those convicted of murder under 18 years of age, as laid out by Lord Bingham in *Smith*.[61] The law requires that a child or young person convicted of murder be sentenced to detention. However, as Lord Bingham pointed out, it is crucial to consider that youth offenders are not necessarily fully developed at the time of committing the crime or at sentencing. Thus, as they mature, it is essential to make 'a more reliable judgment perhaps of what punishment he deserves and certainly of what period of detention will best promote his rehabilitation'.[62]

Lord Bingham believed that terminating a child's or young person's legal right to continuous review at 18, as the case under s.128, would undermine the welfare principle established by statute. This principle recognises children and young people as not fully mature individuals when committing a crime, and they should not be punished as if they were.[63] As a result, Lord Bingham and the Howard League have strongly advocated for the right to a minimum review never being terminated. Given its central importance, it should be accessible to all children and young people who commit murder under the

57 Ibid [329].
58 Ibid [330].
59 Howard League for Penal Reform, *Written Evidence (PCS0396)* <https://committees.parliament.uk/writtenevidence/36293/html/> accessed May 2022.
60 Ibid [2.1].
61 *R v Secretary of State for the Home Department ex parte Smith* [2002] UKHL 51 [12].
62 Ibid.
63 Ibid.

age of 18, regardless of whether they are sentenced before or after reaching the age of 18.[64]

The immediate concern for the Howard League was that S. 128 was 'likely [to] be discriminatory in effect by removing this right from a person who is sentenced after he or she turns 18'.[65] And they were right. In *R (on the application of Jesse Quaye) v Secretary of State for Justice*,[66] the appellant, who was 17 years old at the time of the offence, and another young person (Bile, aged 15) stabbed a man at a party. Both the appellant and Bile were convicted of murder in November 2014. They were each sentenced, contrary to S. 90 of the Powers of Criminal Courts (Sentencing) Act (2000), to detention at His Majesty's Pleasure for a minimum of 15 years in 2015. The appellant subsequently appealed his murder sentence on the grounds that S. 128 PCSC Act is incompatible with Articles 5, 6, 7 and 14 of the ECHR. Although the PCSC Act was not operational when the appellant was sentenced, as I discussed, S. 128 of the PCSC inserted s.27A in the Crime (Sentences) Act (1997). Thus, his right to review his minimum sentence was removed when S. 27A came into force because he could receive a more severe penalty than what was applied in 2014 when he was sentenced.[67]

The Court of Appeal held that S. 128 directly contravened Articles 5 (a person's right to liberty and security)[68] and 14 (everyone should enjoy the rights enshrined in the Convention without discrimination)[69] of the ECHR, finding that the White Paper 'conflated offenders' who committed murder aged 18 and over with those who committed the same offence as minors. Before the PCSC, under Schedule 21 (as amended), it was common practice for youth to receive longer sentences than the minimum 12 years because of aggravating factors in the case.

The Court of Appeal noted that 'a minimum term of 15 years (as imposed on the claimant and his co-accused was commonplace'.[70] Therefore, a judge would not have typically considered the offender's review until they were between 20 and 25. On average, the reviews did not take place exactly at the halfway point of the sentence; in practice, it was delayed for the preparation of the dossier, and 'the nature of the progress ha[d] to be exceptional' before a judge would reduce their sentence.[71] The Court of Appeal,

64 [2002] UKHL 51 [12]; PCS0396, 6.1–6.2.
65 Ibid 6.4.
66 [2024] EWHC 211 (Admin).
67 Ibid a1–4 and 32–36.
68 Article 5 of the ECHR <https://fra.europa.eu/en/law-reference/european-convention-human-rights-article-5> accessed July 2024.
69 Article 14 of the ECHR <https://fra.europa.eu/en/law-reference/european-convention-human-rights-article-14> accessed July 2024.
70 [2024] EWHC 211 (Admin) 51.
71 Ibid.

citing *R v Herbert*,[72] claimed 'it is not uncommon for the crucial progress to be made when an offender has passed their 25th birthday'; thus, there is no reasonable justification to differentiate between those aged 18 at the date of sentencing and those under 18.[73]

The effect of S. 128 is that it removes the prospect of a judge making 'a more reliable judgment', which would likely result in many offenders serving longer in detention than lawfully required, which contradicts Articles 5 and 14.[74] This amounts to arbitrary detention, as highlighted in *Smith*, in that as a child 'grows into maturity a more reliable judgement may be made, perhaps of what punishment he deserves and certainty of what period of detention will best promote his rehabilitation'.[75]

The Court of Appeal has determined that S. 128 is inconsistent with ECHR Articles 5 and 14, particularly for individuals over 18, as it deprives them of the right to a minimum term review. Although the Court did not propose an alternative, it will be interesting to see how Parliament will address this unlawfulness within Section 4 of the Human Rights Act (1998). Next, I critically examine the reform to minimum term starting points, as outlined in S. 127 of the PCSC Act.

The PCSC Reforms of Minimum Sentences

Section 127 of the PCSC Act replaced the 12-year starting point and increased the mandatory detention period for most children and young people convicted of murder based on their age and the seriousness of the offence:

> Starting points for murder committed when under 18
>
> In Schedule 21 to the Sentencing Code (minimum terms in mandatory life sentences), for paragraph 6 substitute –
>
> "5A(1) This paragraph applies if –
>
> (a) the offender was aged under 18 when the offence was committed, and
>
> (b) the offender was convicted of the offence on or after the day on which section 127 of the Police, Crime, Sentencing and Courts Act 2022 came into force.

72 *R v Herbert* [2020] EWHC 216 (Admin).
73 [2024] EWHC 211 (Admin) 51–52.
74 Ibid 59.
75 [2002] UKHL 51, 12 and 59.

(2) The appropriate starting point, in determining the minimum term, is the period given in the entry in column 2, 3 or 4 of the following table that corresponds to –

(a) the age of the offender when the offence was committed, as set out in column 1, and
(b) the provision of this Schedule that would have supplied the appropriate starting point had the offender been aged 18 when the offence was committed, as set out in the headings to columns 2, 3 and 4.

As the table shows, the starting points are categorised into three age groups, and each has its own starting point and four gradients for the seriousness of the offence. These gradients of severity are the same that apply to adults who commit murder, which is set out in Schedule 21.[76]

The Government's justification for changing the starting point is that 'the fixed 12-year starting point for children does not account for the seriousness of the crime, nor does it reflect the different stages of development children go through between the ages of 10 and 17' to create a criminal justice system that is fairer.[77] The Government claimed that these changes would be fairer to young persons as those 'closer to the age of 18, will have higher starting points, while younger children will have lower starting points to reflect their reduced maturity and development'[78] so that there would be 'a more gradual shift to adult sentences, reducing the gap that currently exists'. More specifically, the Government claimed that a 17-year-old required a longer starting point than children because 'a 17-year-old, a week before they turn 18, is likely to have more concept of responsibility than a 11-year-old'.[79]

Table 12.1 Age of Offender and Sentence Starting Point[80]

Age of offender when offence committed	*Starting point supplied by paragraph 3(1) had the offender been 18*	*Starting point supplied by paragraph 4(1) had the offender been 18*	*starting point supplied by paragraph 5 had the offender been 18*
17	27 years	23 years	14 years
15 or 16	20 years	17 years	10 years
14 or under	15 years	13 years	8 years

76 Schedule 21 of the 2(1), 3(1), 4(1) and 5(1).
77 MoJ (2020) 91.
78 Ibid 92.
79 Joint Committee on Human Rights (September 2021) [34].
80 This table was taken from S. 127 of the PCSC (2022).

The latest neuroscientific evidence[81] indicates that neurocognitive and frontal lobe development play critical roles in adolescent decision-making and behaviour. It has been known for some time that adolescents show gradual improvements in mental competence as they age. For example, as they mature, their abilities improve at aligning perspectives, thinking logically, filtering out irrelevant information, and processing data.[82] However, they demonstrate heightened risk-taking and impulsivity and lack an appreciation of the consequences of their actions throughout adolescence due to 'the slow development of the brain regions necessary for cognitive control, subsuming response selection, top-down control and inhibitory processes, and including the prefrontal cortex (PFC)'.[83]

Recently, Mrs Justice May noted in *R v ZA*[84] that when considering the appropriate approach to sentencing children and young people that 'the brains of young people are still developing up to the age of 25, particularly in the areas of the frontal cortex and hippocampus. These areas are the seat of emotional control, restraint, awareness of risk and the ability to appreciate the consequences of one's own and others' actions; in short, the processes of thought engaged in by, and the hallmark of, mature and responsible adults'.[85] The Youth Justice Board criticised S. 127 because

> the Bill [now Act] creates a distinction between younger and older children, so bringing 16 and 17 year-olds into scope for minimum terms does not treat them as individuals and does not take into account their childhood or developmental stage; it treats them as if they are adults.
>
> That is at odds with the convention, which very clearly defines that a child is anyone under the age of 18. There is no sliding scale below the age of 18 at which it is acceptable to treat somebody as more or less of a child; it is everybody under the age of 18.[86]

The board argued that these starting points need to adequately reflect the varying degrees of development and immaturity of those aged between 10 and 17 years old. The problem is that most offenders under 18 who are

81 JN Giedd, J Blumenthal, NO Jeffries et al., 'Brain Development during Childhood and Adolescence: A Longitudinal MRI Study' (1999) 2 *Nature Neuroscience* 861–63; N Gogtay, JN Giedd et al., 'Dynamic Mapping of Human Cortical Development during Childhood through Adulthood' (2004) 101(21) Proceedings of the National Academy of Sciences 8174–79.

82 SJ Blakemore and T Robbins, 'Decision-Making in the Adolescent Brain' (2012) 15(9) *Nature Neuroscience* 1184; BJ Casey, C Simmons, LH Somerville, and A Baskin-Sommers, 'Making the Sentencing Case: Psychological and Neuroscientific Evidence for Expanding the Age of Youthful Offenders' (2021) 5 *Annual Review of Criminology* 327.

83 Blakemore and Robbins (2012) 1184.

84 [2023] EWCA Crim 596.

85 Ibid 52.

86 Joint Committee (30 June 2021) 4.

sentenced for murder are between 15 and 17. During 2017 and 2019, there were 101 sentences for murder: 2% of the offenders were between 12 and 14, 59% were between 15 and 17, and 39% were young adults aged 18 to 20.[87] This means that the majority of young persons sentenced for murder 'face longer tariffs as a result of these changes, although some younger children may receive shorter tariffs',[88] which closely resemble those of adults. For example, a 17-year-old convicted of murder with a weapon will receive a starting point of 23 years in detention, while an 18-year-old will be sentenced to 25 years for the same offence, rather 12 years.[89] It is questionable how these starting points were conceived given the previous judicial dissent over minimum sentences for young people: As Judge LJ stated in *H*, 'no mathematical table can be produced which calculates the culpability of a young offender with any specific age'.[90]

It is concerning that this sliding scale presupposes that young people are less vulnerable and more mature and that 17-year-olds are more responsible than children just because they are nearing adulthood.[91] As discussed, S. 127 directly contradicts the latest neuroscientific evidence that adolescents are impulsive, suggestible, and susceptible to criminal behaviour. Indeed, in 2018, the National Crime Agency reported that the majority of victims who are criminally exploited for drug trafficking are young people between ages 15 and 17.[92] It is also well documented that individuals aged 18 to 25 are significantly more susceptible to peer influences and are prone to more impulsive behaviour than older adults. This is attributed to the delayed maturation of the prefrontal cortex, which reaches full development around 25 years of age.[93]

According to the Howard League, it makes sense 'that adolescence is best understood as a phase of life which extends from around age 10 to age 24 and that young people continue to develop rapidly throughout this period,

87 Home Office, *Youth Measures in the Police, Crime, Sentencing & Courts Bill: Equalities Impact Assessment* (13 May 2021) <www.gov.uk/government/publications/police-crime-sentencing-and-courts-bill-2021equality-statements/youth-measures-in-the-police-crime-sentencing-courts-bill-equalities-impact-assessment> accessed May 2022.

88 Joint Committee on Human Rights (September 2021) [31].

89 [2024] EWHC 211 (Admin) 25.

90 *R v H* [2007] 2 Cr App R (S) 59, 2.

91 PCS0396, 2022 [4.5].

92 See, generally, National Crime Agency, *Country Lines Drug Supply, Vulnerability and Harm 2018* <www.nationalcrimeagency.gov.uk/publications/993-nac-19-095-county-lines-drug-supply-vulnerability-and-harm-2018/file> accessed July 2024.

93 The Royal College of Psychiatrists, *Written Evidence Submitted by the Royal College of Psychiatrists to the Young Adult Offenders Inquiry* (HC937, 13 October 2015) 1.1–1.3. <http://data.parliament.uk/writtenevidence/committeeevidence.svc/evidencedocument/justice committee/the-treatment-of-young-adults-in-thecriminal-justice-system/written/22190.html> accessed July 2024.

including in ways which affect their culpability for offences'.[94] The way S. 127 is written penalises young people for their age irrespective of their developmental vulnerabilities. For example, a 15- or 16-year-old could receive a minimum sentence of 10 to 17 years, while the minimum point for a 17-year-old is between 14 and 23 years, and a child 14 or under will receive a minimum of 8 to 13 years. That is, S. 127 views older youth more as adults than as children.

Conclusion

The PCSC Act significantly changed how children and young people are sentenced for murder in England and Wales. Because the courts are supposed to consider the best interests of the child and recognise their vulnerability, it is vital that they are not unfairly given lengthy detention sentences without the opportunity for review to promote their rehabilitation, considering their age and level of maturity. The current Act does not fully respect the rights of young people conferred upon them under the UNCRC and ECHR.

Neuroscientific evidence of adolescent brain development indicates that young people, due to the slow development of the frontal cortex, are cognitively immature, impulsive, and highly susceptible to peer influences and find it challenging to make effective decisions; youth and young adults are susceptible to peer pressure, and they lack control. The PCSC Act should grant the authority to consider the ages and maturity levels of children, young people, and young adults when setting minimum sentences under domestic case law. Instead, it will continue to undermine the human rights of young people by increasing the amount of time they serve in detention and preventing them from seeking minimum sentence reviews after they turn 18 unless Parliament reverses Sections 127 and 128.

Further longitudinal research is needed to understand the extent to which the PCSC Act impacts the rights and liberties of young people, particularly an in-depth analysis of young people and young adults' reviews, once the court hears more cases on the issues of the Act. This research would help understand how the Act needs to be amended, bringing the sentencing of young people for murder in line with international children's rights and domestic legislation.

94 PCS0396, 2022, 4.5; See also, SM Sawyer, 'The age of adolescence' (2018) 2(3) Lancet Child & Adolescent Health 223–228.

13 Justice for Nature

A Rawlsian Approach

Simon Sneddon

Introduction

This chapter is set in an as-yet-unachieved version of England and Wales in which there is no longer any debate about whether nature can have enforceable rights or not. It is difficult to envisage a nation in which the rights of nature have become legally enforceable but the human right to a clean and healthy environment is not. For the purposes of this chapter, therefore, I treat both rights as being established. Many rights intersect in this hypothetical scenario including constitutional rights, jurisprudential theory, and environmental ethics. The interplay between them is already an evolving area of legal scholarship.[1] Rights for nature, an idea which was almost unthinkable 50 years ago, might not yet be mainstream legal thinking, but it is taking place in debate and in practice, for example in the enshrinement of such rights into the Ecuadorian Constitution in 2008, the Laws of the Rights of Mother Earth in Bolivia in 2010 and the Te Urewera Act 2014, and the Awa Tupua (Whanganui River Claims Settlement) Act 2017 in New Zealand.

Traditionally, the nature of constitutional rights has been anthropocentric: human centred. The focus has been on the recognition and protection of individual and collective liberties and ensuring that justice is served in human societies. Robert Alexy, the German jurist, argued that there is a tension between 'rights' in the abstract, as propounded by philosophers, and rights in a practical, enforceable state in real-world, complex societies.[2] Kirschlaeger makes the interesting point that 'Human rights did not "fall from heaven"; they are not the 'absolute truth'. Every human being is not only a right-holder but also needs to respect the human rights of others.[3] This in many ways aligns with

1 See, for example A Chalabi, 'A New Theoretical Model of the Right to Environment and its Practical Advantages' (2023) 23 *Human Rights Law Review* 1–19; D Hanschel, MG Aguilera Bravo, B Dashpurev, and AK Idris, 'Environmental Rights Between Constitutional Law and Local Context: Reflections on a Moving Target' (2022) 23(7) *German Law Journal* 1012, 1012–28.

2 R Alexy, *Theorie der Grundrechte (suhrkamp taschenbuch wissenshaft)* (Suhrkamp Verlag, 1986).

3 PG Kirchschlaeger, 'Human Rights as Ethical Basis for Science' (2013) 22(2) *Journal of Law, Information and Science* 1, 5–6.

DOI: 10.4324/9781003496823-13

Jeremy Bentham's view that the idea of there being enforceable rights which were not granted by the state as 'nonsense on stilts'[4] but contrasts with the view of inherent human rights. By logical extension, the rights of nature upon which I predicate this chapter also did not 'fall from heaven' but had to be recognised by human society, policymakers, and lawmakers.

I begin the chapter by looking at the concept of rights of nature and what this has meant over time. Drawing on legal, criminological, and philosophical concepts, I trace the development from Christopher Stone in the 1970s[5] through to the granting of rights to different non-human entities. I then look at the idea of proportionality since enforcing one set of rights is likely to impinge on another's. Aharon Barak, among others[6] recognises this need for balance but also recognises the main argument against proportionality, namely incommensurability and irrationality.[7] Having established the importance of proportionality in upholding the rights of nature, I consider the work of John Rawls, particularly his theory of justice and how this has been reinterpreted to fit a 21st-century reality; I also examine the limitations of applying his theories in the context of the rights of nature. I then look at imagined case studies, applying Rawlsian theories in four contexts: state versus nature, human versus nature, non-human (for example corporate bodies or AI) versus nature, and nature versus nature.

The Rights of Nature

The concept of the rights of nature originates from a range of Indigenous worldviews and ecological philosophies that place a strong emphasis on the interdependence of all living things. The natural world is acknowledged by many Indigenous cultures as a living being with rights and obligations of its own. For instance, rivers, mountains, and other natural elements are revered as sacred entities by numerous Native American tribal groups who maintain reciprocal relationships with them.[8] Even in England and Wales, our pre-Christian ancestors venerated nature and natural phenomena.[9]

4 J Bentham, 'Anarchical Fallacies: Being an Examination of the Declarations of Rights Issued During the French Revolution' (c 1795) in John Bowring (ed) *The Works of Jeremy Bentham* (vol 2, William Tait 1843) 489.

5 CD Stone, 'Should Trees Have Standing? Toward Legal Rights for Natural Objects' (1972) 45(2) *Southern California Law Review* 450.

6 See, for example, VC Jackson, 'Constitutional Law in an Age of Proportionality' (2015) 124(8) *Yale Law Journal* 3094–3196; M Teo, 'Proportionality as Epistemic Independence' (2022) 2 Public Law 245–68.

7 A Barak, *Proportionality: Constitutional Rights and Their Limitations* (Cambridge University Press 2012).

8 See, for example, PH Kunesh, 'The Significance of Belonging for Indigenous Peoples: The Power of Place and People – Creating a Vision for Community in Indian Country through Self-Governance and Self-Determination' (2021) 30 *Journal of Affordable Housing & Community Development Law* 1.

9 D Hooke, 'Groves in Anglo-Saxon England' (2017) 38(1) *Landscape History* 5.

Despite this long and wide tradition, the very concept of nature having legal rights will doubtless continue to strike some in England and Wales as an exercise in navel gazing. What I demonstrate in this section is that, to the contrary, acknowledging or granting (as I will show later, the language used here is important) rights to nature is a logical progression of the gradual expansion of rights recognition. The visualisation of nature as being property subject to the 'dominion of man'[10] dates to Genesis and is a shared point between Christianity and Judaism. Other belief systems, notably polytheistic religions such as Hinduism and the systems of Ancient Greece and Rome, and 'trans-polytheistic'[11] ones such as Buddhism, promote a more balanced and equal relationship between human and non-human life. Indeed, it is easy to see the link between concepts such as the Greek Gaia and Māori *kaitiakitanga* (stewardship) with their approaches of balance and mutual respect, and modern legal concepts such as sustainability.

One of the main drivers towards a recognition of the rights of nature has been the loose environmental philosophy and environmental ethics movement. In the West, this movement was popularised in the mid-20th century when Aldo Leopold's *Sand County Almanac* was posthumously published. Leopold envisaged the wilderness as a 'biotic community' and outlined his position simply: 'A thing is right when it tends to preserve the integrity, stability, and beauty of the biotic community. It is wrong when it tends otherwise'.[12] Murray Bookchin took the idea of a less-hierarchical relationship between humans and non-humans a step further and outlined a (possibly utopian) vision of a future where all hierarchies were removed and humans lived better lives.[13]

Stone, writing in the 1970s, was among the first legal scholars to suggest that nature could hold legal rights.[14] He made the very persuasive argument that since medieval times, 'rights' have evolved from a position where they were held by almost no one to where humans of any age, gender, or ethnicity have rights: 'The world of the lawyer is peopled with inanimate rights-holders: trusts, corporations, joint ventures, municipalities, . . . and nation-states, to mention just a few'.[15] Stone further makes the point that conferral of right onto an entity does not guarantee it absolute protection from all things and that 'to say that the environment should have rights is not to say that it should have every right we can imagine, or even the same body of rights as human

10 WG Wood, *The Dominion of Man* (Richard Bentley & Son 1889).

11 P Harvey, *Buddhism and Monotheism* (Cambridge University Press 2019).

12 A Leopold, *A Sand County Almanac and Sketches Here and There* (Oxford University Press 1949) 173.

13 M Bookchin, *The Ecology of Freedom: The Emergence and Dissolution of Hierarchy* (Cheshire Books 1982).

14 CD Stone, 'Should Trees Have Standing? Toward Legal Rights for Natural Objects' (1972) 45(2) *Southern California Law Review* 450.

15 Ibid 452.

beings have. Nor is it to say that everything in the environment should have the same rights as every other thing in the environment'.[16] Boyd, writing four decades after Stone, presents a world where the rights of nature have not yet been widely recognised but where there has been a significant shift from anthropocentrism and ecocentrism and where lawyers are fighting for the recognition of rights for animals kept in captivity.[17] Ecocentrism has as its central tenet the view that nature has its own intrinsic value, as opposed to anthropocentrism which attributes value to nature based on its utility to humans – a 'nice' view, for example.

Identifying that nature 'ought to' have rights of some form is, understandably, far removed from setting these rights into a legal basis. I take the view that just as people had rights before the Universal Declaration of Human Rights, nature had rights before any legal text acknowledged them. Despite the passing of millennia in which human societies recognised that nature had some rights, it was not until 2008 that the first nation state passed legislation recognising this. Ecuador, which passed a new constitution in 2008 (the country's 20th constitution) included a section on the rights of nature as Chapter 7. Article 71 recognised that Pachamama (an 'Earth Mother' type goddess revered by the peoples of the Andes but used in the Ecuadorian Constitution as a cypher for 'nature') 'has the right to integral respect for its existence and for the maintenance and regeneration of its life cycles, structure, functions and evolutionary processes'.[18]

Furthermore, Art 71 sets out how these rights are to be enforced, Art 72 gives nature the right to be restored, and Art 73 places a duty of the state to 'apply preventive and restrictive measures on activities that might lead to the extinction of species, the destruction of ecosystems and the permanent alteration of natural cycles'.[19] Several cases have been successfully brought before the Constitutional Court of Ecuador under these provisions. In 2021, the Court ruled that mangrove ecosystems are right holders and declared that legislative measures which did not offer sufficient respect to the 'maintenance and regeneration of their life cycles, structure, functions and evolutionary processes' were unconstitutional.[20] The following year, the Court ruled that wild animals (in this case a chorongo monkey called Estrellita ('little star')) were rights holders and that the current Ecuadorian rules on keeping wild animals as pets were unconstitutional.[21]

16 Ibid 457–58.
17 DR Boyd, *The Rights of Nature: A Legal Revolution That Could Save the World* (ECW Press 2017).
18 Constitution of Ecuador, 2008, Article 71.
19 Ibid Article 73.
20 Corte Constitucional del Ecuador, Caso No 22-18-IN, Coordinadora Ecuatoriana de Organizaciones para la Defensa de la Naturaleza y Ambiente v Presidente de la Republica, Decisión, para 1
21 Ibid Caso No 253-20-JH

In 2010, Bolivia passed *Ley de Derechos de la Madre Tierra* (The Law of the Rights of Mother Earth). Chapters II and III focused on the definitions and rights of Mother Earth. It emerged from the Indigenous concept of *sumac kawsay* (essentially 'ideal life') which evolved into *buen vivir* ('living well'). Article 3 stated that 'Mother Earth is a dynamic living system comprising an indivisible community of all living systems and living organisms, interrelated, interdependent and complementary, which share a common destiny',[22] and Article 7 outlines the seven rights of Mother Earth: to life, the diversity of life, water, clean air, equilibrium, restoration, and pollution-free living.

Interestingly, whereas Ecuador's steps have been largely seen as positive, there is significant criticism of the operationalisation of the Bolivian Law. Calzadilla and Kotzé argue that subsequent legislation passed by the Bolivian government (for example the Law on Mining and Metallurgy in 2014) has had significant impacts on the rights of nature, 'effectively becom[ing] a statutory device that legalises extractivism as a way of achieving the Vivir Bien'.[23] There is no recorded case law brought before Bolivian Courts under the Mother Earth law, although the (non-juridical) International Rights of Nature Tribunal has ruled that Bolivia breached the laws in the TIPNIS case[24] which concerned the *Territorio y Parque Nacional Isiboro Secure*, a protected area and Native Community Land about 100 km to the east of the capital, La Paz.

New Zealand has not recognised the rights of nature overall but passed the Te Urewera Act 2014 and the Awa Tupua (Whanganui River Claims Settlement) Act 2017, recognising the rights of the Te Urewera area and Whanganui River, which are regarded as sacred by Indigenous communities. What is interesting about this approach is that the rights were granted simply *because* the rivers had value to humans, which seems to go against the ecocentric approach I've outlined. Indeed, Stone himself, in a later update on his original argument, says all such rights systems, while they may be admirable, are 'unavoidably anthropocentric'.[25]

At a more municipal level, in 2006 the Borough of Tamaqua (a 7,000-person town covering just under 10 square miles in Pennsylvania, USA) was the first in the world to recognise the rights of nature in its local legislation. The Tamaqua Borough Sewage Sludge Ordinance[26] was enacted to stop the dumping of toxic sludge by out-of-area contractors: 'Borough residents, natural communities, and ecosystems shall be considered 'persons' for the purposes of the enforcement of the civil rights of those residents, natural communities,

22 Art 3, The Law of the Rights of Mother Earth, 2010.

23 PV Calzadilla and LJ Kotzé, 'Living in Harmony with Nature? A Critical Appraisal of the Rights of Mother Earth in Bolivia' (2018) 7(3) *Transnational Environmental Law* 397–424.

24 IRNT, TIPNIS Judgment, International Rights of Nature Tribunal, 2021.

25 CD Stone, *Should Trees Have Standing? Law, Morality, and the Environment* (3rd edn, Oxford University Press 2010).

26 Ordinance No 612 of 2006.

and ecosystems'.[27] Since the action by Tamaqua, more than 50 other communities have passed similar ordinances.[28] In practical terms, this has had limited value, as industry has not been dissuaded from projects and instead has 'lawyered up and sued, and they have won every case'.[29]

Of course, recognising rights by passing legislation is merely a part of a much larger process. Daly observes that such rights are not necessarily enforceable[30] and may grant powers or duties to particular bodies. As Stone identified earlier, the recognition of some rights does not automatically mean the recognition of all rights, and the absolute or qualified status of any rights also needs to be clarified. Where such rights are enforceable, the question arises as to who should be given the power to enforce them.

This latter point is the least contentious. Section 7(1) of the Human Rights Act 1998 makes it clear that 'a person' may bring proceedings, 'but only if he is (or would be) a victim'. If this procedural rule were repeated in legislation recognising the rights of nature, it would become unworkable. However, in those countries where the rights of nature have been recognised, the relevant legislation clarifies who can bring cases on behalf of nature. In Ecuador, it is 'All persons, communities, peoples and nations'[31] who are empowered; in Bolivia, it is 'all Bolivians'[32]; and in New Zealand, it is a specifically created body consisting of representatives of the Crown and local Māori peoples.[33]

In England and Wales, we already have a system whereby corporate bodies, for example, can be represented by a natural person, since they cannot represent themselves, so this issue will not be hard to resolve.

Proportionality

The principle of proportionality is often stated to be a 'cornerstone' or a 'fundamental' of (human) rights law, but as Möller[34] points out, the principle's start in a constitutional context only dates to the late 1950s. It is used in other contexts, for example in criminal law, where the severity of a penalty for committing a crime should be proportionate to the harm caused by the crime.

27 §260–61 Statements of Law, Para F, Borough of Tamaqua, PA, code, as inserted by Ordinance No 612 of 2006

28 J Smith, 'Rights of Nature and Tribal Sovereignty: Protecting Natural Communities, Wild Rice, and Salmon in the United States' (2023) 38(1) *Maryland Journal of International Law* 11.

29 NM Sachs, 'A Wrong Turn With the Rights of Nature Movement' (2023) 39 *Georgetown Environmental Law Review* 13.

30 E Daly, 'Constitutional Protection for Environmental Rights: The Benefits of Environmental Process' (2012) 17(2) *International Journal of Peace Studies* 71.

31 Constitution of Ecuador, 2008, Article 71.

32 Art 3, The law of the Rights of Mother Earth, 2010.

33 E O'Donnell and J Talbot-Jones, 'Creating Legal Rights for Rivers: Lessons from Australia, New Zealand, and India' (2018) 23(1) *Ecology and Society* 7.

34 K Möller, 'Proportionality: Challenging the Critics' (2012) 10(3) *International Journal of Constitutional Law* 709.

Davis extended this, arguing that 'a punishment [should be] proportioned to that [unfair] advantage (and that advantage alone)'.[35] This approach – of looking at the advantage gained by the perpetrator rather than the harm caused to the victim or society – has been criticised.[36] The principle in the current context is based on the notion that enforcing the rights of one entity can and will sometimes infringe on another's. For instance, in cases involving freedom of expression, courts often must determine whether restrictions on speech are justified by other societal interests such as public order or national security.[37] The principle of proportionality ensures that rights are not restricted more than necessary and that any limitations are justified by a sufficiently important purpose. The principle is itself the final stage in a three-part test for the restriction of rights: Is the restrictive measure pursuing a legitimate aim? Is the measure suitable and necessary to achieve that legitimate aim? Is the measure proportionate? Does it strike a fair balance between the right being restricted and the interest being pursued?[38]

In fact, some of the rights enshrined in the Human Rights Act 1998 are 'qualified' – for example the right to respect for private and family life, to manifest your religion or belief, to expression and assembly[39] – meaning that they can legitimately be restricted to protect the rights of others or in the 'public interest for specific reasons such as the prevention of crime'.[40] Other rights are regarded as absolute, and both the European Court of Human Rights[41] and the UK Supreme Court[42] have recognised the right of individuals to challenge the legality of any decision which interferes with that.

Extending the principle of proportionality to the realm of the rights of nature requires reimagining the anthropocentric rights framework in the UK and recognising, as I have outlined, of the intrinsic value of natural entities. The adversarial nature of the legal system in England and Wales is such that we tend to think of enforcement of rights as a bilateral conflict, and that lends itself well to ideas of proportionality. As we will see later in the chapter, four possible categories of conflict have been identified: state versus nature, human

35 M Davis, 'How to Make the Punishment Fit the Crime' (1983) 93(4) *Ethics* 726, 744.

36 Restorative justice, for example, is predicated upon recognising the impact of a crime on the victim rather than simply looking at the benefit accrued by the offender. See, for example, J-A Wemmers, I Parent, and ML Quirion, 'Restoring Victims' Confidence: Victim-Centred Restorative Practices' (2023) 29(3) *International Review of Victimology*.

37 S. 2(1) of the Terrorism Prevention and Investigation Measures Act 2011 is a good example of this: The liberty of one individual can legitimately be restricted for the purposes of 'protecting members of the public from a risk of terrorism'.

38 R Alexy, *A Theory of Constitutional Rights* (Oxford University Press, 2009).

39 Human Rights Act 1988.

40 EHRC, 'How are your rights protected?' (*Equality and Human Rights Commission*, 2016) <www.equalityhumanrights.com/human-rights/what-are-human-rights/how-are-your-rights-protected> accessed 28 October 2024.

41 *Chahal v UK* (1996) 23 EHRR 413.

42 *R (ex parté Begum) v Special Immigration Appeals Commission* [2021] UKSC 7 per Reed LJ [64].

versus nature, non-human entity versus nature, and nature versus nature. This is not intended to be an exhaustive list, but it gives an idea of the difficulties that proportionality poses in application.

One of the ongoing complexities of the application of proportionality is the differing weights given to competing rights. Conversations about the difference between suppressing news in the public interest and releasing it because it is 'what the public finds interesting' abound in decisions around rights to free speech and privacy.[43] These difficulties, which have to date involved only balancing human rights, will become more complex when the rights of nature are introduced into the process. Part of this complexity will be the untangling of the rights of nature from the rights of humans, although this is perhaps less problematic in the UK, where a (human) right to a clean and healthy environment has yet to be established.

Consider a river which supports various species of bacteria, fungi, gastropods, insects, fish, mammals, birds, and plants. It can only do this effectively if the water contains appropriate levels of oxygen.[44] Pollution from a company with the requisite government licence has reduced the oxygen levels in the river until it is anoxic,[45] effectively a 'dead' river. Reducing pollution in an anoxic river will allow it to recover and support life. In this case, the rights being balanced are on the one hand those of the company causing the pollution but on the other a range of entities from the river itself to the non-human mammal species or the plants.

The Atrato River in Colombia was polluted by legal and illegal gold mines to such an extent that the chemicals, notably mercury, used by these miners were causing 'a terrible toll on the river and the communities that rely on it'.[46] A claim was filed with the *Corte Constitucional de Colombia* against a range of government agencies for not stopping the illegal mining. In 2016, the court recognised that the actions were breaching the rights of local communities and biodiversity and that 'The Atrato River, its basin and tributaries are recognised as an entity subject to rights to protection, conservation, maintenance and restoration by the State and ethnic communities'.[47] Having recognised these rights, the court issued an order for the government and other organisations

43 See, for example, *Campbell v Mirror Group Newspapers Ltd* [2004] UKHL 22, *Mosley v News Group Newspapers* [2008] EWHC 1777 (QB).

44 E Akasal and D Ekinci, 'Effects of Hypoxia and Hyperoxia on Growth Parameters and Transcription Levels of Growth, Immune System and Stress Related Genes in Rainbow Trout' (2021) 262 *Comparative Biochemistry and Physiology Part A: Molecular & Integrative Physiology* 111060.

45 Rivers which have a dissolved oxygen level of under 2 parts per million. Hyperoxic rivers (which have very high levels of oxygen) are also damaging to river life.

46 J-A McNeish and Jenny Morenho Socha, 'Muddy Waters: On the Problematic Political Ecology of the Atrato Ruling, Colombia' (2024) The International Journal of Human Rights (forthcoming) 3.

47 Corte Constitucional de Colombia, Sentencia T-622/16, para 10.2.1

to both design and implement a plan to, in conjunction with the ethnic communities involved, design and implement a plan 'to decontaminate the water sources of Chocó, starting with the Atrato River basin and its tributaries, the riverside territories, recover their ecosystems and avoid additional damage to the environment in the region'.[48]

This exercise in proportionality weighed the actions of the state in not closing down the illegal mining operations against the impact on the river and those who live on or near it and gave the river itself sufficient weight to tip the scales. One of the criticisms of this approach is the potential for bias and influence. Governments and corporate entities are likely to have deeper pockets than environmental NGOs or ethnic communities, so there is an asymmetry here. However, if the model adopted in New Zealand is used, then the state is one of the representatives for nature, so this may go some way to ameliorate the threat of asymmetry.

Not everyone supports the idea of using existing approaches to reset the relationship between humans and nature. Some, for example Cormac Cullinan, propose that rather than adapting existing jurisprudential systems so that they can take into account the rights of nature, what is needed is an entirely new and different system – earth jurisprudence.[49] In fact, Cullinan argues this is not an entirely new system at all but comes out of what he calls the 'Great Jurisprudence', the laws which shape and govern the universe and which inherently recognise the rights and interconnectedness of all things. He acknowledges the challenges of changing the *status quo ante* but also notes that what we currently regard as 'tradition' is, in the context of human history, a relatively recent phenomenon. His conception of the interrelationships of an Earth jurisprudential system is that

> The allegiance that we humans owe Earth is . . . more analogous to that which a cell owes a body. The 'duty' of the cell is to fulfil the functions for which it evolved and to continue acting in a manner that contributes to the health of the body. If it ceases to do so it dies or becomes a cancer. Similarly, our obligation to Earth is to play our proper role in the functioning of the Earth system and to act in a way that maintains the integrity or 'wholeness' of Earth[50]

Proportionality can therefore be seen as a reasonable but not unflawed approach to balancing the competing rights of humans and nature. After two centuries of industrialisation, when the scales were heavily skewed in favour of humans, a form of pre-industrialisation equilibrium can start to be established once again.

48 Corte Constitucional de Colombia, Sentencia T-622/16, para 10.2.2.
49 C Cullinan, *Wild Law: A Manifesto for Earth Justice* (2nd edn, Green Books 2011).
50 Ibid 100.

Rawlsian Theory of Justice

John Rawls was another of those who felt that an over-reliance on proportionality was too much of an unnecessary compromise; the rights claim of one party would always be weaker – or judged as weaker, less valid, or less important – than the other party's. Instead, he reimagined 'justice as fairness',[51] a system where freedom and equality became a seamless whole.

In his 1971 *Theory of Justice*, Rawls set out a 'thought experiment' which he called the 'original position'.[52] To greatly simplify this experiment, he envisaged a group of people who were deciding the political and economic structure they wanted for a new society they knew they would be part of. They operated behind what he called a 'veil of ignorance',[53] meaning that they did not know their level of importance in that society, the roles they would play, or most of their characteristics (e.g. race, wealth, intelligence, gender etc.). Rawls concluded that if the participants behaved rationally (in itself a rebuttable assumption), they would create a much fairer and more equal society. Inequalities would be allowed, but the 'difference principle'[54] would only justify them if they benefitted the most vulnerable in society. One weakness of the model is that even though the model does not encompass the idea of proportionality from a legal, rights perspective, the rational chooser will balance whether protecting the vulnerable is sufficient to justify any permitted inequality.

While Rawls' approach drew considerable approval and agreement for its emphasis on a fairer and more equitable human society, Mandel argued that 'Rawls assumed that animals lack the two moral powers necessary for full participation in a scheme of social cooperation . . . [and] assumed that reciprocity of social justice was not owed to them'.[55] It is this focus on *human* society and exclusion of the broader ecological context which has drawn criticisms in more recent years.[56]

The anthropocentrism of Rawls' work is perhaps most evident in the difference principle and the inherent assumption that the 'most vulnerable' refers solely to the most vulnerable humans. In an environmental context, it is possible to view this as allowing environmental harm if it benefits the most disadvantaged humans. Gold mining by Indigenous people in the Amazon rainforest, for example, would immediately provide a financial benefit to marginalised and disadvantaged humans but cause significant long-term damage – to the

51 J Rawls, *A Theory of Justice* (Harvard University Press 1971).
52 Ibid 102.
53 Ibid 118.
54 J Rawls, *A Theory of Justice* (Harvard University Press 1971) 65.
55 J Mandle, 'The Environment' in J Mandle and DA Reidy (eds) *The Cambridge Rawls Lexicon* (Cambridge University Press 2015).
56 See, for example, MC Nussbaum, *Frontiers of Justice: Disability, Nationality, Species Membership* (Harvard University Press 2006).

environment and to those same humans. Nussbaum argues that this approach risks perpetuating the exploitation of nature, particularly in cases where short-term human gains lead to long-term ecological damage.[57]

However, other writers have taken Rawls' ideas and adapted them to environmental issues. Norton uses a modified version of the veil of ignorance to create a model in which the rational chooser will pick a 'broadly naturalist-preservationist strategy, which imposes constraints on the pervasive exploitation of ecological systems, and therefore protects biological diversity in the long run'.[58] Adams strips away large sections of Rawls' ideas and applies what is left to the Kyoto Protocol,[59] arguing that applying the 'theory of justice shows that the Kyoto Protocol should have included a cap of greenhouse emissions for all nations'.[60]

At its simplest, Rawls' veil of ignorance can be amended to prevent the rational chooser from knowing anything about the environmental conditions of the society which is to be created. The risk aversion inherent in the model, which Adams criticises concerning climate change, can be seen here as an opportunity. If the chooser cannot know whether the society being created is rich in natural resources or suffering from all manner of environmental degradation, then logic would dictate that environmental sustainability will be paramount. With this would come a greater likelihood of ascribing rights to nature as part of a higher level of protection. Even more interesting would be an amendment whereby the rational chooser did not know whether they would enter the new society as a human or as a non-human animal.

Similarly, Rawls' original position was designed with only human actors represented. Clearly, a tree cannot directly represent itself, but neither can human infants, so the model allows for representation by other stakeholders. As Eckersley suggests, 'nonhuman nature knows no human ethics, it simply *is*'.[61] Using representatives of nature to make decisions is not yet widespread. Still, the excellent work of Lawyers for Nature and the Earth Law Centre in getting a Nature Director appointed to the Board of Directors of the British beauty company Faith in Nature[62] demonstrates that this is possible. Recreating Rawls' thought experiment with representatives of nature in general

57 MC Nussbaum, *Frontiers of Justice: Disability, Nationality, Species Membership* (Harvard University Press 2006).

58 BG Norton, 'Intergenerational Equity and Environmental Decisions: A Model Using Rawls' Veil of Ignorance' (1989) 1(2) Ecological Economics 137.

59 The 1997 Kyoto Protocol to the 1992 United National Framework Convention on Climate Change was an international agreement which set 'legally binding' targets for reducing national emissions of greenhouse gases.

60 TB Adams, 'Rawls' Theory of Justice and International Environmental Law: A Philosophical Perspective' (2007) 20(1) *Global Business and Development Law Journal* 1, 13.

61 R Eckersley, *Environmentalism and Political Theory: Toward an Ecocentric Approach* (Routledge 1992) 59 (emphasis in original).

62 Lawyers for Nature, *Nature-Positive Corporate Governance* (2021) <www.lawyersfornature.com/npcg/> accessed 12 September 2024.

(or specific species) allows for the outcomes to align more closely with ideas of interdependence of all species and all generations and with the views of Attfield, who argues that the flourishing of all living beings is intrinsically of value.[63]

The third part of Rawls' model, which could be reimagined, is the difference principle. As stated earlier, the principle as Rawls intended applies only to humans, but it would not be a significant conceptual leap to include non-human animals and ecosystems. The 'most vulnerable' epithet could then be applied across the board: to humans, species other than humans, or an ecosystem. This has the potential to cause problems if not handled carefully, however. If the non-human participants are assumed to be vulnerable as a matter of policy, then the framework will naturally prioritise their well-being. This could mean that vulnerable humans are treated less favourably and suffer.

What we have seen here is that despite being its designed for a different approach, it is possible to take Rawls' model and with only minor tweaking make it work for ascribing rights to nature. Acting alone, the model is perhaps insufficient. It requires as a starting point a deep ecology[64] or wild law/earth jurisprudence[65] stance that recognises the inherent rights of nature, and that starting point is a long way from reality in the UK. Despite these difficulties, Rawlsian principles highlight the potential for achieving more just and fair outcomes and look likely to contribute significantly to current and future debates around justice for nature.

Hypothetical Case Studies

Having examined some of the theoretical concepts associated with the existence and enforcement of the rights of nature, I turn to considering some brief examples based on hypothetical scenarios. They are all simplified, bilateral conflicts geographically sited in the UK landscape and temporally placed in the UK, which recognises the rights of nature. I acknowledge that in reality, there are likely to be many more parties involved, as in the Atrato case discussed earlier demonstrates.[66] This will be an exercise in applying a revised Rawlsian framework to the scenarios in an attempt to demonstrate the applicability within a UK context. This is beyond what has actually happened in the legislative approaches taken by Bolivia, Ecuador, and New Zealand; none of these was created under a Rawlsian framework, and all those involved in the drafting knew the role they would be playing in the future world. The conflicts

63 R Attfield, *Environmental Ethics: An Overview for the Twenty-First Century* (2nd edn, Polity Press 2014).

64 A Naess, 'The Shallow and the Deep, Long-Range Ecology Movements: A Summary' (1973) 16(1–4) *Inquiry* 95.

65 C Cullinan, *Wild Law: A Manifesto for Earth Justice* (2nd edn, Green Books 2011).

66 Corte Constitucional de Colombia, Sentencia T-622/16.

are categorised into four groups, but it is easy to see that the groups are not discrete and there is significant overlap.

The State Versus Nature

One of the more contentious areas of state activity in the 21st century is the approach to climate change. In this example, the UK government is debating whether to increase the percentage of electricity generation produced by hydroelectric power by damming the River Severn. This will flood large areas of farming and other land; displace local wildlife (including at a nearby site which is a Site of Special Scientific Interest,[67] a Special Protection Area,[68] and a wetland of international importance under the Ramsar Convention[69]); and change the flow of the river. For this example, these impacts will be collated under the umbrella of the river ecosystem.

Using an amended Rawlsian framework, the decision-makers are placed behind the veil of ignorance and thus unaware of whether they would be impacted as a beneficiary of any electricity generated by the dam or as the river ecosystem negatively impacted by the plans. The revised original position that Norton outlined encourages decision-makers to adopt principles which would ensure maximum fairness for *all* parties, both human and non-human. The difference principle would likely identify the river as one of the most disadvantaged stakeholders, as it is particularly vulnerable to human exploitation. As such, the dam building would be permissible if it could be demonstrated that this would not disproportionately harm the river ecosystem. This would require balancing human energy needs with the intrinsic value of the river, ensuring that the least advantaged (i.e. the river ecosystem) is not sacrificed for the benefit of others.[70]

As I have shown so far, despite the best interests of lawmakers in Bolivia and Ecuador, both countries' legislative frameworks have been exploited by industry, which has largely been able to carry on in business as usual. By normalising the use of an adapted Rawlsian approach, state and industrial decision-makers will no longer have the ability to exploit nature for their own benefit.

Humans Versus Nature

The second example considers a scenario where the town of Northampton plans to expand its urban infrastructure eastwards along the River Nene to accommodate the rising human population. This development would disrupt

67 Wildlife and Countryside Act 1981 as amended.

68 Conservation of Habitats and Species Regulations 2017, as amended.

69 Ramsar. *United Nations Educational, Scientific and Cultural Organization Convention on Wetlands of International Importance especially as Waterfowl Habitat* (1971) <www.ramsar.org/sites/default/files/documents/library/scan_certified_e.pdf> accessed 28 October 2024.

70 B Baxter, *A Theory of Ecological Justice* (Routledge 2017).

the river's ecosystem (including wildlife and the flow of the river as in the last example). The conflict arises between the human need to develop housing versus the river's right to maintain its ecological integrity.

From our amended Rawlsian perspective, the veil of ignorance means that the decision-makers do not know whether they will be the humans benefitting from the development, the humans being harmed by the development (e.g. local farmers), or the river ecosystem itself. The original position is the same as in the previous example, where decision-makers are encouraged to adopt policies that give the most fairness to the broadest range of participants. As Eckersley points out,[71] the river cannot advocate for itself, and thus, the imagined mechanism put in place in the UK will need to be used to advocate on its behalf. As a result, the difference principle would again identify the rights of the river as one of the least advantaged entities, alongside the human community. Thus, decision-makers would have to consider whether the proposed urban expansion disproportionately will harm the river's ecosystem and whether alternative plans would be less damaging but still benefit the human population. This could include measures like designing green or blue-green infrastructure[72] or expanding areas of protection.

Non-Human Versus Nature

For these examples, I look at corporations, which have held legal personality in England since medieval times, and AI, which currently does not have separate legal personality but could in the future.[73]

Corporations

In this example, a multinational corporation uses advanced technological processes to decide whether to start logging in Kielder forest in the north-east of England. This activity will be of great benefit to the corporation but threatens to degrade the forest's biodiversity and ecosystem.

In the Rawlsian framework, the decision-makers are behind the veil of ignorance and do not know if they represent the corporate interest or the interests of the forest. As with the rivers Severn and Nene, the forest cannot advocate for itself, but then neither can the corporation. In such an example, the interests of both sides in the conflict will be represented by advocates and, as I have shown, those who cannot advocate for themselves are usually regarded

71 R Eckersley, *Environmentalism and Political Theory: Toward an Ecocentric Approach* (Routledge 1992).

72 CE Little, *Greenways for America: Creating the North American Landscape* (Johns Hopkins University Press 1995); A Walmsley, 'Greenways and the Making of Urban Form' (1995) 33 *Landscape and Urban Planning* 81, 81–127.

73 S Chesterman, 'Artificial Intelligence and the Limits of Legal Personality' (2020) 69(4) *International and Comparative Law Quarterly* 819.

as vulnerable in the difference principle stage. Is the forest most vulnerable because it will be damaged by the logging operations? Or, to take a *reductio ad absurdum* approach, is the corporation most vulnerable because without the logging operations, it will be damaged? Although these two options are both possible, realistically, the river is clearly more vulnerable and thus deserving of protection. The decision is therefore likely to be one which protects the forest ecosystem, either by not logging at all or by requiring the corporation to engage in reforestation or other biodiversity preservation measures.

Artificial Intelligence

The second example in this category is a farmer using an AI-driven system to maximise crop yields in East Anglia. The decisions made by AI have led to soil degradation and loss of soil fertility, which can be seen as interfering with the soil's right to maintain its ecological functions.

Using the revised Rawlsian model, the original position and veil of ignorance need no further exploration, as they follow the pattern I have established. The soil is the most vulnerable, as its ability to regenerate and repair itself has been significantly undermined. The model would therefore require the farmer to use more sustainable practices to ensure the improvement and long-term stability of the soil. Interestingly, this would also be future generations of humans, demonstrating both the interconnected nature of these rights and how a revised Rawlsian framework can indirectly benefit future generations.

NATURE VERSUS NATURE

The final example is a non-location-specific scenario involving competing rights of a river and a tree: The river's right not to have its flow impeded competes with the tree's right to grow across the river and in the process impede its flow. Unlike in the previous examples, the tree and the river each form part of the other's ecosystems and are intrinsically linked; the veil of ignorance ensures that the fairest outcome for the wider ecosystem will be reached. The part of the model which needs unpacking is the difference principle. Neither party can advocate for itself, but unlike the corporate example, this is a genuine comparison: The river is essential to the downstream ecosystem, and if the flow is impeded too much, this will have widespread ecological consequences; the tree is an ecosystem in its own right but has a less far-reaching ecological impact. This leads us to a possible compromise solution where the river's rights are slightly prioritised but not so much as to overrule the tree's right to exist. This could involve minor human intervention to maintain the river's flow while allowing the tree to remain.

What these examples demonstrate is that an adapted Rawlsian approach to environmental decision-making makes it considerably more likely that 'better' and more balanced decisions will be made. The need to consider the interests of all parties is enhanced, as none of the decision-makers knows which of the players they would become. The beauty of this system is that it can be retrofitted to existing legal frameworks which speak of consultation with affected parties, for example through the creation of environmental impact assessments and environmental statements. While these may be statutory requirements, they are often one-sided, and since they are produced largely by the party wishing to carry out the development, they are often partisan in nature. Using the adapted Rawlsian framework to create these statutory documents is much more likely to result in impartial, objective results which will give greater recognition to the rights of nature.

Conclusion

In this chapter, I used an imagined future to highlight the complex, evolving, and increasingly urgent legal, ethical, and philosophical discourse surrounding the recognition of non-human entities as rights-bearing entities. An analysis of concepts like proportionality, environmental ethics, and the Rawlsian Theory of Justice demonstrated that while the recognition of the rights of nature is still far from universal, significant strides have been made in both theory and practice, especially in Ecuador, Bolivia, and New Zealand.

One of the takeaways from this chapter is the recognition that the concept of the rights of nature is not a radical break from legal tradition but rather a logical progression in the expansion of rights that have, over time, extended from privileged individuals to all humans and now to non-human entities. This broadening of rights serves as an acknowledgement of the interconnectedness of all life and the intrinsic value that ecosystems and natural entities hold.

Proportionality, a cornerstone of human rights law, provides a structured framework for resolving conflicts between competing rights. Extending this principle to include the rights of nature requires reimagining the anthropocentric foundations of traditional legal frameworks through a more ecocentric, wild law, or Earth jurisprudence lens. Courts and governments must balance the rights of natural entities, such as rivers or forests, against the rights of humans, corporations, and even the state itself. This balancing act will go a long way to ensuring that no right is disproportionately curtailed without justification and that justice is not denied. The application of proportionality to real-world scenarios, such as the Atrato River case in Colombia, illustrates that it is indeed possible to strike a fair balance between state actions and the protection of natural ecosystems.

Applying Rawls to environmental conflicts adds to the conversation around the rights of nature. Although the original framework was developed within an anthropocentric context, it can be adapted to accommodate non-human rights. Using the 'original position' and 'veil of ignorance' requires decision-makers to impartially consider the interests of all players, leading to more equitable outcomes. Moreover, by extending the difference principle to include the most vulnerable elements of the environment, such as rivers, forests, or endangered species, Rawlsian justice can provide a foundation for fair and sustainable environmental governance.

The brief hypothetical case studies presented offered a practical lens through which the Rawlsian framework and the principle of proportionality can be applied to various conflicts. Whether the dispute involves the state's desire to construct hydroelectric dams, human expansion into natural habitats, corporate resource extraction, or even natural entities in conflict with each other (such as rivers and trees), the application of these legal and philosophical principles can guide decision-makers towards solutions that respect both human and ecological rights. These case studies illustrate that justice for nature is not only possible but necessary for long-term ecological and societal sustainability.

In conclusion, the recognition and enforcement of the rights of nature are part of a broader movement towards an ecocentric legal and ethical framework that prioritises the intrinsic value of all life. While challenges remain – particularly in balancing human and non-human rights in an increasingly industrialised and anthropocentric world – the theoretical tools provided by proportionality and Rawlsian justice offer a way forward. As environmental crises continue to escalate, it is imperative that legal systems evolve to protect the Rights of Nature, not just as a matter of ethical duty but as a necessity for the survival and flourishing of all species including humans. By ensuring that nature is afforded the same protections and considerations as humans, we take the crucial step toward a more just, equitable, and sustainable future for the planet. Given the interconnectedness of all species, justice for nature is justice for all.

Bibliography

Abdelaaty L, 'Do Rights Violations Deter Refugees?' (2023) 49(1) Journal of Ethnic and Migration Studies

Achebe C, 'The Politics of Language' in Ashcroft B, Griffiths G and Tiffin H (eds) *The Postcolonial Studies Reader* (2nd edn, Routledge 2006)

Adams TB, 'Rawls' Theory of Justice and International Environmental Law: A Philosophical Perspective' (2007) 20(1) Global Business and Development Law Journal 1

Akasal E and Ekinci D, 'Effects of Hypoxia and Hyperoxia on Growth Parameters and Transcription Levels of Growth, Immune System, and Stress-Related Genes in Rainbow Trout' (2021) 262 Comparative Biochemistry and Physiology Part A: Molecular & Integrative Physiology 111060

Alexy R, *A Theory of Constitutional Rights* (Oxford University Press 2009)

Alexy R, 'The Dual Nature of Law' (2010) 23(2) Ratio Juris 167

Alge D, 'The Effectiveness of Incentives to Reduce the Risk of Moral Hazard in the Defence Barrister's Role in Plea Bargaining' (2013) 16(1) Legal Ethics 162

Ali H, 'Why Has Sabina Nessa's Murder Not Dominated the News? Take a Wild Guess' *The Independent* (London, 22 September 2021)

Allely CS, 'Experiences of Prison Inmates with Autism Spectrum Disorders and the Knowledge and Understanding of the Spectrum Amongst Prison Staff: A Review' (2015) 6(2) Journal of Intellectual Disabilities and Offending Behavior 55–67

Allely CS, Kennedy S and Warren I, 'A Legal Analysis of Australian Criminal Cases Involving Defendants with Autism Spectrum Disorder Charged with Online Sexual Offending' (2019) 66(101456) International Journal of Law and Psychiatry 1–11

Allely CS, Kennedy S and Warren I, 'Psychiatric and Legal Issues Surrounding the Extradition of WikiLeaks Founder Julian Assange: The Importance of Considering the Diagnosis of Autism Spectrum Disorder' (2022) 28(4) Psychology, Public Policy, and Law 630–643

Alsalem R, 'Report of the Special Rapporteur on Violence against Women and Girls, Its Causes and Consequences' UNGAOR 53rd Session UN DOC A/HRC/53/56 (2023) <www.dropbox.com/scl/fi/0tuwx2l3ffzm4q28bozev/9.-United-Nations-Report.pdf?rlkey=m22h220et30d51d9p8abocp3c&e=1&dl=0>

Ames J, 'Victims Abandon Rape Trials Due to Acute Backlog of Cases' *The Times* (25 July 2024)

Andersson H and Jutvik K, 'Do Asylum-Seekers Respond to Policy Changes? Evidence from the Swedish-Syrian Case' (2023) 125(1) The Scandinavian Journal of Economics 3

Andrew Malkinson Inquiry, 'Chronology' <https://andrewmalkinson.independent-inquiry.uk/andrew-malkinson/>

Angiolini E, *The Angiolini Inquiry: Part 1 Report, HC 530* (The Stationery Office, 2024)

Aqui L, Kenny M and Pearce N, 'The Empire of England: Enoch Powell, Sovereignty, and the Constitution of the Nation' (2021) 32(2) Twentieth Century British History 238–260

Armstrong LM, 'Is Restorative Justice an Effective Approach for Children and Young People Who Sexually Harm' (2021) 10(4) MDPI Laws 86

Arnull A, 'The Law Lords and the European Union: Swimming with the Incoming Tide' (2010) 35(1) European Law Review 57

Arthur R, 'Protecting the Best Interests of the Child: A Comparative Analysis of the Youth Justice Systems in Ireland, England and Scotland' (2010) 18 International Journal of Children's Rights 217

Arthur R, 'Rethinking the Criminal Responsibility of Young People in England and Wales' (2012) 20(1) European Journal of Crime, Criminal Law and Criminal Justice 13

Ashworth A and Roberts JV, 'The Origins and Nature of the Sentencing Guidelines in England and Wales' in Ashworth A and Roberts JV (eds) *Sentencing Guidelines: Exploring the English Model* (OUP 2013)

Attfield R, *Environmental Ethics: An Overview for the Twenty-First Century* (2nd edn, Polity Press 2014)

Attorney General's Office, *Attorney General's Guidelines on Disclosure: For Investigators, Prosecutors and Defence Practitioners* (2024)

Backhouse C, McRae D and Lyer N, *Report of the Task Force on Misogyny, Sexism and Homophobia in Dalhousie University Faculty of Dentistry* (Dalhousie University, 2015)

Baldwin J and McConville M, *Negotiated Justice* (Martin Robertson 1977)

Baldwin MP, 'Subject of Empire: Married Women and the British Nationality and Status of Aliens Act' (2001) 40 Journal of British Studies 522

Baraister P et al, 'Improving Experience of Medical Abortion at Home in a Changing Therapeutic, Technological and Regulatory Landscape: A Realistic Review' (2022) 12(11) British Medical Journal 1

Barak A, *Proportionality: Constitutional Rights and Their Limitations* (Cambridge University Press 2012)

The Bar Council, *Access Denied: The State of the Justice System in England and Wales in 2022* (The Bar Council, 2022)

Barlow A, Hunter R, Smithson J and Ewing J, *Mapping Paths to Family Justice: Resolving Family Disputes in Neo-Liberal Times* (Palgrave Macmillan, 2017)

Baroness Casey Review, 'An Independent Review into the Standards of Behaviour and Internal Culture of the Metropolitan Police Service' *Final Report* (2023) <www.met.police.uk/police-forces/metropolitan-police/areas/about-us/about-the-met/bcr/baroness-casey-review/>

Barr W and Picton J, *Pearce and Stevens' Trusts & Equitable Obligations* (8th edn, OUP 2022)

Barry-Walsh JB and Mullen PE, 'Forensic Aspects of Asperger's Syndrome' (2004) 15(1) Journal of Forensic Psychiatry and Psychology 96

Bashford A and McAdam J, 'The Right to Asylum: Britain's 1905 Aliens Act and the Evolution of Refugee Law' (2014) 32(2) Law and History Review 309

Baxter B, 'Ecological Justice and Justice as Impartiality' (2000) 9(3) Environmental Politics 43

Baxter B, *A Theory of Ecological Justice* (Routledge 2017)

Beccaria C, *On Crimes and Punishments* (Hackett Publishing Company 1986)

Behrens J, 'Meeting the Needs of Victims of Domestic Violence with Family Law Issues: The Dangers and Possibilities of Restorative Justice' (2005) 1(3) International Journal of Law in Context 215

Bellamy C, *Independent Review of Criminal Legal Aid* (29 November 2021)

Belloni F and Hodgson J, *Criminal Injustice* (Macmillian 2000)

Bentham J, 'Anarchical Fallacies; Being an Examination of the Declarations of Rights Issued during the French Revolution' (c 1795) in Bowring J (ed) *The Works of Jeremy Bentham* (vol 2, William Tait 1843)
Bentham J, *An Introduction to the Principles of Morals and Legislation* (Reprinted 1948 Hafner Press)
Berryessa CM, 'Judiciary Views on Criminal Behaviour and Intention of Offenders with High-Functioning Autism' (2014) 5(2) Journal of Intellectual Disabilities and Offending Behaviour 97
Berryessa CM, 'Brief Report: Judicial Attitudes Regarding the Sentencing of Offenders with High Functioning Autism' (2016) 46(8) Journal of Autism and Developmental Disorders 2770
Berryessa CM, 'Educator of the Court: The Role of the Expert Witness in Cases Involving Autism Spectrum Disorder' (2017) 23(6) Psychology, Crime and Law 575
Bertea S, 'Certainty, Reasonableness and Argumentation in Law' (2004) 18 Argumentation 465
Billings P, 'Alienating Asylum Seekers: Welfare Support in the Immigration and Asylum Act 1999' (2002) 9(3) Journal of Social Security and Law 115
Bird JC, *Control of Enemy Alien Civilians in Great Britain, 1914–1918 (Routledge Revivals)* (Routledge 2015)
Blakemore SJ and Robbins T, 'Decision-Making in the Adolescent Brain' (2012) 15(9) Nature Neuroscience 1184
Blitz CL, Wolff N and Shi J, 'Physical Victimization in Prison: The Role of Mental Illness' (2008) 31(5) International Journal of Law and Psychiatry 385
Bookchin M, *The Ecology of Freedom: The Emergence and Dissolution of Hierarchy* (Cheshire Books 1982)
Bowen P, 'Building Trust: How Our Courts Can Improve the Criminal Court Experience for Black, Asian and Minority Ethnic defendants' (2017) <https://justiceinnovation.org/publications/building-trust-how-our-courts-can-improve-criminal-court-experience-black-asian-and/>
Bowling B and Westenra S, 'A Really Hostile Environment: Adiaphorization, Global Policing and the Crimmigration Control System' (2020) 24(2) Theoretical Criminology 163
Boyd DR, *The Rights of Nature: A Legal Revolution That Could Save the World* (ECW Press 2017)
Braithwaite J, *Crime, Shame and Reintegration* (Cambridge University Press 1989)
Braithwaite J, 'Restorative Justice' in Tonry M (eds) *The Handbook of Crime and Punishment* (Oxford University Press 1998)
Braun V and Clarke, V, *Thematic Analysis: A Practical Guide* (Sage Publications 2021)
Briggs M, *Civil Courts Structure Review: Interim Report* (HMSO, 2015)
British Government by the Public Law Project, *Public Law Project Briefing on the Illegal Migration Bill – House of Commons second reading* (March 2023)
Brooke P, 'India, Post-Imperialism and the Origins of Enoch Powell's "Rivers of Blood" Speech' (2007) 50(3) The Historical Journal 669
Brown P et al, 'Prevalence of Mental Disorders in Defendants at Criminal Court' (2022) 8(3) BJPsych Open 1
Bury SM, Jellett R, Spoor JR and Hedley D, '"It Defines Who I Am" or "It's Something I Have": What Language Do [Autistic] Australian Adults [on the Autism Spectrum] Prefer?' (2020) 53(2) Journal of Autism and Developmental Disorders 677
Byrne B and Brooks K, *Post Yot Youth Justice Working Paper 19/2015* (Howard League for Penal Reform, 2015)
Cardozo BN, *The Nature of the Judicial Process* (Yale University Press, 1921)
Carlen P, 'The Staging of Magistrates' Justice' (1976) 16(1) The British Journal of Criminology 48

Carnegie A and Roth R, 'From Grassroots to the Oireachtas: Abortion Law Reform in the Republic of Ireland' (2019) 21(2) Health and Human Rights Journal 109
Carter HDE and Bowsher GM, 'Hunt's Priorities on Entitlement to Use the NHS Are Wrong' (2013) British Medical Journal 347
Cartwright A and Lucas S, 'Report of the Committee on the Working of the Abortion Act' *Lane Report* (vol 1, 1974)
Carty H, 'Precedent and the Court of Appeal: Lord Denning's Views Explored' (1981) 1(1) Legal Studies 68
Casciani D, 'Andy Malkinson: DNA Evidence Identified Three Years after Eape Conviction' (*BBC News*, 16 August 2023)
Case S, *Youth Justice A Critical Introduction* (Routledge 2018)
Casey BJ, Simmons C, Somerville LH and Baskin-Sommers A, 'Making the Sentencing Case: Psychological and Neuroscientific Evidence for Expanding the Age of Youthful Offenders' (2021) 5 Annual Review of Criminology 321
Casseus M, 'Prevalence of Co-Occurring Autism Spectrum Disorder and Attention Deficit/Hyperactivity Disorder among Children in the United States' (2022) 26(6) Autism 1591
'Census 2011' <www.ons.gov.uk/census/2011census/>
'Census 2021' <www.ons.gov.uk/census/>
The Centre for Women's Justice 'Women Who Kill: How the State Criminalises Women We Might Otherwise Be Burying' (13 February 2021) <https//www.centreforwomensjustice.org.uk/news/2021/2/13/women-who-kill-how-the-state-criminalises-women-we-might-otherwise-be-burying>
Chalabi A, 'A New Theoretical Model of the Right to Environment and Its Practical Advantages' (2023) 23 Human Rights Law Review 1
Chapman B and Niven S, *A Guide to the Criminal Justice System in England and Wales* (Home Office 2000)
Chapman T, 'Connecting People to Restore Relationships, Practice Guide on Values and Standards for Restorative Justice Practices' (European Forum for Restorative Justice, 2018) <https://efus.eu/wp-content/uploads/2022/02/Concept-paper-Tim-Chapman-Restorative-Justice-an-approach-that-contributes-to-the-prevention-and-mitigation-of-polarisation-at-the-local-and-regional-level.pdf>
Chesterman S, 'Artificial Intelligence and the Limits of Legal Personality' (2020) 69(4) International and Comparative Law Quarterly 819
Clements R and Abass A, *Complete Equity and Trusts: Text, Cases, and Materials* (5th edn, OUP 2018)
Clough A, 'Coercive Control: Transforming Partial Defences to Murder in England and Wales' (2023) 87(2) Journal of Criminal Law 109
Coates RB, Umbreit MS and Vos B, 'Responding to Hate Crime through Restorative Justice Dialogue' (2006) 9(1) Contemporary Justice Review 7
Cohen I, Gal T and Enosh G, 'Two Roads Converge: The Interchange between the Mental Health and Legal Discourses in Sexual Assault Trials' (2022) 32(2) Social & Legal Studies 441
Coker D, 'Enhancing Autonomy for Battered Women: Lessons from Navajo Peace-Making' (1999) UCLA Law Review 47
College of Policing, 'New Code and Guidance for Non-Hate Crime Incidents' (2023) <www.college.police.uk/article/new-code-and-guidance-non-crime-hate-incidents>
Commission for Countering Extremism, P*redicting Harm among Incels (Involuntary Celibates)* (2024)
Cooper P and Allely CS, 'You Can't Judge a Book by Its Cover: Evolving Professional Responsibilities, Liabilities and "Judgecraft" When a Party Has Asperger's Syndrome' (2017) 68(1) Northern Ireland Legal Quarterly 35

Coskun D, *Law as a Symbolic Form: Ernst Cassirer and the Anthropocentric View of Law* (Springer 2007)
Cotello C and Mann I, 'Border Justice: Migration and Accountability for Human Rights Violations' (2020) 21 German Law Journal 311
Crawford A and Newburn T, *Youth Offending and Restorative Justice* (Willan 2003)
Crenshaw K, 'Mapping the Margins: Intersectionality, Identity Politics and Violence against Women of Colour' (1991) 43(6) Stanford Law Review 1241
Criminal Cases Review Commission, *Annual Report and Accounts 2022/23* (2023)
Crown Prosecution Service, 'CPS Sets Out the Law on Street Based Sexual Harassment' (2022) <www.cps.gov.uk/cps/news/cps-sets-out-law-street-based-sexual-harassment>
Crown Prosecution Service, 'Hate Crime' (2022) <www.cps.gov.uk/crime-info/hate-crime>
Crown Prosecution Service, *Public Order Offences Incorporating the Charging Standard* (2022)
Cullinan C, *Wild Law: A Manifesto for Earth Justice* (2nd edn, Green Books 2011)
Cusworth L et al, *Uncovering Private Family Law: Who's Coming to Court in Wales? Summary* (Nuffield Family Justice Observatory, 2020)
Cusworth L, Bedston S, Broadhurst K, Alrouh B, Akbari A and Griffiths LJ, *Uncovering Private Family Law: Who's Coming to Court in England? Summary* (Nuffield Family Justice Observatory, 2021)
Daicoff SS, 'Families in Circle Process: Restorative Justice in Family Law' (2015) 53(3) Family Court Review 427
Daly E, 'Constitutional Protection for Environmental Rights: The Benefits of Environmental Process' (2012) 17(2) International Journal of Peace Studies 71
Daly K, 'Restorative Justice: The Real Story' (2002) 4(1) Punishment and Society 55
Daly K, 'Restorative versus Retributive Justice' (2005) 60 CJM 28
Daly K, 'Restorative Justice and Sexual Assault: An Archival Study of Court and Conference Cases' (2006) 46 British Journal of Criminology 334
Daly K, *South Australia Juvenile Justice Research on Conferencing Technical Report 2. Research Instruments in Research 2 (1999) and Background Notes* (School of Criminology, Griffith University) <www.aic.gov.au/criminal_justice_system/rjustice/sajj/~/media/aic/rjustice/sajj/tech-report-2.pdf>
Daly K, 'What iIs Restorative Justice? Fresh Answers to a Vexed Question' (2015) 11(1) Victim and Offenders 9
Daly K and Stubbs J, 'Feminist Engagement with Restorative Justice' (2006) 10(1) Theoretical Criminology 9
Daly T and Dawkins C, 'The Illegal Migration Bill Is Not Only Deeply Cruel: But Also a Shameless Attempt to Embolden Extremism' *The Bristol Cable* (Bristol, 13 March 2023)
Daquin JC and Daigle LE, 'Mental Disorder and Victimisation in Prison: Examining the Role of Mental Health Treatment' (2018) 28(2) Criminal Behaviour and Mental Health 141
Dathan M, 'Thousands of Prisoners Recalled to Hail after Early Release', *The Times* (1 November 2024)
Davis M, 'How to Make the Punishment Fit the Crime' (1983) 93(4) Ethics 726
de Londras F and Enright M, *Repealing the Eighth: Reforming Irish Abortion Law* (Policy Press 2018)
Dickens BM, *Abortion and the Law* (MacGibbon and Kee 1966)
Dodd V, 'Two Met Officers Jailed over Photos of Murdered Sisters' *The Guardian* (London, 6 December 2022)
Douglas H and Reed A, 'The Role of Loss of Self-Control in Defences to Homicide: A Critical Analysis of Anglo-Australian Developments' (2021) 72(2) NILQ 271
du Bois-Pedain A, *Transitional Amnesty in South Africa* (Cambridge University Press 2007)

Du Cann R, *The Art of the Advocate* (Penguin 1964, Reprinted 1993)
Duff RA, *Punishment, Communication, and Community* (Oxford University Press 2021)
Duggan M and Mason-Bish H, 'A Feminist Theoretical Exploration of Misogyny and Hate Crime' in Zempi I and Smith J (eds) *Misogyny as Hate Crime* (Routledge 2022)
Dunbar I and Langdon A, *Tough Justice – Sentencing and Penal Policies in the 1990s* (Blackstone 1998)
Dworkin R, *Law's Empire* (Hart Publishing 1986)
Dworkin R, *Freedom's Law: The Moral Reading of the American Constitution* (Harvard University Press 1996)
Dwyer P, Hodkinson S, Lewis H and Waite L, 'Socio-Legal Status and Experiences of Forced Labour among Asylum Seekers and Refugees in the UK' (2016) 32(3) Journal of International and Comparative Social Policy 182
Easton S and Piper C, *Sentencing and Punishment: The Quest for Justice* (4th edn, OUP 2016)
Eckersley R, *Environmentalism and Political Theory: Toward an Ecocentric Approach* (Routledge 1992)
Edwards S, 'Justice Devlin's Legacy: Duffy a Battered Woman Caught in Time' (2009) 12 Criminal Law Review 851
Edwards S and Koshan J, 'Women Who Kill Abusive Men: The Limitations of Loss of Control, Provocation and Self-Defence in England and Wales and Canada' (2023) 87(2) Journal of Criminal Law 75
Eekelaar E, 'Beyond the Welfare Principle' (2002) 14 Child and Family Law Quarterly 237
EHRC, 'How Are Your Rights Protected?' (Equality and Human Rights Commission, 2016) <www.equalityhumanrights.com/human-rights/what-are-human-rights/how-are-your-rights-protected>
Emanuel D, Mawer C and Janes L, 'The Sentencing of Young Adults: A Distinctive Group Requiring a Distinctive Approach' (2021) 3 Criminal Law Review 203
The Fabian Society, *The Crisis in the Justice System in England and Wales: The Bach Commission on Access to Justice – Interim Report* (The Fabian Society, 2016)
Fair Trials, *Young Minds, Big Decisions* (October 2022)
Falkoner C, 'National-Strategy-for-the-Recruitment-of-Lay-Magistrates' (2003) <http://webarchive.nationalarchives.gov.uk/+/www.dca.gov.uk/magist/recruit/natstrat_magrecruit_full.pdf>
Fazel S and Danesh J, 'Serious Mental Disorder in 23000 Prisoners: A Systematic Review of 62 Surveys' (2002) 359(9306) Lancet 545
Fazel S, Hayes AJ, Bartellas K, Clerici M and Trestman R, 'Mental Health of Prisoners: Prevalence, Adverse Outcomes, and Interventions' (2016) 3(9) Lancet Psychiatry 871
Fazel S, Lichtenstein P, Grann M, Goodwin GM and Långström N, 'Bipolar Disorder and Violent Crime: New Evidence from Population-Based Longitudinal Studies and Systematic Review' (2010) 67(9) Archives of General Psychiatry 931
Fazel S and Seewald K, 'Severe Mental Illness in 33,588 Prisoners Worldwide: Systematic Review and Meta-Regression Analysis' (2012) 200(5) British Journal of Psychiatry 364
Ferris P, *The Nameless: Abortion in Britain Today* (Hutchinson 1966)
Fionda J, 'Case Commentary, R v Secretary of State for the Home Department Ex Parte Venables and Thompson, the Age of Innocence? – the Concept of Childhood in the Punishment of Young Offenders' (1998) 10 Child & Family Law Quarterly 1358
Fish S, 'Policing Misogyny as a Hate Crime – the Nottinghamshire Police Experience' in Zempi I and Smith J (eds) *Misogyny as Hate Crime* (Routledge 2022)
Fleming G, 'Review of Migration Decision-Making: Rival Goals and Values' (1999) 10 PLR 131

Fleming PJ, Patterson TL, Chavarin CV, Semple SJ, Magis-Rodriguez C and Pitpitan E, 'Are Men's Misogynistic Attitudes Associated with Poor Mental Health and Substance Use Behaviours? An Exploratory Study of Men in Tijuana, Mexico' (2019) 19(2) Psychology of Men and Masculinities 314

Flew A, 'The Justification of Punishment' in Acton HB (ed) *The Philosophy of Punishment* (MacMillan 1954)

Forrester A and Hopkin G, 'Mental Health in the Criminal Justice System: A Pathways Approach to Service and Research Design' (2019) 29(4) Criminal Behaviour and Mental Health 207

Forrester A, Samele C, Slade K, Craig, T and Valmaggia L, 'Demographic and Clinical Characteristics of 1092 Consecutive Police Custody Mental Health Referrals' (2017) 28(3) Journal of Forensic Psychiatry & Psychology 295

Forrester A, Till A, Simpson A and Shaw J, 'Mental Illness and the Provision of Mental Health Services in Prisons' (2018) 127(1) British Medical Bulletin 101

Foster S, 'Autism Is Not a Tragedy – Ignorance Is: Suppressing Evidence of Asperger's Syndrome and High-Functioning Autism in Capital Trials Prejudices Defendants for a Death Sentence' (2015) 2(1) Lincoln Memorial University Law Review 9

Fouzder M, 'Sunak Criticised for "Startling Ignorance" over "Lefty Lawyer" Attack' (*Law Society Gazette*, 8 March 2023) <www.lawgazette.co.uk/news/sunak-criticised-for-startling-ignorance-over-lefty-lawyer-attack/5115357.article>

Freckelton I, 'Autism Spectrum Disorders and the Criminal Law' in Mohammadi MR (ed) *A Comprehensive Book on Autism Spectrum Disorders* (Intech Press 2011)

Freckelton I, 'Expert Evidence by Mental Health Professionals: The Communication Challenge Posed by Evidence about Autism Spectrum Disorder, Brain Injuries, and Huntington's Disease' (2012) 35(5–6) International Journal of Law and Psychiatry 372

Freckelton I and List D, 'Asperger's Disorder, Criminal Responsibility and Criminal Culpability' (2009) 16(1) Psychiatry, Psychology and Law 16

Garland D, 'Penality and the Penal State' (2013) 51(3) Criminology 475

Garner R, 'Towards a Theory of Justice for Animals' (2012) 2(1) Journal of Animal Ethics 98

Garner R, *A Theory of Justice for Animals: Animal Rights in a Nonideal World* (Oxford University Press 2013)

Gavin P, Kite C, Porter C, McCartan K and Cawley P, 'Restorative Justice in Cases of Sexual Violence: Current and Future Directions in the UK' (2024) 26(4) Contemporary Justice Review 393

Gavrielides T, *Restoring Relationships: Addressing Hate Crime through Restorative Justice* (City Parochial Foundation, 2007)

George M and Layard A, *Thompson's Modern Land Law* (8th edn, OUP 2022)

George R and Marsh R, 'Do We Need Physical Family Courts?' (2024) 46(1) JSWFL 59

Gibbs P, 'Judged by Peers? The Diversity of Lay Magistrates in England and Wales' (2014) <https://howardleague.org/wp-content/uploads/2016/04/HLWP_6_2014.pdf>

Gibson B and Gordon W, *Introduction to the Magistrates' Court* (Waterside Press 2008)

Giedd JN, Blumenthal J and Jeffries NO, 'Brain Development during Childhood and Adolescence: A Longitudinal MRI Study' (1999) 2 Nature Neuroscience 861

Godden-Rasul N, 'Repairing the Harms of Rape of Women through Restorative Justice' in Zinsstag E and Keenan M (eds) *Restorative Responses to Sexual Violence: Legal, Social and Therapeutic Dimensions* (Routledge 2017)

Gogtay N and Giedd JN, 'Dynamic Mapping of Human Cortical Development during Childhood through Adulthood' (2004) 101(21) Proceedings of the National Academy of Sciences 8174

Goodmark L, 'Restorative Justice as Feminist Practice' (2018) 1(3) The International Journal of Restorative Justice 372

Goss R, *Criminal Fair Trial Rights: Article 6 of the European Convention on Human Rights* (Hart, 2014)
Gower M and Hawkins M, 'Immigration and Asylum: Changes Made by the Coalition Government 2010–2015' (House of Commons Library, 24 March 2015). Available at: Immigration and Asylum: Changes Made by the Coalition Government 2010–2015 – House of Commons Library
Gray VF and Kelly L, 'Contested Gendered Space: Public Sexual Harassment and Women's Safety Work' (2020) 44(4) International Journal of Comparative and Applied Criminal Justice 265
Grey C, 'The Rights of Migration' (2014) 20 Legal Theory 25
Grey J, Davies C and Llewellyn T, '20mph Wales: Some Roads to Revert to 30mph after Backlash' (*BBC News*, 20 April 2024) <www.bbc.co.uk/news/uk-wales-68859568>
Griffiths M and Yeo C, 'The UK's Hostile Environment: Deputising Immigration Control' (2021) 41(4) Critical Social Policy 521
Habermas J, *Between Facts and Norms* (Polity Press 1997)
Hansard (HC Debates), '27th of July (1993) Column 864: Written Answer' <https://hansard.parliament.uk/commons/1993-07-27/debates/a3942995-fa01-44d4-8885-0d79bb7e7fac/WrittenAnswers>
Hanschel D, 'Environmental Rights between Constitutional Law and Local Context: Reflections on a Moving Target' (2022) 23(7) German Law Journal 1012
Hansen R, 'The Politics of Citizenship in 1940s Britain: The British Nationality Act' (1999) 10(1) Twentieth Century British History 67
Hart HLA, 'Positivism and the Separation of Law and Morals' (1957–58) 71 Harvard Law Review 593
Hart HLA, *The Concept of Law* (first published 1961, 3rd edn, OUP 2012)
Harvey P, *Buddhism and Monotheism* (Cambridge University Press 2019)
Haydon D and Scraton P, '"Condemn a Little More, Understand a Little Less": The Political Context and Rights Implications of the Domestic and European Rulings in the Venables-Thompson Case' (2007) 27 Journal of Law and Society 416
Herman JL, 'Justice from the Victim's Perspective' (2005) 11(5) Violence against Women 571
Hill C, 'Debating Britain's Role in the World: From Decolonisation to Brexit' (2023) International Politics 10.1057/s41311-023-00454-8
Hindell K and Simms M, *Abortion Law Reformed* (Peter Owen Publishers 1971)
Hirschler S, *Hostile Homes: Violence, Harm and the Marketisation of UK Asylum Housing* (Palmgrave Macmillan 2021)
Hitchings E, Bryson C, Douglas G, Purdon S and Birchall J, 'Fair Shares? Sorting Out Money and Property on Divorce' *Final Report* (University of Bristol, Nuffield Foundation, and Bryson Purdon Social Research, 2023)
HM Courts and Tribunals Service, 'Form: Apply for a Court Order to Make Arrangements for a Child or Resolve a Dispute about Their Upbringing: Form C100' (2024) <www.gov.uk/government/publications/form-c100-application-under-the-children-act-1989-for-a-child-arrangements-prohibited-steps-specific-issue-section-8-order-or-to-vary-or-discharge>
HM Courts and Tribunals Service, 'Guidance: Family Courts Fees (EX50)' (2024) <www.gov.uk/government/publications/fees-in-the-civil-and-family-courts-main-fees-ex50>
Hodgson J, *Gender, Power and Restorative Justice: A Feminist Critique* (Palgrave Macmillan 2022)
Hollingsworth K, 'Judicial Approaches to Children's Rights in Youth Crime' (2007) 19 Child and Family Law Quarterly 42
Home Office, *Report of the Departmental Committee on the Treatment of Young Offenders* (HMSO, The Moloney Report, London, 1927)
Home Office, *Sovereign Borders: International Asylum Comparisons Report, Section I: Drivers and Impact on Asylum Migration Journeys. Migration and Border Analysis*

(September 2020). Available at: Microsoft PowerPoint – Annex A – Sovereign Borders International Asylum Comparisons Report – Section 1 Drivers and impact on asylum migration journeys with references

Home Office, *Youth Measures in the Police, Crime, Sentencing & Courts Bill: Equalities Impact Assessment* (13 May 2021). <www.gov.uk/government/publications/police-crime-sentencing-and-courts-bill-2021equality-statements/youth-measures-in-the-police-crime-sentencing-courts-bill-equalities-impact-assessment>

Hood R, *Race and Sentencing* (OUP 1992)

Hooke D, 'Groves in Anglo-Saxon England' (2017) 38(1) Landscape History 5

Hopkins K, Uhrig N and Colahan M, 'Ministry of Justice Associations between Ethnic Background and Being Sentenced to Prison in the Crown Court in England and Wales in 2015' (2016) <https://assets.publishing.service.gov.uk/media/5a814a3d40f0b62305b8e241/associations-between-ethnic-background-being-sentenced-to-prison-in-the-crown-court-in-england-and-wales-2015.pdf>

Horder J, *Ashworth's Principles of Criminal Law* (10th edn, OUP 2022)

House of Commons, *Attitudes towards Women and Girls in Educational Settings* (5th Report of Session, Women and Equalities Committee, 2023)

House of Commons Justice Committee, *Impact to Changes of Civil Legal Aid under Part 1 of LASPO 2012* (8th Report, HMSO, 2015)

Hudson B, 'Restorative Justice and Gendered Violence: Diversion or Effective Justice?' (2002) 42(3) The British Journal of Criminology 616

Hunter R, Burton M and Trinder L, *Assessing Risk of Harm to Children and Parents in Private Law Children Cases Final Report* (Ministry of Justice, 2020) <https://assets.publishing.service.gov.uk/government/uploads/system/uploads/attachment_data/file/895173/assessing-risk-harm-children-parents-pl-childrens-cases-report_.pdf>

Hymas C, 'Ministers Threaten to Quit over Rwanda Flights Law' *The Daily Telegraph* (London, 5 December 2023)

Hymas C, 'Reducing Court Case Backlog "Unachievable", Says Audit Office', *The Telegraph* (24 May 2024)

Hynes S, *Austerity Justice* (Legal Action Group 2012)

Jackson E, *Regulating Reproduction, Law, Technology and Reproduction* (Hart Publishing 2001)

Jackson VC, 'Constitutional Law in an Age of Proportionality' (2015) 124(8) Yale Law Journal 3094

Jenkins A, *Law for the Rich* (V Gollancz 1960)

Johnston E and Smith T (eds), *The Law of Disclosure – a Perennial Problem in Criminal Justice* (Routledge 2021)

Jones C, Farrelly N and Barter C, 'UK Prevalence of University Student and Staff Experiences of Sexual Violence and Domestic Abuse: A Systematic Review from 2002 to 2022' (2024) European Journal of Higher Education 1

Judicial Appointments Commission, 'Diversity Update 2020' <https://judicial-appointments.gov.uk/wp-content/uploads/2020/11/Diversity-Update-Sept-2020-PDF.pdf>

Justice Committee, *Restorative Justice: Fourth Report of Session* (HC 2016–17 164)

Kazi T, 'Restorative Justice, Hate Crime and Migrant Integration' [online] (European Forum for Restorative Justice) <www.euforumrj.org/en/restorative-justice-hate-crime-and-migrant-integration>

Khai Liew Y, 'Making Sense of Agreement-Based Constructive Trusts in the Commercial Context' (2022) 4 JBL 330

Kidder DL, 'Restorative Justice: Not "rights" But the Right Way to Heal Eelationships at Work' (2007) 18(1) International Journal of Conflict Management 4

Kirchschlaeger PG, 'Human Rights as Ethical Basis for Science' (2013) 22(2) Journal of Law, Information and Science 5

Kirk T, 'More Than 2,000 Criminal Trials Abandoned Due to Crumbling Courts and Lawyer Shortages' *The Standard* (23 September 2023)

Kirwan S, 'Law and the "Stbx": Online for a and the "Delegalised Space" of Family Law' (2017) 7(7) Oñati Socio-Legal Series 1421

Koss M, 'The Restore Program of Restorative Justice for Sex Crimes: Vision, Process and Outcomes' (2014) 29(9) Journal of Interpersonal Violence 1

Krasnostein S, '*Boulton v the Queen*: The Resurrection of Guideline Judgments in Australia?' (2015) 27(1) Current Issues in Criminal Justice 41

Krishnadas J, 'Legal Needs across the Family Justice System: Who Needs What, Where, and When? The Contribution of CLOCK, a Community Outreach System in England and Wales' in Maclean M, Treloar R and Dijkterhuis B (eds) *What Is a Family Justice System for?* (Bloomsbury 2022)

Kunesh PH, 'The Significance of Belonging for Indigenous Peoples: The Power of Place and People – Creating a Vision for Community in Indian Country through Self-Governance and Self-Determination' (2021) 30 Journal of Affordable Housing & Community Development Law 1

Lammy, D., 'Lammy Review: An Independent Review into the Treatment of, and Outcomes for, Black, Asian and Minority Ethnic individuals in the Criminal Justice System', (2017), <www.gov.uk/government/uploads/system/uploads/attachment_data/file/643001/lammy-review-final-report.pdf>

Law Commission, *Partial Defences to Murder* (Law Com No. 290, 2004)

Law Commission, *Hate Crime: Consultation Paper Summary* (2020) <https://lawcom.gov.uk/document/hate-crime-consultation-paper/>

Law Commission, *Hate Crime Laws: Final Report* (Law Com No 402, 2021) <https://lawcom.gov.uk/document/hate-crime-report/>

Law Commission, *Hate Crime: Final Report Summary* (2021) <https://lawcom.gov.uk/document/hate-crime-report/>

Law V, 'Against Carceral Feminism' *Jacobin* <https://jacobin.com/2014/10/against-carceral-feminism/>

Lee R, Birch T and Humphries M, *Survey of Civil Legal Aid Providers in England and Wales: Informing the Review of Civil Legal Aid* (PA Consulting 2024)

Legg S and Nottingham Citizens, 'No Place for Hate' (2021) 22(8) Social and Cultural Geography 1164

Leopold A, *A Sand County Almanac and Sketches Here and There* (Oxford University Press 1949)

Lester A, 'English Judges as Law Makers' (1993) Public Law 269

Leveson B, 'Review of Efficiency in Criminal Proceedings' *Final Report* (January 2015)

Levine K and Cameron ST, 'Women's Preference for Method of Abortion and Management of Miscarriage' (2009) 35(4) Journal and Family Planning and Reproductive Healthcare 233

Lewis A, Pritchett R, Hughes C and Turner K, 'Development and Implementation of Autism Standards for Prisons' (2015) 6(2) Journal of Intellectual Disabilities and Offending Behaviour 68

Lewis C, 'Misogyny as a Hate Crime: Is It All That It Seems?' (South Wales Business Research School) <https://business.research.southwales.ac.uk/law-research/law-research-blog/misogyny-hate-crime-it-all-it-seems/?utm_source=Twitter&utm_medium=social&utm_campaign=Orlo>

Lewis H, Waite L and Hodkinson S, 'Hostile' UK Immigration Policy and Asylum Seekers' Susceptibility to Forced Labour' in Vecchio F and Gerard A (eds) *Entrapping Asylum Seekers: Social, Legal and Economic Precariousness* (Palgrave Macmillan 2017)

Lewis O, 'Written Evidence: Legislative Scrutiny: Illegal Migration Bill (IMB0045)' (April 2023) <https://committees.parliament.uk/writtenevidence/119978/html/>

Lewis O and Gilbert G, 'Human Rights of Asylum Seekers in the UK' (Written Evidence to the Human Rights Joint Committee of the UK Parliament ASU0004, 2023). <https://committees.parliament.uk/writtenevidence/114168/html/>

Lister M, 'Justice and Temporary Labor Migrations' (2014) 29(1) Georgetown Immigration Law Journal 95

Little CE, *Greenways for America: Creating the North American Landscape* (Johns Hopkins University Press 1995)

Llewellyn J, MacIssac J and MacKay M, *Report from the Restorative Justice Process at the Dalhousie University Faculty of Dentistry* (1 May 2015)

Lord D, *The Discipline of Law* (Butterworths 1979)

Lord J, 'Triumphs and Trials with UK Abortion Law: The Power of Collaboration in Abortion Reform' (2024) 164(1) International Journal of Gynaecology and Obstetrics 5

Lord M, 'Should the Law be Certain?' (The Oxford Shrieval Lecture, 11 October 2011) 3 <www.supremecourt.uk/docs/speech_111011.pdf>

Lowestoft Heritage, 'The History of Justices of the Peace' <www.lowestoftheritage.org/research/prominent-lowestoft-personalities/the-history-of-justices-of-the-peace>

Lyons B, 'Dying to Be Responsible: Adolescence, Autonomy and Responsibility' (2010) 30(2) Legal Studies 257

Maboloc C, 'The Moral Argument for Migration' (2020) 48 Philisophia 1501

Maduro MP, 'Interpreting European Law: Judicial Adjudication in a Context of Constitutional Pluralism' (2007) 1(2) European Journal of Legal Studies 137

Mahmood S, *Lord Chancellor Sets Out Immediate Action to Defuse Ticking Prison "Time-Bomb"* (Government Press Release, 12 July 2024)

Mandle J, 'The Environment' in Mandle J and Reidy DA (eds) *The Cambridge Rawls Lexicon* (Cambridge University Press 2015)

Manne K, *Down Girl: The Logic of Misogyny* (Penguin Books Ltd 2017)

Mant J, *Litigants in Person and the Family Justice System* (Hart Publishing 2022)

Mar G, 'Ethnic Minorities, Probation and the Magistrates' Courts' (1986) 26(2) British Journal of Criminal Law

Marsh L, 'Leveson's Narrow Pursuit of Justice: Efficiency and Outcomes in the Criminal Process' (2016) 42(1) Common Law World Review 51

Marsh L, 'The Wrong Vaccine: Custody Time Limits and Loss of Liberty during Covid-19' (2021) 41 Legal Studies 693

Marsh L, 'A Portrait of Guilt from England and Wales: Defending against State-Induced Pleas' in Langer M, McConville M and Marsh L (eds) *Research Handbook on Plea Bargaining and Criminal Justice* (Edward Elgar 2024)

Marshall T, 'The Evolution of Restorative Justice in Britain' (1996) 4 European Journal on Criminal Policy and Research 21

Masson I and Österman L, 'Working with Female Offenders in Restorative Justice Frameworks: Effective and Ethical Practice' (2017) 64(4) Probation Journal 354

Mayor of London, 'What Is Misogyny?' (*Gov.UK*, 2024) <www.london.gov.uk/what-misogyny>

McAuliffe M and Jayasuriya D, 'Do Asylum Seekers and Refugees Choose Destination Countries? Evidence from Large-Scale Surveys in Australia, Afghanistan, Bangladesh, Pakistan and Sri Lanka' (2016) 54 International Migration 4

McCarthy L and Taylor S, 'Misogyny and Organization Studies' (2023) 45(3) Organization Studies 457

McCold P and Watchel T, 'In Pursuit of Paradigm: A Theory of Restorative Justice' (2003) International Institute for Restorative Practices 1

McConville M and Marsh L, *Criminal Judges* (Edward Elgar 2014)

McConville M and Marsh L, 'Adversarialism Goes West: Case Management in Criminal Courts' (2015) 19(3) The International Journal of Evidence and Proof 172

McConville M and Marsh L, 'Criminal Justice in a Time of Covid-19: Paralysis and Prognosis' (2020) 170 New Law Journal 7906

McConville M and Marsh L, *The Myth of Judicial Independence* (OUP 2020)

McConville M and Marsh L, 'Tipping the Scales of Justice – Covid-19 and Detention without Trial' in Johnston E (ed) *Covid-19 and Criminal Justice – Impact and Legacy in England and Wales* (Routledge 2023)

McDiarmid C, *Childhood and Crime* (Dundee University Press 2007)

McGlynn C, 'Challenging Anti-Carceral Feminism: Criminalisation, Justice and Continuum Thinking' (2022) Women's Studies International Forum 93

McGuire K, 'Extending the Concept, or Extending the Characteristics? Misogyny or Gender?' in Zempi I and Smith J (eds) *Misogyny as Hate Crime* (Routledge 2022)

McKeegan M, 'The Politics of Abortion: A Historical Perspective' (1993) 3(3) Womens Health Issues 127

McKinney CJ, Gower M and Dawson J, *Research Briefing – Illegal Migration Bill: Progress of the Bill* (24 April 2023)

McKinnon I and Grubin D, 'Health Screening in Police Custody' (2010) 17(4) Journal of Forensic and Legal Medicine 209

McNeish JA and Socha JM, 'Muddy Waters: On the Problematic Political Ecology of the Atrato Ruling, Colombia' (2024) The International Journal of Human Rights (forthcoming)

Melissaris E, 'Is Common Law Irrational? The Weberian "England Problem" Revisited' (2020) 55(4) Northern Ireland Legal Quarterly 378

The Michael Sieff Foundation, *1908–2008: The Children Act 100 Years on Young Defendants Today* (Report on the Conference Hosted on Tuesday the 28th of April, 2009 at Church House, Westminster, London, Published July 2009)

Michna I and Trestman R, 'Correctional Management and Treatment of Autism Spectrum Disorder' (2016) 44(2) Journal of the American Academy of Psychiatry and the Law Online 253

Miller D, *Principles of Social Justice* (Harvard University Press 1999)

Miller WB, 'Ideology and Criminal Justice Policy: Some Current Issues' (1973) 64 Journal of Criminal Law and Criminology 141

Ministry of Justice, 'Code of Practice for Victims of Crime' (2015) <https://assets.publishing.service.gov.uk/government/uploads/system/uploads/attachment_data/file/974376/victims-code-2020.pdf>

Ministry of Justice, Lord Chief Justice of England and Wales and Senior President of Tribunals, *Transforming Our Justice System* (MoJ, 2016)

Ministry of Justice, *A Smarter Approach to Sentencing Consultation Paper 292* (HMSO, London, September 2020)

Ministry of Justice, *Guide to Family Court Statistics* (MoJ, 2021)

Ministry of Justice Statistics Bulletin, 'Criminal Justice Statistics 2014 England and Wales' <https://assets.publishing.service.gov.uk/media/5a80a9b2e5274a2e8ab51739/criminal-justice-statistics-december-2014.pdf>

Möller K, 'Proportionality: Challenging the Critics' (2012) 10(3) International Journal of Constitutional Law 709

Monckton-Smith J, 'Intimate Partner Femicide: Using Foucauldian Analysis to Track an Eight Stage Relationship Progression to Homicide' (2019) 26(11) Violence against Women 1267

Moore MS, *Placing Blame: A Theory of the Criminal Law* (Oxford University Press 1997)

Moore S and Newbury A, *Legal Aid in Crisis: Assessing the Impact of Reform* (Policy Press 2017)

Moore S and Newbury A, 'Pursuing Family Justice before, during, and after the COVID-19 Pandemic: The Changing Role of Legal Companions and the New Invisibility of Unmet Legal Need' (2024) 2 CFLQ 155

Moorhead R and Sefton M, *Litigants in Person: Unrepresented Litigants in First Instance Proceedings* (DCA Research Series 2005)

Morgan R and Russell N, 'The Judiciary in the Magistrates' Courts' (November 2000) <https://web.archive.org/web/20120328133820/http://library.npia.police.uk/docs/homisc/occ-judiciary.pdf>

Murray K, *Data Matters: Recording Sex and Gender Identity in the Criminal Justice System* (Understanding Inequalities, 2024)

Naess A, 'The Shallow and the Deep, Long-Range Ecology Movements: A Summary' (1973) 16(1–4) Inquiry 95

National Audit Office (comptroller and auditor), 'Mental Health in Prisons' (*National Audit Office*, 26 June 2017) <www.nao.org.uk/wp-content/uploads/2017/06/Mental-health-in-prisons.pdf> accessed 10 June 2024

National Audit Office, *Early Progress in Transforming Courts and Tribunals* (National Audit Office, 2018)

National Audit Office, *Transforming Courts and Tribunals – a Progress Update* (National Audit Office, 2019)

National Crime Agency, *Country Lines Drug Supply, Vulnerability and Harm 2018* <www.nationalcrimeagency.gov.uk/publications/993-nac-19-095-county-lines-drug-supply-vulnerability-and-harm-2018/file>

National Highways, 'Privacy Notice' <https://nationalhighways.co.uk/about-us/privacy-notice/mobile-phone-and-seatbelt-detection-trial-ends-march-2025-privacy-notice/>

Neeley JE, 'Addressing Sexual Assault in Criminal Justice, Higher Education and Employment: What Restorative Justice Means for Survivors and Accountability' (2021) 31(1) The Kansas Journal of Law and Public Policy 1

Newman D, *Legal Aid Lawyers and the Quest for Justice* (Hart 2013)

Noonan JT, *The Morality of Abortion: Legal and Historical Perspectives* (Harvard University Press 1970)

Norton BG, 'Intergenerational Equity and Environmental Decisions: A Model Using Rawls' Veil of Ignorance' (1989) 1(2) Ecological Economics 137

Nussbaum MC, 'Rawls and Feminism' in Freeman S (ed) *Cambridge Companions to Philosophy* (CUP 2002)

Nussbaum MC, *Frontiers of Justice: Disability, Nationality, Species Membership* (Harvard University Press 2006)

Nussbaum MC, 'The Future of Feminist Liberalism' (2013) American Philosophical Association Centennial Series 679

O'Callaghan C and Smith KI, *Femicide Census Report* (Femicide Census, 2021)

O'Donnell E and Talbot-Jones J, 'Creating Legal Rights for Rivers: Lessons from Australia, New Zealand, and India' (2018) 23(1) Ecology and Society 7

Official Statistics, 'Diversity of the Judiciary: Legal Professions, New Appointments and Current Post-Holders – 2024 Statistics' (July 2024) <www.gov.uk/government/statistics/diversity-of-the-judiciary-2024-statistics/diversity-of-the-judiciary-legal-professions-new-appointments-and-current-post-holders-2024-statistics#magistrates-in-post>

O'Mahony LF and Sweeney JA, 'The Exclusion of (Failed) Asylum Seekers from Housing and Home: Towards an Oppositional Discourse' (2010) 37(2) Journal of Law and Society 285

O'Sullivan J, *O'Sullivan & Hilliard's the Law of Contract* (10th edn, OUP 2022)

O'Sullivan OP, 'Autism Spectrum Disorder and Criminal Responsibility: Historical Perspectives, Clinical Challenges and Broader Considerations within the Criminal Justice System' (2018) 35(4) Irish Journal of Psychological Medicine 333

O'Sullivan OP and Eastman N, '"Out of the Penal System and into the Hospital Regime?" Judicial Challenges in Sentencing Mentally Disordered Offenders and the

Likely Impact of the 2020 Sentencing Council *Guideline*' (2023) 87(5–6) Journal of Criminal Law 417

Page P and Hossain T, 'State Violence against Migrants: How Immigration Removal Became Normal and How We Are Challenging It Now' (2018) 32(4) Journal of Immigration Asylum and Nationality Law 385

Parsons J, '2017–19 Governmental Decisions to Allow Home Use of Misoprostol for Early Medical Abortions in the UK' (2020) 124(7) Health Policy 679

Payne D, 'Record Numbers of Irish Women Visit Britain for Abortion' (1999) 319 British Medical Journal 592

Pellew J, 'The Home Office and the Aliens Act, 1905' (1989) 32(2) The Historical Journal 369

Penner JE, *The Law of Trusts* (12th edn, OUP 2022)

Polden P, 'Mingling the Waters: Personalities, Politics and the Making of the Supreme Court of Judicature' (2002) 61(3) CLJ 575

'Practice Guidance: Using Restorative Circles' (Devon County Council, 2020) <https://proceduresonline.com/trixcms1/media/9641/restorative-circles-practice-guidance.pdf>

Pritchard-Jones L, 'Palm Tree Justice': The Inherent Jurisdiction in Adult Welfare Cases' (2023) 86(6) MLR 1358

Quinlan C, 'Policing Women's Bodies in an Illiberal Society: The Case of Ireland' (2017) 27(1) Women and Criminal Justice 51

Quirk H, 'The Post Office Scandal and the Separation of Powers' (2024) 2 Criminal Law Review 91

Raban O, *Modern Legal Theory and Judicial Impartiality* (Glasshouse Press 2003)

Radburch G, 'Statutory Lawlessness and Supra-Statutory Law' (first published 1946, Paulson BL and Paulson SL (trs)) (2006) 26(1) Oxford Journal of Legal Studies 1

Radziwinowiczowna A and Lewis O, 'The New Grounds for Deportation of European Union Citizens in the UK' (2023) 61(5) International Migration 1

Raleigh D, 'Serving Soldier Who Beat Woman Unconscious and Boasted about It on Social Media Gets Suspended Sentence' *The Irish Times* (Dublin, 20 June 2024)

Rawls J, *A Theory of Justice* (revised edn, Harvard University Press 1999)

Raz J, 'Legal Principles and the Limits of Law' (1972) 81 Yale Law Journal 823

Reagan LJ, *Dangerous Pregnancies: Mothers, Disabilities and Abortion in Modern America* (University of California Press, 2010)

Rebbapragada N, Furtado V and Hawker-Bond GW, 'Prevalence of Mental Disorders in Prisons in the UK: A Systematic Review and Meta-Analysis' (2021) 7(1) BJPsych Open 283

Reinecke C, 'Governing Aliens in Times of Upheaval: Immigration Control and Modern State Practice in Early Twentieth-Century Britain, Compared with Prussia' (2009) 54 International Review of Social History 39

'Restorative Justice APPG Inquiry into Restorative Practices in 2021/2022' <https://rjappg.co.uk/wp-content/uploads/2021/09/RJ-APPG-Inquiry-Report.pdf>

Restorative Justice Council, 'Restorative Justice and the Judiciary Information Pack' (2015) <https://restorativejustice.org.uk/sites/default/files/resources/files/Restorative%20justice%20and%20the%20judiciary%20-%20information%20pack.pdf>

Robertson CE and McGillivray JA, 'Autism behind Bars: A Review of the Research Literature and Discussion of Key Issues' (2015) 26(6) Journal of Forensic Psychiatry and Psychology 719

Robeyns I, 'Sen's Capability Approach and Feminist Concerns' in Comim F, Qizilbash M and Alkire S (eds) *The Capability Approach: Concepts, Measures and Applications* (Cambridge University Press 2008)

The Royal College of Psychiatrists, *Written Evidence Submitted by the Royal College of Psychiatrists to the Young Adult Offenders Inquiry, HC937*

Rumgay J, 'Twice Punished: When Women Victims Become Offenders' (2005) 60(1) Criminal Justice Matters 16
Runciman Commission, *Report of the Royal Commission on Criminal Justice* (Cm 2263, 1993)
Rutherford A, *Criminal Justice and the Pursuit of Decency* (OUP 1993)
Sachs NM, 'A Wrong Turn with the Rights of Nature Movement' (2023) 39 Georgetown Environmental Law Review 13
Sawyer SM, 'The Age of Adolescence' (2018) 2(3) Lancet Child & Adolescent Health 223
Schaap A, 'The after Rights of the Citizen of the UK and Its Colonies: Who Is the Subject of the Rights of the Citizen in Britain's Hostile Environment?' (2024) The International Journal of Human Rights 1
Schatzberger E, 'The Immigration Act 2014: "Not on the List You're Not Coming in; Landlords Forced to Discriminate"' (2015) 79(5) Conveyancer and Property Lawyer
Schonberg D & Ors, 'The Accuracy of Using Last Menstrual Period to Determine Gestational Age for First Trimester Medication Abortion: A Systematic Review' (2014) 90(5) Contraception 480
Scullion L, 'Sanctuary to Sanction: Asylum Seekers, Refugees and Welfare Conditionality in the UK' (2018) 25(3) Journal of Social Security and Law 158
Seddon P, 'Tories Must Back ECHR Exit to Survive, Says Jendrick' (*BBC News*, 30 September 2024) <www.bbc.co.uk/news/articles/cy0lqzjwqx8o>
Sentencing Council, 'Sentencing Guideline, Theft – General' (1 February 2016) <www.sentencingcouncil.org.uk/offences/magistrates-court/item/theft-general>
Sentencing Council, *New Guideline for Sentencing Offenders with Mental Disorders Published* (Sentencing Council, 22 July 2020)
Sentencing Council, Overarching Principles: Sentencing Offenders with Mental Disorders, Developmental Disorders, or Neurological Impairments – Response to Consultation (Sentencing Council, July 2020)
Sentencing Council, 'Sentencing Basics' <www.sentencingcouncil.org.uk/sentencing-basics/> accessed 10 June 2024
Shalal A, 'Biden Warns Supreme Court Presidential Immunity Ruling Is "dangerous Precedent"' (*Reuters*, 2 July 2024) <www.reuters.com/world/us/biden-make-remarks-Monday-evening-immunity-ruling-by-supreme-court-2024-07-01/>
Shaw J, Creed F, Price J, Huxley P and Tomenson B, 'Prevalence and Detection of Serious Psychiatric Disorder in Defendants Attending Court' (1999) 353(9158) Lancet 1053
Sheldon S, Davis G, O'Neill J and Parker C, *The Abortion Act 1967: A Biography of a UK Law* (Cambridge University Press 2023)
Smart C, *Feminism and the Power of Law* (Routledge 1989)
Smith E, 'From the Aliens Act to the "Hostile Environment" the Making of the British Border Control System' in le Louvier K and Hough KL (eds) *UK Borderscapes Sites of Enforcement and Resistance* (Routledge 2023)
Smith J, 'Rights of Nature and Tribal Sovereignty: Protecting Natural Communities, Wild Rice, and Salmon in the United States' (2023) 38(1) Maryland Journal of International Law 11
Smith L and Hitchings E, 'Professionals and Partisans: Lessons for Family Lawyers from a Study of Fee-Charging McKenzie Friends' (2019) CFLQ 362
Smith M, *Jurisprudence* (Columbia University Press 1909)
Smyth A, 'The X Case: Women and Abortion in the Republic of Ireland, 1992' (1993) 1 Feminist Legal Studies 163
Smyth CM, 'Restrictive Abortion Laws as Torture in International Law' (2016) 34(9) Irish Law Times 127
Solum LB, 'District of Columbia v. Heller and Originalism' (2009) 103(2) Northwestern University Law Review 9

Stark E, *Coercive Control: How Men Entrap Women in Personal Life* (Oxford University Press 2007)

Statista, 'Arrest Rate Per 1,000 People in England and Wales from 2006/07 to 2023/24, by Ethnicity' <www.statista.com/statistics/1230734/arrest-rate-england-and-wales-by-ethnicity/> accessed 6 December 2024

Steffensmeier D and Chester L, 'Judges' Race and Judicial Decision Making: Do Black Judges Sentence Differently?' (December, 2002) Britt, Social Science Quarterly 749

Stensvold A, *A History of Pregnancy in Christianity: From Original Sin to Contemporary Abortion Debates* (Taylor Francis 2015)

Stone CD, 'Should Trees Have Standing? Toward Legal Rights for Natural Objects' (1972) 45(2) Southern California Law Review 450

Stone CD, *Should Trees Have Standing?: Law, Morality, and the Environment* (3rd edn, Oxford University Press 2010)

Stone N, 'Children Who Murder: Indeterminate Sentencing in Law and Practice' (2018) 18 Youth Justice 82

Strang H and Sherman LW, 'Repairing the Harm: Victims and Restorative Justice' (2003) Utah Law Review 15

Stürup-Toft S, O'Moore EJ and Plugge EH, 'Looking behind the Bars: Emerging Health Issues for People in Prison' (2018) 125(1) British Medical Bulletin 15

Tata C, 'Sentencing as Craftwork and the Binary Epistemologies of the Discretionary Decision Process' (2007) 16(3) Social and Legal Studies 425

Tata C, *Sentencing as a Social Process: Re-Thinking Research and Policy* (Palgrave Macmillan 2020)

Taylor B, 'Immigration, Statecraft and Public Health: The 1920 Aliens Order, Medical Examinations and the Limitations of the State in England' (2016) 29 Social History of Medicine 512

Taylor D, 'Illegal Migration Bill Could Topple World Refugee System, Lawmakers Told' *The Guardian* (London, 29 March 2023)

Taylor PJ, Eastman N, Lathan R and Holloway J, 'Sentencing Offenders with Mental Disorders, Developmental Disorders or Neurological Impairments: What Does the New *Sentencing Council Guideline* Mean for Psychiatrists?' (2021) 218(6) British Journal of Psychiatry 299

Teo M, 'Proportionality as Epistemic Independence' (2022) 2 Public Law 245

Tewksbury R, 'Qualitative versus Quantitative Methods: Understanding Why Qualitative Methods Are Superior for Criminology and Criminal Justice' (2009) 1(1) Journal of Theoretical & Philosophical Criminology 38

Thomas C, 'Ethnicity and Fairness of Jury Trials in England and Wales 2006–2014' (2017) 9 Criminal Law Review

Thomas D, 'Judicial Discretion in Sentencing' in Gelsthorpe L and Padfield N (eds) *Exercising Discretion – Decision-Making in the Criminal Justice System and Beyond* (Willan Publishing 2003)

Thomas R, 'The Impact of Judicial Review on Asylum' (2003) PL 479

Thomas R, 'Evaluating Tribunal Adjudications: Administrative Justice and Asylum Appeals' (2005) 25 LS 462

Tomlinson S, 'Enoch Powell, Empires, Immigrants and Education' (2017) 21(1) Race Ethnicity and Education 1

Tonry M, 'Setting Sentencing Policy through Guidelines' in Rex S and Tonry M (eds) *Reform and Punishment – the Future of Sentencing* (Willan Publishing 2002)

Tonry M, *Punishment and Politics – Evidence and Emulation in the Making of Crime Control Policy* (Willan Publishing 2004)

Townsend KCS, *Inaugural Address* (Lincoln's Inn, 9 January 2024)

Tracy LJ, 'Letter to the Editor' (2016) 7 Criminal Law Review 489

Trinder L et al, *Litigants in Person in Private Family Law Cases* (Ministry of Justice 2014)
Uhrig N, 'Black, Asian and Minority Ethnic Disproportionality in the Criminal Justice System in England and Wales' (2016) <https://assets.publishing.service.gov.uk/media/5a75928440f0b6360e475224/bame-disproportionality-in-the-cjs.pdf>
Valentini L, 'Justice, Disagreement and Democracy' (2013) 43(1) British Journal of Political Science 177
van Reekum R and Schinkel W, 'Instituting the Global: The Racial Analytics of Migration' (2024) Migration Studies 12
Villavicencio Calzadilla P and Kotzé LJ, 'Living in Harmony with Nature? A Critical Appraisal of the Rights of Mother Earth in Bolivia' (2018) 7(3) Transnational Environmental Law 397
von Hirsch A, *Doing Justice: The Choice of Punishments* (North Eastern University Press 1976)
Wacks R, *Understanding Jurisprudence: An Introduction to Legal Theory* (6th edn, OUP 2020)
Wade KCC, 'Domestic Homicide Sentencing Review Government Response to the Independent Review' (July 2023) <https://assets.publishing.service.gov.uk/media/64b802acef537100147aeeee/domestic-homicide-sentencing-review-case-review-response.pdf>
Wager NM, 'A Scoping Review Considering the Applicability of Restorative Justice to Cases of Sexual Assault' *Conference Paper* <www.researchgate.net/profile/Nadia-Wager/publication/263653926_A_SCOPING_REVIEW_CONSIDERING_THE_APPLI CABILITY_OF_RESTORATIVE_JUSTICE_TO_CASES_OF_SEXUAL_ASSAUL/links/0deec53b6e2be85740000000/A-SCOPING-REVIEW-CONSIDERING-THE-APPLICABILITY-OF-RESTORATIVE-JUSTICE-TO-CASES-OF-SEXUAL-ASSAUL.pdf>
Walmsley A, 'Greenways and the Making of Urban Form' (1995) 33 Landscape and Urban Planning 81
Walsh PW and Sumption M, 'UK Policies to Deter People from Claiming Asylum' (The Migration Observatory at the University of Oxford, 2023). Available at: UK policies to deter people from claiming asylum – Migration Observatory – The Migration Observatory (ox.ac.uk)
Walters MA, *Hate Crime and Restorative Justice: Exploring Causes, Repairing Harms* (Oxford University Press 2014)
Walvisch J and Carroll A, 'Sentencing Offenders with Personality Disorders: A Critical Analysis of *DPP (Vic) v O'Neill*' (2017) 41(1) Melbourne University Law Review 417
Webber F, 'On the Creation of the UK's "Hostile Environment"' (2019) 60(4) Race & Class 76
Welsh L, Skinns L and Sanders A, *Sanders & Young's Criminal Justice* (5th edn, OUP 2021)
Wemmers JA, Parent I and Lachance Quirion M, 'Restoring Victims' Confidence: Victim-Centred Restorative Practices' (2023) 29(3) International Review of Victimology
White H, 'Illegal Migration Bill Highlights How Expectations of Legislative Scrutiny Have Plummeted' (Institute for Government, 2023). Available at: Illegal Migration Bill highlights how expectations of legislative scrutiny have plummeted | Institute for Government
Wilcock CA, 'Hostile Immigration Policy and the Limits of Sanctuary as Resistance: Counter-Conduct as Constructive Critique' (2019) 7(4) Social Inclusion 141
Williams G, *The Sanctity of Life and the Criminal Law* (Cambridge University Press 1957)
Wolff N, Blitz CL and Shi J, 'Rate of Sexual Victimisation in Prison for Inmates with and without Mental Disorders' (2007) 58(8) Psychiatric Services 1087

Wong S and Cain R, 'The Impact of Cuts in Legal Aid Funding on Private Family Law Cases' (2019) 41 JSWFL 3
Wood WG, *The Dominion of Man* (Richard Bentley & Son 1889)
Wrisley SM, 'Feminist Theory and the Problem of Misogyny' (2021) 24(2) Feminist Theory 188
Wundisch J, 'Towards a Non-Ideal Theory of Climate Migration' (2022) 25(4) Critical Review of International Social and Political Philosophy 496
Yeo C, 'Everything You Need to Know about the "Hostile Environment Policy" for Immigrants' (*Freemovement*, 29 May 2017) <Everything you need to know about the "hostile environment" for immigrants – Free Movement>
York S, 'The "Hostile Environment": How Home Office Immigration Policies and Practices Create Perpetual Illegality' (2018) 32 Journal of Immigration, Asylum and Nationality Law 363
Young S and Cocallis K, 'ADHD and Offending' (2021) 128(7) Journal of Neural Transmission 1009
Yuval-Davis N, Wemyss G and Cassidy K, 'Everyday Bordering, Belonging and the Reorientation of British Immigration Legislation' (2018) 52(2) Sociology 228
Zehr H, *Changing Lenses: A New Focus for Crime and Justice* (Herald Press 1990)
Zehr H, *The Little Book of Restorative Justice* (Good Books 2002)
Zehr H, 'Restorative Justice? What's That?' [online] <https://zehr-institute.org/what-is-rj/>
Zinsstag E and Keenan M (eds), *Restorative Responses to Sexual Violence: Legal, Social and Therapeutic Dimensions* (Routledge 2017)

Index

FSC
www.fsc.org
MIX
Papier | Fördert
gute Waldnutzung
FSC® C083411

Kolibri 360 GmbH
Ferdinand-Jühlke-Straße 7
99095 Erfurt, Deutschland
produktsicherheit@kolibri360.de